A HISTORY OF BRITAIN FROM 1867

JOHN MARTELL

Nelson

Acknowledgements

The author and publishers are grateful to the following for permission to reproduce copyright material.

Photographs and cartoons
All Saints Church, Margaret Street, London W1, p. 67; Associated Press, pp. 184, 256; BBC Hulton Picture Library, pp. 5, 22, 27, 44, 51, 60, 72, 103, 158; British Library, p. 227; Daily Telegraph Cartoon, pp. 140, 232; ET Archives, p. 87 (bottom); Express Newspapers, pp. 150, 151, 161, 172, 176, 199, 217, 219; Mary Evans Picture Library, pp. 9 (left), 30, 50, 62, 89 (left), 134; Gernsheim Collection, p. 34; GLC Photo Library, p. 97; Glasgow Art Gallery and Museum, p. 141. Iron Bridge Gorge Museum, p. 48; Imperial War Museum, pp. 115, 119, 121, 124 (bottom), 125, 182; Keystone Collection (Fox Photos), pp. 85, 93, 139, 160, 163, 177, 181, 194, 195, 201, 203, 225, 231, 236, 241, 245; London School of Economics, p. 100; Mansell Collection, pp. 13, 18, 28, 32, 39, 40, 63, 68, 89 (right), 107, 112, 113, 124 (top), 146; Museum of London, p. 108; National Museum of Ireland (Lawrence Collection), p. 38; National Museum of Labour History, p. 53; National Army Museum, p. 94; Olney Collection (D.C. Harrod), p. 74; Popperfoto, pp. 76, 87, 180, 183, 190, 222; Press Association, pp. 249, 251; Public Record Office of Northern Ireland, p. 110; Punch Publications, pp. 6, 244; Royal Commission for Historical Monuments of Great Britain, p. 162; Sunday Telegraph, pp. 212, 247; Reece Winstone, p. (right).

Extracts and statistics
Page 8, Longman Group UK Ltd for population statistics from K. Robbins, *The Eclipse of a Great Power, Modern Britain 1870–75*, 1983; pp. 12, 41, 45, 159, 164, 220, Her Majesty's Stationery Office (Crown © reserved) for extracts from Hansard, *Parliamentary Debates*; pp. 20, 38, 123, Times Newspapers Ltd for extracts from *The Times*, 14.9.1872, 12.11.1880 and April 1915; p. 62, Macmillan Publishers Ltd for an extract from J. Wroughton, *Documents on British Political History, 2, 1815–1914*, quoted from *Journals of Gordon at Khartoum*; pp. 74, 102, Oxford University Press for extracts from Flora Thompson, *Lark Rise to Candleford*, 1939; p. 75, Basil Blackwell for an extract from Elizabeth Roberts, *A Woman's Place, An Oral History of Working Class Women*, 1984; p. 78, Manchester University Press for an extract from R. Roberts, *The Classic Slum*, 1966; pp. 94, 95, Weidenfeld & Nicolson Ltd for a passage from Thomas Pakenham, *The Boer War*, 1977, taken from E. Hobhouse, *Brunt of War*, 1902; p. 105, Macmillan Publishers Ltd for an extract from D. Fraser, *The Evolution of the Welfare State*, 1973; p. 108, Unwin Hyman Ltd for an extract from Emmeline Pankhurst's speech from the dock in 1908, quoted from L. Baily, *Leslie Baily's BBC Scrapbook 1*, Allen and Unwin, 1966; p. 116, Methuen London for an extract from J. Grigg, *Lloyd George, The People's Champion, 1902–11*, 1978; p. 121, Macmillan Publishers Ltd for two extracts from Tony Ashworth, *Trench Warfare, the Live and Let Live System*, 1980; p. 138, Hamish Hamilton Ltd for an extract from Robert Rhodes James, *British Revolution, British Politics 1880–1939*, (vol 2); p. 144, the estate of the late Sonia Brownell Orwell and Martin Secker and Warburg Ltd for the extract from George Orwell, *The Road to Wigan Pier*; pp. 147, 154, Routledge and Kegan Paul for four passages from J. H. Bettey, *English Historical Documents 1906–39*; pp. 179, 181, Martin Secker and Warburg Ltd for an extract from William Shirer, *The Rise and Fall of the Third Reich*, 1960; p. 188, Hodder and Stoughton Ltd for an extract from J. Beveridge, *Beveridge and His Plan,* 1954; pp. 195, 206, Macmillan Publishers Ltd for two passages from P. Lane, *Documents on British Economic and Social History, 3, 1945–67*, 1969; p. 203, A. D. Peters & Co Ltd on behalf of The Bodley Head, for statistics from *Britain in the Century of Total War* by Arthur Marwick, 1968; p. 226, A. D. Peters & Co Ltd on behalf of Hodder and Stoughton, for an extract from Colin Cross, *The Fall of the British Empire*, 1968; p. 240, Constable Publishers for an extract from Anthony Nutting, *No End of a Lesson*, 1967; p. 244, Oxford University Press for an extract from R. W. Breach, *Documents and Descriptions, The World since 1945,* 1966, quoted from the *Annual Register* for 1963.

Every effort has been made to contact the holders of copyright material, but if any have been inadvertently overlooked the publishers will be pleased to make the necessary arrangements at the first opportunity.

Nelson History Titles for GCSE

Assignments in British Social and Economic History by Nicholas Tate
Twentieth-Century World Affairs by Geoffrey Regan
The Twentieth-Century World by John Martell

Thomas Nelson and Sons Ltd
Nelson House, Mayfield Road
Walton-on-Thames, Surrey
KT12 5PL, UK

51 York Place
Edinburgh
EH1 3JD, UK

Thomas Nelson (Hong Kong) Ltd
Toppan Building 10/F
22A Westlands Road
Quarry Bay, Hong Kong

Distributed in Australia by
Thomas Nelson Australia
480 La Trobe Street
Melbourne, Victoria 3000
and in Sydney, Brisbane,
Adelaide and Perth

© John Martell 1988
First published by Thomas Nelson and Sons Ltd 1988
ISBN 0-17-435016 3
NPN 9 8 7 6 5 4 3 2 1
Printed in Great Britain by Butler and Tanner Ltd., Frome

All Rights Reserved. This publication is protected in the United Kingdom by the Copyright Act 1956 and in other countries by comparable legislation. No part of it may be reproduced or recorded by any means without the permission of the publisher. This prohibition extends (with certain very limited exceptions) to photocopying and similar processes, and written permission to make a copy or copies must therefore be obtained from the publisher in advance. It is advisable to consult the publisher if there is any doubt regarding the legality of any proposed copying.

CONTENTS

Preface	4
Introduction: The economy, the people and the governing of Britain	5
1 Gladstone, the Liberal party and the ministry of 1868–74	15
2 Disraeli, the Conservative party and the ministry of 1874–80	25
3 Ireland and the issue of home rule	36
4 Trade unions, Socialism and the Labour party	47
5 Domestic and foreign issues in late Victorian times	57
6 Religion and society in late Victorian and Edwardian times	67
7 The growth of the British Empire	80
8 Politics and reform during the Edwardian era	97
9 Britain and Europe in the early twentieth century	112
10 Britain and the First World War	120
1867–1918: Chart of Events	130
11 Political and economic change in the post-war years	134
12 The General Strike and the 1931 crisis	144
13 British society during the 1930s	156
14 British foreign policy during the inter-war years	167
15 Britain and the Second World War	180
16 Readjustment within Britain during the post-war decade	193
17 Conservative and Labour policies 1955–70	205
18 The British Empire and Commonwealth in the twentieth century	216
19 Britain and the world 1945–73	233
20 Britain in the 1970s and 1980s	246
1919–1987: Chart of Events	258
Glossary	263
Index	265

Maps

Afghanistan and Persia (today Iran)	29
The Balkans in the late 1870s	33
Egypt and the Sudan in the late nineteenth century	61
British possessions in Africa	81
British possessions in South-East Asia and the Far East	82
South Africa at the time of the First and Second Boer Wars	91
Europe in 1914	118
The Western Front in the First World War	122
The Ottoman Empire at the time of the First World War	128
Ireland	137
The peace settlement of 1919	168
Czechoslovakia and Germany at the time of the Munich conference	175
North Africa and Italy during the Second World War	185
Europe during the Second World War	189
The Indian sub-continent at the time of independence	221
The Middle East in the 1940s and 1950s	239
The Falklands campaign of 1982	250

PREFACE

This history textbook is intended for use by those preparing for GCSE history syllabuses in modern British history. Attention is given to political, economic and social developments in Britain, as well as to Britain's relations with foreign powers and with its own Empire and Commonwealth.

The years since 1867 have been of vital importance in the emergence of modern Britain. The book seeks to present a comprehensive factual outline of developments during this period, while also directing attention to the reasons for them and to their importance in the continuing history of the country. Contemporary photographs, cartoons and documentary extracts, together with maps illustrating foreign and imperial policy, form an important part of the book. Those who use it are encouraged to examine this evidence from the past in a critical way and to appreciate it as the basis on which history is written.

Each chapter concludes with a set of exercises appropriate for GCSE candidates. The first two exercises consist of structured essay questions, focused essentially though not exclusively on the chapter's content. The third exercise views historical events from the standpoint of people in the past. The fourth is based on source material used in the chapter and affords opportunity to relate understanding of the past to the evidence that survives from it; a suggested mark allocation is given in brackets at the end of each part of this fourth question.

The author is much indebted to two colleagues for their help in the book's preparation. At an early stage, drawing on his considerable experience as a teacher and examiner of history, Ed Rayner gave helpful encouragement of draft chapters that he reviewed. At a later stage Nicholas Tate, Senior Lecturer in History at Moray House College of Education, Edinburgh, read virtually the entire typescript. His perceptive and detailed comments were of great value in deciding the book's final content and form.

INTRODUCTION: THE ECONOMY, THE PEOPLE AND THE GOVERNING OF BRITAIN

British people living at the end of the nineteenth century – a time only just outside the memories of older people today – were conscious that their country was one of the great powers of the world. They had a stable system of government, an empire that was increasing in size and a well developed industrial economy. Some people within Britain were also conscious that theirs was a land of many injustices. Educational provision was slight, conditions of work were hard, the right to vote was limited to a privileged minority. The years covered by this book see a gradual decline in Britain's international greatness. They also see a gradual development of fairer opportunities for the people of Britain.

British industry

Britain's greatness as a world power was based on its industry. Already by the late 1860s, Britain could look back on a longer industrial history than any other country in the world. Good raw materials, plentiful labour supplies and new manufacturing methods had together helped Britain to begin its industrialisation early. But why was the successful industrialisation of Britain the foundation of the country's greatness? Because Britain was able to export the products of its industry and to gain money from foreign countries in return. Though industrial profits were also made from sales within Britain, it was the exporting of industrial products that was the key to British success.

Trade Britain was most successful in what were known as the country's **staple industries**. These consisted of textiles, iron and steel, coal mining and ship building. By the middle years of the nineteenth century all of these industries were showing big increases in their export figures. Politicians and most people within Britain attributed this recent success in exports to one major reason: the economic policy of **free trade**. Trade with foreign countries was quite unrestricted. The goods of British manufacturers could be exported freely. The goods of foreign manufacturers could be imported freely, without payment of tariffs

The Crystal Palace, constructed to accommodate the Great Exhibition of 1851, became a symbol of the greatness that industrial and commercial leadership had brought to Britain in the mid-nineteenth century. Though the Crystal Palace has since been destroyed, many buildings of the time survive to suggest the pride that Victorians felt in their country's achievements.

A HISTORY OF BRITAIN FROM 1867

(import taxes) when entering the country. As the economy succeeded so well under the free trade system, few doubted its value for Britain. In such circumstances it is not surprising that sterling was regarded as the world's leading currency or that the City of London was regarded as the world's financial centre.

Great Depression But Britain's leadership of the world's economy was beginning to be challenged. During the last three decades of the nineteenth century the economy was less successful than it had earlier been. The term Great Depression has sometimes been applied to the economic problems experienced by Britain in these years. Britain still kept its leadership in industry, but was now less confident. The main cause of the Great Depression was foreign competition. Germany, only

Foreign competition in trade is suggested by this cartoon of the 1880s as the basic reason for the desperation of British workers and their families. The value of free trade, long held as the basis of Britain's commercial prosperity, was increasingly called in question.

UNFAIR TRADE WINDS.

recently united as a country, was beginning to apply new industrial methods. A similar trend was to be found in the United States, now that the troubles of its Civil War (1861–65) were over. In France, industrial development had already taken firm root; Russian industry was also developing. Nor did competitor countries automatically adopt the free trade principles that Britain itself held to so strongly. Some were using tariffs, making it difficult for British goods to be traded abroad. An article at the time put it in this way:

> Thirty years ago England had almost a monopoly of the manufacturing industries of the world; she produced everything in excess of her consumption, other nations comparatively nothing. The world was obliged to buy from her, because it could not buy anywhere else.... Well, that was thirty years ago; now France and America and Belgium have got machinery and our workmen and our capital, and they are sending us a yearly increasing surplus that is driving our own goods out of our own markets; and every year they are more completely closing their markets to our goods.

THE ECONOMY, THE PEOPLE AND THE GOVERNING OF BRITAIN

> Foreigners form their own opinions from their own observations. When they see industries dying out under Free Trade in England, and springing into vigorous life under Protection in France, Belgium, Germany and America... they do not look much further for arguments against Free Trade. 'After all,' they say, 'the proof of the pudding is in the eating. If this is the result of thirty years of Free Trade, perhaps we are just as well without it.'
>
> Edward Sullivan, 'Isolated Free Trade', in *The Nineteenth Century*, August 1881.

Part of the reason for these difficulties lay within Britain itself. The success of the staple industries made British industrialists unwilling to develop new industries or exploit new methods of production. Meanwhile, other countries were beginning to develop the new power of electricity, instead of that of steam, to which Britain still kept. British industrialists remained suspicious of the mass production methods that were beginning to be used in the United States. While the new chemical industry became important in other countries, it made only slight progress in Britain.

Unemployment

The result of these different developments did not mean complete disaster for British industry. Exports were still increasing in the late nineteenth century, but they failed to increase as strongly as the exports of other countries and Britain could no longer maintain its lead in world trade. Nor did these developments have any noticeable effect on the living conditions of British workers. Because prices of goods were declining and wages were remaining fairly constant, many found that their living costs went down in these years. Problems were, however, serious for those who became unemployed. As figures of unemployment were not then kept, it is impossible to know how many were affected in this way. Unemployment existed, but on a far lesser scale than later in the 1930s, or in recent years.

British agriculture

The problems facing British agriculture in the late nineteenth century were more serious. Like industry, agriculture met serious competition, especially in wheat and meat. The 1870s and 1880s were years when large-scale wheat growing was developing in countries such as the United States, Canada and Australia. Improved transport led to heavy wheat imports into Britain. Under the free trade system no tariffs were placed on this wheat, which could therefore be sold in Britain more cheaply than British-grown wheat. Improvements in shipping, and particularly the introduction of refrigerators in ships, allowed bulk importation of meat from Argentina, Australia and New Zealand. Those who reared cattle thus found their livelihood threatened. To make up for the losses caused by this competition, there was diversification into other branches of farming. It was in these years that fruit growing, market gardening and milk production began to be developed. Nevertheless, some farmers did go out of business in these years and some farm labourers became unemployed. However, falling prices and stable wages were to the advantage of the employed country labourers just as they were to those in employment in the towns.

Industry and agriculture needed therefore to adjust to changing circumstances. To do so was not easy, nor was it entirely successful. Many British people became disillusioned with their prospects in these years and sought better opportunities abroad. During the last three decades of the nineteenth century approximately seven million people emigrated from Britain. The developing economy of the towns and prairies of the United States attracted some five million of these emigrants. Others went to settle in Canada, Australia, New Zealand and South Africa.

A HISTORY OF BRITAIN FROM 1867

Britain and its monarchy

Population

The population figures given below are based on the results of the census (counting of the population) that was taken at the beginning of every decade throughout the years covered by this book. They provide useful evidence of the strength of England's position as a part of Britain.

	Total British population, in millions	Proportion of the population, in percentages			
		England	Ireland	Scotland	Wales
1871	31 398	67.5	17.2	10.7	4.5
1971	55 515	82.9	2.8	9.4	4.9

Notice, from the figures in the first column, how Britain's total population had almost doubled during the hundred years to which the figures relate. Notice, from the figures in the second column, how the proportion of that population living in England had risen from just over two-thirds to just over four-fifths. Containing a greater and an increasing part of the population gave England a strong position. England's capital, London, was also the capital of Britain. It was in London, at Westminster, that parliament met and it was in London that the government of Britain was based. Much – though not all – of the industrial development of these years took place in England and provided a powerful attraction for immigrants from Ireland, Scotland and Wales.

Study of the last three columns of these figures shows that while the proportions for Scotland and Wales remained much the same between 1871 and 1971, the proportion for Ireland was very much reduced. The particular reason for that reduction is the creation in 1921 of the Irish Free State; only the six counties of Northern Ireland then remained under British rule and it is on the smaller population figures for those six counties that Ireland's population proportion for 1971 is based. In the early years covered by this book, Ireland, Scotland and Wales formed with England what was known – until the time of the Irish separation – as **Great Britain**. Another term, which is often used for all four areas presently under the British monarchy, is the **United Kingdom**.

Ireland

The relationship of Ireland with the British government is given attention in later chapters. The difficulties in this relationship were nothing new and had existed ever since the English had begun to settle in Ireland during the middle ages. Control of Irish affairs from Westminster had been strengthened by the Act of Union of 1801. This abolished Ireland's separate parliament and allowed instead for Irish representation in the parliament at Westminster. Many Irish continued to dislike the links that bound them to the rest of Britain. They considered that of all the parts of the United Kingdom, theirs was the least well treated and the most despised.

Scotland

Much less controversy surrounded the links that bound Scotland and Wales within the United Kingdom. For Scotland, another Act of Union (of 1707) had similarly abolished the Scottish parliament and provided for Scottish representation at Westminster. There was general satisfaction at the way in which this Anglo-Scottish union worked. Though the people of the Scottish Highlands had in the past shown their opposition to the connection with England, the force of such feeling was of little importance by the late nineteenth century. While the links with Scotland were therefore generally trouble-free, Scotland retained many features that made it different from the rest of the United Kingdom. It had its own church, its own legal system and its own educational system. Above all, the Scots possessed a distinct pride in themselves as a nation and in their

THE ECONOMY, THE PEOPLE AND THE GOVERNING OF BRITAIN

contribution to the history of Britain. A similar national identity was to be found among the people of Wales and a similar harmony in Anglo-Welsh relations was to be found in the late nineteenth century. A common loyalty to the British monarch held together these different parts of the United Kingdom, though the degree of loyalty was less strongly felt in Ireland than it was elsewhere.

Queen Victoria

At the time this book opens, Queen Victoria's long reign of 64 years (1837–1901) still had its greater part to run. A few years earlier, in 1861, her husband's death had been for the Queen a personal tragedy which she found very difficult to bear. A widowed woman in the last century, and earlier in this, was expected to withdraw from society. But in Victoria's case her seclusion in her Scottish castle at Balmoral was so lengthy that, for most people, Britain appeared to have no monarch at all. Victoria became unpopular, and there were some demands that the British system of government should be changed from a monarchy to a republic. By the late 1870s the Queen had largely overcome her grief and she again became a familiar figure. She also became an increasingly popular one, as the festivities surrounding her Golden Jubilee in 1887 and her Diamond Jubilee in 1897 were to show.

Two contrasting views of the British monarchy in the second half of the nineteenth century. The cartoon of the late 1860s makes a harsh criticism of Victoria's lengthy retirement from public life in her early years as a widow. The photograph of 30 years later, with bunting and banners for the Silver Jubilee of 1897, shows how the Queen had by then recaptured the affection of her subjects.

Parliamentary government

Despite the popularity surrounding Queen Victoria, the importance of the monarchy in the governing of Britain was decreasing. The real business of governing the country lay with the Prime Minister and the cabinet, who together formed the **government** of the country. These men were members of the political party or group of parties which had a majority in the House of Commons. Their policies and their actions had to be approved by **parliament**. This consists of the elected House of Commons and also of the House of Lords, whose members were there by right of birth or as a result of having been created an aristocrat by the monarch, not as a result of election. This system of government is known as **parliamentary government**. It had developed over many centuries, starting with the early parliaments of the middle ages. By Victoria's reign, the way in which parliamentary government functioned was regarded by many British people with great pride. It seemed much better than the way in which foreign countries were governed. It was, for example, contrasted favourably with the autocratic rule of the Tsar in the Russian Empire, with the changeable systems found in France and with what were considered to be the dangers of full democracy as practised in the United States.

Parliamentary seats

But by the 1860s there was concern about the whole system. It could be criticised in two particular ways. One was the **distribution of seats**. Since the time of the middle ages, a member of parliament had been elected either as a **county member** or as a **borough member**. Over the centuries the pattern of population had changed so that the system was no longer as representative as it had been when it began. In particular, during the previous hundred years, the sharp increase in population and the growing numbers living in towns had made parliament even less representative than earlier. Under the terms of the First Parliamentary Reform Act, passed in 1832 after much controversy, there had been a readjustment of the county and borough representation. Though this had made the system fairer, it had not solved the problem entirely. In any case, the distribution of population had changed further since that time. The basic problem by the mid-1860s was that the north of England had too few MPs for its population and the south of England had too many.

The right to vote

Those who had the right to vote were said to possess the **franchise** or the **suffrage**. The restricted nature of the franchise in these years was the other way in which the system was criticised. The ownership or the renting of property was the basis on which the franchise was allowed; and it was allowed only to men. The amount that a man paid in rent to the property's owner or in rates to the local authority decided whether or not he had the franchise. Thus in the counties the franchise was allowed to those who were called the **40 shilling freeholders**, persons who owned property that was valued at 40 shillings (£2) for the payment of the annual rate to the local authority. This group of people had been the traditional holders of the county franchise. The 1832 Act had enfranchised others in the counties. These people were referred to as the £10 copyholders, the £10 long leaseholders, the £50 medium leaseholders and the £50 tenants. These technical terms refer to various different ways in which property was valued for the annual rate payment. In the boroughs the system was simpler. Here the franchise was allowed to those who were called **£10 householders**, persons who either owned or rented town property which was valued at £10 or more each year for rate payment. The uniform £10 qualification was introduced in 1832 when various earlier qualifications had been abolished.

Demand for parliamentary reform

In its time, the 1832 Parliamentary Reform Act had been of great importance. Though it had not increased the electorate very dramatically, it had resulted in better representation for the middle classes. It was the middle classes who had pioneered and made money from the industry which had so much changed Britain during the half-century before the Act had been passed. Some politicians closely associated with the 1832 Act believed that the changes it had brought about were final, that there was no further need to adjust the distribution of seats or the availability of the franchise.

Few things in history are ever 'final'. By the 1860s there were demands for further reform. The idea of the franchise becoming available for all adult males got little support. That would be too dangerous. It was generally considered that to use the vote responsibly, a man should have had some education. In the 1860s

THE ECONOMY, THE PEOPLE AND THE GOVERNING OF BRITAIN

many lacked education and there was fear that such people might use the vote irresponsibly and elect unsatisfactory MPs. The idea of extending the vote to women was scarcely considered.

Palmerston's opposition to reform

In 1865 the death of the Prime Minister, Lord Palmerston, had opened the way for change. Palmerston had been Prime Minister almost continuously for the previous ten years, leading a coalition government of Whigs and Liberals. He would have described himself as a Whig, a member of a political party with a long history, going back into the previous century and earlier. Though Palmerston and the Whigs were not completely opposed to change and reform, they were much more cautious in their approach than the Liberals. Having developed significantly during the mid-nineteenth century, the Liberals were able to press more forcefully for parliamentary reform now that Palmerston's long dominance was ended. In doing this, the Liberals were assured of useful support from the Radicals, a minority political group, loosely allied to the Whigs and the Liberals. The attitudes of these different political groups and their relationships with each other in these years are more fully considered in the following chapter on pages 15–17.

Gladstone and reform

The acknowledged leader of the Liberals at this time was W.E. Gladstone, one of the leading statesmen of the nineteenth century, who became Prime Minister on four occasions. His achievements as a politician and his standing among the Liberals are also considered in the following chapter. On parliamentary reform, his main argument was that there was no point in refusing the vote to better-educated working-class men, the **skilled artisans** as they were often called in the language of the time. The further development of industry in mid-Victorian times had increased the number of men in this category. They played a vital part in the prosperity which Britain enjoyed, yet they had no vote because they failed to meet the requirements of the 1832 Act. Was there really any good reason why they should not be allowed to take part in the election of their country's government? If the franchise continued to be refused to them, might they not oppose the government? The view of the Liberals was that the country would not only benefit by giving these men the vote, but might also avoid future difficulties.

There was much to suggest that the Liberals were putting forward a sensible course of action. But they had another and more direct reason for wanting to widen the franchise to include the skilled artisans. Though this was not a time of careful surveys and polls such as those familiar to us today, some useful observations were nevertheless made in the 1860s about the likely ways in which people might vote. There were many social similarities between the skilled artisans who did not have the vote and the lower middle classes who did. The general tendency was for the latter to vote Liberal. There was therefore a strong likelihood that enfranchising the skilled artisans would directly benefit the Liberal party. The opposition Conservatives also believed this to be likely.

The controversy surrounding the Second Parliamentary Reform Act

Lord John Russell, the Whig politician who some 30 years before had played a leading role in the passage of the 1832 Act, became Prime Minister on Palmerston's death in October 1865. He favoured a moderate approach to parliamentary reform and intended to appoint a commission to suggest how the present electoral system might be changed. However, Russell's government relied on the support of the Radicals in order to stay in power. The price for continuing this support was an immediate bill to reform parliament and Russell had no alternative but to yield.

The 1866 bill

The bill that was introduced in 1866 had many references to the amounts paid in rent or rates by those to whom the franchise was to be allowed in counties and boroughs. All this was designed to achieve the goal which men such as the Prime

Minister and Gladstone, now Chancellor of the Exchequer, had set themselves: the extension of the vote to skilled artisans. This moderate goal soon ran into criticism from among the government's supporters. Though they did not urge universal suffrage, the Radicals had hoped for a wider extension of the franchise than the government now planned. On the other hand, some Whigs were concerned that the bill's provisions would result in the enfranchisement of people not capable of using the vote wisely. These differences among the government's own supporters boded ill for the bill's chances.

Robert Lowe

The greatest trouble was caused to the government by Robert Lowe. This experienced Whig politician had developed a fear of democracy. This fear was based on what he had seen of the way in which democracy worked in the United States and in Australia. In a number of speeches early in 1866 he painted a grim and exaggerated picture of the effects of democracy in countries where it was practised.

> **We see in America, where the people have undisputed power, that they do not send honest, hard-working men to represent them in Congress, but traffickers in office, bankrupts, men who have lost their character and been driven from every respectable way of life and who take up politics as a last resource. In the colonies they have got Democratic Assemblies. And what is the result? Why, responsible government becomes a curse instead of a blessing.**
>
> Hansard, *Parliamentary Debates*

The blunt fact was that Lowe greatly mistrusted the working classes; and he was not even satisfied with the government's modest proposals that the vote should go only to the better-off among them. He foresaw other problems. An extension of the franchise would increase the importance of parliament; as a result, the government would become more powerful and this would have unhappy results for the country as a whole.

> **Under democracy, individual men are small, and the government is great. That must be the character of a government which represents the majority, and which absolutely tramples down and equalises everything except itself. And democracy has another strong peculiarity. It looks with the utmost hostility on all institutions not of immediate popular origin, which intervene between the people and the sovereign power which the people have set up.**
>
> Hansard, *Parliamentary Debates*

Lowe's fears, however unfounded they may now appear, were shared by many in the 1860s. He soon became the acknowledged leader of those among the government's supporters who were opposed to the Reform Bill. These politicians formed themselves into an opposition group, known as the **Adullamites**. This name came from the Old Testament story of David being chased to the cave of Adullam (*1 Samuel*, Chapter 22, Verse 1), a reference that would have been well understood in the nineteenth century, when the details of the Bible were better known than they generally are today. The existence of the Adullamites showed the government as divided and presented a great opportunity to the main opposition party in parliament, the Tory party.

The defeat of the Liberals

Lord Derby in the House of Lords and Benjamin Disraeli in the House of Commons were the leaders of the Tory party. From the opening of this controversy Disraeli had seen it as providing excellent means of advancing the fortunes of his party and of establishing more firmly his own position within it. He certainly succeeded in doing the latter, and his achievements as a politician are considered more fully in Chapter 2. Disraeli and the Conservatives were careful never to show outright opposition to parliamentary reform, as such opposition might make them unpopular among new voters. Instead, they preferred to criticise the particular proposals of the government. In June 1866,

THE ECONOMY, THE PEOPLE AND THE GOVERNING OF BRITAIN

Tory and Adullamite opposition resulted in the government's defeat. Gladstone, the main force behind the government's proposals for parliamentary reform, hoped to have the chance of fighting an election on the issue. Russell, however, lacked enthusiasm for such a course. He resigned as Prime Minister, advising the Queen to appoint Lord Derby in his place.

Disraeli and reform

What is usually called the **Derby–Disraeli ministry** of 1866–68 was then formed. Lord Derby was Prime Minister, keeping (as any aristocrat had to until the late 1950s) his position in the House of Lords. Disraeli was Conservative leader in the House of Commons and the real force in the government. There could be no backing away from the issue of reform, to which Disraeli had earlier committed himself. In any case the summer of 1866 was marked by serious rioting, suggesting that worse might follow if some measure of reform were not allowed. The most serious rioting occurred in London's Hyde Park, as a result of the banning of a meeting in favour of parliamentary reform. All this showed that the issue could not be dropped. Nor had Disraeli any intention of dropping it, as in his judgement parliamentary reform could be made to work to the advantage of his party. Disraeli felt that an even wider extension of the franchise would be of benefit to the Tories. This view was based on the feeling that many of the working classes would vote for a traditional party such as the Tory party was.

The Tory bill was introduced in the spring of 1867. Like the previous bill, it had a difficult passage through the House of Commons, where Disraeli proved himself a more able pilot for his bill than Gladstone had been in the previous year. His greatest achievement in this respect was to hold the Tory party together in these difficult months and to avoid the serious type of split which the Adullamites had caused for the Liberals. The Tories were not, however, in a strong position in the House of Commons, where a combination of the opposition parties could have defeated them. It was only to be expected that the bill would be amended as it went through the House of Commons. The House of Lords scarcely adjusted what came to it from the House of Commons and in August 1867 the Second Reform Act became law.

THE DERBY, 1867. DIZZY WINS WITH "REFORM BILL."
Mr. Punch. "DON'T BE TOO SURE; WAIT TILL HE'S *WEIGHED.*"

Mr Punch makes a shrewd comment on the success of Disraeli ('Dizzy') in securing the passage of the Second Parliamentary Reform Act.

The terms and importance of the Second Reform Act

Terms

The terms of the Second Reform Act can be considered in three sections. In the boroughs, the franchise was now allowed to all householders and to lodgers occupying lodgings with an annual value of £10 for the payment of rates. In the counties, the franchise was now allowed to those who owned property with an annual value of £5 and to those who rented property with an annual value of £12. Additionally, the Act redistributed a fairly small number of parliamentary seats: these were mainly ones removed from small boroughs and given to larger boroughs or to counties. The Act applied only to England and Wales. Two acts of 1868 extended some very similar provisions concerning franchise and redistribution to Scotland and Ireland.

Voters and parliamentary seats

The number of British people able to vote increased from approximately one and a half million just before the Act to approximately two and a half million afterwards. One man in every three now had the vote. Most of the new voters were to be found in the boroughs among the newly enfranchised householders. It was the skilled artisan in the towns who benefited most from the Second Reform Act.

In other respects, the Act produced little change. The most glaring feature of the earlier system that still remained was the division into county constituencies and borough constituencies. Earlier reference has been made to the unjust distribution of seats before the 1867 Act. It was essentially the county–borough division which caused that injustice; the minor adjustments of 1867 made very little difference to this. There were still, after the Act, many boroughs

A HISTORY OF BRITAIN FROM 1867

of small population which returned an MP. There were still areas of heavy population, such as Lancashire, London, Yorkshire and the Lowlands of Scotland, which were seriously under-represented.

Importance of the Act

The 1867 Act can be seen today as an important step in the development of democratic parliamentary government. It could not, of course, be seen in that way by people at the time. Its opponents were not alone among those who were nervous of its effects. 'A leap in the dark' was the way in which the Prime Minister, Lord Derby, regarded what had been done. 'Shooting Niagara' was another description given to it. This would have been well understood at the time as a reference to the acrobat Blondin, who had achieved world-wide renown for his courage in crossing Niagara Falls on a tightrope, while blindfolded. In practice, the 1867 Act appears to have had little direct effect on the way in which Britain was governed. Although, as we shall see, the 20 years or so after 1867 were more notable for reforms than were those leading up to the Act, it is not easy to say whether these reforms were a direct result of the Act itself. The Act did, however, show that what had been done in 1832 was not final; the fundamental reforms of that year had now been taken further. For the future, there was no reason why that process should not continue.

That is what happened. Over the next half-century further steps were taken in parliamentary reform. In the following pages, attention will be directed to the Ballot Act of 1872, the Corrupt Practices Act of 1883, the Third Parliamentary Reform Act and the Redistribution Act of 1884–85, the Parliament Act of 1911, the Representation of the People Act of 1918 and the Equal Franchise Act of 1928. On another level, similar changes in local government were made by acts of 1888, 1894, 1929 and 1973. All were further steps along the road that led to universal suffrage and a system in which the government became fully responsible to the people of Britain rather than to any privileged group. This book therefore opens in a year of early significance and great importance on that road. For the present, however, attention will be directed towards the way in which politicians tackled other immediate issues in Britain during the years after the passage of the Second Reform Act.

---------- EXERCISES ----------

1. 'British greatness as a world power was already being challenged in the late 1860s.' Show how far you agree with this statement by reference to:
   (a) British industry, and
   (b) British agriculture.

2. (a) Explain why there were demands for the reform of parliament in the late 1860s.
   (b) Describe the various attempts to secure reform in 1866–67.
   (c) Outline the terms of the 1867 Reform Act.

3. Imagine that before the passage of the 1867 Reform Act you were not allowed to vote. Write a letter for publication in a newspaper, explaining why in your opinion you should be allowed to vote. Write a second letter, after the passage of the 1867 Act, explaining the course of events that led to your securing of the vote in that year.

4. Study the cartoon on page 13 and then answer questions (a) to (d) which follow.
   (a) (i) Identify the Prime Minister, shown as the winner of this race.
       (ii) Identify the Prime Minister's main political rival, shown as the runner up.
       (iii) What is the attitude of the cartoonist towards each of these men? By reference to the events of 1866–67 show in what ways this attitude is justified. (1+1+4)
   (b) Describe the terms of the 'Reform Bill' as passed by parliament. (5)
   (c) (i) What do you understand by the words that Mr Punch is speaking?
       (ii) Show in what ways those words were proved to be accurate. (2+3)
   (d) By reference to the words and portrayals in the cartoon, indicate its value as a piece of historical evidence. (4)

GLADSTONE, THE LIBERAL PARTY AND THE MINISTRY OF 1868–74

For about a dozen years after the passage of the 1867 Reform Act, political life within Britain was dominated by two of the greatest politicians of the nineteenth century: William Ewart Gladstone and Benjamin Disraeli. Both had been active in politics for some years and both had risen to the position of party leader: Gladstone in the Liberal party and Disraeli in the Conservative party. We have already seen the important part each played in the events leading to the 1867 Act and their concern to get political advantage for their party as a result of the wider franchise. There the similarities end. In their characters and their ideals each man was markedly different from the other.

William Ewart Gladstone

Background

By upbringing, Gladstone came from a wealthy Tory family that had made money from the cotton trade and that had much influence in Liverpool. In later life Gladstone never lost touch with the north-west and returned whenever he could to his house and extensive estates at Hawarden, in Cheshire. Political life came naturally to him. He entered the House of Commons as a Tory MP in 1833 at the age of only 24, and joined the government in 1841, while still quite young. Like some other great politicians in the years covered by this book, Gladstone changed parties during the course of his career. In 1846 the government in which he served and which was headed by Sir Robert Peel, a politician whom the young Gladstone greatly admired, had taken a decision of great importance. The early nineteenth-century Corn Laws, which prevented the importing of cheap foreign corn, were repealed. Only by doing this – and thus allowing into the country cheap foreign corn – could adequate relief be given to the Irish, at that time suffering a famine from which thousands were dying. Many Tories were angered at what they regarded as a 'betrayal' of their own interests by Peel; others were glad that he had acted in such a humane way.

Gladstone gave his support to the **Peelite** group that pledged their support to the Prime Minister. The crisis of 1846 was seen by Gladstone as a moral crisis. What was the right thing to do? Was it right to support his party and the landowners or was it right to help the starving people of Ireland? For Gladstone there could only be one answer to such a question. His decision in 1846 – to support the giving of aid to the Irish – became typical of his approach to politics: at all times to seek and do what he considered to be morally right.

Attitudes and personality

In supporting this view Gladstone drew inspiration, even more than most Victorians, from the Christian faith. He was a devout member of the Church of England, and committed to the high church way of thinking within it. Earlier in his life he had intended becoming a clergyman of the Church of England. In his manner and attitudes as a politician later in life he bore many resemblances to a conscientious Anglican vicar. He had no fear of hard work or of hostile opinions. Additionally, he was a man of great intellectual brilliance, well demonstrated earlier in his life while a schoolboy at Eton and student at Oxford.

These varying qualities made William Ewart Gladstone a powerful politician. After his involvement in the Peelite split from the Tories in 1846, he moved towards the Whig party, though still for some years keeping his Peelite identity. As Chancellor of the Exchequer in the years 1852–55 and for a longer period in the years 1859–66, Gladstone's main concern had been to develop more fully the free trade policies which Peel had worked for in the early 1840s. These were years in which Gladstone gained experience in a senior government position and in which he developed skills which were to serve him well as Prime Minister in later life.

Opponents

Not everyone was filled with enthusiasm and admiration for Gladstone. He aroused great dislike among many of his opponents. His policies were often considered by them to be likely to lead the country to disaster. He was often tactless in dealing with people. When he expressed firmly held views at great length and with much intensity, many felt he was a pompous bore. He never succeeded in achieving the confidence of Queen Victoria, who complained that he spoke to her at private audiences as if he were addressing a public meeting. To his supporters he may have become, in the popular expression of the time, the 'Grand Old Man'; to his opponents he was known as 'God's One Mistake'.

The Liberal party and the general election of 1868

Whigs and Radicals

The 1850s and 1860s were years of crucial development for the political opponents of the Tories, among whom Gladstone now found himself. The Whigs were the main opponents of the Tories in the mid-nineteenth century. Like the Tories, they traced their history back for at least 200 years. In many respects leading Whigs would not be particularly different from leading Tories in background and attitude. Though Whigs did claim to support the idea of reform more whole-heartedly than Tories, the reforms they looked for were certainly limited. The recently formed Radicals pushed more vigorously for reform. They were regarded with suspicion by the Whigs, with whom they were allied, and were of course regarded with much suspicion by the Tories. In the middle years of the century the Peelites were steadily attaching themselves to this loose Whig–Radical alliance. These three political groups formed the basis of what was to develop as the Liberal party.

The Liberal party

Gladstone, more than any other politician, breathed life into the new Liberal party. Though he did not become its leader until 1868, just a few months before his victory in the general election of that year, he had much influence in the party by the mid-1860s. Gladstone knew that these were years of change in Britain and he was convinced that the newly formed party could respond to those changes. The new party was in any case assured of varied support throughout the country. Members of most of the Nonconformist Churches, who had traditionally supported the Whigs, were won over without much difficulty to the Liberals. They were a valuable catch as in the mid-nineteenth century Nonconformists were probably more numerous than Anglicans, many of whom traditionally supported the Tory party. Gladstone also sought to attract members of the trade union movement. Here was a new force in Britain. It was developing in these years and it could identify itself with the reform demands of the Liberals. The timing was fortunate for the Liberals in another way, as in these years the circulation of newspapers was increasing. In an age before radio and television, newspapers had deep impact and became a means of spreading the Liberal message. The extension of the franchise by the 1867 Reform Act presented even further opportunities.

The 1868 general election

The general election in the autumn of 1868 was a test of how far the new party and its new leader could respond to these favourable circumstances. When the results were all gathered in from the constituencies they showed that the Liberals had scored an impressive victory.

General Election: November 1868	
Conservatives	274
Liberals	384

With a result such as this to his credit, Gladstone's prestige within his party could not be challenged. His Liberal ministry which followed was to be a long one. Until the early twentieth century the gap between general elections could be as long as seven years. Few ministries lasted for such a time, but Gladstone's first ministry lasted for six years (1868–74) and, like Disraeli's second ministry which followed (1874–80), was one of the longest in the nineteenth century. It has also been regarded as one of the most important.

Gladstone and Ireland

The issue to which Gladstone attached greatest importance in this ministry, as in his later ones, was Ireland. Violence in Ireland and violence in Britain because of Irish problems had been much in evidence throughout the 1860s. Irish issues had dominated the 1868 general election campaign. On hearing the news of his success in the election, Gladstone declared that to bring peace to Ireland was his 'mission', thus further emphasising the religious basis on which he approached his work. As it is useful to see how Gladstone's work in Ireland linked with that of other politicians, the history of Ireland in the late nineteenth century is considered as a whole in Chapter 3. It should at this point be remembered that Ireland loomed very large indeed during Gladstone's first ministry. In his later ministries it was to dominate almost entirely. In the end, it was to frustrate and defeat even the Grand Old Man's political skill.

The 1870 Education Act

Public and elementary schools

School education in the second half of the nineteenth century was of two kinds: a public school education for the minority and an elementary school education for the majority. The public schools were privately financed and provided a particular type of education for the sons of wealthy families. Elementary education was provided by two voluntary Christian societies: the National Society (of the Anglican Church) and the British and Foreign Society (of the Nonconformist Churches). Such schools were usually known as **voluntary schools**. The societies had been receiving financial grants from the state since the 1830s. In recent years these grants had led to an increase in the number of schools and teachers at the elementary level. The increased provision for education by the time of Gladstone's first ministry was one of the most important ways in which the lives of ordinary people had improved in the middle years of the century.

Religious issues

The improvement was not without its problems. As the number of schools had increased so there came demands for the state to take a more active part in education. It was argued that the state ought not to limit its activities to providing the voluntary societies with money. Instead it should provide state-run schools. If it did that, the vital question arose as to whether the religious teaching in the schools should be Anglican or Nonconformist. Today such a question would be unlikely to cause serious problems. But in nineteenth and early twentieth-century Britain, relations between the different churches were often unfriendly. No politician wished to deal with the dangerous question of what type of religious teaching should take place in a state school. So the simplest approach was to allow the voluntary societies to continue with government help and to postpone the setting-up of state schools.

Demand for more schools

State schools, however, could not be postponed indefinitely. There was much general demand for more schools. Many felt that only state schools could really fulfil that demand and that it was no good continuing to rely just on the voluntary schools. Those who pressed this demand did so due to a real belief in the value of education for the working classes. They believed that as education became more widely available to them, so there would be a lessening of crime and an improvement in behaviour. Men and women would become better civilised people. Additionally, the expansion of industry and commerce meant that there was a growing need for skilled workers and clerks.

After 1867 another very strong argument existed. Surely some provision should be made to see that the new voters were educated people? Many of those who obtained the vote under the 1867 Act certainly were educated; many were not. In any case, the number of people entitled to vote was likely to be further increased before very long. If no action were taken, many future voters would remain illiterate. There was real danger to the country in allowing people who had no education to exercise control over the country's affairs by their votes. Robert Lowe, a politician who had played an important part in educational policies during the 1860s and whose opposition to parliamentary reform at that time has been noted in the previous chapter, summarised the attitude of many on this key issue.

> I suppose now it will be absolutely necessary to educate our masters.... From the moment you entrust the masses with power, their education becomes an imperative necessity; and though I believe the existing system is one superior to the much vaunted Continental system: it is not quality but quantity we shall require. You have placed the government of this country in the hands of the masses, and you must therefore give them education.

It was only natural that a government such as Gladstone's would respond to these pressures.

THE THREE R'S; OR, BETTER LATE THAN NEVER.

RIGHT HON. W. E. FORSTER (CHAIRMAN OF BOARD). "WELL, MY LITTLE PEOPLE, WE HAVE BEEN GRAVELY AND EARNESTLY CONSIDERING WHETHER YOU MAY LEARN TO READ. I AM HAPPY TO TELL YOU THAT, SUBJECT TO A VARIETY OF RESTRICTIONS, CONSCIENCE CLAUSES, AND THE CONSENT OF YOUR VESTRIES – YOU MAY!"

This cartoon gives some idea of the tensions surrounding provision for education in the early 1870s. The author of the 1870 Act has some difficulty in explaining these tensions to those whom the Act was to benefit directly.

Terms The Act of 1870 by which they did so is often termed the **Forster Education Act** from the minister who guided it through the House of Commons. It had two main provisions, one to create a new system and the other to maintain the old one. The new system was the setting-up of state schools that became known as **board schools**. These were to be controlled by local school boards and were to be financed not by the central government but by a locally raised **education rate**. As for the tricky problem of religious teaching in these schools, it was agreed in the Cowper-Temple clause of the Act that this should be of an **undenominational** kind: it was to be neither Anglican nor Nonconformist in type and was to be based strictly on Bible study. It was in this way that the likelihood of conflict between the Christian denominations was reduced. Alongside this new system, the Act maintained the old. In districts where parents were already able to send their children to local voluntary schools, no board schools were to be set up. In addition to these main provisions, the Act is also important for not doing two things for which many had hoped. It did not make school attendance compulsory and it did not make school attendance free.

Importance

The Forster Education Act marks a vital stage in the development of elementary education. It showed, in particular, that the state was now ready to be far more fully committed to providing education than it had previously been. Nevertheless it met much opposition. This opposition was the more dangerous for the government as it came from its own Nonconformist supporters. They disliked the continued absence of compulsory attendance and the continued payment of fees. They also felt the Act gave too much to the Anglicans. The Nonconformists strongly supported the board schools, but by not providing them in districts already adequately supplied with voluntary schools, the Act was in practice giving a distinct advantage to the Anglicans. Anglican schools were already more numerous than Nonconformist schools, so the Act really upheld this Anglican lead. The Nonconformists also disliked a minor clause in the Act which allowed the fees of poor children to be paid from the rates. In this way public money was used to finance voluntary schools; their fear was that Anglican schools would get far more advantage from this clause than their schools would.

The abolition of privilege: the Ballot Act

Gladstone and his government were prepared to face the opposition which the 1870 Education Act aroused, as they believed in the Act's basic principles. In spite of its limitations, what it was doing was to provide greater opportunity for young people to make a success of life by providing them with an elementary education. Other acts took this basic principle further, by providing greater opportunity in life for adults. To do this, the government launched attacks on long-established privileged positions in the conduct of politics, in the civil service and in the armed forces.

Voting at the hustings

The 1872 Ballot Act was the government's contribution to parliamentary reform. Before this Act, voting was done in public at what were known as the **hustings**. How a man voted became a matter of public knowledge. Politicians seeking election could therefore see some point in bribing their prospective voters, as they would know on election day exactly how each of them voted. Local landowners were also able to assert influence on voters who were dependent on the landowner for their land and living. If the voter used his vote to support a politician of whom the landowner disapproved, he might have to face victimisation, which at times resulted in eviction from his land. With the recent extension of the franchise by the 1867 Act the results of bribery and victimisation became even more widespread. In these respects the general election of 1868 was about the worst of the whole century.

Given such voting conditions, it is surprising that there were still those who defended the system of voting at the hustings. These defenders of the old ways valued the hustings as a place where a man would openly and unashamedly declare his political loyalty. In their view there was something 'manly' about open voting, and something rather cowardly about secret voting. Surely, they argued, a man should stand up for his political opinions and not try to make a secret of them?

The secret ballot

Arguments such as this now carried little weight. Gladstone had become convinced of the need for secret voting. The Act of 1872, providing for secret voting in a ballot box, did not arouse much controversy. The following newspaper account of an 1872 by-election emphasised the contrast with the previous system.

A HISTORY OF BRITAIN FROM 1867

> Usually an election day here has been a day of great political tumult and uproar. But to-day the general aspect of things is changed. When the poll opened the principal streets of the town were almost as quiet as usual. At the polling booths, thirty-seven in number, there was very little crowding, and generally the town seemed to have got up no earlier than usual this morning, though in an extreme state of mystification. At each polling booth there was erected, under contract with the Corporation, the compartments prescribed by the Act to secure privacy to the voter while marking his ballot paper. These compartments consisted of an open movable box, with four stalls or recesses, each supplied with a small ledge to serve as a desk, and placed back to back, so that four voters might be engaged in marking their papers at one and the same time.
>
> *The Times*, 14 September 1872

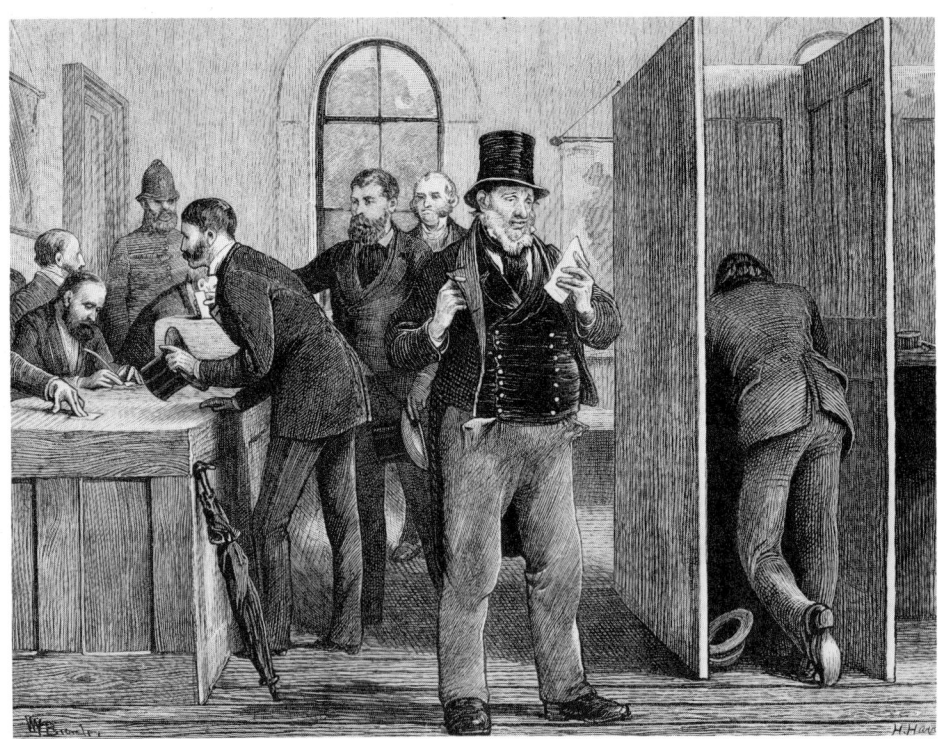

The introduction of the secret ballot by the Act of 1872 was an essential step in the developing provision within Britain for democracy. The orderliness in this scene would contrast sharply with voting at the hustings earlier.

Elections were therefore conducted in a more orderly way. But deep-rooted attitudes of deference towards the local landowner were not readily abandoned, and such men continued to assert influence on the outcome of elections for the next decade or so, in spite of the secrecy in which their tenants now voted. More important were the effects the Act had at the next general election on the development of the Nationalist party in Ireland and the success later in the century of Socialist politicians in England and Scotland. No longer fearful of the possible effects of voting, many now voted for new parties which appeared to represent their interests better than the old ones did. The importance of the Act for the Irish Nationalist party and for Socialism is considered more fully in Chapters 3 and 4.

The abolition of privilege: the civil service and the universities

The civil service

The Liberals made other important inroads against privilege. Both the civil service and the ancient universities of Oxford and Cambridge played a vital part in British life: the civil service in the administration of the country and the ancient universities in the education of its leaders. Until the middle years of the nineteenth century, the civil service was recruited entirely by **patronage**. Under this system, young men were merely recommended for entry into the civil service by some older acquaintance, regardless of how well qualified they might or might not be for the posts. Such a system of recruitment failed to build up the civil service as the really efficient body it needed to be in these times, when the administration of various acts of parliament was now creating more work for civil servants. Already some reforms had been made by requiring senior posts to be filled by examinations. In 1870 the government made it compulsory for almost all grades in the civil service to be filled by examinations. But the government was not prepared to make entry into the civil service fully competitive. Senior posts in the Foreign Office were excluded from the new system and continued to be filled by patronage.

Oxford and Cambridge

Similar measures were taken at Oxford and Cambridge. Here privilege was not that of wealth, but the position of the Church of England. Anglican influence in these universities had been strong since the Reformation. It was only in the middle years of the century that non-Anglicans had been allowed to enter these universities as students. Now, by the Universities Tests Act of 1871, it was no longer necessary for those who taught and researched at them to be Anglicans. Gladstone did not like this Act. As a high church Anglican he favoured the old system. But he took a realistic view and could see that the position of the Church of England in these universities was difficult to defend. It might become subject to even sterner measures in the future if this reform were not made.

The abolition of privilege: the armed forces

Need for reform

There were many reforms affecting the British Army in the early 1870s and these were long overdue. In the 1850s, the Crimean War had shown the bad organisation of the Army. In that war there were many examples of inefficiency that led to unnecessary loss of life and that almost led to loss of the war. Since then, little attention had been given to the Army and the number of soldiers had decreased. The man whom Gladstone appointed as Secretary for War during his first ministry was Edward Cardwell. Events on the Continent usefully played into Cardwell's hands. In the autumn of 1870 the Prussian Army had advanced swiftly and successfully into France in the opening stages of the Franco-Prussian War. There was fear in Britain – bordering on panic in some areas – that the Prussians might obtain similar success if they were to attempt an invasion of Britain. Against this background, the House of Commons readily approved Cardwell's proposals for Army reform.

Opposition to reform

Nevertheless, Cardwell's proposals were strongly opposed elsewhere. Foremost among his opponents was the Commander-in-Chief of the British Army, the Duke of Cambridge. Few men in authority at that time were so determined in their opposition to change. It was his view that the system worked well enough as it was and no good purpose would be served by changing it. The House of Lords supported him and their opposition became a real stumbling block for Cardwell.

Purchase of commissions

The reform that was more strongly opposed than any other was the abolition of the purchasing of commissions in the Army. Until this time it had been possible for young men from wealthy backgrounds to become commissioned (to become officers) in the Army merely on payment of money and not as a result of suitability for the job. Some of the setbacks in the Crimean War had been caused by the incompetence of officers who had joined the Army in this way. The wealthy regarded the purchasing of commissions as a right which should not be taken from them. Their view was vigorously put forward in the House of Lords.

A HISTORY OF BRITAIN FROM 1867

In order to overcome their opposition the government persuaded the Queen to sign what was called an **order in council**. It was therefore on the Sovereign's authority that the purchasing of commissions was abolished.

Other Army reforms

Gladstone's other Army reforms were less controversial. Some were directed at making the life of the ordinary soldier more humane. An early reform had been the abolition of flogging as a military punishment. Soldiers had previously often been sentenced to this brutal punishment for quite trivial offences. At the same time the practice of branding an army deserter with the letter 'D' was also dropped. Previously soldiers on enlistment in the Army had to sign on for a period of 12 years. This was now reduced to six years, though for a further six years they were in the reserves and could be called on to fight if need arose.

Other reforms were directed at improving efficiency. Until this time there had been confusion whether the Secretary for War or the Commander-in-Chief was ultimately in control of the British Army. Cardwell made it clear that the Secretary for War, the man with direct responsibility to parliament, held final control. The different **regiments** of the Army consisted of various **battalions**. Now a system of **linked battalions** was set up, one serving in Britain and the other abroad. Some ten years after these reforms, in the hope of attracting local recruits, the regiments took on the names of their counties.

The Cardwell reforms of the 1870s did much to improve the efficiency of the British Army. Like many photographs that survive from the late nineteenth century, this military one shows the popularity of a formal group portrait in those years. (Compare those on page 76 and top of page 87.)

Gladstone's first ministry: foreign affairs

Britain and the Franco-Prussian War

It was during Gladstone's first ministry that the Franco-Prussian War of 1870–71 took place. This war was the product of increasing tension between France and Prussia over a number of years. Its consequences were crucial for the future of both countries: in France it resulted in the fall of the Second French Empire of the Emperor Napoleon III and in Prussia it resulted in the creation of the Second German Empire under the Kaiser (Emperor) Wilhelm I. The First and Second World Wars, though very much longer and more widespread, were to share an essential feature with the Franco-Prussian War, as they also centred on a violent conflict between continental Europe's two great powers.

Belgian neutrality

Yet, unlike the two twentieth-century world wars, Britain played no part in the Franco-Prussian War. No vital British interests were involved in the issues for which the war was fought and so Britain remained neutral. Britain successfully insisted that both combatants in the war should respect the independence of Belgium. There were fears in the early stages of the war that France might invade Belgium, but these fears were to prove groundless. During the nineteenth century and early twentieth century, preserving Belgian neutrality was always a major objective of British foreign policy. Belgium is so close to British shores that control of it by an unfriendly power was considered a serious danger to Britain. The natural defence provided by the Channel would be made less secure; additionally, Britain's overseas trade might be more readily threatened.

Relations with Russia

More serious were the consequences the war had on Britain's relations with Russia. For much of the nineteenth century Britain's relations with the vast Russian Empire were unfriendly. Its government was viewed as autocratic and backward. More seriously Russia was viewed as an aggressive power, whose ambitions were a danger to Britain in two particular respects. Its infiltration of lands such as Persia, Afghanistan and Tibet were seen as a threat to Britain's hold on India. Its influence in the Balkans and Middle East was seen as a challenge to the decaying power of the Ottoman Empire in those areas. Any opportunity of curbing Russian might was seized upon by successive British governments. In the mid-1850s, Russia had been defeated in the Crimean War and as part of the peace terms imposed by Britain and France had agreed not to keep warships on the Black Sea. The point of denying Russia this right was to prevent it from being able to threaten the Ottoman Empire. But the Russian government seized the opportunity of the diversion caused by the Franco-Prussian War to break what were known as the **Black Sea clauses** and to send warships there. Much popular anti-Russian feeling was produced in Britain by this action and there were demands in some quarters for war with Russia. The government did not however respond to these demands. Gladstone and his Foreign Secretary knew that the Black Sea clauses had in the first place been particularly hard on Russia. The government therefore instead became involved in a complex series of negotiations that led at the start of the following year to an agreement among the great powers of Europe that the clauses should be abandoned and Russia given the right to keep warships on the Black Sea.

***Alabama* settlement**

A similar spirit of compromise was also found in relations with the United States. Some ten years earlier a British-made ship, the *Alabama*, had fought for the South in the US Civil War. After the North had won, the US government claimed compensation against the British government. Negotiations on these claims were lengthy and bitter. It was Gladstone's government which brought them to an end in 1872 by agreeing to pay fifteen million dollars to the United States as a fair settlement. The way in which the *Alabama* claims were settled provides an important early example of the use of international arbitration in solving an international dispute. In years to come there were to be many further examples of this approach, but at the time it was seen as an example of weakness. The government, so its opponents claimed, had shown weakness in facing Russia over the Black Sea clauses and in facing the United States over the *Alabama* claims.

'A range of exhausted volcanoes'

The Gladstone government of 1868–74 had an impressive record of reform. Not all of it has been considered in this chapter. His work for Ireland is considered in Chapter 3 (pages 36–44) and his work in connection with the trade unions is considered in Chapter 4 (page 48). The reforms he undertook, though important, were all modest in scope. None of them involved direct state intervention in the lives of the people in Britain. Yet his record of reform was to be the main cause of his loss of the general election in February 1874. Disraeli likened the Liberal ministers to 'a range of exhausted volcanoes', suggesting by that expression that not only were they tired by the work they had done, but that much of their work had caused needless upheaval.

Varied opposition to the government

Even the government's Nonconformist supporters had severe reservations about the Education Act of 1870. Few of them probably went so far as to vote against the government in 1874, but there is evidence that on this issue a number of Nonconformists abstained from voting. Reforms such as those connected with the ballot, the civil service, the universities and the Army led many to wonder what further changes Gladstone might introduce if re-elected. The government's foreign policy was criticised as lacking in the qualities expected from the government of a great power; in this connection, the acceptance of the Alabama award was particularly disliked. Trade unionists, whose movement was still in a formative stage, were angered by the ungenerous terms of the Criminal Law Amendment Act of 1871 (page 48). Though much of Gladstone's Irish legislation in these years had been useful for the Irish, it had alienated others. There was Anglican criticism of the Irish Church Act of 1869 (page 36) and criticism from landowners of the Land Act of 1870 (page 36).

Licensing Act

Gladstone himself attributed the Liberal defeat to one particular cause: the Licensing Act of 1872. This had been the work of Gladstone's Home Secretary, H.A. Bruce, and should be seen as part of the continuing concern about the problem of drink. The Act limited the hours of opening of pubs and it imposed stricter regulations for the granting of licenses to run pubs. It was a highly unpopular Act. Public houses, so the Liberals maintained, virtually became committee rooms for the Conservative party. In such places, doubtless, other points of criticism against Gladstone and his government would be eagerly discussed. The Licensing Act played an important part in Gladstone's downfall, but it should be seen against the general decline of the government's popularity, which was based on a variety of causes.

EXERCISES

1. Explain how the lives of the following would have been affected by the work of Gladstone during his first ministry:
   (a) school children
   (b) soldiers, and
   (c) civil servants.

2. Why did the Liberal government of Gladstone fail to secure re-election in 1874? In the course of your answer refer to:
   (a) domestic affairs, and
   (b) foreign affairs.

3. Imagine you are a political supporter of Gladstone during his ministry of 1868–74. Write a letter to a friend who in the election of 1874 is likely to vote for Disraeli showing why, in view of his record of achievement, Gladstone is the person for whom your friend should vote.

4. Study the cartoon on page 18 and the illustration on page 20 and then answer questions (a) to (d) which follow.
   (a) Identify by name and date the Act of Parliament with which:
      (i) the cartoon on page 18 is associated, and
      (ii) the illustration on page 20 is associated. (2)
   (b) (i) Explain why the work of the men shown in the cartoon on page 18 was considered necessary at that time.
      (ii) Explain why there was so much controversy over the terms of the Act with which this cartoon is associated, making particular reference to the role in that controversy of men such as the one shown on the extreme right.
      (iii) Give the terms of the Act as finally agreed.
      (iv) What do you learn from the cartoon about attitudes towards this controversy? (2+2+2+3)
   (c) (i) What do you learn from the illustration on page 20 about the way in which elections were held under the terms of the Act you have identified in (a) (ii)?
      (ii) Indicate how the illustration shows an improvement on the ways in which elections had been held earlier.
      (iii) Indicate the main effects that these improvements had on politics in Britain. (2+3+2)
   (d) What general principle might the Gladstone government be said to have furthered by its work in the two acts associated with this cartoon and this illustration? (2)

DISRAELI, THE CONSERVATIVE PARTY AND THE MINISTRY OF 1874–80

Benjamin Disraeli – in later life known as the Earl of Beaconsfield – was a distinct contrast in both personality and outlook to his great political rival, William Gladstone. On almost all the great issues of their time each took a different view from the other. Their backgrounds also were very different. Disraeli's family was Jewish, though he himself was baptised into the Church of England. His early career in politics was closely linked with his work as a writer of novels, in which he put forward some of his developing political ideas. He entered the House of Commons as a Conservative MP in 1837 at the age of 33, but he was not invited to join the Conservative government which Peel formed in 1841. Disraeli never forgave Peel for overlooking him in those years. When in 1846 Peel faced rebellion within his own party over the repeal of the Corn Laws (see page 15 for a summary of this episode) Disraeli took on the leadership of the rebel party members. By doing so he identified himself with the most traditional men among the Tories: the landowners, the men for whom Peel's abandonment of the Corn Laws had been an act of betrayal.

Disraeli's Conservatism

Disraeli and the Tories

Disraeli did not allow himself to be dominated by these wealthy supporters. As has been shown in the introduction, he played a key role in the events leading to the passage of the 1867 Reform Act. The doubts many of his supporters had about the usefulness of this Act appeared to be confirmed by the Tory loss of the next general election in 1868. But Disraeli, who had taken on the leadership of the party early in 1868, knew better than some among his supporters that it was essential for the party to accept change. If it failed to do so, it would not survive as a major party in the changing Britain of the late nineteenth century. The Liberals under Gladstone, by the extensive legislation of their years in power between 1868 and 1874, had shown that they certainly realised the need to respond to changed circumstances. How could the Tories fail to do otherwise?

The Conservative party

It is at around the time of Disraeli's leadership that the term **Conservative party** comes generally to replace the term **Tory party**. Disraeli has sometimes been called the founder of the modern Conservative party. During the time of Gladstone's first ministry he was responsible for improving party organisation. A Conservative Central Office was set up in London. Conservatives were encouraged to organise themselves into local associations capable of encouraging support for their party at election time. This work helped considerably towards the Conservative success in 1874. Better known were plans he publicly put forward in speeches for Britain's future under a Conservative government. The best known and most important of these speeches was one he gave in June 1872. The speech was made in the Crystal Palace, a fantastic structure in glass erected for the Great Exhibition of 1851, some 20 years previously, and a symbol of British pride in British achievements. Here Disraeli outlined the main aims of his party.

> It is the first duty of England to maintain its institutions, because to them we principally ascribe the power and prosperity of the country. Gentlemen, there is another and second great object of the Tory party. If the first is to maintain the institutions of the country, the second is, in my opinion, to uphold the Empire of England. If you look to the history of this country since the advent of Liberal-

ism you will find that there has been no effort so continuous, so subtle, supported by so much energy, and carried on with so much ability and acumen, as the attempts of Liberalism to effect the disintegration of the Empire of England. Gentlemen, another great object of the Tory party, and one not inferior to the maintenance of the Empire, or the upholding of our institutions, is the elevation of the condition of the people.

These aims might be summarised as the maintaining of Britain's institutions, supporting Britain's Empire and improving the conditions of the people of Britain. The Crystal Palace speech was a bid to secure wider support for the Conservative party. Traditional supporters would welcome the first objective; new working-class voters would welcome the third objective; all who felt keenly about Britain's position in the world would welcome the second objective. Nor was the Crystal Palace speech the only one in which Disraeli urged these aims. He was an active speaker in many parts of the country during the early 1870s.

The 1874 general election

Though better organisation and new thinking in the Conservative party set the scene for success in the 1874 general election, this was probably not the main reason for it. As seen at the end of the previous chapter, it was really their own policies which led to the Liberal collapse. One of the promises which Disraeli made in 1874 was that his government would give the country a rest from the constant changes which the Liberals had brought about. Most of the ministers whom he brought into his government would have supported this attitude. There was a notable exception among them. This was Richard Cross, a man who had never held office before, and whose work as Home Secretary was to result in as large a package of acts of parliament as the Liberals had produced in the previous six years.

Social legislation

Richard Cross

It was really the extensive work of Richard Cross that gave Disraeli's government a reputation for its social legislation. Disraeli generally supported what his Home Secretary did. But the Prime Minister was now aged over 70 and his health was not strong. He did not himself become closely involved in the details of social legislation. Some historians have termed this social legislation **Tory democracy** and seen it as a sign that the Conservative party really was responding to the changed circumstances of the time. Other historians have been more doubtful about this. They have pointed out that the legislation of these years was not removing privileges in society. Gladstone's reforms in the previous ministry, though modest, had at any rate widened opportunities for people. The legislation of Disraeli's government was restricted to the improvement of living conditions and making life more tolerable for working-class people.

Public Health Act

The Public Health Act of 1875 was a vital part of Cross's social legislation. **Public health** was a term which in the nineteenth century covered many of the factors that controlled people's living conditions. It was concerned with the provision of adequate drainage and waste disposal, the purity of water and proper arrangements for burials. All of these were matters of crucial importance in preventing the spread of disease. In the middle years of the nineteenth century there had been many acts of parliament dealing with these matters. The importance of Cross's Act of 1875 was in bringing together these different acts. It placed a legal responsibility on local government to see they were carried out and it strengthened local government powers to do so. The most noticeable effect of the Act was seen in Birmingham which under the direction of its (Liberal) mayor, Joseph Chamberlain, used the clauses of the Act to full effect. Vast improvements were made in Birmingham in these years. Overall, however, the

DISRAELI, THE CONSERVATIVE PARTY AND THE MINISTRY OF 1874-80

A row of terraced houses. This style of housing became widespread in British towns during the late nineteenth century, encouraged by the 1875 Artisans Dwellings Act and later housing legislation.

effect of the Act should not be exaggerated. There was still evidence of much squalor and poor sanitation in many British towns in the late nineteenth century.

Other health reforms A similar concern with matters of health was shown by two other acts of lesser importance. Throughout the nineteenth century food suppliers had improved their profits by the **adulteration** of their goods. Such common items as beer, tea and flour were more often than not sold in an impure condition, with consequent ill-effects on health. The Sale of Food and Drugs Act of 1875 was a step towards improving food quality. The River Pollution Act of 1876 was an attempt to curb the practice of channelling untreated sewage and industrial waste directly into rivers and streams. As with the Public Health Act, such powers as these acts gave to local authorities in these matters were permissive and not compulsory. Consequently impure food and polluted rivers continued as problems, though less serious ones than earlier. Other social legislation followed a similar pattern. The Artisans Dwellings Act of 1875 gave powers to local authorities to pull down slum dwellings of the artisan classes (skilled workers) and to purchase land on which to rehouse them. But the Act did not compel local authorities to do this. In practice, the slum clearance provided for by the Act was carried out more extensively than the rehousing.

Factory Acts Attention was also given to working conditions. The ministry produced two Factory Acts. One in 1874 fixed ten hours as the maximum length of the working day in factories and raised to 14 the age at which young people could start work in factories. Probably more people benefited from the terms of this Act than by those of any of the others. The Factory Act of 1878 produced nothing new; it merely brought together under one Act of Parliament the provisions of the Factory Acts of the previous half-century.

Merchant Shipping Act The Merchant Shipping Act of 1876 was the result of pressure from a back-bench MP, Samuel Plimsoll. In the House of Commons he condemned in strong and emotional terms the sending of overladen ships to sea. This practice enabled unscrupulous ship owners to get high profits either from the sale of so much merchandise or from its insurance value if the overladen ship sank. Concern for their profits completely over-rode any sense of responsibility for the sailors, whose lives were ruthlessly put at risk in this way. The government supported the legislation that Plimsoll proposed. The Act of 1876 made compulsory the painting of a load line on a ship. This **Plimsoll Line**, as it became known, was intended to prevent overloading. Only to an extent did it do so, as the Merchant Shipping Act allowed the ship owners themselves to paint the Plimsoll Line at whatever level they felt best. This defect in the Act was eventually removed by a further Act of 1890 which provided for the line to be fixed by the Board of Trade.

Equality of opportunity

In encouraging equality of opportunity, this government was less significant than the previous one. But it did not ignore the issue. The Sandon Education Act of 1876 was an important step towards making school attendance compulsory. School Attendance Committees were set up to ensure that all parents sent their children to school. Financial help was to be given to poor parents who for financial reasons wanted their children to work rather than attend school. The Employers and Workmen Act of 1875 put right a long standing injustice. Breach of contract was now made a civil offence for both employers and their employees. Previously it had been a criminal offence for the employee, carrying a possible prison sentence. The government also secured some popularity among trade unionists by the Conspiracy and Protection of Property Act, considered more fully on page 48.

The purchase of the Suez Canal Company

Suez Canal

The Suez Canal, constructed by French engineers in the 1860s, had been hailed as an outstanding technical achievement. The company which controlled it was directed jointly by the governments of France and Egypt. But the country to which it was of the greatest value was Britain. The canal provided a direct route to India via the Mediterranean and the Indian Ocean, and British ships were the ones most usually to be found sailing through it. The fear always existed that if a hostile power were to gain control of the canal the result could be fatal for Britain's hold on India. It was therefore understandable that British governments cast an envious eye on the Suez Canal Company and that an opportunity to take part in its direction was readily seized upon.

This opportunity presented itself as a result of the activities of the government of Egypt. Its ruler, who had the title of **Khedive**, was faced with bankruptcy. So in November 1875 he offered for sale his shares in the Suez Canal Company. Disraeli responded swiftly to this splendid opportunity. Without consulting parliament – an omission for which he was criticised at the time – he borrowed the necessary four million pounds from bankers and bought up the 44 per cent of the shares held by the government of Egypt. In this way the British government became the main shareholder in the company and the passage of British ships through the canal was now completely guaranteed. Control of the canal was to prove over the years profitable to Britain, in spite of Gladstone's fears to the contrary. It also gave Britain a closer interest in Egypt that was to lead to full British control of the country in 1882 (pages 59–60).

India and Afghanistan

The speed with which Disraeli acted over the Suez Canal shows how strongly he was concerned for the security of Britain's hold on India. In the following year, by the Royal Titles Act, the British sovereign was given the title of Emperor or Empress of India. This title was used by Queen Victoria and her successors from 1876 until British rule in India ended in 1947. Though it made no practical difference to Britain's relationship with India, the new title did emphasise very strongly the importance that was attached to Britain's connection with its Indian Empire.

EMPRESS AND EARL;
OR, ONE GOOD TURN DESERVES ANOTHER.

Queen Victoria's granting of a peerage to Disraeli, creating him Earl of Beaconsfield, could be seen as reward for his own recent gesture in giving the Queen the title of Empress of India.

DISRAELI, THE CONSERVATIVE PARTY AND THE MINISTRY OF 1874-80

Afghanistan

The government was also concerned to protect its Indian Empire from possible attack. As has been indicated in the previous chapter, the threat in this respect came mainly from Russia. It focused on Afghanistan, the country lying between the Russian Empire and Britain's Indian Empire. Afghanistan was an independent country, which generally favoured British interests. But the Conservatives became suspicious that the Russians were infiltrating Afghanistan and therefore sent agents to try to keep the Afghan government loyal to Britain. Firmer action was taken later in 1878 when a British force was sent into the country to compel its loyalty to Britain.

Lord Roberts

This force was under the command of General Roberts, a soldier of many years experience in India and much concerned to defend it. By his achievements in the Afghan campaigns of 1878-79, Roberts made a reputation for himself among the heroes of late nineteenth-century British imperialism, a reputation that was to be strengthened by further military exploits both in India and in South Africa (see pages 59 and 94). By the summer of 1879 Roberts had forced the Afghans to accept as their new ruler a man of known British loyalties; a British envoy was left behind in the capital, Kabul, to have oversight of the situation in the country. In spite of the popular acclaim in Britain that greeted Roberts's achievements, they did not solve the Afghan problem.

In the autumn of the same year, Afghan soldiers rose in a rebellion against the newly imposed British influence and murdered the new envoy. Roberts once again entered the country in order to deal with this rebellion. Roberts followed up his successful action in his second Afghan campaign by taking forceful measures against the rebels, many of whom were hanged. Such action – intended to deter others from rebellion – was a normal British response to such circumstances in these years. After 1880 the Afghan problem had to be faced by the incoming Liberal government of Gladstone. As the Liberals had been critical of the Afghan campaign, it was only to be expected that their Afghan policies would be more moderate. But, for the sake of India, they insisted on continued British influence there and, like the Conservatives, they also had to face Afghan opposition, as is shown later on pages 58 and 59.

Afghanistan and Persia (today, Iran)

Southern Africa

Boers and British

South Africa was another area where the government showed its concern for British power abroad. The British were not alone in colonising South Africa. Dutch settlers, known as **Boers** (today known as **Afrikaners**), had been there for a couple of centuries before a British presence was established in the early nineteenth century. The always uneasy relationship between those two groups worsened considerably in the late 1860s when large quantities of diamonds were discovered. Many outside South Africa now saw in it more exciting prospects than farming, previously the only settler occupation.

The amount of outside interest in South Africa and the number of new settlers there now increased substantially. With so much more now involved, the conflict heightened over which South African territories were Boer and which were British. Furthermore, the increased number of settlers and the increased conflict between them had serious impact on the blacks of South Africa. These earlier inhabitants were now pushed out of areas which ambitious new settlers considered likely to be rich in diamonds. Not unnaturally, such policies stimulated much opposition among the blacks.

The British Lion, shown under attack from many quarters. This cartoon of the summer of 1879 suggests Britain's pride in its position abroad and the consequences that may face those who attempt to challenge it.

Annexation of the Transvaal

The British in South Africa were therefore challenged by the Boers and by the blacks. Disraeli's government was unlikely to ignore these challenges. The first positive step taken by this government was the annexation of the Transvaal in April 1877. Political and economic circumstances within this Boer republic had become so chaotic that there was virtually no resistance to the British annexation. The Boers were assured by their new masters in the Transvaal that British military strength would be invaluable in meeting the threat from the blacks. Undoubtedly that was a major reason for the annexation, though it was not the only one. The British government was also anxious to create in South Africa a union of British and Boer territories, in which the British authority would be supreme.

Disraeli's government failed to achieve either of these objectives. The British annexation of the Transvaal increased the Boer hostility towards the British and was a major factor leading to the outbreak of the First Boer War in 1881. Certainly the British presence in the Transvaal did mean that the blacks faced sterner opposition in this area. From the Boer point of view this was the only advantage the new situation held for them.

DISRAELI, THE CONSERVATIVE PARTY AND THE MINISTRY OF 1874–80

The Zulu War

Conflict with Cetewayo's Zulus

Those amongst the blacks who were the most opposed to the increasing strength of the white presence in South Africa were the Zulu people, who inhabited Natal. Under the warlike leadership of Cetewayo, the Zulus had increased the strength and numbers of their armed forces. The British and the Boers were aware that the Zulus were dangerous enemies of both settler groups. In what was therefore a challenging and changing situation, Disraeli's government at Westminster had to rely upon the British in South Africa to decide when action was needed. Sir Bartle Frere, the British High Commissioner in South Africa, was the man who bore this responsibility. Alarmed at the 'massing' of the Zulus around the borders of the Transvaal, he decided the time had come for attack. The strength of the Zulus was greater than Frere had imagined and the armed forces he sent against them were not adequate for the task. In January 1879 the British were badly defeated at Isandhlwana. After this humiliation, the necessary reinforcements were secured and the disaster reversed by a British victory against the Zulus at their capital of Ulundi in July. British rifles proved on that occasion decisive against Zulu numbers.

The importance of the war

Disraeli's government received little credit for its success in the Zulu War. Isandhlawana produced much criticism at home of the government's handling of the situation, criticism which contributed to the Conservative failure in the general election of the following year. More seriously for the future, it had the effect of undermining the confidence of those few Boers who had welcomed the annexation of the Transvaal as a means of combatting the Zulus more vigorously, as the British had been shown to be unsteady protectors. In any case, the eventual victory over the Zulus made British protection less necessary. The British–Boer divide in South Africa was now stronger than ever and conflict between the settler groups could not be long postponed.

The Eastern Question

Nature of the problem

From time to time in the nineteenth century, the Eastern Question arose to trouble the British government of the day. Gladstone in his first ministry had been lucky to avoid it. Disraeli in his second ministry was less fortunate. The Prime Minister was also to find that it was his policies towards the Eastern Question in the mid-1870s that provoked the sharpest criticism of his government.

The **Eastern Question** concerned the problem of the declining power of the Ottoman (Turkish) Empire. From the capital city of Constantinople (today, Istanbul), the Ottoman Sultan had control of substantial territories in both the Middle East and the Balkans. The essence of the problem was to be found in the Balkans. Here, the Russian Empire, and to a lesser extent Austria-Hungary, were keen to advance their power.

The Balkans in the mid-1870s

In the mid-1870s Balkan nationalists took advantage of the serious financial problems then facing the Ottoman government. Rebellion took place in Bosnia in 1875 and in Bulgaria in 1876. Disraeli wanted to prevent Russia from advancing its influence in the Ottoman Empire through the giving of its support to these rebels. In taking this anti-Russian stand, Disraeli's main concern was to prevent Russian dominance at Constantinople, as this could lead to a Russian threat in the Mediterranean to Britain's route to India. To support his words with actions, he sent a British fleet to the Dardanelles in May 1876 to act as a warning against Russian ambition. By adopting these policies and taking these actions, Disraeli was also giving his support to the Ottoman Empire. It seemed therefore that he supported its harsh policies of suppressing the rebels.

A HISTORY OF BRITAIN FROM 1867

Gladstone's criticisms

This point was seized upon by Gladstone. The Russian challenge that concerned Disraeli meant much less to the Liberal leader. He approached the matter from the moral standpoint which was the basis of so many of his actions. Was it right for Britain to support the Ottoman Empire and its policies of suppression in the Balkans? This theme was given even greater force in the summer of 1876 by news of widespread atrocities by Ottoman soldiers in the rebellious Bulgarian provinces. These atrocities were vividly described in the press and became the basis of many speeches by Gladstone in condemning Disraeli's policies.

Gladstone's strong criticisms had another role to play. So far in this ministry it had been difficult for Gladstone to find major issues on which to criticise the Conservatives. Their domestic record, though limited, was useful and it was not possible to criticise the government very strongly in this respect. The foreign policy issues of 1876 were useful to Gladstone in enabling him to assert leadership over his party by attacking his opponents in this way.

Russian advances

Under such vigorous political attack, both Disraeli's government and the policy of support for the Ottoman Empire became less popular. However, a second phase of the whole issue began in 1877 and with it renewed support for the government's position. In April 1877 the Russian Army invaded the Ottoman Empire through the Balkans. Disraeli's earlier fear about Russian ambitions in this part of the world were thus shown to be well based. Advance towards Constantinople was less swift and more difficult than the Russians had originally thought. It took them a full 12 months to get there. When their army was at last successful, the Russian government imposed on the Ottoman Empire, in March 1878, the harsh Treaty of San Stefano, named after the suburb of Constantinople in which it was signed.

The British Lion shows some suspicions of the motives of the Russian Bear in becoming involved in the problems within the Ottoman Empire in the late 1870s.

FRIENDS OR FOES?
THE BEAR. "*THAT'S MY ROAD!*"
THE LION. "IT'S MINE, TOO! LET'S GO TOGETHER!
WHEN WE CAN'T, IT WILL BE TIME TO QUARREL!!"

Impact of the Treaty of San Stefano

News of the terms of the Treaty of San Stefano was received with anger in a number of European countries, not least in Britain. The most important of the terms provided for the creation of a big Bulgaria. The old Ottoman-controlled Bulgarian provinces were enlarged by western additions, and the entire area was to be under Russian influence. Additionally, some border areas of Asia Minor were to be acquired by Russia. San Stefano thus allowed a substantial advance of Russian power at the expense of the Ottoman Empire.

DISRAELI, THE CONSERVATIVE PARTY AND THE MINISTRY OF 1874–80

The Balkans in the late 1870s

Public opinion in Britain was now thoroughly aroused. Demand for some form of retaliation became widespread. The early summer of 1878 was a time when Victorian **jingoism** was at its height. The term originated in a popular music hall song, whose words vividly illustrated the strong feeling which gripped much of the country on this matter.

> **We don't want to fight;**
> **But by jingo, if we do,**
> **We've got the men, we've got the ships,**
> **We've got the money too.**

Gladstone's policies towards the Eastern Question were now much out of favour, while Disraeli's known anti-Russian stand was held by popular opinion to be the right attitude to take. With this support, Disraeli insisted that the Treaty of San Stefano must be revised. Austria–Hungary, whose own interests in the Balkans had also been challenged by San Stefano, joined Britain in this demand. In June 1878 a major European congress was held at Berlin. The combined pressure of the other European powers forced Russia to abandon its gains at San Stefano and accept instead the more modest terms of the Treaty of Berlin. In securing this agreement, Disraeli played a key role and became one of the best respected participants in the Congress.

The Treaty of Berlin   The key change made at Berlin was the total abandonment of 'big Bulgaria'. It was to be divided into three provinces; two were to become independent, while Ottoman rule was to be restored in the third province of Eastern Rumelia. Russia was permitted to retain the border areas that it had acquired in Asia Minor, but in compensation Britain was to secure the island of Cyprus. Thus Britain acquired a foothold in the eastern Mediterranean and a useful base from which to challenge any later Russian attempt to disturb the Berlin settlement.

Disraeli returned from Berlin to a triumphant homecoming. His own comment that the Treaty of Berlin represented 'peace with honour' was widely echoed throughout the country. Gladstone did not agree. His main criticism of the Treaty of Berlin was that it re-imposed Ottoman rule and was therefore unjust to the Balkan people. Ottoman promises of improved rule in the Balkans, made as a part of the treaty, were held by Gladstone to be worthless. Few supported Gladstone on these issues. Had Disraeli called a general election after his Berlin triumph there is little doubt that the Conservatives would have won. What therefore happened to produce the defeat at the polls which they suffered less than two years later?

The Midlothian campaigns

Gladstone's opposition

The answer lies in the exceptional nature of Gladstone's political opposition. In 1879 and again in 1880 he set out on what became known as his **Midlothian campaigns**. In a series of speeches, mainly delivered in his new Scottish constituency of Midlothian, he used all his considerable powers of oratory to condemn the immorality of Disraeli's imperial and foreign policies. The reason why so much attention was given to the Midlothian campaigns was not just Gladstone's brilliance as a speaker. It was also the novelty of this type of approach by a leading politician to current issues. Never before had the leader of a major political party travelled around to denounce the government of the day in such strong and colourful terms, as in this speech given by Gladstone towards the end of 1879.

William Gladstone speaking to a group of people from a train during his election campaigns of 1879–80. The photograph suggests something of Gladstone's tireless energy and also his determination to rally support at a time when the extended franchise made efforts of this kind more necessary than they previously had been.

> Go from South Africa to the mountains of Central Asia. Go into the lofty hills of Afghanistan, as they were last winter, and what do we there see? I fear a yet sadder sight than was to be seen in the land of the Zulus. You have seen during last winter from time to time that from such and such a village attacks have been made upon the British forces, and that in consequence the village has been burned. Have you ever reflected on the real meaning of those words? Those hill tribes had committed no real offence against us. We, in the pursuit of our political objects, chose to establish military positions in their country. If they resisted, would not you have done the same? And when, going forth from their villages they had resisted, what you find is this, that those who went forth were slain, and that the village is burned. Again, I say, have you considered the meaning of these words? The meaning of the burning of the village is that the women and the children were driven forth to perish in the snows of winter.... Remember the rights of the savage, as we call him. Remember that the happiness of his humble home, remember that the sanctity of life in the hill villages of Afghanistan among the winter snows, is as inviolable in the eyes of Almighty God as can be your own.

Many – not least Queen Victoria – disapproved of the new tactics which Gladstone was using. But they produced good political results for the Liberals who under this vocal and inspiring leadership developed as a powerful challenge to the government.

Other difficulties of the government

Gladstone generally avoided domestic issues in his Midlothian campaigns. Yet these issues also contributed to the unpopularity of Disraeli's government. It was towards the end of the 1870s that Britain was beginning to experience the effect of the **Great Depression**, considered at the start of this book. For many in Britain this brought unemployment, and its effects were particularly severe in the countryside. Disraeli's government appeared to have no solution to the problems people were experiencing. Nor did it show towards the end of the 1870s the same interest in improving the conditions of the people of Britain as it had in its earlier years.

The 1880 general election

It was not therefore very surprising that when Disraeli called a general election in the spring of 1880, the Liberals won. The results showed an almost exact reversal of the situation in the previous general election.

DISRAELI, THE CONSERVATIVE PARTY AND THE MINISTRY OF 1874-80

General Election: March 1880	
Conservatives	238
Liberals	353

Much of the material in this chapter concerns domestic legislation; much has been concerned with imperial and foreign affairs. There is no reference to Ireland. Disraeli's second ministry had virtually ignored the increasing problems that existed there. Disraeli attributed his election defeat of 1880 to the failure of his government to tackle the problems of Ireland. Yet despite firmer efforts by successive governments in the 1880s this was to prove the most obstinate of all problems facing British governments in the late nineteenth century.

EXERCISES

1. (a) Describe and explain the approach of the Disraeli government towards domestic issues.
   (b) By selecting three acts passed during his ministry of 1874–80, show how Disraeli attempted to put this approach into practice.

2. (a) Describe the policies pursued by Disraeli during his ministry of 1874–80 within two of the following: Egypt, Afghanistan, southern Africa.
   (b) What advantages and disadvantages resulted from these policies?

3. Imagine you are a political supporter of Disraeli during his ministry of 1874–80. Write an account of the domestic and foreign work undertaken by the government in those years, explaining why you felt your support for the Prime Minister was justified.

4. Study the cartoon on page 32 and then answer questions (a) to (d) which follow.
   (a) In what ways and for what reasons were the first two areas shown on the left of the signpost disturbed in the mid-1870s? (3)
   (b) (i) Explain why, in your opinion, the bear makes the statement given for him in the caption, and carries the document fastened into his belt.
   (ii) Explain why, in your opinion, the lion speaks the first six words given for him in the caption, and is dressed and shown carrying the simple knapsack.
   (iii) How fair had the cartoonist been in his portrayal of the bear and the lion? (2+2+3)
   (c) Describe the quarrel that occurred between the two countries represented by these animals and which the lion appears to expect. (5)
   (d) In the summer of 1878 this quarrel was resolved at an important European Congress.
   (i) Name the city in which the Congress was held and the man who presided over it.
   (ii) Name the Prime Minister and Foreign Secretary who represented Britain at this Congress,
   (iii) Explain for what reasons one of the animals in the cartoon would have been pleased by the outcome of this quarrel. (1+1+3)

3 IRELAND AND THE ISSUE OF HOME RULE

The relationship between Britain and Ireland has been troublesome for centuries, but it became particularly difficult during the years covered by this book. The Irish had many grievances against the British. There was dislike of the privileged position of the Church of Ireland, a minority Protestant body in a land where most of the population was Roman Catholic. There was dislike of the ownership of much of the Irish soil by absentee British landowners and the difficulties this created for many Irish peasantry. Above all else, there was a legacy of hatred among the Irish for a far-off government that appeared to ignore their problems and to treat them with contempt. This hatred, built up over the centuries, had in the mid-nineteenth century increased as a result of the feeble action taken by the British government to curb the ravages of the great Irish famine of the 1840s. Millions of Irish had died in this famine or had been forced to emigrate.

Gladstone and Ireland: the first ministry

The British politician who more than any other in the late nineteenth century made it his concern to tackle Ireland's problems was Gladstone. To this task he dedicated himself when, at a particularly disturbed time in Ireland's history, he first became Prime Minister in 1868. Its problems were to dog his steps for the rest of his life.

Irish Church Act Early on, his main concern was to remove the causes of discontent among the Irish. Despite his own position as an Anglican, he decided to disestablish the Church of Ireland. This he did by the Irish Church Act of 1869. By this Act, the Church of Ireland was **disestablished**: it was to have no official connection with the British government. More important for the Irish people was the provision in the Act that the Church was also to be **disendowed**: it was to lose all its possessions in land and buildings. By removing the complete dominance of a Protestant Church in a Roman Catholic land, the British government had taken an important step towards meeting one of the Irish objections to the British connection.

Land Act Gladstone's other measure was designed to deal with landlord–tenant relations. His Land Act of 1870 contained two main provisions. On leaving a rented property, a tenant was to receive fair compensation for any improvements he had made to the property. Tenants who were evicted for reasons other than non-payment of rent were to be similarly compensated. Few peasants in fact benefited by the latter clause, as the reason in almost all cases of eviction was non-payment of rent.

Gladstone's failure Similar ill fortune surrounded the Irish University Bill of 1873. This was an attempt to bring together the Roman Catholic and the Protestant colleges at Dublin into a new University of Dublin. But the proposals were opposed in both England and Ireland; within the House of Commons opposition was strong enough to bring an end to the scheme before it began. In spite of his concern about Ireland, Gladstone was no nearer accomplishing his 'mission' at the end of his first ministry than he was at its start. Part of his failure is explained by the inadequate nature of much of the legislation. But much is explained by the increasing strength within Ireland during these years of the home rule movement.

The Home Rule/Irish Nationalist party

Part of the reason for the increasing strength of the home rule movement lies with the Ballot Act of 1872. No longer compelled for fear of a landlord to vote for the candidate he favoured, Irish voters now gave support to the **Irish Nationalist party**, often called the **Home Rule party**. This was fully illustrated in the 1874 general election when a majority of the Irish MPs elected were from the Home Rule party.

Isaac Butt

Two Irishmen were crucial during the 1870s in making this new party one of the most powerful forces in British politics at the time: Isaac Butt and Charles Parnell. Butt was responsible for setting up the Home Rule party in the early 1870s. He came from a Protestant family, was moderate and in no way violently revolutionary. These features were in fact to characterise the Home Rule party throughout the half-century of its existence. Butt simply wanted Ireland to look after its own internal affairs and at the same time to acknowledge the overall authority of the British government at Westminster. He pointed out that there was nothing new about this idea. The British government had already, by an Act of 1867, provided for this type of relationship between Britain and Canada; Butt now wanted Ireland to be treated in the same way. Nor did he see religion as a problem. In his time the Home Rule party had many Protestants as well as Catholics within it. Butt's achievement was to set up this party and provide it with definite aims.

Charles Parnell

As the party gathered strength in the mid-1870s, however, Butt's weaknesses as a leader became noticeable. He failed to give as much attention to the leadership as was needed if the new party were to achieve success. Charles Parnell, who entered the House of Commons as an Irish Nationalist MP in 1875, was to succeed Butt as leader of the party in 1877. Though his wealthy Protestant background was similar to that of Butt, the two men had little else in common. The most noticeable feature about Parnell was the forcefulness with which he spoke in public to argue the case for home rule. This was a marked contrast to Butt's approach, which by the mid-1870s was getting the movement nowhere. Nor was Parnell's forceful approach restricted to words. He was prepared to use forceful tactics both at Westminster and in Ireland.

Obstruction in parliament

Parnell gave full support and encouragement to the practice of **obstruction** increasingly employed by Irish Nationalist MPs in the 1870s. They constantly interrupted speakers, proposed amendments to bills and generally misused the rules of parliament in order to obstruct or delay its work. Naturally, other members of the House of Commons were angered by these tactics. Certainly the cause of home rule was not advanced in parliament as a result of them, but their supporters in Ireland could feel that at least some protest was being made about Ireland's position.

The Land League

Michael Davitt

Within Ireland itself this protest, with Parnell's approval, took even stronger form. Here the dominant influence was an Irishman of very different background from that of either Butt or Parnell. Michael Davitt was from a peasant family and knew at first hand the hardship and bitterness of life in the Irish countryside and the Irish towns. As a child factory worker his arm had been severed in a hideous industrial accident caused by unguarded machinery. Davitt brought to his cause a commitment that even Parnell could not equal. Landlords were the object of his hatred. At the end of the 1870s the Great Depression worsened further the conditions among the Irish peasantry. Such conditions favoured a campaign against landlords and in 1879 Davitt formed the **Land League**, to take on this work. Its immediate aim was to protect the interests of tenants; its eventual aim was to get rid of landlords altogether.

The forceful eviction of an Irish family for non-payment of rent. Sad episodes such as this formed part of the ever-present land problem of Ireland which no British government really solved in the late nineteenth century.

Boycotting

Evictions were at the root of the discontent in the rural areas in these years. One of the most effective methods of the members of the Land League was their refusal to have any dealings with those who replaced evicted tenants. This became known as the practice of **boycotting**, from an obscure Captain Boycott against whom it was first directed. *The Times* gave the following account of the treatment of Captain Boycott.

> The persecution of Captain Boycott is only a typical instance of the system by which the peasantry are attempting to carry into effect the instructions of the Land League. Captain Boycott has been beleaguered in his house near Ballinrobe; he is excluded from contact not merely with people around him, but with the neighbouring towns; his crops are perishing because such is the organised intimidation in the district that no labourers would dare to be seen working in his fields. It is certain that any ordinary workman whom Captain Boycott might hire would be subjected to brutal violence, as, indeed, has already happened to servants who ventured to fetch his letters for him from the nearest post office.
>
> **The Times, 12 November 1880**

More violent methods such as cattle maiming and attacks on landlords were also characteristic of the Land League. Parnell supported the aims and methods of the Land League: as it had captured so fully the support of the Irish, it was wise of him to do so.

Irish issues were crucial in the general election of 1880. Obstruction at Westminster and boycotting in Ireland both brought the problems of Ireland to public attention, yet neither major political party was willing to yield on the matter of home rule. The Conservatives were its firmest opponents. In their view the granting of home rule would signify the break-up of the United Kingdom and would be disastrous for Britain's prestige and prosperity. They had little to offer on the Irish issue other than this severely negative policy, to which they held consistently until after the First World War. The Liberals in 1880 did not commit themselves to home rule, but Gladstone did commit himself to further reform within Ireland. He intended once again to try to make the union of the two countries work adequately.

Gladstone and Ireland: the second ministry

After his election in 1880, Gladstone endeavoured to put his promises into practice. The situation he faced in Ireland could scarcely have been more difficult. Increasing disorder there compelled Gladstone to introduce a Coercion Act in 1881. This was a severe measure. Its most important feature was the abolition of the long-established principle of freedom from arrest without trial, as guaranteed under **habeas corpus**. So strong was dislike of it within Ireland that its effects offset those of other more reforming legislation of the same year. At Westminster the Coercion Act was greeted by further obstruction. But on this occasion the Speaker (Chairman) of the House of Commons declared the debate closed. In this way the impact of parliamentary obstruction was brought to an end.

Three Fs Act

1881 was also the year of one of the most important of the Land Acts: the **Three Fs Act**, as it has commonly been called. **Fair rents** were to be established by a local land court. **Fixed tenure** gave security to the tenant provided the rent was paid. **Free sale** enabled the sale of a tenancy once it had expired. Under the terms of free sale the tenant would be paid for improvements made to the property. Though some in Ireland welcomed the 1881 Act, many were critical that it did not go far enough. Parnell defiantly urged that in view of the Act's inadequacies, the Irish must now take steps to set up their own laws themselves.

Kilmainham Treaty

Parnell's views were taken by the British government as treasonable and, under the terms of the Coercion Act, he was sent to Kilmainham Gaol. While he was imprisoned there, the Land League encouraged violence and disorder throughout Ireland on an altogether new scale. The Coercion Act proved a feeble instrument in dealing with this dangerous situation. Compromise was necessary. The government undertook this by making an arrangement with the imprisoned Parnell, an arrangement usually known as the **Kilmainham Treaty**. The government agreed to widen the benefits of the 1881 Land Act and to protect tenants whose rents were in arrears. Parnell agreed to use his influence to curb violence. But the promise contained in this arrangement was threatened almost as soon as the Kilmainham Treaty had been signed. In May 1882 a new Secretary for Ireland, Lord Frederick Cavendish, was murdered in Phoenix Park, Dublin, shortly after arriving in Ireland to take up his new work. The murder was the work of extremists, whose real objective had not been Cavendish but the unpopular Under Secretary, with whom Cavendish was walking at the time of the attack. In these difficult circumstances it was Parnell's achievement to ensure that the Kilmainham Treaty was kept to on his side. He denounced the Phoenix Park murders, and violence within Ireland slackened, helped by the government's fulfilling of its part of the bargain.

This led to an improvement in the agrarian situation in Ireland by the mid-1880s. No longer was such importance attached to the Land League, which came to be replaced by the National League, a new organisation completely loyal to Parnell. Home rule, the clear objective of the National League, came now to dominate the Irish question.

THE BILL-STICKER.

The Irish question was foremost in Gladstone's policies as Prime Minister. This cartoon shows him as a bill-sticker giving priority to the 1881 Land Act over all other legislation.

The British political scene in 1885

Lord Salisbury's first ministry

The support of the National League for the Home Rule party came at a vital time. Recent legislation at Westminster also assisted the party's fortunes. The Third Parliamentary Reform Act of 1884 (page 58), by allowing the franchise to all householders and lodgers, was likely further to increase the number of their MPs in the House of Commons. The two leading parties fully realised how important it was to secure the support of these new members. Already the Irish Nationalists were asserting their strength. In June 1885 it was their support for the Conservatives in the House of Commons that brought about the fall of

Gladstone's second ministry. Irish Nationalist support of the Conservatives seemed to be a sensible policy during Lord Salisbury's brief first ministry between June and November 1885. The Ashbourne Land Act of these months made it possible for tenants to receive, on very favourable terms, a government advance for the purchase of the property they previously rented. But home rule had now become a more important issue than land reform. The Conservatives even appeared to suggest that they might grant home rule to Ireland. As in the meantime there was no positive offer from the Liberals, the Irish Nationalists gave their support to the Conservatives in the general election.

The 1885 general election

The results of the general election in November 1885 confirmed the newly found importance of the Irish Nationalist party.

General Election: November 1885	
Conservatives	249
Irish Nationalists	86
Liberals	335

Study of the above figures will show the powerful position in which Parnell and his party were now placed. It was possible for them either to keep out both parties by maintaining a neutrality or it was possible for them to put the Liberals in by giving support to them. Parnell's course of action was decided by a reliable newspaper report that Gladstone had at last reached a decision that Ireland should be given home rule. The Irish Nationalist support now went to

At a crossroads in Irish policy in the mid-1880s, Gladstone ignores the direction of Joseph Chamberlain and pursues the course to which he had become committed. In attempting to reach his destination Gladstone brought disaster on the political fortunes of his party.

AT THE CROSS ROADS.
JOE (THE COW-BOY). "HOI!—*THIS* BE YOUR ROAD, MEASTER!"

the Liberal party and with that support Gladstone was able to form his third ministry at the beginning of 1886. Lord Salisbury had meanwhile made it clear that any home rule sympathies which the comments of some Conservatives may have suggested during 1885 were now at an end; from this time onwards the Conservative party was to be a stern foe of home rule.

The First Home Rule Bill

Terms

In introducing his Home Rule Bill into the House of Commons, Gladstone emphasised that the Irish now needed more than a series of reforms undertaken by Westminster.

IRELAND AND THE ISSUE OF HOME RULE

> I do not deny the general good intention of parliament on a variety of great and conspicuous occasions, and its desire to pass good laws for Ireland. But let me say that, in order to work out the purposes of government, there is something more in this world occasionally required than even the passing of good laws. It is sometimes requisite not only that good laws should be passed, but also that they should be passed by the proper persons. The passing of many good laws is not enough in cases where the strong permanent instincts of the people, their distinctive marks of character, the situation and history of the country require not only that these laws should be good, but that they should proceed from a congenial and native source, and besides being good laws should be their own laws.
>
> Hansard, *Parliamentary Debates*

The bill provided for an Irish parliament to take control of internal Irish affairs, while the Westminster parliament was to keep control of defence and foreign affairs. There was to be no Irish representation at Westminster. Irish Nationalists were disappointed that Westminster still had control over them, yet without the chance of any Irish MPs influencing its decisions. Nevertheless, they were united as a party in giving the bill their support. There was, however, no such unity in the Liberal party. The Home Rule Bill showed it to be seriously divided. The Whigs under Lord Hartington and the Radicals under Joseph Chamberlain became bitterly opposed to what their party leader was preparing to do. Their attitude towards home rule was very similar to that of the Conservatives. When the time came for a decisive vote in June 1886, 93 members of the Liberal party voted against the bill. These defectors were sufficient for the bill's defeat.

Opposition Judged by the arrangements eventually made in the early 1920s for Irish independence, the home rule proposals of 1886 were very modest. Yet the Conservative and the Liberal opposition reflected a strong hostility throughout much of Britain to Irish home rule. Why was there this hostility? Among many in England there was a contempt for the Irish, who were considered unfit to govern themselves. Recent campaigns such as those of the Land League, with their accompanying disorder and violence, suggested to many people that they were right to hold this opinion. Others took a broader approach to the subject: if Ireland were to separate from British rule in this way, why should not other parts of the British Empire do the same? Their view was based on a profound respect for the British Empire and a fear of what might follow if it collapsed.

Ulster Probably the strongest reason for opposition to home rule is to be found in the **Ulster question**. It was in the north-east province of Ulster that most of Ireland's Protestants lived. They were concerned that the Irish Nationalist party had become by the 1880s a strongly Roman Catholic party. Any grant of home rule to Ireland would therefore lead to a dominance of the Roman Catholic Church in the government of Ireland. Many in England sympathised with Ulster. Partly this was due to their admiration of the loyalty that Ulster showed; partly it was due to mistrust of the Roman Catholic Church, a distrust which was widespread in Britain in the late nineteenth century. From this time onwards, the Ulster question dominated all other issues involved in Ireland's links with Britain.

Conservative policies towards Ireland

Liberal Unionists The home rule attempt of 1886 had profound effects on British politics. The fact that 93 Liberals had voted against their party on this major issue shows a fundamental split within the party. Those who had voted in this way became known as **Liberal Unionists**. They generally sympathised more with Conservative than Liberal policies and by the beginning of the twentieth century the link between the two was complete. The Conservative party was much strengthened by the events of 1886 and was able to keep itself in power for almost 20 years, under Lord Salisbury and subsequently his nephew, Arthur Balfour, as Prime Ministers. The Liberals managed to get back to power for three of these years, from 1892 to 1895. In 1886 Gladstone's immediate reaction to the rejection of home rule was to summon another general election. The Conservatives were returned to power, though dependent on Liberal Unionist support.

General Election: July 1886	
Conservatives	316
Irish Nationalists	85
Liberal Unionists	78
Liberals	191

The general election gave further evidence of the unpopularity of any policy of home rule. Nevertheless, Conservative policy toward Ireland was not as negative as it had been in Disraeli's time.

Arthur Balfour

For most of Salisbury's second ministry, the Chief Secretary of Ireland was his nephew, Arthur Balfour. He approached the problems of Ireland in two ways: firm government combined with agrarian reform. It was circumstances within Ireland which assisted him most strongly in putting these policies into effect. Bad harvests in Ireland in the mid-1880s had once again focused attention on the land problem. Tenants were finding difficulty in keeping up with rent payments and in spite of the provisions of the 1881 Land Act, the number of evictions rose. Emigration figures increased during these years. So also did the activities of the National League. They developed a new approach, known as the **Plan of Campaign**, which relied on solidarity among tenants. To meet rent difficulties, reduced amounts were to be offered to the landlord by the tenants of an estate. If the landlord rejected these, the money was paid instead into a fund used to assist those among the tenants who suffered eviction. These tactics were well supported within Ireland, but were strongly opposed by Balfour. Full advantage was taken by him of the terms of a new Coercion Act to undermine both the Plan of Campaign and the National League itself. Arrests and imprisonments dominated the early years of Balfour's time as Secretary. Towards the end of the 1880s his tactics appeared to be getting results.

Parnell's difficulties

Balfour was further helped in getting the better of the Irish situation by the personal difficulties of Parnell. For some years Parnell had conducted a love affair with Mrs Kitty O'Shea, the wife of one of his followers, and three children had been born of this liaison. When in November 1890 action for divorce was taken, Parnell's involvement became public knowledge. Thus broke one of the greatest scandals of late Victorian times. The Liberal party, responding to its close links with the Nonconformists, became outraged by these reports of Parnell's personal conduct, and cut off their support of him. The Irish Nationalist party, inclined at first to take a less severe attitude, knew how important to them the recently formed Liberal connection was. Many members now urged Parnell to resign, while the Roman Catholic Church in Ireland became outspokenly critical of him. In his attempts to gather support for his leadership Parnell spoke at countless meetings throughout Ireland. But he was often badly received and it was clear that he had lost his earlier popularity. The strain of this campaigning led to physical collapse and to his death in the autumn of 1891. Parnell's achievement had been to build up the Irish Nationalist party to a position in which, by its links with the Liberal party, it stood a chance of achieving home rule.

Agrarian reform

Towards the end of the 1880s Balfour was able to turn away from his pursuit of firm government and give more attention to the other part of his Irish policy: agrarian reform. He encouraged tenants to buy their property instead of renting it. He foresaw the development of a class of **peasant proprietors**, for whom the problems of landlords and rents would be a thing of the past. The Ashbourne Act of 1885 had already pointed the way towards this policy. Balfour went further along this road by two Land Purchase Acts of 1888 and 1891 and prospective Irish purchasers benefited by their terms.

The government also tackled other practical problems in Ireland. Overseas competition in agricultural products was affecting Ireland as much as England in these years. To relieve this situation the government set up the Congested Districts Board to help the areas – mainly in the west – that were the most seriously affected by the Great Depression. With the help of government funds, useful practical work was done by this Board. Encouragement was given to the improvement of agriculture and development of other sources of income, such as fishing and small scale industry.

The Second Home Rule Bill

Balfour proved himself in the years 1887–92 a far-sighted Irish Secretary. Though his earlier coercion in Ireland had made him unpopular there, many came to recognise the solid and stable work that he did for the Irish. In England this work established his reputation as one of the country's leading politicians. He saw his Irish policies as the best means of winning the Irish away from home rule, to which in his judgement they were not very strongly committed anyway.

The 1892 general election

Nevertheless, the success achieved by the Irish Nationalists in the general election of July 1892 showed how little he had succeeded in diminishing support within Ireland for home rule.

General Election: July 1892	
Conservatives	268 ⎫ 314
Liberal Unionists	46 ⎭
Irish Nationalists	81
Labour	1
Liberals	272

The above figures show that a Liberal government might again be formed only with Irish Nationalist support. Though the Irish MPs were still divided on the issues concerning Parnell that had so rent their party in the previous year, home rule remained the policy around which they could all unite. It formed also a key part of the Liberal programme.

Terms

All other approaches to Irish issues now once more gave way before the policy of home rule. The Second Home Rule Bill was introduced into the House of Commons by Gladstone in June 1893. Now aged 84, the Grand Old Man spoke with fervour of the need for home rule as the essential basis on which to build sound Anglo-Irish relations for the future. The young Winston Churchill – who was present on the occasion – gave this account.

> Well do I remember the scene and some of its incidents. The Grand Old Man looked like a great white eagle at once fierce and splendid. His sentences rolled forth majestically and everyone hung upon his lips and gestures, eager to cheer or deride. He was at the climax of a tremendous passage about how the Liberal Party had always carried every cause it had espoused to victory. He made a slip. 'And there is no cause,' he exclaimed (Home Rule), 'for which the Liberal Party has suffered so much or *descended so low*.' How the Tories leapt and roared their delight! But Mr Gladstone, shaking his right hand with fingers spread claw-like, quelled the tumult and resumed, 'But we have risen again.'
>
> **Winston S. Churchill,** *My Early Life*

A portrait of the interior of the House of Commons in 1893, showing Gladstone at the despatch box, introducing the Second Home Rule Bill. Arrangements in the House have changed little since then, and this portrait should be compared with that on page 141. The Speaker presides, with three clerks seated in front of him; to his right are the MPs supporting the government and to his left are those supporting the opposition.

The second bill was similar to the first, except that it made provision for 80 Irish MPs at Westminster. Thus what had been seen as a particular problem of the first bill – the continuing control by Westminster without Irish representation there – was to be overcome. Throughout the summer of 1893 the bill survived a difficult passage through the House of Commons. But in September, when it was sent for approval by the House of Lords, it was immediately and decisively defeated.

Importance

The Second Home Rule Bill and its rejection have an importance in a number of different ways. The most obvious was the role of the House of Lords in its rejection. Those who belonged to the House of Lords at this time came mainly from landed families and their political sympathies were largely Conservative. The House of Lords had power to reject any piece of legislation if a majority of the lords voted to do so. There was inevitably much criticism of their action among supporters of home rule. The House of Lords' rejection in 1893 marked for the time being the end of home rule. Gladstone, in the immediate aftermath of defeat, wanted to hold a general election on the whole issue of the power of the House of Lords. He was, however, persuaded by his fellow ministers that such an election at that time might well be lost. Nevertheless criticism of this rejection became an important part of a more generalised criticism of the House of Lords that was to lead during the next 20 years to a substantial curbing of its powers.

Ulster opposition

Ulster also played an important part in opposing the bill. Ulster opposition to home rule had grown since the time of the first bill. The Ulster MPs now formed a distinct group in parliament under the leadership of Edward Saunderson. A devoted Protestant, Saunderson was responsible at this time for encouraging widespread fears of the dangers of Roman Catholic influence in an Ireland that had been granted home rule. Much pressure was exerted on the Conservative party – and through them on the House of Lords – to ensure that this did not occur. If it did, the Ulster Defence Union, which Saunderson formed at the time of the debates on the Second Home Rule Bill, would be prepared to fight to keep Ulster united with Britain.

Nationalism and Unionism

The Liberals had nothing further to offer to Ireland after the defeat of the Second Home Rule Bill. In the following year Gladstone retired and in the year after that the brief premiership of Lord Rosebery came to an end with the Liberal defeat in the general election of July 1895.

IRELAND AND THE ISSUE OF HOME RULE

General Election: July 1895	
Conservatives	340 ⎫ 411
Liberal Unionists	71 ⎭
Irish Nationalists	82
Liberals	177

By this time, almost ten years after the first rejection of home rule, the approach of the Conservatives and Liberal Unionists was identical on almost all political issues and the term **Conservative and Unionist**, or even just **Unionist**, was often used to describe the combination of both parties.

Wyndham Act

Firmly setting its face against any possibility of furthering home rule, the government sought instead to continue during the next ten years the Irish policies that Balfour had been pursuing until some three years previously. The most important piece of legislation by which it did so was the Land Purchase Act of 1903, sometimes called the Wyndham Act from the name of the Irish Secretary of the time. This was a continuation of the policies put forward in earlier land purchase acts.

In a speech in the House of Commons, Wyndham expressed the close links that the Conservatives held to be necessary in these years between agrarian reform and the policies of firmness in government.

> **If the prosperity of agriculture in Ireland shrinks, it induces stresses and contradictions throughout every layer of society, so that, there is a tendency towards disruption and catastrophe. I have always held the view, and I hold it now, that if any illegality ensues it is the duty of any government to make those guilty of illegalities amenable to the law. I have never hesitated to express that view or to give effect to it when, to my regret, the occasion seemed to demand it. But may we not, ought we not, ought we not to consider the possibility of alleviating these social stresses? And if we ought to do so, is it not an obligation at a moment when testimony reaches us of a general desire, of all classes, all creeds, and all parties – throughout the whole community of Ireland – that some lasting basis of agrarian peace shall be found?**
>
> Hansard, *Parliamentary Debates*

The Wyndham Act applied to large estates as well as to the small holdings covered by the earlier acts. It provided more generous terms all round. Former landlords were to receive payment from the government in cash and the amount of the agreed sale price would be increased by an additional state grant of 12 per cent. Former peasants were to pay back the government at the rate of 3.25 per cent annual interest on their loans, which could be spread over $68\frac{1}{2}$ years and thus be passed on within the family. Wyndham's Land Purchase Act can probably be described as one of the few pieces of British legislation that had long-term use for large numbers of Irish. Many tenants bought their land under its terms and repayment of the loans were made regularly until the Act's repeal by the Irish Free State government in the early 1930s.

Devolution proposals

The promise of the 1903 Act encouraged Wyndham to go further. Throughout 1904 civil servants under Wyndham's direction worked on a scheme for devolution of power in Ireland. According to the scheme, an Irish Council would be set up to take control of many aspects of Ireland's internal affairs. When these plans – which never were a part of official government policy – became known in September 1904, they aroused a storm of protest. However forward looking they may have seemed, opponents of home rule viewed them as a measure of bringing about 'home rule by instalments'. Amidst the ensuing protests, Wyndham was compelled to resign and such devolution plans as existed made no further progress.

A HISTORY OF BRITAIN FROM 1867

Gaelic League Twentieth-century Irish nationalism was in a formative stage of development during these years. The Irish were rediscovering and re-emphasising a sense of pride simply in being Irish. The Gaelic League, founded in 1893, was the most powerful means by which this was brought about. Its emphasis was on Irish culture. Interest in Irish history, involvement in Irish customs, the use of the old Gaelic language of Ireland were all encouraged by the Gaelic League. The Irish, the League urged, should cease to think of themselves as an offshoot of England: they should assert their role as Irish men and women.

Sinn Fein It was but a short step from a cultural to a political revival. In 1902, the **Sinn Fein party** was founded by Arthur Griffith, who was later to play a key role in attempting to implement its policies. The use of the Gaelic name **Sinn Fein** – it translates as 'We Ourselves' – was typical of these years. Its main aim was to set up an Ireland that was independent of Britain and that was Republican in its style of government. Its members worked closely with the militant **Irish Republican Brotherhood**. Between them the Sinn Fein party and the Irish Republican Brotherhood attracted the support of younger nationalists.

In spite of these developments, home rule still remained the goal of most Irish. It continued to be pressed at Westminster by the Irish Nationalist party, now led by John Redmond, the party's most effective leader since the time of Parnell. Their chances of success revived considerably with the landslide electoral victory secured by their allies, the Liberals, in January 1906. But Redmond failed to realise that many younger Irish were no longer satisfied in aiming just at home rule. Sinn Fein's wider objectives appealed more strongly. As is shown later, particularly on pages 109–11 in Chapter 8 and on pages 136–8 in Chapter 11, they were to become the dominant feature in the increasing bitterness of Anglo-Irish relations in the early twentieth century.

EXERCISES

1. (a) What were the main problems in Ireland at the end of the 1860s?
   (b) Describe the measures taken by Gladstone to resolve these problems during his first ministry (1868–74).
   (c) Describe the measures taken by Gladstone to resolve these problems during his second ministry (1880–85).
   (d) Why, in spite of these measures, was Ireland still a troubled land in the mid-1880s?

2. (a) Give the terms of the First Irish Home Rule Bill (1886). Explain why it was introduced into parliament and why parliament rejected it.
   (b) Give the terms of the Second Irish Home Rule Bill (1893). Explain why it was introduced into parliament and why parliament rejected it.
   (c) What alternative solutions to the problems of Ireland did the Conservatives offer in the years 1886–1905?

3. Imagine you are a Liberal Unionist MP at the time of the first two home rule bills. Write your memoirs of both 1886 and 1893, describing the actions you took in each of those years and explaining your reasons for opposing home rule.

4. Study the photograph on page 38 and the cartoons on pages 39 and 40 and then answer questions (a) to (d) which follow.

(a) With reference to the photograph on page 38 and the cartoon on page 39:
   (i) Describe the evidence they provide of the poor treatment of Irish peasants.
   (ii) How do you explain the frequency in Ireland of episodes such as that shown in the photograph?
   (iii) How did the legislation illustrated in the cartoon help to prevent episodes such as this? (3+2+2)
(b) With reference to the two cartoons and to your own knowledge, show to what extent you agree that the two cartoons accurately portray the changing attitudes of the central character. (4)
(c) With reference to the cartoon on page 40:
   (i) Explain the reasons why the man on the right is directing his horse along this particular course.
   (ii) Explain why the cowboy is trying to persuade him to take a different course. (4)
(d) With reference to the cartoon on page 40:
   (i) For what reasons did the man on the horse fail on two occasions to reach his destination?
   (ii) To what extent did the course favoured by the cowboy prove more successful? (5)

4 TRADE UNIONS, SOCIALISM AND THE LABOUR PARTY

In the early part of the nineteenth century, the great struggle of trade unionists had been merely to exist. Men of wealth viewed the early development of trade unions as a sinister threat. As such men were well represented in parliament they were able to create many difficulties for the trade unions, so that it was not until 1825 that parliament gave them legal recognition. Even after that, the movement developed only slowly. It still faced much hostility from magistrates and from employers. By the 1850s such trade union development as had taken place was limited to well-off workers, those who practised skilled crafts and who at that time were referred to as **artisans** rather than workers. By the 1860s the unions in Britain were all of this type, such as the Amalgamated Society of Engineers and the Amalgamated Society of Carpenters and Joiners.

The work of these unions was limited to such tasks as providing help for their members when sick or unemployed. To bring improvement in wages was virtually impossible. Such action was widely thought to be wrong, as increases in pay in one trade would – so it was held – lead automatically to increases in another. Though restricted in their activities, the unions in the 1860s got advantage from the rapidly developing economy in Britain during these years. Money for trade union subscriptions became more readily available. The unions were thus strengthened and made more effective in bargaining and negotiating with employers.

The Royal Commission and trade union legislation

Hornby versus Close In the late 1860s much controversy centred on the increasing role of trade unions. The legal case of **Hornby versus Close** in 1867 arose when the Boilermakers Society took legal action against the treasurer of its branch in Bradford, who owed them money from the branch's fund. The case was heard by the Lord Chief Justice, who decided that the treasurer was not guilty of any offence, as the funds of a trade union were not to be allowed the protection of law. The Lord Chief Justice made his decision on the grounds that trade unions were still illegal, as in order to achieve some of their objectives they were prepared to take strike action. The Hornby versus Close decision was important for two reasons. It removed legal protection from the funds of trade unions and it illustrated the continuing hostility of the British judicial system towards the trade union movement.

Sheffield outrages At much the same time, throughout the mid-1860s, events in the city of Sheffield focused unfavourable attention on the trade unions. The city was plagued by many acts of violence, caused largely by the attempts of union workers in the cutlery industry to persuade non-union workers to join them in their union. Some of the violence was of a petty kind and had been taking place for many years; a common feature of it, known as **rattening**, was the removal of the wheel bands of the machines of non-union men. But in 1865 and 1866 violence became more serious, culminating in the destruction of the house of a non-union worker in October 1866. These disturbances – **outrages**, as they were called at the time – provoked widespread hostility towards the unions, especially among the middle classes.

Royal Commission In response, the government appointed a Royal Commission to enquire into the whole position of trade unions in Britain. The Commission consisted of a mixed body of men. While in John Roebuck, MP for Sheffield, the unions had a

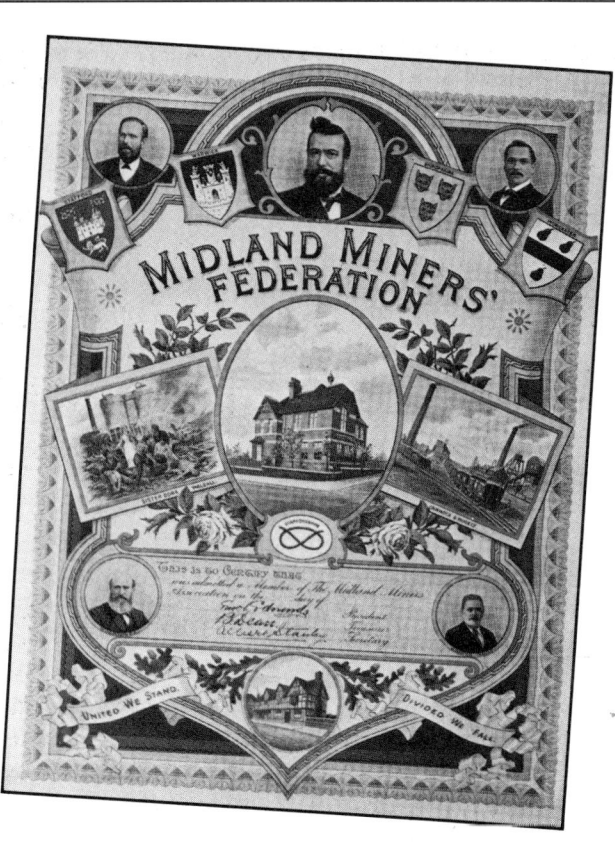

Two trade union membership certificates of the nineteenth century. The one on the left is typical of the unionism of mid-century; the one on the right is typical of the new unionism later in the century. Notice the difference of emphasis in the slogans (at the top of the certificate on the left and at the bottom of the certificate on the right).

determined foe, they had an advantage by the presence on the Commission of William Applegarth, the able leader of the Amalgamated Society of Carpenters. Eventually, in 1869, the Commission reported favourably on the trade unions, urging that they be given the legal status of which they had been robbed by the Hornby versus Close judgement. The unions were further helped by the Royal Commission's view that they were not a hindrance to the development of the country's trade. The most important effect of the Royal Commission was to reassure the country that trade unions were not sinister organisations and that they had a useful part to play in society.

Gladstone's trade union legislation

Trade unionists looked confidently to Gladstone's Liberal ministry to take up the proposals that the Royal Commission had made, but such government action as followed was a disappointment to them. Two acts were passed in 1871. The Trade Union Act gave legal status to the trade unions, and this was obviously acceptable to them. But the Criminal Law Amendment Act of the same year made the practice of picketing illegal. Trade unionists could not therefore take any steps to persuade fellow workers to join them on a strike. Though glad of the first Act, they were thoroughly dissatisfied with the second. The newly formed Trades Union Congress (see next page) had appointed a **parliamentary committee** which was to try to promote trade union interests through parliamentary action. Generally speaking, the trade unions had little cause for satisfaction with the performance of Gladstone's first ministry.

Disraeli's trade union legislation

The parliamentary committee – and many trade unionists throughout the country – were surprised to find that the legislation of the Conservatives under Disraeli was more acceptable to them. The Conservative Home Secretary, R.A. Cross, steered through the House of Commons two bills strengthening the position of trade unions in 1875. The Conspiracy and Protection of Property Act restored the right of peaceful picketing to trade unionists, so the strike weapon could again be employed. The Employers and Workmen Act reversed another trade union grievance by making it a civil and not a criminal offence for a worker to break the terms of his contract of employment. No longer could a worker be imprisoned for breach of contract, as had previously been possible.

TRADE UNIONS, SOCIALISM AND THE LABOUR PARTY

Skilled and unskilled workers

Altogether during the 1860s and 1870s trade unions had been able to secure a firmer place in British society. Some trade unionists felt that there was now nothing more for the movement to achieve. Others were eager for fuller involvement of unskilled workers in the movement. It must be remembered that membership of trade unions was still limited to the skilled workers. The vast mass of workers in Britain were unskilled, and had no trade union to take up their many grievances.

Increasing trade union activity

Trades Union Congress

Trade unions were becoming far more active on behalf of their members. The formation of the **Trades Union Congress** (TUC) in 1868, and its first meeting in Manchester, was one of the most notable ways in which this was shown. It was an attempt to co-ordinate the work of the different trade unions. Though the TUC played a fairly minor role in the trade union movement in its early years, it was eventually to become a forceful means of impressing trade union opinion on employers.

Collective bargaining

The idea of **collective bargaining** by the trade unions also came to be more widely accepted. This involved trade unionists entering into formal discussion with employers so that collectively they could bargain to produce an agreed wage or an agreement on working hours or working conditions. Workers could now see that the trade unions were regarded by the employers as important and respectable organisations. Recruitment of workers to trade unions consequently increased.

Co-operative Movement

Many working-class people were by now taking advantage of the Co-operative Movement, which had begun earlier in the century at Rochdale. There in 1844 a group of workers had set up a shop and had distributed its profits among the customers as a **dividend**, the size of which depended on the value of the purchases made. Towards the end of the nineteenth century the setting up of a number of **Co-ops** had helped improve living standards in many households. A government report at the start of the twentieth century shows the importance of the movement in different parts of Britain by that time.

> The factories of the English society are grouped for the most part around Manchester, Newcastle and London, but boots are made at Leicester, clothing at Leeds and cocoa at Luton. The society has also creameries in Ireland, a bacon factory in Denmark, as well as one in Ireland, and a tallow and oil factory in Sydney. The Scottish society began manufacturing in 1881, with the making of shirts; soon added tailoring, upholstering and cabinet-making; then went on to the making of boots, hosiery, printing, clothing, confectionery, tobacco.
> It may be said that the chief success of co-operation has been among the artisan class – not to any considerable extent either among the poorest classes or the better off; and that, in towns where the co-operative stores have taken a firm hold, the retail trade tends more and more to be divided between them and the owners of other shops. Royal Commission on the Poor Laws, 1909

The New Unionism and the Great Dock Strike

Unskilled workers

In the 1880s and 1890s unskilled workers were drawn into the trade union movement. An early start was made among the agricultural workers. For centuries, those who worked on the land had been exploited by landowners. Poor wages, long hours, crude hovels for homes were to be found in most of the rural areas of Britain in the nineteenth century. Unlike those who worked in industry, agricultural labourers were so widely spread throughout the country that it was difficult to organise them into a union.

Farm workers

After a number of uncertain starts, this was done by Joseph Arch. In the early 1870s a number of individual unions of agricultural labourers came into being in different parts of the country. Arch, who had organised the labourers in Warwickshire, brought these different unions together to form the National Agricultural Labourers' Union. By the mid-1870s it had 100 000 members. They formed a determined body of men and women, capable of taking strike action to press their demands. They met serious difficulties. Local squires were often joined by Anglican (though not Nonconformist) clergy in opposing the union and victimising its members. The union also had to face the realities of the economic situation in the 1870s. Agriculture in Britain was suffering from the competition of foreign-produced wheat and in these circumstances there was little point in using the strike weapon. The union in fact gave more attention in these years to organising the emigration of agricultural workers to Canada, Australia and New Zealand.

Railway workers

Other groups of workers, similarly widely spread, also began to organise themselves. A union of building labourers came into being in the 1870s, though it petered out in the 1880s. In 1871 the Amalgamated Society of Railway Servants was set up. Railway workers were treated at this time with almost military discipline. Their employers considered that the railways had to be run in this way if they were to be run safely. There was therefore strong opposition from employers to the formation of this union. Though much of the union's work was concerned with providing financial help to injured railwaymen and pensions for the retired, the union also involved itself in strike action.

A group of young workers on strike in the match-making industry in 1888. The courage shown by these unskilled workers did much to encourage the dockers in their strike of the following year.

Strike by the match-makers

The 1880s saw an even wider spread of trade unions and increased strike action by their members. The London Dock Strike of 1889 marked the high point in this development, but it should not be seen in isolation from other events in East London. In the previous year, much publicity surrounded a strike among the workers in the match-making factories. The health of the women in these places was much weakened by the phosphorous-laden atmosphere in which they worked. For many years they had put up with these conditions and the pittance wages that went with them. Encouraged by Annie Besant, the women went on strike and were able to win better conditions and better pay. Another group of unskilled workers secured similar success in the spring of the following year. The gas workers at Beckton in East London organised themselves into a union and demanded an eight-hour day.

TRADE UNIONS, SOCIALISM AND THE LABOUR PARTY

Striking London dockers, meeting outside the dock gates in 1889, listen to a speech by John Burns. The events of that year gave much encouragement to non-skilled workers to involve themselves in trade unions.

The dockers

The examples of these two strikes were not lost on another, larger group of workers in East London: the dockers. Employment in the docks was always insecure and payment was low. There was much dislike among the dockers of the **call-on** system by which they were employed. The dockers had to wait at the docks until selected by the foreman. There was no guarantee of regular employment. The uncertainties of the system were later described in the following terms by one of the leaders of the dock strike.

> At that time the 'call-ons' took place frequently in the day and they seemed to be calculated to inflict upon the dock workers the maximum amount of inconvenience, discomfort, anxiety and misery. The first call of the day was at 7 o'clock in the morning. A second took place just before 8 o'clock, a third forty-five minutes later, and a fourth at a quarter to one. In the interval of calls the unfortunate wage-slaves who had not caught the foreman's eye had to loaf about and kill time as best they could. In wet and cold weather their misery can better be imagined than described.
>
> Ben Tillett, *Memories and Reflections*

Under the forceful leadership of Ben Tillett, Tom Mann and John Burns, the dockers demanded a minimum employment period of four hours and a minimum wage of 'a tanner' (six old pence/$2\frac{1}{2}$p) an hour. The employers rejected these demands and the summer of 1889 was a time of determined struggle by the dockers to secure them. The dockers got encouragement from many quarters. Each afternoon, after their own meeting in East London, they marched through the City of London. Their peaceful and dignified marches did much to win the sympathy of the general public for their cause. The leader of Britain's Roman Catholics, Cardinal Manning, identified himself with them. From Australia came generous contributions to the strike fund. This Australian aid virtually ensured the dockers' success. Arbitration organised by London's Lord Mayor eventually brought the five-week dispute to a successful end for the dockers.

Importance of the Great Dock Strike

The strike had not lasted long and was not accompanied by violence. The new unionism received much encouragement from the dockers' victory. As has been seen, unions of unskilled workers, pledged to use the strike weapon to secure their demands, had been developing for a number of years. After the events of 1889 their commitment to strike action was shown to be worthwhile. Low subscription rates were a further encouragement to mass membership. Additionally, their use of outside support, particularly from a number of the new Socialist organisations, was an important element in their successful use of the strike weapon. Membership among unskilled workers, use of the strike weapon, and links with Socialism all made the new unionism different from unionism in the middle of the century. Though the older unions continued, the future lay with the more broadly-based and more militant new unionism. It also lay in closer links with the developing Socialism.

The early development of Socialism

As has been seen in the introduction, the terms of the Second Reform Act had not been generous. Those seeking to secure wider working-class representation now began to press their claims more forcefully. The half-century after the Second Reform Act was a vital time for the development of working-class interests in parliament and local government.

In 1869 a Labour Representation League was set up with the aim of securing better parliamentary representation for working-class people. Throughout the 1870s it lacked funds. More seriously, it lacked interest among working-class people in what it was trying to do for them. They saw the Liberal party satisfactorily representing their interests. But Gladstone's trade union legislation caused disillusion with the Liberal party among a number of trade unionists. Some were attracted to the Conservative party.

The ideas of Karl Marx

Though the 1870s had therefore been a time of only slight political advance by the working classes, the 1880s were to be very different. Socialism was beginning to be of importance. Socialism was much opposed to the **capitalist system** which had brought wealth to many Victorian businessmen through the skilful investment of capital (money). Their success, Socialists argued, was really based on their exploitation of the working classes, who were compelled to work for long hours, in poor conditions, for minimal pay. Through the united action of the working classes, Socialists aimed to bring about a redistribution of wealth, so that all could benefit from the industrialisation of recent years. In the middle of the nineteenth century this type of thinking had been developed by Karl Marx, in particular. Though Marx had worked in Britain, his ideas had initially more support in continental Europe. By the 1880s, however, some trade unionists within Britain were beginning to see Socialism as the type of political programme that would advance their cause.

Social Democratic Federation

In 1881 the Social Democratic Federation (SDF) was founded. Its twin aims were further parliamentary reform and the improvement of social conditions. The main influence in the SDF was H.M. Hyndman, a man from a wealthy background and formerly a member of the Conservative party. The SDF got much inspiration from the recent successes achieved by Socialism in Bismarck's Germany. Under Hyndman's leadership it continued in the 1880s to put forward Socialist thinking on many different subjects and it continued to attract support. But the people it attracted came from the middle classes. Though designed to advance working-class interests, it failed to secure working-class membership.

Fabian Society

This same problem affected another important organisation, established in 1884: the Fabian Society. The new society took its name from a soldier of Ancient Rome, Fabius, whose tactic in securing the defeat of his enemy was to wait and, while waiting, to prepare for the right moment to launch a full attack. In their own tactics, the Fabians were similarly cautious, and devoted their efforts to thinking out a Socialist policy for Britain. Though there were other smaller groups advancing the Socialist cause – some with religious connections – the Social Democratic Federation and the Fabian Society were crucial in laying the foundations of Socialism and of the future Labour party.

TRADE UNIONS, SOCIALISM AND THE LABOUR PARTY

Working-class activity

Nevertheless, neither group was able to achieve much success in either local or central government elections. Both were seriously short of money. Only the dedication of their members kept them going. In the mid-1880s they had no impact among voters enfranchised under the Third Reform Act of 1884 (page 58). Receptive audiences for their teaching were however provided in the late 1880s among the unemployed, whose numbers had increased as a result of the Great Depression. In February 1886 a Trafalgar Square meeting of unemployed men was addressed by Federation leaders and broke up in disorder. Attacks were made by these unemployed on fashionable clubs and expensive shops in the West End of London. Similar outbreaks took place later that year and in the following one. Through these demonstrations and through the court cases which followed them, the Federation got much publicity for its cause. Even so, working-class support in these years was short-lived. When trade revived in the late 1880s, unemployment dropped and Socialism in Britain again lacked a section of society to which it could make a direct appeal.

What helped Socialism at this difficult stage in its history was the new unionism, whose success in these years has already been considered. Working-class candidates now stood more frequently at elections. Sometimes they stood as Liberals and sometimes they stood as independent candidates. Though in most cases they failed to be elected, in their election campaigns they made a direct appeal to those who had seen in the new unionism a way of improving their working conditions. Thus closer links were established between the new unionism, which was already achieving a notable success, and the developing Socialism, which had still to make itself felt.

VOTE FOR
Home Rule.
Democratic Government.
Justice to Labour
No Monopoly.
No Landlordism
Temperance Reform.
Healthy Homes.
Fair Rents.
Eight-Hour Day.
Work for the Unemployed.
KEIR HARDIE.

An election poster at the West Ham election that resulted in the return of the first Labour MP to Westminster. Increased involvement in national politics was a vital feature in the development of Socialism within Britain during the closing years of the nineteenth century.

The Independent Labour party

An important stage in the political development of Socialism was the election of Keir Hardie, a prominent trade unionist, as member for the London constituency of West Ham in an 1891 by-election. For some years Hardie had built up a popular following. When he arrived in parliament for the first time, he wore a worker's cloth cap and a tweed jacket, thus making himself very different in appearance from the other MPs in their formal clothes. Within parliament he stuck firmly to his principles of seeking to advance the interests of the working classes. He was, however, an isolated member within parliament.

In 1893 the Independent Labour party (ILP) came into being. Its birth was a result of encouragement by Hardie and by the new unionism. Its first achievement was to get better representation for Socialist views in the TUC. Within parliament, the ILP was initially less successful. In the general election of 1895, Hardie was defeated and not a single ILP candidate was elected. Nevertheless it continued to put forward its programme of Socialism. In the late 1890s, as the Conservative government of Lord Salisbury took so few steps to help working-class people, the ILP became more successful in local elections.

Labour Representation Committee

In 1900 the Labour Representation Committee was set up to take further steps to secure working-class representation in parliament. The SDF, the Fabians and the ILP all participated, though the SDF shortly withdrew. It was dissatisfied with what it considered to be a less than complete commitment to Socialism on the part of the Committee. The Secretary of the new organisation was James Ramsay MacDonald, destined a quarter-century later to be the first Labour Prime Minister. Soon after its formation, the Labour Representation Committee received the backing of the TUC. Though it was not called the Labour party at this time, the Labour Representation Committee was that in all but name. In the general election of 1906 it secured its first notable success with the election of 30 Labour MPs. Another achievement was the publication of a daily newspaper, *The Daily Herald*, which was able to put forward Labour's views to a wider public from 1912.

The Taff Vale case and the Osborne judgement

Taff Vale railway strike

Early in the twentieth century the trade union movement suffered two legal setbacks. The first of these concerned the Taff Vale Railway Company in South Wales. In August 1900 the railway workers struck for improved wages. They claimed such increases were overdue and they were convinced their employers could pay more. The strike was only partially successful, as the Company had brought in blackleg labour to keep some of their trains running. Up to this point the strike was following a pattern similar to that of many others in these years.

Its importance

What was to make the Taff Vale case different was the result of legal action later taken by the directors of the company. They took to court the Amalgamated Society of Railway Servants, which had principally organised the strike. In court the company sued the union for loss of profits as a result of the strike action. The case eventually reached the House of Lords in July 1901. There, judgement was given in favour of the company which was able to secure £23 000 from the union. The effect of this judgement was that any trade union might find itself facing similar costs for any company's loss of profits during a strike. The strike weapon, which had seemingly been confirmed by the Conspiracy and Protection of Property Act of 1875, was now useless.

Trade Disputes Act

The Conservative government in power at the time did nothing to change this situation. Their failure to do so was an important reason for working people to continue support of the newly developing Labour party. Later under the new Liberal government, parliament passed in 1906 the Trade Disputes Act which reversed the judgement. The Labour MPs elected in 1906 had put much pressure on the government for the passage of this Act.

Osborne judgement

The Labour party itself was also badly affected by another judgement reached by the House of Lords in 1909. Until this judgement the infant Labour party had been receiving financial help from the trade unions. The money the trade unions gave to the Labour party came from the trade union subscriptions. But in 1909 a railway trade unionist, W.V. Osborne, who happened to be a member of the Liberal party, objected to a part of his trade union subscription going to a party which he did not support. The Osborne case eventually reached the House of Lords, where judgement was given against the trade unions and the Labour party. It was therefore no longer possible for any part of the funds of a trade union to go to the support of the Labour party. The situation was eased to a certain extent by the payment of a salary of £400 per year to MPs in 1911.

Trade Union Act

Later, in 1913, this difficult situation was amended by the Trade Union Act. This permitted trade union members to **contract out** of what was termed the **political levy** if they did not wish any part of their subscription to go to the support of the Labour party. There was satisfaction at this solution. It was thought unlikely that most trade unionists would bother to contract out and would be content for part of their subscription to go to a party that was the direct political expression of trade unionism.

Number of working days lost through strike action	
1906	3029
1907	2162
1908	10 834
1909	2774
1910	9895
1911	10 320
1912	40 915
1913	11 631
1914	9878

Industrial unrest before 1914

Strikes in the few years before 1914 were noticeably bitter. They did not involve all workers. They were generally confined to the lower paid, especially those who worked in the coal mines and docks and on the railways. The early increases shown in these figures were largely caused by trouble on the railways. They were closed down completely in 1911 by a nationwide strike, from which the workers got improved pay and fuller recognition of their union. In the same year the dockers and the miners struck. The miners' strike became lengthy. The bitterness of the struggle was increased by the government's decision to send troops to South Wales, to assist the police in maintaining order while the strike

TRADE UNIONS, SOCIALISM AND THE LABOUR PARTY

lasted. The figures show 1912 to have been the worst year of all, in which once again the problems of the coal mining industry were the main cause of discontent. There were also strikes by the London dockers in that year.

Causes of industrial unrest

What caused this wave of strikes? These years were generally ones of expansion in which many industries flourished as never before. A basic trouble was that working-class people failed to benefit in any noticeable way from this expansion. Prices of a wide variety of everyday products were rising, while the wages of the working classes failed to keep pace. The difference between what working people received for their work and what they paid out to support their families became wider. Thus the standard of living of working-class people declined, while the wealthy sections of the population became even more wealthy.

Triple Industrial Alliance

The number of trade union members had doubled from two million at the start of the century to over four million at the outbreak of the First World War. Coupled with this impressive increase in numbers was a fuller determination by the trade unionists to succeed in their struggle with employers. As trade union membership increased, there was a tendency for union amalgamations to take place. In 1914 the **Triple Industrial Alliance** of the miners, railway workers and transport workers was created. Unions were further assisted by the full employment which the successful economy of Edwardian times had created. Employers confronted by a strike would find it difficult if not impossible to employ blackleg workers.

Syndicalism

Most of the industrial struggles of these years were concerned mainly with the improvement of wages, though partly also with the improvement of hours and working conditions. There is, however, some evidence of political motives among the strikers. Among some workers, the idea of **Syndicalism** was gaining popularity. This was an idea which French trade unionists had developed. The aim of the Syndicalists was to create widespread havoc through a series of strikes that would develop into a general strike of all workers. Then it would be possible for the government to be taken over by the strike leaders and for the country to be run according to the interests of the workers. Syndicalism, in thus seeking the destruction of parliament and government, was virtually a call for revolution.

The government and the property owners were naturally worried by Syndicalism. It had particular influence among the South Wales miners, who in 1912 produced a book entitled *The Miners' Next Step*, urging miners to adopt Syndicalism and to spread its message. The force of that message is shown in this extract.

> Alliances to be formed, and trades organisations fostered, with a view to steps being taken, to amalgamate all workers into one National and International union, to work for the taking over of all industries, by the workmen themselves ...
>
> It will be noticed that nothing is said about Conciliation Boards or Wage Agreements. ... Conciliation Boards and Wage Agreements only lead into a morass ... the suggested organisation is constructed to fight rather than to negotiate. It is based upon the principle that we can only get what we are strong enough to win and retain.
>
> *The Miners' Next Step*

But Syndicalism never received widespread support from the British working class. Most had no wish for over-turning the way in which the country was governed. Their aim was the more direct one of obtaining a wage that would allow them to live without the fear of poverty. In spite of the intensity of the industrial struggles of these years, nothing more than that was the objective of the majority of those who were involved in strikes.

EXERCISES

1. With reference to the years 1867–1914 describe one way in which the trade union movement was able to achieve each of the following, and explain why each was important for the movement:
   (a) legal protection for its funds,
   (b) the right to picket peacefully,
   (c) wider membership among unskilled workers, and
   (d) firm links with the Labour party.

2. (a) Explain what you understand by the term *Socialism* and show how each of the following wanted to achieve Socialism:
   (i) the Social Democratic Federation,
   (ii) the Fabians, and
   (iii) the Independent Labour party.
   (b) Trace the stages by which in the years 1900–14 a Labour party emerged in Britain.

3. Imagine you are a trade unionist in late Victorian times. Write an article which might be published in a trade union journal, explaining in what ways those years were ones of important advance.

4. Study the two membership certificates on page 48 and the poster on page 53, and then answer questions (a) to (e) which follow.
   (a) With reference to the membership certificate on the left of page 48:
   (i) What does the slogan at the top suggest to you about the nature of this union?
   (ii) How is this impression strengthened by some of the other details on the certificate? (4)
   (b) With reference to the membership certificate on the right of page 48:
   (i) What does the slogan at the bottom suggest to you about the nature of this union?
   (ii) How is this impression strengthened by some of the other details on the certificate? (4)
   (c) What do you think was the value to different trade unions of elaborate certificates such as these two? (3)
   (d) Study the poster on page 53:
   (i) In what ways does the appearance of the man in the poster show him as different from most MPs at that time?
   (ii) Why do you think he made himself appear in this way in this poster? (4)
   (e) (i) Identify two of the listed causes that the politician shown in the poster would have shared with those who held the trade union certificates. Explain your choice of these two causes.
   (ii) Show in what ways in the late nineteenth and early twentieth centuries trade unionism attempted to strengthen itself by forming political links. (5)

5 DOMESTIC AND FOREIGN ISSUES IN LATE VICTORIAN TIMES

Political life in Britain changed as the century drew to a close. Entry into the House of Commons of Labour MPs was to lead in the twentieth century to the virtual replacement of the Liberal party by the Labour party. Other changes are also noticeable in these years. The separation of the Liberal Unionists from the Liberal party in 1886 on the issue of Irish home rule has already been considered in Chapter 3. The party was so weakened by those events that for the next 20 years, with the exception of the period 1892–95, the Conservatives had little difficulty in maintaining themselves in power.

Gladstone's second ministry: domestic policies

The Liberals in the 1880s

Gladstone's second ministry (1880–85) was to disappoint those who saw him as a great reforming leader. Partly this was due to the diversions caused by events in Ireland, in South Africa and in Egypt. Partly it was due to the continuing effects of economic depression throughout the British Isles. But it was in large measure due to Gladstone's failure to set out a clear reform programme at the time of the general election of 1880. In winning that election, members of the Liberal party – and Gladstone in particular in his Midlothian campaigns – had relied almost entirely on criticising the Conservatives. This approach had brought the Liberals success.

Once in power, however, they appeared uncertain about the direction in which they should go. Nor were they helped by their own internal divisions in the early 1880s. The Radical element within the Liberal party was not so favourably treated by the Prime Minister as the Whig element was. The Radicals had few cabinet positions; Joseph Chamberlain was the sole Radical of any importance to be included and he was given only a minor cabinet office. Dissatisfied by the way in which he was treated, Chamberlain was well poised to become the main leader of political revolt in 1886 (page 41).

Gladstone's legislation

Ireland was Gladstone's main domestic concern during this ministry and has been considered in Chapter 3 (pages 39–40). Gladstone's second ministry had fewer domestic reforms to its credit than his first ministry. The Mundella Education Act of 1880 ensured that school attendance between the ages of five and ten was compulsory. This made firmer the rather loose provision on compulsory attendance contained in the acts of 1870 and 1876. It was certainly a necessary piece of legislation, as before the Act more than a third of children in the age range did not attend school. But in spite of now being compulsory, school attendance was still not free. The Married Women's Property Act of 1882 permitted a woman to retain her property in her own name when she married; previously her property had automatically become that of her husband. This Act marked a step in the development of women's rights, a development that made much progress in the late nineteenth century and early twentieth century and which is more fully considered in the next chapter.

But these and other acts of lesser importance were a disappointment to some Liberals, and especially to the Radicals among them. Chamberlain expressed their frustration in a number of fiery speeches. In the 1885 election he put forward what became known as his **Unauthorised Programme**. This contained far-reaching proposals for the redistribution of wealth, and the riches of the aristocracy were his main target of attack.

Further parliamentary reform

Corrupt and Illegal Practices Act

Excluding legislation concerning Ireland, it was work for further parliamentary reform that was the main feature of domestic policy in Gladstone's second ministry. The Corrupt and Illegal Practices Act of 1883 contained reforms vitally necessary if parliament were to function fairly and properly. It might have been thought that the secret ballot, established in 1872, would have made bribery pointless. But in attempting to secure election, prospective MPs were still bribing voters and the recent general election of 1880 had afforded many examples of this. Quite apart from wanting to rid the country of an evil practice, the Liberals were worried that in this situation it was they, the less wealthy of the two major parties, who would come off worse if the situation were to continue. The new Act was thorough and effective. Large fines and terms of imprisonment were to be imposed on candidates found guilty of a wide range of election offences.

Passage of the Third Reform Bill

The Third Reform Bill was introduced in the summer of 1884 and had a fairly easy passage through the House of Commons. It met more serious Conservative opposition in the House of Lords. Here the Conservative leader, Lord Salisbury, made the redistribution of seats the price of Conservative approval. In this way he hoped to get advantage for his own party. Though Chamberlain was keen to face and fight the House of Lords on this issue, Gladstone preferred compromise. Political discussions between both parties in the autumn of 1884 led to a satisfactory agreement and the two acts – one extending the franchise and the other redistributing the seats – then passed both houses of parliament.

Terms

The terms of both these acts were to have far-reaching effects. The Parliamentary Reform Act of 1884 gave the vote to all male householders in the counties, thus treating county householders in the same way as the 1867 Act had treated borough householders. The effect of this was almost to double the number of voters, allowing the vote to two out of every three men and raising the total number of voters to about five million. More fundamental change accompanied the Redistribution Act of 1885. Since medieval times MPs had represented either **county constituencies** or **borough constituencies**. Most counties, and a number of boroughs, returned two MPs. The county–borough distinction and the return of MPs for a county now came to an end. Instead the vast majority of constituencies were to be **single-member constituencies** returning one MP. Previous wide variations in constituency population were equalled out, and each now had an approximate population of 50 000. This made for fairer, more equal representation.

Importance

These changes had important effects. The dividing up of the old county constituencies led to a reduction in the power of the landed families. It also reduced the number of Whigs returned to the House of Commons, as previously they had often paired with a Radical in the two-member county constituencies. In Ireland its impact was even more profound. As has been seen in Chapter 3, the seat redistribution coupled with the wider franchise led at the next general election to a large increase in the number of Irish Nationalist MPs. All political parties had now to readjust and improve their organisation – both nationally and locally – in order to secure the advantages offered by the new political situation.

Gladstone's second ministry: Afghanistan, South Africa and Egypt

Afghanistan

Two main problems in foreign affairs were inherited by Gladstone from Disraeli: Afghanistan and South Africa. He had been highly critical of Disraeli's policies in both these areas. In Afghanistan the Liberal government withdrew from the strong involvement that Disraeli had favoured. Nevertheless, for the

DOMESTIC AND FOREIGN ISSUES IN LATE VICTORIAN TIMES

sake of the British control of India, the government insisted that British influence in Afghanistan should continue. A new British-approved ruler was established at the capital, Kabul. Shortly after he took control his rule was challenged by rebels who besieged the British-controlled fortress at Kandahar, some 300 miles from the capital. This challenge was suppressed by General Roberts in the summer of 1880. The difficult countryside of the long journey from Kabul to Kandahar was covered by Roberts with his 10 000 men in less than a month and the fortress successfully relieved. The march from Kabul to Kandahar was regarded in late Victorian Britain as an epic journey and General Roberts – 'Bobs' as he became popularly known – one of the best loved imperialists of his time. The immediate importance of his march was to confirm the British-controlled government in Afghanistan. British interests were maintained in this buffer state between India and Russia for the rest of the century.

First Boer War

No similar success was achieved by Gladstone in South Africa. The Boers had been greatly angered by the recent British annexation of the Transvaal. In spite of Gladstone's assurances in opposition that the Transvaal would be restored to the Boers if he secured power, once in power he was slow to do this. Boer impatience grew, and in December 1880 a Boer attack on the British was made. Thus began the First Boer War of 1880–81, which was to prove a total disaster for Britain.

A major feature of the opening British campaign against the Boers was an attack on the Transvaal through the Drakensberg Mountains. In February 1881 a British force was sent to occupy Majuba Hill, commanding one of the crucial passes through the Drakensbergs into the Transvaal (see the map on page 91). Their Boer opponents, well acquainted with the mountains, got to know of their movements and successfully attacked them in force. An unco-ordinated and humiliating retreat by the British soldiers resulted. Majuba Hill was an event British imperialists preferred to forget.

Convention of Pretoria

Abandonment of the Transvaal was now certain and in 1881 was agreed in the Convention of Pretoria. Further terms in this Convention did however provide for an over-riding British control – referred to as British **suzerainty** – in the Transvaal, including control of its foreign policy. Neither the 1881 agreement nor a further agreement of 1884 made exactly clear what rights Britain had in the Transvaal, and this uncertainty contained the seeds of the Second Boer War, which was to break out in 1899.

Arabi Pasha

Problems originating in Egypt in the 1880s were to prove more long-lasting and, in their final outcome, more damaging for the government. The basic trouble was one which had been familiar to Disraeli in the previous decade: the bankruptcy of the Egyptian government. Bankruptcy had led to a worsening in the already poor administration of Egypt and provided fertile ground for rebellion. In these circumstances two strong leaders had arisen: Arabi Pasha in Egypt itself and the Mahdi in the Sudan. Arabi Pasha, an Egyptian army officer who detested British influence in his country, was initially the more troublesome. His following by the autumn of 1881 was so numerous and so strong that he was able to force the Khedive to appoint a government favourable to his own nationalist position. He had therefore become a serious threat to the British. There was fear that Britain's recently acquired interest in the Suez Canal might now be threatened and thus the security of India put at risk.

British action in Egypt

His activities were also of concern to the French government, which shared many of Britain's financial interests in Egypt and which, since 1878, had also shared the administration of the country with Britain. The continuing violence of Arabi Pasha's followers, and particularly some attacks they made on Europeans and European property inside Egypt, alarmed both governments. The British government decided that Arabi's forces must be suppressed, but was unable to persuade the French government to join in the action they proposed. In July 1882 British forces bombarded the town of Alexandria from the sea,

One of the forts at Alexandria, at the time of the bombardment of July 1882. British action in that year was considered necessary if Britain were to retain security for its route to India.

thereby bringing disorders in the city to an end. This naval action was followed in September by victory over Arabi's forces at Tel-el-Kebir, one of Britain's most impressive military achievements of the late nineteenth century. As the French had refused to assist in the suppression of Arabi, they now abandoned their share in the administration of Egypt. Britain was now dominant and the government took practical steps to ensure that this dominance would last. In the following year Sir Evelyn Baring (later in life known as Lord Cromer) was appointed Consul-General of Egypt, a position he held until well into the twentieth century. It was his practical reforms in Egypt and close supervision of the Khedive's government that kept Egypt peaceful and under secure British control.

Gladstone's second ministry: the Sudan

Britain's policies in the Sudan, the large region south of Egypt and loosely under Egyptian control, were far less successful. Gladstone's policies in the Sudan were very different from his policies in Egypt. The reason for this is to be found in his attitude towards British power abroad. To him, the acquiring of foreign territories had little purpose unless essential British interests were involved. As British interests were involved in Egypt, he had no doubts that it was right to take action. But in his judgement British interests were not involved in the Sudan and he was unwilling to pursue any similar policy in this vast area, little known to Europeans.

The Mahdi The people of the Sudan had rallied to the support of a fanatical religious leader known as the Mahdi. His powerful hold over the Sudanese was based partly on rebellion against foreign influence and partly on faith in Islam. The combination of these two elements made the Mahdi and his warriors formidable enemies. Evidence of this was conclusively provided in the autumn of 1883 when an Egyptian force under a British mercenary commander, Colonel Hicks, was killed by the Mahdi's warriors while attempting to bring them under control. The isolated Egyptian garrisons in the Sudan were at risk, and there was fear that Egypt itself might be threatened. In Britain, public opinion clamoured for action. Though the cabinet failed to reach full agreement on the action that was needed, Gladstone's view that the Sudan should be evacuated in as orderly a manner as possible became the government's policy.

DOMESTIC AND FOREIGN ISSUES IN LATE VICTORIAN TIMES

General Gordon The government was unwise in its choice of a commander to carry out this policy: General Charles Gordon. His main recommendation for the job was that he knew the Sudan well. In the 1870s he had been responsible for the suppression of the slave trade in the Sudan and for establishing order in the area before the Mahdi was heard of. But Gordon was a committed imperialist, who had served Britain in many other parts of the world, in China, in India and in Africa. He was a Christian of firm Evangelical beliefs. He was also an adventurer, who would stop at nothing once committed to a cause. Given these characteristics, was he really the right man to conduct an imperial retreat?

Events at Khartoum Once arrived in the Sudanese capital of Khartoum as Governor-General in the spring of 1884, General Gordon quickly showed that he was not. Instead of organising the retreat, he embarked on a plan of his own for Britain to secure control of the whole upper valley of the Nile. Unfortunately for Gordon, however, the forces of the Mahdi achieved success after success. By the summer of 1884 Gordon found himself under siege in Khartoum itself. Gordon's determination to go his own way in the Sudan had imperilled his own safety and that of his men. The government now had to take steps to get Gordon out of the difficulty that he himself had created.

To do so was no easy task. In any case the government – preoccupied in the summer of 1884 with the details of the Third Reform Bill – was slow to give orders for the sending of a relief force. Eventually in the autumn of 1884 Sir Garnet Wolseley, the commander at the battle of Tel-el-Kebir, was sent southwards. Only in January 1885 did an advance party of Wolseley's force reach Khartoum. They discovered that a few days previously the garrison had fallen to the besieging forces and Gordon had been killed.

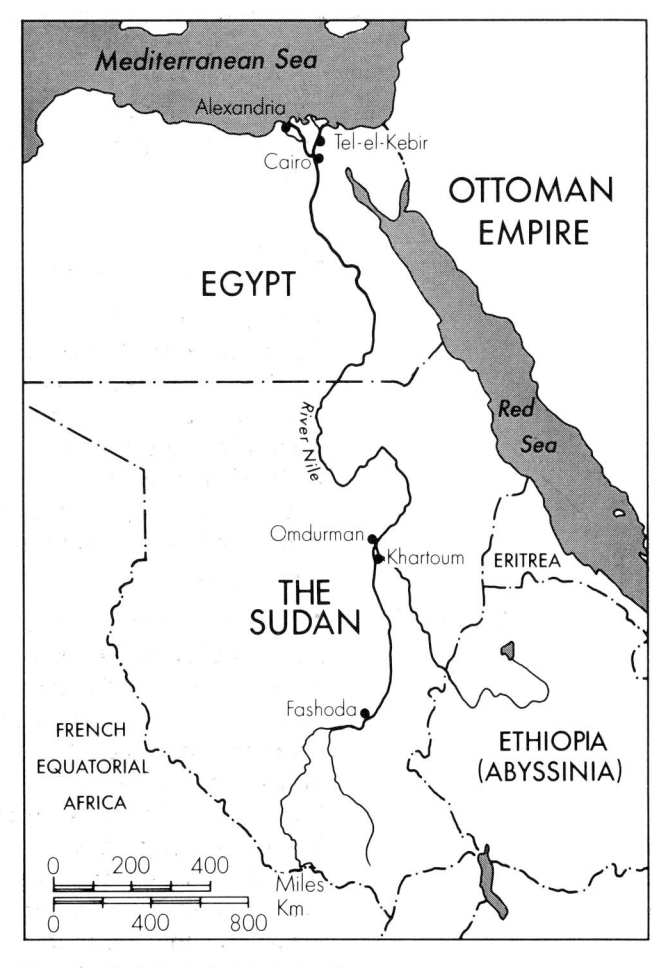

Egypt and the Sudan in the late nineteenth century

A HISTORY OF BRITAIN FROM 1867

The importance of the death of General Gordon

The emotion caused in Britain by news of the death of Gordon was immense. His stand at Khartoum had captivated the enthusiasm of many in Britain who until that time may never even have heard of the Sudan. News of his death now gave him the status almost of a martyr. The government was attacked from all sides for its failure to give adequate protection to him and the Queen was particularly critical of their conduct. Gladstone was singled out for the crudest, most emotional criticism. Yet it was Gordon's refusal to obey the government that was really at fault. The following extracts from the diary he kept while besieged at Khartoum illustrate this well.

> *19 September 1884*: I own I have been very insubordinate to Her Majesty's government and its officials, but it is my nature and I cannot help it. I know if *I* was chief I would never employ *myself*, for I am incorrigible. To the government, I must be *perfect poison*. I wonder what the telegrams about the Sudan have cost Her Majesty's government?
>
> *13 December 1884*: If some effort is not made before ten days time the town will fall. It is inexplicable, this delay. If the expeditionary forces have reached the river and met my steamers, one hundred men are all that we require, just to show themselves.... I have done my best for the honour of our country.
>
> **The Journals of Major-General C.G. Gordon at Khartoum**

TOMMY ATKINS MOUNTED ON TOO LATE
BY
VERBOSITY OUT OF VACILLATION

Gladstone's failure to send an adequate relief force to rescue General Gordon at Khartoum in 1885 was a matter for which he was much criticised. This cartoon of the time shows a British 'Tommy' (soldier) mounted on 'Too Late', a camel bearing Gladstone's head.

Given Gordon's unpredictable nature, there was no certainty that he would have allowed himself to be relieved at Khartoum, even had Wolseley's forces arrived a few days earlier in January 1885.

Combined with memories of Majuba Hill, Gordon's death brought a drastic reduction in the popularity of Gladstone and the Liberals. But Gladstone made no apology for his actions and appeared almost to enjoy the outcry of opposition that greeted him. Shortly afterwards, on a different issue, he showed that he could be quite firm when vital British interests were threatened. In March 1885 Russian forces crossed the Afghan border (as it then was) to bring down the fortress at Pendjeh. The government interpreted this action as a threat to India, prepared for war, but at the same time entered negotiations. These were continued by the Conservatives later in the year and resulted in an agreement on boundary adjustments.

Lord Salisbury's Conservatism and Randolph Churchill's Fourth party

1885 and 1886 were years of much political change, in which Irish affairs dominated. The formation of Lord Salisbury's first Conservative government in June 1885, the election towards the end of that year, the formation of Gladstone's third ministry in February 1886, the home rule issue, the separation of the Liberal Unionists from the Liberal party and the consequent general election of July 1886 were all events so strongly influenced by Irish issues that they have been considered in connection with Ireland, in Chapter 3.

Lord Salisbury and the Cecil family

Lord Salisbury was to be Prime Minister on three occasions: the first during the brief months of 1885–86, the second 1886–92, and the third 1895–1902. He had previously served Disraeli as Foreign Minister at the time of the Congress of Berlin. He came from the distinguished and wealthy Cecil family. A sixteenth-century predecessor had for many years been Chief Minister to Queen Elizabeth I and since that time the Cecils had always been prominent in British life. They were even more prominent in the Conservative party. When Salisbury retired in 1902 he handed the premiership to his nephew, Arthur Balfour, almost as a family legacy. The Cecil family continued to have strong influence in the Conservative party even until the 1960s. Lord Salisbury would probably

DOMESTIC AND FOREIGN ISSUES IN LATE VICTORIAN TIMES

have preferred to be described as a Tory rather than a Conservative. He himself described his political views in these terms.

> **The Tory party is composed of varying elements, and there is trouble in trying to make them work together. I think the 'classes and dependants of class' are the strongest ingredients in our composition, but we have so to conduct our legislation that we shall give some satisfaction to both classes and masses. This is specially difficult with the classes – because all legislation is unwelcome to them, as tending to disturb a state of things with which they are satisfied. It is evident, therefore, that we must work at less speed and at a lower temperature than our opponents. Our bills must be tentative and cautious, not sweeping and dramatic. The opposite course is to produce drastic measures, hitting the 'classes' hard, and consequently dispensing with their support, but trusting to public meetings and the democratic forces generally to carry us through. I think such a policy will fail.**
>
> Letter of Lord Salisbury to Lord Randolph Churchill, 7 November 1886

The progressive ideas of Disraeli meant little to Lord Salisbury. He was out of sympathy with the recent extensions of the franchise and had no programme of domestic reforms to implement. He sought, rather, to resolve problems at home and abroad as and when they occurred. And he expected his ministers to do the same.

Lord Randolph Churchill and the Fourth party

Most did. But the newly appointed Chancellor of the Exchequer wanted the Conservative party to develop a more dynamic course. Lord Randolph Churchill had already attracted much attention to himself earlier in the 1880s by the forming of what was known as the **Fourth party**. It consisted of four leading Conservative politicians, and it could also be regarded as a 'Fourth' party after the Conservatives, Liberals and Irish Nationalists. Though its name made it sound separate from the Conservative party, it in fact always remained within it. The immediate purpose of the Fourth party was to create a sharper opposition to the Liberals in the House of Commons. It also developed the idea of **Tory democracy** which, its members suggested, had been begun by Disraeli in the 1870s. They tried to attract the newly enfranchised voters and to widen the basis of Conservative support.

Randolph Churchill's restless energy was to prove his own downfall. He did not last long as Chancellor of the Exchequer. He continued to take close interest in all aspects of government policy and in the autumn of 1886 put forward proposals for various domestic reforms and new foreign policies. The Prime Minister and his cabinet colleagues feared that this young Chancellor of the Exchequer would prevent them from developing as the unified and stable government they hoped to be. When towards the end of 1886 the Minister of War objected to proposed budget cuts for the Army, Churchill resigned as Chancellor of the Exchequer. From then onwards his influence declined. His political promise, a great talking point of the early 1880s when he was often suggested as a future Prime Minister, had come to nothing. Yet his work was important for the Conservative party. By his friendship with Chamberlain he had helped link more closely the Conservatives with the Liberal Unionists. By his urging of Tory democracy he had helped to show that the Conservative party needed a broader base than the rather solemn government Lord Salisbury suggested.

Lord Randolph Churchill – father of Winston Churchill – was regarded in the 1880s as a bold supporter of the 'Tory democracy' earlier associated with Disraeli. But political misjudgements and ill-health prevented him from making any significant contribution to political life.

Lord Salisbury's government: domestic legislation

Local Government Act

Lord Salisbury's government had an unimpressive record in domestic legislation. Such legislation as there was tended to be produced as a result of the urgings of the Liberal Unionists, on whom the government depended for votes. Chamberlain had long wanted a reform that would bring to local government the types of change which the 1867 and 1884 acts had brought to parliament.

The Local Government Act of 1888 achieved this. This Act created a county council for each county. The new county councils did not, however, have any authority over the older established borough councils. These continued to administer built-up areas, some of them widening their boundaries in order to administer areas with a population of 50 000. The London County Council was set up as a special unit. Voting rights for local councils were now the same as those for parliamentary elections. A concession was, however, made to women. If qualified by the property they inhabited and if single, they were permitted to vote in local elections though they were still denied this right in parliamentary elections. Those whose powers were threatened by the new Act were the justices of the peace who had previously been solely responsible for county administration.

Two acts of these years were concerned with developments in education. The Technical Instruction Act of 1889 allowed the new county councils to make an additional charge on the rates in order to provide for technical education. In 1891 school fees in elementary schools were abolished.

Housing

As is shown in the following chapter, the period of the 1890s was a time in which the public was becoming more aware of the problems of poverty within Britain. Lord Salisbury's governments did not entirely neglect these problems. The Housing of the Working Classes Act of 1890 was the government's response to the findings of a Royal Commission which had made a study of working-class housing. Like the previous Conservative measure on housing, the Artisans Dwellings Act which had been passed 15 years earlier, the 1890 Act continued to place responsibility for housing on local authorities. It made better provision for the granting of loans to them for this purpose by central government. This made easier their task of slum demolition. Soundly built terraced housing – much of it still inhabited a century later – was the main product of the house-building done in these years. Provision was further made for working-class people to grow their own crops on allotments (by an Act of 1887) and smallholdings (by an Act of 1892).

Workmen's Compensation Act

The working classes were also able to benefit from the Workmen's Compensation Act of 1897. This legislation, in Salisbury's third ministry, was largely a result of the urgings of Chamberlain. He had joined the ministry in 1895 and had persuaded the Prime Minister that a fuller commitment should be made to introduce social reforms. As Colonial Secretary he was not in a position to influence domestic policy very strongly. Nevertheless the Workmen's Compensation Act established an important principle. It was now to be the responsibility of an employer to pay compensation to any of his workers who were injured while at work. The categories of workers and the types of accident for which benefit could be obtained under the terms of the 1897 Act were limited. More were added by the terms of further, similar acts passed over the next few years.

The Liberals in the 1890s

Gladstone's retirement

The election in the summer of 1892 returned the Liberals to power. Gladstone, now well into his eighties, formed his fourth ministry. His political position was, however, insecure. In the House of Commons he relied on the votes of the Irish Nationalists to maintain him in power, while his party was still weakened by the effects of the Liberal Unionist split. Gladstone's energies were devoted almost entirely to his unsuccessful second attempt to secure home rule for Ireland, the details of which have been considered in Chapter 3. In February 1894 he retired, disappointed by his failure at the end of a long political life to fulfil the 'mission' to which he had pledged himself many years earlier and for which he had devoted so much of his tireless energy.

DOMESTIC AND FOREIGN ISSUES IN LATE VICTORIAN TIMES

Lord Rosebery as Prime Minister

Lord Rosebery succeeded Gladstone as Prime Minister. Rosebery came from a Whig family whose wealth was based on its extensive landed possessions. He was also a man of much intellectual brilliance and had served successfully as Foreign Secretary during Gladstone's fourth ministry. He had been selected for the premiership by the Queen, not by the Liberal party or Gladstone. His background and his ability were certainly recommendations. He was known to be, almost alone among leading Liberals, a convinced imperialist. That probably was the decisive factor in Queen Victoria's choice. Yet Rosebery was unhappy as Prime Minister and its responsibilities taxed his nervous personality cruelly. In June 1895 he appeared almost to welcome the opportunity of resigning when the government was defeated by a vote in the House of Commons. The more solid Lord Salisbury, who formed his third ministry on the resignation of Rosebery, was confirmed in office in the general election that followed almost at once.

Newcastle Programme

When the Liberal party had taken on the governing of Britain in 1892 it had done so with a clear reputation as a reforming party. This was based on its recent record in office, but had been particularly emphasised by the **Newcastle Programme** which the party had accepted in October 1891. Home rule was the main item in the programme, but it included many others. There was to be further reform of parliament and general elections were to be called at least every three years. Democracy in local government was to be taken further by the setting up of district and parish councils. Working-class conditions were to be improved by making employers liable for accidents, by limiting hours of work and by encouraging the use of allotments. The Anglican Church in Wales and the Church of Scotland were to be disestablished. This was a programme for reform that went far beyond earlier Liberal commitments.

The acceptance of the Newcastle Programme by the Liberal party would hardly have been possible before the events of 1886. Most of the old aristocratic Whig families, who would have viewed the Newcastle Programme with alarm, had left the party with the Liberal Unionists. In this respect, Whig aristocrats such as Lord Rosebery were an exception. The Liberals now hoped to get the support of many newly enfranchised voters. To an extent they did so in 1892 though, as has been seen on page 43, their victory in that year was only a narrow one. Their failure in the general elections of 1895 and 1900 may be attributed to the important place they gave in the Newcastle Programme to home rule, never a truly popular issue with British voters in these years.

Opposition from the House of Lords

The Liberals in the years 1892–95 found the House of Lords solidly against them. The fortunes of the Second Home Rule Bill were dashed by the opposition of the House of Lords. Similar fate met other Liberal measures of these years. It is for this reason that so much of the Newcastle Programme remained unfulfilled. The tactics of the Conservative and Unionist majority in the House of Lords were unwise. Neither Gladstone nor Rosebery felt confident enough at the time to challenge the power of the House of Lords, but it is from the resentments of these years that there developed the sharp hostility of the Liberal party towards the House of Lords. This was to form the basis of their successful challenge to the Lords' power in the political conflicts of 1909–11 (pages 104–6).

Further Conservative legislation

Yet in spite of these troubles some important legislation was passed. Further local government reforms had been promised in the Newcastle Programme, as the 1888 Local Government Act had brought about little real change in the people who controlled local affairs. The Liberals wanted to add to the councils provided for in the 1888 Act other, more localised councils that would better represent local opinion. The Conservatives feared these elected councils would undermine the traditional authority of local landowners and local justices of the peace. As eventually passed in 1894, after much opposition in both houses, the new Local Government Act created parish councils, rural district councils and urban district councils. Those who qualified as electors under the 1888 Act were allowed to vote for these new councils, with an important addition in favour of women. If qualified, they were now allowed to vote whether married or single (under the 1888 Act only qualified single women had been allowed to vote). Qualified women voters were also allowed to stand for election, though their right to do so continued to be disputed until 1907. As the Conservative opposition had insisted that the rate-levying power of the new councils should be strictly limited, they were unable in the early years to undertake really useful work in their localities. But the terms of the new Act did mark an important extension of the principle of democracy and at a level which affected people more closely than county or central government did.

Death duty tax

In the budget of 1894 the Chancellor of the Exchequer, Sir William Harcourt, introduced death duty. The budget of that year needed to raise extra money in order to pay for increased spending on the Navy. Higher income tax and higher duties on drink would not produce enough. So Harcourt decided on what was then the novel idea of taxing the total value of a person's possessions at death. Such a tax would certainly produce much revenue. Socialists and some Liberals welcomed it for the more fundamental reason that over the years it would lead to a more even distribution of income among the people of Britain. Conservatives feared that it would weaken the landowning classes. As it was a well established tradition that the House of Lords did not challenge government budgets, the death duties were able to pass both houses without any direct conflict from the Conservatives.

EXERCISES

1. Show in what ways and with what success during his second and third ministries of 1880–85 and 1886, Gladstone tried to:
   (a) create a fuller democracy within Britain,
   (b) defend British interests abroad, and
   (c) satisfy the demands of the Irish.

2. (a) Why were the Conservatives able to secure power in 1886?
   (b) What was the approach of the Conservatives towards the governing of Britain in the years 1886–1905?
   (c) Describe the main reforms which they undertook in England and Ireland during these years.

3. Imagine you are opposed to Gladstone's policies abroad and in Ireland during his second ministry of 1880–85. Write three letters, each for different years of the ministry, to explain why you oppose these policies of the Prime Minister.

4. Study the extract and the cartoon on page 62 and then answer questions (a) to (c) which follow.

(a) (i) What do you learn from the extract about the character and attitudes of General Gordon? In your answer, refer to specific words and phrases.
(ii) Describe the situation in the Sudan at the time that Gordon was sent there.
(iii) From the words in the extract and from your own knowledge of Gordon, explain why he might be considered unsuited for his work in the Sudan.
(3+4+3)
(b) (i) By reference to the words and features of the cartoon, show what was the cartoonist's attitude towards Gladstone.
(ii) By describing Gladstone's policy towards Gordon in the Sudan, show whether or not you agree with the cartoonist's interpretation. (3+3)
(c) Giving reasons for your choice, indicate whether the extract or the cartoon is the more reliable source for an understanding of events in the Sudan in the 1880s. (4)

6 RELIGION AND SOCIETY IN LATE VICTORIAN AND EDWARDIAN TIMES

The earlier chapters of this book have shown how the lives of individual people were beginning to benefit directly from government policies. As these were years of crucial importance for the extension of democratic rights and the passage of reforming legislation, these features have so far been given much emphasis. But government policies are not alone in making up the history of any country. Many important developments that took place during the later years of Queen Victoria's reign and those of her son Edward VII (1901–10) had no close connection with government policies or legislation. Yet they are of much importance in British history.

Religion: the Christian denominations

Importance of religion

Religion formed a vital part of life in Britain during the late nineteenth century. Most people attended a church or a chapel (the name usually applied to Nonconformist places of worship). Many new churches, usually in styles imitating medieval gothic, were constructed to cater for the large number of worshippers. Many are still used and their size suggests the importance of religion in people's lives during these years. That importance is further illustrated by the intense feeling which controversies about religion were capable of arousing.

Conflict within the Church of England

The roots of these controversies go back before the period covered by this book. Within the Church of England, the denomination that attracted the most number of worshippers, much turmoil had been created by the Oxford Movement, which had started in the 1830s. This movement had emphasised the position of the Church of England as a spiritual society, not subject to control by outside forces, such as the government of the day. It also encouraged Anglicans

A photograph taken in the 1930s during a celebration of High Mass at the London church of All Saints, Margaret Street. The use of ritual in Anglo-Catholic churches such as this became a matter of much controversy in the early years covered by this book.

to be more fully aware of the heritage their church possessed from pre-Reformation times. By the 1860s and 1870s many of the **high church** clergy, those who were loyal to the ideals of the Oxford Movement, had begun to practise what was generally termed **ritualism**. The description **Anglo-Catholic** was often applied to such clergy. They gave greater attention to beautifying the worship in their churches by the use of crosses, candles, chants and incense. They wore vestments such as had been used in medieval times and they adjusted the Prayer Book in order to use forms of prayer similar to those used in the Roman Catholic Church. The **low church** or **Evangelical** element within the Church of England was profoundly disturbed by these tendencies, which it viewed as a betrayal of the Protestant principles established at the Reformation.

Public Worship Regulation Act

So bitter had the conflict between high churchmen and low churchmen become by the 1870s that the Archbishop of Canterbury feared that the unity of the Church of England was under threat. It was this fear that prompted him to get the agreement of Disraeli to legislation prohibiting ritualism. In agreeing to this legislation, Disraeli was much influenced by Queen Victoria's known hostility towards ritualism. 'The Queen,' she had said on one occasion, 'is Protestant to the very heart's core', and she had expressed a particular dislike of 'high church young curates'. But the Public Worship Regulation Act of 1874

"BLACK SHEEP."

The Archbishop of Canterbury's Public Worship Regulation Act of 1874 was a misguided attempt to use the law to curb the development of ritualism among Anglican clergy. Some preferred to escape the Act by joining another church in which the use of ritual was more favourably regarded.

proved unworkable. Although a number of high church clergy were sent to prison under its terms, the legal machinery set up by the Act was difficult to apply. There was much sympathy for the imprisoned clergy, even from those who did not support their actions. Legislation was clearly not a proper solution to an internal Anglican problem. The controversy over ritualism nevertheless continued within the Church of England until well into the twentieth century.

Roman Catholics

Quite apart from the unpleasantness of this controversy, the Church of England had unfriendly relations with other denominations. Roman Catholics were comparatively few in number, many were descendants of Irish people who had earlier settled in mainland Britain. Their Church was the subject of much suspicion and hostility, some of it crudely and abusively expressed in newspapers and magazines. Partly this was on account of the general contempt in which the Irish were held; partly it was due to prejudice against the papacy that went back to Reformation times. The allegiance of Roman Catholics to a power outside the British Isles led even such a seriously minded statesman as Gladstone to doubt if a Roman Catholic could be regarded as a fully loyal citizen.

RELIGION AND SOCIETY IN LATE VICTORIAN AND EDWARDIAN TIMES

Nonconformists More numerous were the churches generally known as **Nonconformist** or **Dissenting**. These mainly consisted of old-established denominations such as the Baptists and Congregationalists and those which had emerged in the previous century, such as the Methodists. Even these three denominations were further divided and there were numerous smaller ones. The Church-Chapel (Anglican–Nonconformist) conflict was the one that was the most noticeable in English life, both in town and country. Families would generally give their loyalty to the one or to the other. The division had a distinct political significance. It was more usual for Anglicans to be Conservatives and even more likely for Nonconformists to be Liberals. The Church of England tended to attract rather wealthier people than the Nonconformist churches. As the **established** Church of the land, possessing the ancient cathedrals and parish churches, it had a standing which no other Church could hope to equal. Yet though in the late nineteenth century its membership figures were larger than those for all the Nonconformist Churches combined, the latter formed a close second. With their emphasis upon hymn singing and the preaching of fiery sermons – in which political views were often expressed – Chapel was a powerful attraction. Though it was usually poorer families who attended, ambitious middle-class families were often prominent in Chapel congregations.

Disestablishment Within Britain the Church of England was just one of two **established** churches. The Church of Scotland had a similar status, yet its Presbyterian structure – involving an absence of bishops – gave it strong points of similarity with the Nonconformist Churches in England. South of the border, **disestablishment** of the Church of England was the goal of many Nonconformists. Only such drastic action could remove the inequalities which still aroused Nonconformist anger in late Victorian times.

The disestablishment of the Church of Ireland in 1869 was a great encouragement to them. So in 1914 was the disestablishment of the Anglican Church in Wales. Yet they never achieved their object of disestablishing the Church of England. Partly this was due to the removal of some of the more glaring Nonconformist disabilities during these years. An Act of 1868 abolished the payment of a local rate for the support of the local Anglican church. An Act of 1871 (page 21) permitted Nonconformists to hold teaching and research posts at Oxford and Cambridge. An Act of 1880 allowed for Nonconformist burial in Anglican churchyards (often the only burial place in rural areas) without an Anglican service.

By the early twentieth century, the fire had gone out of the disestablishment cause. Yet Nonconformist feeling could still be aroused. Especially through the Liberal party it could still evoke sharp opposition on such issues as education, licensing, or what was judged to be immoral conduct in foreign affairs. In these respects, Nonconformity was to show itself as a powerful force of opposition to Balfour's Conservative ministry of 1902–05, considered in Chapter 8.

Religion: doubt and atheism

The ideas of Darwin In the middle years of the nineteenth century few households in Britain would have been unaware of the name of Charles Darwin. After extensive travels in the regions of the Pacific Ocean, this Cambridge scholar had constructed theories about the evolution of human beings. The theories were put forward in *The Origin of the Species* (1859) and *The Descent of Man* (1871). The first of these books cast doubt on a literal belief in the seven-day origin of the world as given in the biblical book of *Genesis*. In the early 1860s many churchmen entered into lively debate with Darwin on these difficult matters. Yet the force of this controversy subsided quite quickly. By the 1870s most churchmen were willing to accept the general accuracy of Darwin's scientific discoveries, while maintaining that the creative processes he so carefully described were the act of God.

Their view that it was no longer necessary to believe literally in the book of *Genesis* accorded with the current thinking of churchmen who were researching the writing of the books of the Bible. Quite independently, the suggestion was being made by such churchmen that complete belief in all parts of the Bible was not necessary for a Christian.

Doubts about Christianity

Even though ideas about evolution had therefore become accepted by most Christians in the late nineteenth century, doubts about Christianity were now openly expressed. Swinburne, in many of his poems of the 1860s and 1870s, had poured scorn on Christianity. To him it was a joyless religion, sapping men and women of their full potential as human beings.

> Thou hast conquered, O pale Galilean;
> the world has grown grey from thy breath ...
>
> Though all men abase them before you in spirit, and all knees bend,
> I kneel not neither adore you. ...

Swinburne had a wide popular following. In an age of increasing literacy, before the arrival of the radio or the television, the writings of poets were widely read. Swinburne, in his own highly effective style, put his doubts more directly than other poets, but he was not alone in doing so. Tennyson, possibly the most highly respected of all Victorian poets, had similar doubts, though he expressed them with greater caution and subtlety. *In Memoriam* was his greatest poem, written while he mourned the death of a friend. Its marked popularity in the second half of the nineteenth century suggests that many found its wording a meaningful expression of their own inner doubts about Christianity.

However doubtful people were about the truth of Christianity, the numbers attending places of worship at the end of the century were still high. Among those who did not attend, some would acknowledge themselves as **agnostics**, people who doubted God's existence. Only very few went so far as to say they were **atheists**, people who denied God's existence.

Charles Bradlaugh

Foremost among Victorian atheists was Charles Bradlaugh, a politician who as well as denying God's existence also advocated a republic in place of the British monarchy. Atheism and republicanism combined to make Bradlaugh appear, in his time, as a man of very extreme and dangerous views. In the general election of 1880, he was elected as a Radical MP. On arrival in the House of Commons, he stood by his principles in refusing to take the oath required from new MPs, as the oath had to be sworn on the Bible and contained references to God. The Speaker of the House of Commons therefore refused to allow him to take his seat in parliament and referred the matter to a committee. After the committee had reported in favour of what the Speaker had done, Bradlaugh decided to defy them and to take his seat in the House of Commons regardless of their views. By this time he faced much opposition within the House of Commons.

As a measure of compromise he now said that he was prepared to take the oath. But a majority of MPs, encouraged very much by members of the Fourth party, opposed his doing so as it was known that he still held to his atheistic views. He was ejected by the police, imprisoned and declared not to be an MP. Undaunted, he stood again for parliament and was re-elected. Again, on the same grounds, he was denied the right to take his place in the House of Commons. This weary process was repeated no less than three times during Gladstone's second ministry. Only in 1886, by the action of a new Speaker, was it brought to an end and Bradlaugh allowed to take his rightful place. In 1888 the Oaths Act was passed, having been proposed by Bradlaugh as a result of his earlier experiences. New MPs could now, if they wished, affirm rather than swear an oath; at the same time similar provision was made in law courts.

A changing society

Newspapers

Increasing literacy made for other fundamental changes in Britain. Even before the 1870 Education Act it is probable that about three-quarters of the population could read. During the years after that Act there were certainly many more. This was the main reason for the big increase towards the end of the century in the number and variety of newspapers. New methods of printing – particularly the introduction of rotary presses – led to a reduction in newspaper prices, often to as low as a penny or a half penny a copy. Newspapers were no longer expensive. Their content was also changing and they were beginning to be identified with political attitudes. In this way the new papers were distinctly different from *The Times*, which had begun publication in the late eighteenth century, and which maintained its long-established position of political neutrality. Among the new publications with the highest circulation were *The Daily Telegraph* (originally Liberal, but later Conservative), *The Standard* (Conservative), *The Daily News* (Liberal), and *The Echo* (Liberal). Until towards the end of the century their circulation was mainly restricted to London, but these were years in which many new local newspapers also flourished.

Alfred Harmsworth

In an age when many were exercising the right to vote for the first time, newspapers had a vital role to play. Much of their content was strongly political; many of their reports were about political events. But as the century drew to a close newspapers tended to contain fewer political references. The lead was mainly taken by some new weekly newspapers which used new techniques to attract new readers. Cartoons, photographs, interviews, headlines and competitions began to appear. Much of this innovation was a deliberate copying of techniques that had proved successful in boosting newspaper circulation in the United States. Foremost in introducing them into Britain were men such as William Stead and Alfred Harmsworth. In 1896 Harmsworth began publication of the *Daily Mail*, which by using these techniques and selling at only a half penny a copy very soon became the first paper to have a mass circulation. Harmsworth's influence in the newspaper world was increased early in the twentieth century by his publication of the *Daily Mirror* and his purchase of *The Times*. Harmsworth – later known as Lord Northcliffe – was a new type of newspaper proprietor, one who aimed at making high profits from increased circulation among middle-class and working-class people. Not only did he succeed handsomely in both these aims, but he also influenced the style and presentation of the other newspapers whose circulation figures were threatened by his success.

Entertainment

Music halls

So newspapers were increasingly welcomed by people for their entertainment value as well as for their news value. It was an age when fuller provision was being made for the entertainment of all social classes. The music halls had developed in the middle of the century from the entertainments staged in pubs. They provided cheap, lively entertainment that by the 1870s and 1880s had gained a wide popularity. Drinking was as much a part of the entertainment provided in them as were stage personalities and communal singing. An important position in any music hall belonged to the 'Chairman'. It was he who made introductions to the acts and who tried – by a mixture of tact and bravado – to keep his audience both happy and controlled. These were not easy tasks and it sometimes proved beyond the ability of a Chairman to fulfil them. But communal singing – which always had an important place in the music halls – often enabled a Chairman to unite a difficult audience in a collective activity which they all enjoyed. Music hall songs became well-known.

A music hall audience of the 1890s. By this time, the music hall had become one of the most popular forms of entertainment for both the middle classes and the working classes.

Jingoism

At times of national emergency – such as the Balkan crisis of the late 1870s or the Second Boer War at the turn of the century – patriotism was the main theme in music hall songs. The most famous of these (reproduced on page 33) gave the word **jingoism** to the English language, suggesting determination to defend and to extend British authority abroad. When criticism of jingoism was voiced, the music halls retaliated further.

> If it's jingo to love honour, then jingoes sure are we,
> If it's jingo to love England, then jingoes sure are we,
> There are jingoes in our colonies who love the dear old land,
> Who are ready too when wanted by the brave old flag to stand,
> From our proud and right position England never will retreat
> And if cowards be amongst us, let them take a far back seat.

How far did this type of patriotism really represent the views of music hall audiences? It is not easy to say. But songs that were far from patriotic also found popularity, as when a miserable army recruit sang, in parody of the more famous song.

> I don't want to fight, I'll be slaughtered if I do!
> I'll change my togs and sell my kit and pop my rifle too!
> I don't like the war, I ain't no Briton true,
> And I'd let the Russians have Constantinople.

As the century drew to a close, music hall entertainment became more varied. Emphasis was placed upon the variety of entertainment that could be provided by them. In the 1890s some began to show moving films as part of this variety, and here lay the seeds of the decline of the music halls. A decade later the new cinemas were beginning to attract audiences away from the music halls which, in the inter-war years, they largely replaced.

Changes in transport

Railways

In the first half of the nineteenth century the construction of railways had begun for Britain a far-reaching revolution in its transport system. By the 1870s the country was covered by a network of railway lines, all of them privately owned. The British people were proud of the railways, and governments were convinced of their benefit. By providing for the quick and efficient transport of goods the railways had made a vital contribution to the country's prosperity. They had also speeded the postal services, provided cheap transport for people of all classes and encouraged a boom in seaside holiday towns, which could now be reached more easily. Another important effect of the railways was to standardise time throughout the country. Until the late nineteenth century different parts of the country kept to different time. Efficient use of the railways demanded that everyone in the country should keep to the same time. By the Definition of Time Act of 1880 Greenwich time became accepted throughout the country.

Changes in railway travel

Though during the period covered by this book the greatest period of railway construction was over, developments in the system were nevertheless made. Railways were renowned for being dangerous. In the early 1870s, when more than a thousand people were killed each year on the railways, a Royal Commission was set up to enquire into the causes of these accidents. Improved safety precautions were developed, though in the late nineteenth century a rail journey was still regarded as by no means free from danger. In these years also more attention was given to the comfort of passengers. Third class carriages, in which the vast majority of passengers travelled, were now upholstered, while restaurant cars and sleeping cars were beginning to form part of long distance trains. These years also saw the taking over by the larger railway companies of many of the small companies that had earlier pioneered railway development.

The development of suburban lines and the increased use of third class accommodation were two of the notable features of railway development in the second half of the nineteenth century. This print of the mid-1860s shows passengers leaving a train after its arrival at London's Victoria Station.

New railway lines

Construction of new lines had not, however, entirely ended by this time. In the late nineteenth century lines were being constructed in the Scottish Highlands and in the suburban areas of large towns. The latter development, by providing quick access between work and home, did much to encourage further suburban growth. An allied development within many large towns during these years was the construction of electrically powered tramway systems. Trams had many

A HISTORY OF BRITAIN FROM 1867

advantages. They were cheap and speedy and were a considerable improvement on horse-drawn public transport. Another major enterprise was the construction of much of the present London Underground system, originally serviced by steam trains. During the 1890s travel in the poorly ventilated tunnels became much more pleasant with the introduction of electricity as the motive power for the system.

The bicycle

The greatest transport innovation of these years was the bicycle. Its development began in the early 1870s with the penny-farthing bicycle, one enormously large wheel balanced with a very small one. By the 1880s bicycles had been designed along simpler lines. With wheels of equal size, protected by the new pneumatic tyres, bicycles had become easier to manage and more comfortable to ride. Tricycles also enjoyed popularity, as did a number of cycles of very curious design. In the early years, cycling was almost entirely a pastime of members of cycling clubs, who wore distinctive uniforms and who were often ridiculed as they went on their way. But cycling very quickly became popular. Before the end of the century – by which time bicycles had become cheap – almost all households owned one. The importance of the arrival of the bicycle in an English village is shown in this extract from memoirs of the 1880s.

> **Cycling was looked upon as a passing craze and the cyclists in their tight navy knickerbocker suits and pillbox caps with the badge of their club in front were regarded as figures of fun. None of those in the hamlet who rushed out of their gates to see one pass, half hoping for and half fearing a spill, would have believed, if they had been told, that in a few years there would be at least one bicycle in every one of their houses, that the men would ride to work on them and the younger women, when their housework was done, would lightly mount 'the old bike' and pedal away to the market town to see the shops.**
>
> Flora Thompson, *Lark Rise to Candleford*

The last sentence of this extract pinpoints the real importance of the bicycle. People were no longer restricted to their immediate home area; nor were they restricted by the times and routes of trains. They now had their own, cheap means of transport. Those who lived in the town could get out to the open country, while those who lived in the village found life to be no longer quite so restricted.

Members of a cycling club pose with their penny-farthings and tricycles while leaving town for a country outing. The bicycle boom of the 1880s and 1890s brought about one of the most important social changes of the nineteenth century.

RELIGION AND SOCIETY IN LATE VICTORIAN AND EDWARDIAN TIMES

Early motor cars

In the mid-1890s, while the bicycle boom was at its height, the motor car began to appear on British roads. It was not so happily received as the bicycle had been. The early motor cars were handsome machines and, by the standards of the times, speedy ones. But they created noise, they threw up dust and mud on roads unused to them and they caused accidents. Until the 1930s a motor car could only be afforded by the more wealthy. The motor car became in these years a status symbol that emphasised the class divisions of Victorian and Edwardian society. It was sad that the quiet transport revolution of the bicycle was so quickly overtaken by that of the motor car.

The position of women

Work

It is in the last decade of the nineteenth century that a beginning was made on removing some of the social discrimination which women suffered in Britain. Most noticeable in this respect was the widening of opportunities for women's employment. Traditionally, the only women who took on jobs were from the working classes. For such women, work was a necessity if reasonable standards were to be maintained in the home. Usually such women worked in factories or in agriculture or they entered domestic service. The two photographs on the next page illustrate both these types of employment. In the north, textile factories provided work for many women. Life in such factories is described in these memoirs of a woman worker.

> When I went full-time from 6 on a Monday morning till 12 o'clock Saturday dinner-time, I got my full money. I got six shillings a week. You could say good old days or bad old days. I don't know what you would say. I was happy somehow.
>
> *Did you like the mill?*
>
> I hated it. It was a job.
>
> *What did you hate especially?*
>
> I don't know. I used to like going to school.... I wish I could have stopped at school, but no, I had to go to work and that was that. As time went on, it was coloured pyjamas and nightdresses and I couldn't see the coloured work. I got many a knock from the Missus as I passed a flaw. They weren't happy days in the mill, not to me. I had to go and I went....
>
> *Was it hot in the mill?*
>
> Oh yes. You kept wiping the perspiration off, and you daren't stop, there was no stopping.
>
> Interview with Miss Ainsworth, who started mill work in 1911, quoted in Elizabeth Roberts, *A Woman's Place, An Oral History of Working Class Women*

Others took on piece work – such as tailoring – at home. But the changing society of the late nineteenth century created better opportunities for the employment of women. Women teachers increased in numbers after the passage of the 1870 Education Act. As medical treatment improved, more nurses were needed; from the 1870s women were able to qualify and practise as doctors. Women were increasingly found working in shops and in offices.

Advances in women's education

If women were to be able to take advantage of these new opportunities, improvement in the education of women was essential. Pioneering work had been done in the middle of the century by two Anglican Evangelical women. Miss Frances Buss had set up the North London Collegiate School as a girls' day school; Miss Dorothea Beale had set up the Cheltenham Ladies College as a girls' boarding school. The success achieved by these schools led to the foundation of others and the development of a system of girls' public schools similar to that which already existed for boys. In the 1870s similar developments took

A HISTORY OF BRITAIN FROM 1867

place at Oxford and Cambridge, where colleges for women students were set up. Not everyone welcomed these advances and there were instances of serious opposition to them.

Married women

Married women who did not take up a career themselves had few legal rights. Possessions owned by a woman while single automatically became the property of her husband once her marriage had taken place. A Married Women's Property Act of 1870, and a similar more effective Act of 1882, removed this injustice and allowed a married woman to possess property in her own legal right. Until the passage of the Matrimonial Causes Act of 1878 a wife had little legal protection against violence from her husband. By the terms of this Act, legal separation and maintenance could be obtained from the courts. As for divorce, this tended to be more difficult for a woman to obtain than it was for a man. Legal proceedings for divorce were in any case expensive and tended to be taken only by the more wealthy.

Women's suffrage

Demands that women should be allowed to exercise the democratic right of voting first came to prominence at the time of the Second Reform Act. J.S. Mill, a philosopher and a Liberal MP, attempted unsuccessfully to amend the 1867 Bill so that the word 'person' replaced that of 'man'. But the idea of granting **women's suffrage** at that time stood no chance of success. It scarcely entered the minds of most people that the government of the country was anything other than a man's job. Women first obtained the parliamentary vote in 1918, after an immense struggle during the years just before the First World War and as a result of the circumstances of the war itself. These events are considered more fully in Chapter 8 and on page 125 in Chapter 10.

In other ways the last three decades of the nineteenth century did see important advances in women's political rights, though it was in local rather

By the late nineteenth century there were still many rights denied to women, and many professions where entry was difficult. But large numbers found employment as domestic servants in houses or as manual labourers in industry.

RELIGION AND SOCIETY IN LATE VICTORIAN AND EDWARDIAN TIMES

than central government that most advance was made. After 1888 single women ratepayers were allowed to vote in local elections and married women were allowed to do so after 1894 (see pages 65–6). In 1907, after much legal argument, it was established that women should be allowed to stand for election in local government. Opposition to the extension of these political rights to women was not particularly strong. The thinking at the time was that as local government dealt with matters concerning the home – regarded as the place for women – there seemed to be nothing seriously wrong in granting them political rights in this limited way.

Women in political parties

With the gradual extension of the parliamentary vote for men in the late nineteenth century, political parties needed to make closer contact with voters. Women were beginning to play an active role in party organisation, even though most of them would hold to the view that the vote in parliamentary elections was not for them. In the 1880s the Primrose League of the Conservatives and the Women's Liberal Federation both came into being. Within the Women's Liberal Federation there was a minority who asserted the right of women to the parliamentary vote. Some of these women were to find their way into a number of organisations that aimed to achieve this right.

Poverty

Artisans and the poor

Fortunes were made in the nineteenth century by those who invested skilfully and successfully in the newly developing industries. By the late nineteenth century some workers were not always badly off either. The **artisan** class of skilled workers, who were generally assured of secure jobs, experienced a rise in income and were able to maintain a comfortable standard of living. Below this class were the **poor**. They were seen by the more wealthy as an unfortunate but inevitable part of society. Nevertheless, the more prosperous sections of society felt that the poor should be treated in a kindly way.

Assistance for the poor

The Christian denominations, in spite of the intensity of many of their quarrels outlined earlier in this chapter, took an active part in such work. The Church of England set up 'settlements' in working-class areas, where their members gave practical as well as spiritual help to the people of the neighbourhood. Many of the churches in slum districts were devotedly served by Anglo-Catholic clergy. The Salvation Army began work in the 1870s under the firm control of 'General' William Booth. Its use of a military style among the poor, both in seeking conversions and in providing help, was greeted with suspicion in its early years. By the end of the century, however, the Salvation Army was regarded with much respect.

Drunkenness

Salvationists were particularly critical of the problem of drink. In this they were joined by members of a number of **temperance societies** who considered drink to be the underlying cause of the many social ills in Victorian and Edwardian times. Their activities were concentrated on getting people to sign 'the pledge' that they would totally abstain from alcohol. Useful work was also undertaken voluntarily among children and orphans. Particularly notable in this respect was the work of Dr Barnardo's Homes in providing accommodation for unwanted children and in organising the emigration of many of them to dominion countries.

Fear in the lives of working-class people

Despite all these efforts, the suffering caused by poverty persisted. Only after the First World War was there a noticeable reduction in the extent of extreme poverty. The economic problems of the late nineteenth century, considered in the introduction, made for uncertainty of employment among unskilled workers. In spite of the advances made by the trade union movement these workers were not well organised. They were at the mercy of their employers and had little alternative but to accept the low wages they were paid. These

These two photographs – taken with a concealed lens – show aspects of working-class life in a northern town during the early years of the twentieth century. On the left, two boys look through the window of a corner shop. On the right is a group of men at a pub entrance.

reminiscences of the time recall the dominance of fear in the lives of working-class people in a northern industrial town.

> In children – fear of parents, teachers, the Church, the police, and authority of any sort; in adults – fear of petty chargehands, foremen, managers and employers of labour. Men harboured a dread of sickness, debt, loss of status; above all of losing a job, which could bring all other evils fast in train. Most people in the undermass worked not, as is fondly asserted now, because they possessed an antique integrity which compelled 'a fair day's work for a fair day's pay' (whatever that means); they toiled on through mortal fear of getting the sack. Fear was the key feature of their lives, dulled only now and then by the Dutch courage gained from drunkenness.
>
> R. Roberts, *The Classic Slum*

The workhouse was what the poor most feared. Life in a workhouse was to be made so unpleasant that only the really destitute would seek to enter it. By the late nineteenth century there were marked differences between the standards applied in particular workhouses. Nevertheless the workhouse remained a place that most of the poor hoped they could manage to avoid. It has been estimated that by the end of the century about 10 per cent of the population were compelled to enter a workhouse in old age and then to die there.

Charles Booth

In the 1880s and 1890s the extent of poverty within Britain was more carefully measured than previously. Everyone had earlier been made aware of poverty, either by seeing it or by reading novels that focused on it as a problem. In the middle years of the century, Charles Dickens, Benjamin Disraeli and Elizabeth Gaskell had all brought poverty into their novels as a central theme. But no one seriously attempted to study and define poverty until later in the century. Foremost in doing so was Charles Booth (not to be confused with William Booth of the Salvation Army) who made extensive studies of London poverty. The results of his work were published between 1889 and 1903 in his multi-volume *Life and Labour of the London Poor*. Here was clear and precise evidence that about one-third of the population of the capital city subsisted in a state of poverty. In analysing the causes of their poverty Booth gave emphasis particularly to the problems of insecure work and old age.

RELIGION AND SOCIETY IN LATE VICTORIAN AND EDWARDIAN TIMES

Seebohm Rowntree

Seebohm Rowntree used a similar approach to a study of the northern town of York in his *Poverty: A Study of Town Life*, published in 1901. His conclusions for York were very similar to those of Booth for London. The most important point to emerge from the work of Booth and Rowntree was that any solution to the problem was quite beyond the scope of private charity. If the problem were to be properly tackled, then it must be done by government action. The solution lay in the hands of politicians. To this view, the Conservative government of the time made no response. These surveys were nevertheless to form the basis of much of the social work of the Liberal ministries before the First World War and were to lead to a fuller involvement by government in the problems of the poor as the twentieth century progressed.

EXERCISES

1. Show how the closing years of Queen Victoria's reign might be described as a time of change in respect of each of the following:
   (a) the education and rights of women,
   (b) the knowledge and treatment of poverty,
   (c) the development and use of transport, and
   (d) the publication and reading of newspapers.

2. Describe each of the following developments in late Victorian times and explain the importance that each had:
   (a) the controversy about evolution,
   (b) the controversy about ritualism,
   (c) the Bradlaugh affair, and
   (d) doubt in matters of religious faith.

3. (a) Imagine you are a person living in Britain in late Victorian times, worried about either ritualism or Darwinism. Write a letter to a friend, explaining your worries.
   (b) Imagine you are a woman employed in late Victorian times in either domestic service or manual labour. Write a letter to a friend, describing your life and your thoughts about it.

4. Study the photographs on pages 76 and 78 and then answer questions (a) to (d) which follow.
   (a) Explain in what ways the two photographs on page 78 help you to understand the lives in late Victorian times of:
      (i) children from poor homes, and
      (ii) working-class men. (5)
   (b) Explain in what ways the two photographs on page 76 help you to understand the work done in late Victorian times by women employed as:
      (i) domestic servants, and
      (ii) manual workers. (5)
   (c) How valuable do you find these four photographs as evidence of the lives of ordinary people at this time? (4)
   (d) In each of the following cases, give one example of how those living in poverty in late Victorian and Edwardian times were helped by:
      (i) a published report, and
      (ii) an act of parliament. (6)

7 THE GROWTH OF THE BRITISH EMPIRE

References have been made quite frequently in the earlier chapters of this book to examples of the extension of British power abroad. This extension is known as **British imperialism** and, as a result of it, the size of the **British Empire** was greatly increased. The last 20 years of the nineteenth century were crucial years for its development. Yet it was not to last for long. Though it might be said that the British Empire reached its fullest extent during the first half of the twentieth century, by the 1960s it had ceased to exist.

British imperialism in the 1880s and 1890s

Dominions and India

By the 1880s Britain already occupied many territories overseas. Some of these, known as the **dominions**, already had their own parliaments in which white settlers were represented. New Zealand had acquired self-government in 1856, Canada had become a dominion in 1867; Australia was to become a dominion in 1901. The rest of the Empire came directly under British control. All the different parts of the Empire had been acquired over recent centuries in a variety of ways. A number of West Indian islands were the result of settlement and warfare in the seventeenth and eighteenth centuries. In South Africa, Cape Colony and Natal had been secured by treaty in the early nineteenth century. Successful mid-nineteenth century wars had confirmed various different possessions by Britain along the Chinese coast. Most important, and in a category of its own, Britain held India. The concern of British governments for the security of India was the underlying reason for their expansionist policies of the 1870s and 1880s towards Afghanistan and Egypt. In the case of Afghanistan (pages 29 and 58–9), to prevent a Russian threat to India; in the case of Egypt (pages 59–60), to protect the Suez Canal sea route to India. Even the British policies in South Africa (pages 30–1 and 59) were partly designed to ensure the safety of the Cape route to India.

Africa

The African continent was to be the great area of European colonisation in the 1880s and 1890s. In the first half of the nineteenth century, apart from South Africa, there had been little European settlement in the continent. The African interior was unknown to Europeans. In the middle years of the century a number of courageous European explorers made extensive surveys of these regions. Full coverage was given in Britain to their exploits. Such men as David Livingstone and Henry Stanley became popular heroes in many Victorian homes. They deserved the respect in which they were held, as immense endurance and unshakeable determination were needed in those who ventured into the unknown interior of Africa. As Africa was 'opened up' to Europe by the explorers, many imagined that the profits now being acquired by businessmen in India might be found in Africa also.

Africa and trade

The trouble was that British businessmen were not alone in seeking fortunes in the African continent. Had they been so, British governments would have preferred to have left their businessmen to their own devices. Africa would not have become a concern of the British government. But competition came from other European powers: France, Belgium, the Netherlands and, especially, Germany. The last 30 years of the nineteenth century was for Europe generally a time of peace and stability, a time which provided excellent opportunities for the development of industry and trade. For many European countries the commercial expansion of these years was so rapid that European markets appeared no longer capable of absorbing their products. Africa provided potential opportunities as an alternative market.

THE GROWTH OF THE BRITISH EMPIRE

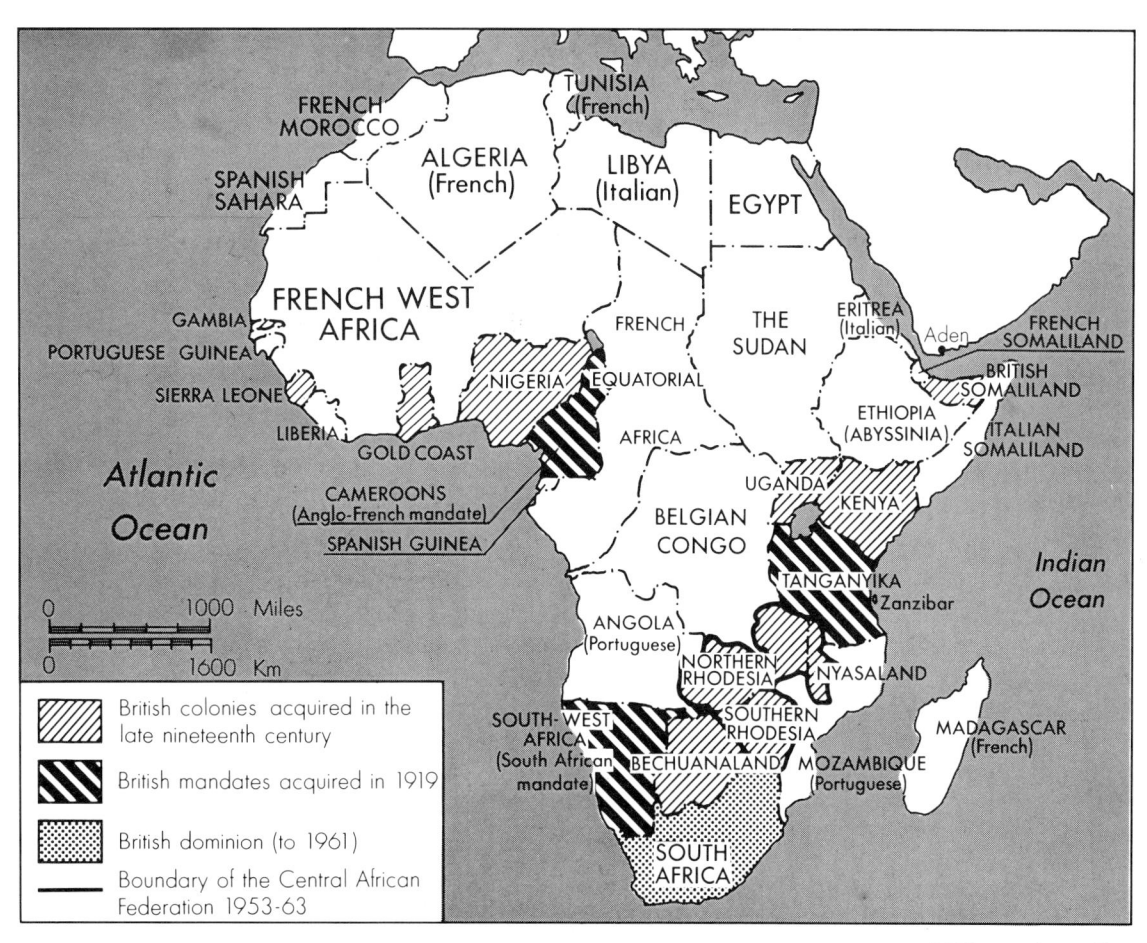

British possessions in Africa

The British in Africa

Arguments such as these provided a major stimulus for British imperialism in the 1880s and 1890s. The British government therefore secured control over certain areas of Africa, where British trade and investments were already being developed and where they were likely to be threatened by another European power. Other European powers were doing the same in other areas. All felt they had a perfect right to this course of action without any need to consult African opinion. In any case they did not mean to exercise any very strong control over the areas they acquired. The terms **protectorate** or **sphere of influence** were usually applied to these areas and suggested a loose type of control. The term **colony**, suggesting firmer control, was less often used.

Areas under British control

This limited imperial role partly explains the speed with which the African continent was divided up. British influence extended out from three areas where British interests were already being protected. The way in which the British had asserted control of Egypt and had involved themselves in the Sudan has already been shown (pages 28 and 59–62). Claim was now staked to neighbouring areas in eastern Africa: the territory then known as British East Africa (and later known as Kenya) and the smaller territories of Somaliland and Uganda. Britain's concern for its South African possessions had already led to the First Boer War (page 59). There was now to be extension northwards into the territories known as Bechuanaland and Rhodesia. Penetration by Britain in West Africa had gone no deeper than a few coastal trading stations, but the hinterlands were now claimed and four territories marked out: Nigeria, Gold Coast, Sierra Leone and Gambia. Africa was not the only place subject to this type of treatment. British power was extended in Burma, was established in North Borneo and was shared with Germany in New Guinea. A number of Pacific islands were also acquired. Probably of greatest importance in these areas was the Malay peninsula, valuable for its natural resources and for the

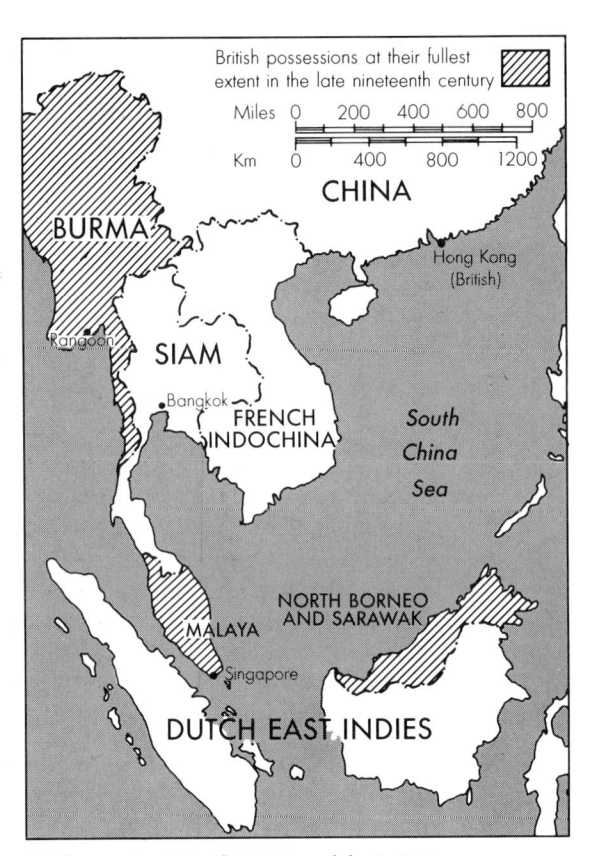

British possessions in South-East Asia and the Far East

strategic usefulness of Singapore. But in the development of British overseas power in these years, the Pacific and South-East Asia never had the same importance as Africa.

The chartered companies

Benefits The main way in which business consolidated the vague control that the government had established was through the working of **chartered companies**. Those seeking to exploit more fully the potential economic advantages of a territory formed themselves into such a company and secured a royal charter, allowing them the sole right to operate in a particular area. Chartered companies held many advantages. For the government, they provided a cheap method of administering the newly acquired territories. For the members of the company, they provided the chance of much wealth. It was suggested at the time that the introduction of Western techniques by a chartered company provided a stimulus to the economy of the area and, as a result, everyone who lived there would benefit.

Extent of activity Three companies in particular illustrate this process at work in Africa: the Imperial British East African Company, the Royal Niger Company and the British South Africa Company. All proved that they could consolidate British interests most effectively and defend them against threats from other European countries. The first two of these companies were, respectively, highly successful in combating the Germans in east Africa and the French in west Africa. Yet both went out of business in the 1890s when their own pioneering work was completed. The government then felt ready to take control of the areas administered by the companies and accorded them the status of **crown colonies**, with direct administration by the British government.

THE GROWTH OF THE BRITISH EMPIRE

Cecil Rhodes The third company, the British South Africa Company, was founded in 1889, slightly later than the others. It was to last longer and to have a greater importance. Its founding chairman was one of the most adventurous imperialists of his time: Cecil Rhodes. While still young, he had become a millionaire through successful diamond mining in South Africa. In founding the British South Africa Company, Rhodes sought to extend British control further into southern Africa. Thus the British position in relation to the Boers would be strengthened and a firm base set for an even more ambitious extension of British power from 'the Cape to Cairo'.

Rhodes shared with other imperialists the fear that if Britain did not secure promising African territories, other Europeans would. But there was more to the South Africa Company than merely this defensive concern. It aimed at high profits and it was based on firm idealism. Minerals recently mined in South Africa had prompted many to imagine that even greater wealth might be discovered there. Many of the young men who joined the company and went out as pioneers into the interior of southern Africa were attracted by such prospects. Idealism was also present in the company. Rhodes was convinced that the British could benefit those who lived in these parts by bringing Western civilisation to them and expressed his views in this way.

> I contend that... the more of the world we inhabit the better it is for the human race. I contend that every acre added to our territory means the birth of more of the English race who otherwise would not be brought into existence. Added to this, the absorption of the greater portion of the world under our rule simply means the end of all wars.... The furtherance of the British Empire, for the bringing of the whole uncivilised world under British rule, for the recovery of the United States, for the making of the Anglo-Saxon race but one Empire. What a dream! But yet it is probable. It is possible.

Rhodesia The name of Rhodes and the work of his company have become inseparably linked with that of Rhodesia (today, Zimbabwe). The immediate purpose in founding the company had been the settlement of the lands occupied by the Matabele and Mashona peoples of central Africa. During the 1890s, white settlements were established throughout these lands and those to the north of them. The capital, Salisbury, was named after the British Prime Minister. Those who had any real hope of prospering through their settlement in Rhodesia needed determination and courage if they were to achieve their hopes.

But the decade contained disappointments for the settlers. The African inhabitants felt exploited by them and rebellion broke out among the Matabele in 1896. These people were related to the Zulus, and the settlers were determined not to face defeats such as those in the early stages of the Zulu War of 1879. The rebellion was therefore firmly suppressed, the fighting of the rebels being no match for the machine guns of the settlers. Further disappointment faced the settlers over their failure to find the expected mineral resources. Losing hope in Rhodesia's prospects, many of these early settlers moved to exploit the known potential of the neighbouring Boer republic of the Transvaal. Their settlement there as **Uitlanders** was to have important consequences, explained later in this chapter.

'The white man's burden'

Rudyard Kipling The idealism which was an important part of Rhodes's attitude to the British Empire got greater emphasis as the century came to a close. No man expressed this idealism more vividly than the writer Rudyard Kipling. He was born in India and he had got to know at first hand many different parts of the expanding Empire. His extensive travels formed the basis of many published works. Kipling's stories and poems on imperial topics had a ready public and did much to influence the way people thought about the Empire. He approached his subject as a writer and not as a historian. Hence little reference was made by Kipling to the development of the Empire for commercial gain or for protection against competitor nations. Kipling saw imperial expansion as a moral duty that destiny had placed on the British people. British expansion overseas would permit more and more people of the world to receive the benefits of British culture, British technology and British justice. Imperialism was to Kipling a means of spreading civilisation. Nor in taking up what he called 'the white man's burden' should the British necessarily expect gratitude from those whom they now ruled.

> Take up the White Man's burden
> And reap his old reward:
> The blame of those ye better,
> The hate of those ye guard.

Another Kipling verse – this time part of a hymn – puts the British Empire into a Christian context and considers the responsibility the British have, under God's guidance, to rule the 'lesser breeds without the law'.

> God of our fathers, known of old,
> Lord of our far-flung battle-line,
> Beneath whose awful hand we hold
> Dominion over palm and pine –
> Lord God of Hosts, be with us yet,
> Lest we forget – lest we forget!
>
> If, drunk with sight of power, we loose
> Wild tongues that have not thee in awe,
> Such boastings as the Gentiles use,
> Or lesser breeds without the law –
> Lord God of Hosts, be with us yet,
> Lest we forget – lest we forget!

Lord Cromer Lord Cromer in Egypt and Lord Lugard in Nigeria afford examples of Kipling's approach to imperialism. Both had no doubt that the 'natives' would benefit from British rule and that if British rule were well administered there was less likelihood of rebellion against it. From 1883 to 1907, Lord Cromer was the virtual ruler of Egypt on behalf of the British crown. As has been shown earlier (page 60) he was appointed after a time of much bad administration; there was therefore good scope for reform. Cromer threw himself into this task with vigour. The taxation system of the country was totally reformed, the archaic system of forced labour was abolished, essential irrigation works were constructed and new railway lines were laid. The work that Cromer did in Egypt was in the best traditions of the British imperialism of his day. Yet he ruled Egypt almost as a dictator and never gave serious thought to the idea that the Egyptians might one day become competent enough to administer their own country.

Lord Lugard Lord Lugard's approach was similarly dictatorial. After earlier work in eastern and central Africa, he devoted his energies to the administration of Nigeria. Here he put into practice a method of governing a colony known as **indirect rule**. This method required the British authorities not to interfere too closely with the traditional tribal structure that had been in existence long before the British arrival. Cromer in Egypt had developed a system in which the British played a fully involved role in government. Lugard in Nigeria developed a system in which the British role in government was more restricted. Nevertheless both of them showed their determination to bear 'the white man's burden' and further the best interests of those whom they governed.

Dual mandate

Lugard was a highly skilled administrator and his system of indirect rule became the usual method of administration in the twentieth century throughout the British West African colonies. He later developed another view of Britain's role in West Africa: the **dual mandate**. There was nothing startling or new in this. It simply emphasised that Britain's responsibility (or mandate, in this general sense) was both for the welfare of the colonies' original inhabitants and for the development of the colonies' economic potential. This idea of Britain's dual mandate in its colonies was long-lasting and widely accepted. Only with the beginning of demands for independence in the middle of the twentieth century was it to become out of date.

Lord Lugard photographed in old age with West African chiefs. The method of indirect rule that he encouraged in West Africa in the late nineteenth century was to become a principal means of administering many of Britain's African colonies.

Colonial administrators

The work of men such as Cromer and Lugard, and also Curzon in India (considered later on page 88), provides practical example of the idealism which by the turn of the century had become a very noticeable part of imperialism. Such men did not stand alone in seeking to bear this 'burden'. The colonies provided a variety of careers for young men, as administrators, as soldiers, as missionaries or as men of business. Between 1870 and 1914 over ten million people left Britain to settle in British territories overseas. Those men among them who took on positions of major responsibility would have come from reasonably wealthy families and would have been educated at Britain's boys' public schools.

Imperialism was very closely linked with these schools in the late nineteenth century, to such an extent that the boys' public schools could almost be regarded as training centres for work in the Empire. Public schoolboys were encouraged to think themselves superior to others, just as colonial administrators thought themselves superior to those they ruled. The prefects in public schools were expected to take on wide responsibilities; to carry them out they were given much power and authority. Such young men would find their work in the colonies very similar in style. The public schools were therefore well adjusted to supply the Empire's manpower needs, and continued to do so until the middle of the twentieth century.

Missionaries

A quite distinct service was performed by missionaries. Every committed Christian would feel a responsibility to spread the Christian faith and convert people to it. Given the intensity of Christian faith in Victorian times it is not surprising that missionaries went in large numbers to the developing Empire. Many of the explorers of unknown regions in Africa were concerned to convert as well as to explore. Livingstone, the best known and most popular of the Victorian explorers, was as well known for his missionary work as for his work of exploration. In some parts of the Empire missionaries were brutally treated by those they hoped to convert. Martyrs were produced in these years, especially in the New Hebrides where missionaries were sometimes victims of cannibalism. Usually, however, the missionaries were able to preach unmolested by such direct violence. Even so their task was a hard one. They were dealing with people whose religion – whatever variety it took – was firmly embedded within the traditions of their society. Nor was it easy to get such people to understand the Christian faith which, with its long history of development in Europe, was in most ways alien to them.

Missionary methods

Existing religious practices and social customs seemed primitive in the eyes of the missionaries, and often shocked them deeply. Their usual approach was to pour contempt on these practices and customs, while preaching the greater benefits of Christianity. Conversion was helped by the offering of the medical facilities which often formed a vital part of the services offered by mission stations. Problems often arose for the converts themselves. They tended to be shunned by those among whom they lived on account of their identity with the missionaries and, as a consequence, with the colonising power. The story of the Victorian missionaries is a mixed one. Misunderstanding and harm form as much a part of it as heroism and dedication. Yet the missionaries also illustrate the way in which the Victorians took seriously the responsibility of 'the white man's burden'.

India

Among Britain's overseas possessions, India came into a category of its own. In 1857 there had been a real prospect that India might slip from British control. In that year had occurred the Indian Mutiny, which British military power had managed to suppress. After the mutiny, the way in which India was administered by the British was changed.

Viceroy and Secretary of State

The power of the East India Company, which had played a vital part in the development of India during the previous century, was reduced. Two men were now to share responsibility in exercising the control of the British government. In India there was to be a **Viceroy**. This word means 'in place of the king'. The Viceroy was treated in India with the type of respect and ceremonial which in Britain would be given to the reigning sovereign. In Britain there was to be a **Secretary of State for India**. By having this particular appointment for India, the unique connection between Britain and the sub-continent was again emphasised. Disraeli's decision in 1877 to proclaim Queen Victoria as Empress of what was now referred to as the Indian Empire should be seen as part of the same process. Though Queen Victoria never visited her Indian Empire, as heirs to the throne both her son and grandson did. George V and Queen Mary received a coronation in India at an Imperial Durbar (celebration) held at Delhi in 1911.

Administration

In administering the vast population of the sub-continent, the Viceroy was assisted by the Indian Civil Service. This was supplied with recruits by British public schools, who regarded entry to it as carrying more prestige than entry to similar work in Africa. Its members were expected to take on heavy responsibilities, often as **district officers** posted to remote parts. The efficiency and fairness with which they carried out their tasks made the Indian Civil Service an institution of which the British Empire had good reason to be proud.

There were additionally soldiers serving in India to protect the Empire against attack or against internal rebellion. Unlike the Indian Civil Service,

THE GROWTH OF THE BRITISH EMPIRE

A senior administrator of Britain's Indian Empire meets formally with Indian princes during the 1870s. Both the British rulers and the Indian princes found it useful to support each other's authority in India.

which consisted almost entirely of whites, Indians were more numerous in the armed forces. Of particular importance in helping Britain to maintain its control were the Indian princes. Treaties signed between them and the British authorities had guaranteed their continued control of lands their families had held for centuries. The princes controlled, in lands of varying size, about one quarter of the total population. The links with the princes gave some suggestion that British rule in India was acceptable to those whose land it originally was.

Economic advantages of India

The British had already begun to exploit the economic advantages that India offered. Tea planting and jute cultivation developed considerably in the middle years of the century and brought handsome return for investors. After the cotton industry in Lancashire had experienced shortage of raw cotton from the United States as a result of the US Civil War, Lancashire businessmen urged cotton cultivation in India. This was undertaken so successfully that by the early twentieth century a cotton industry had developed in India as a serious challenge to Lancashire's own interests. As railways were generally regarded to have played an essential part in the successful development of Britain's industry, their construction in India was given priority, as was improvement in road communications.

Tea being loaded by Indian workers for shipment to Britain. During their administration of the Indian sub-continent, the British did much to develop its economic potential.

Lord Curzon and the partition of Bengal

Much of what was done in these respects would have been valuable to the Indians. The appalling effects of periodic famine could be reduced by prompt British action and sensible use of the railways. Unfortunately the British were sometimes tactless in the way they approached issues in India. Tactlessness was particularly shown by Lord Curzon, Viceroy at the turn of the century. Curzon was a dedicated imperialist and in this respect a first-rate administrator. He had great respect for Indian culture and was determined that Indians should be fairly treated. But in his approach to issues in Bengal, in the north-east of the sub-continent, he showed uncharacteristic insensitivity. Bengal, with its large population, had proved difficult to administer efficiently. Civil servants had long spoken of the need to partition Bengal, and Curzon decided to do so. Opinion in Bengal became intensely hostile to the idea of partition: there were boycotts of British goods and much violent protest throughout the province. Curzon resigned in the course of the disturbances his policies had produced, and his successor, Lord Minto, had to implement the partition and attempt to deal with the situation as best he could.

Morley-Minto reforms

The disturbances accompanying the partition of Bengal gave a foretaste of problems that were to become more serious for the British in India during the twentieth century. Already there had been founded in 1885 the Indian National Congress to assert Indian interests in the affairs of their country. In 1906 the Moslem League was formed to protect Moslem interests. The new Viceroy was aware that he had taken over at a time when British rule was beginning to be seriously challenged. Minto's view was that only by making reforms could the British hope to retain control in India. Together with the Secretary of State for India, John Morley, he produced in 1909 what became known as the **Morley-Minto reforms**. The essential feature of these reforms was provision for Indians to advise the British more closely and to bring Indians more fully into local government. Though moderate opinion accepted these reforms, it was clear that India was already before 1914 the area of the world where British rule overseas was beginning to receive its most serious challenge.

Imperial rivalries

It was only to be expected that rivalries with other European powers would develop in imperial affairs. Britain was among the 15 countries with African interests which attended the Berlin Conference of 1884–85. It had largely been the concern of Britain about Belgian and French expansion in the Congo and German expansion in East Africa and the Cameroons that led to the summoning of this conference. These and other issues were settled and the conference came to agreed decisions on spheres of influence in Africa. The great achievement of the conference was to avoid any prospect of war in Europe on colonial issues.

Relations with Portugal

In 1890, largely through the work of Lord Salisbury, Britain negotiated three colonial agreements that further helped to reduce tensions. Portugal had claimed possession of the area then established as Rhodesia and the area of Nyasaland to its east. The whole of this part of central Africa was seen by Portugal as providing a link between its colonies of Angola and Mozambique, respectively on Africa's western and eastern shores. An agreement of 1890 established Britain's right to Rhodesia and Nyasaland, and compensated Portugal by increasing the size of her two African colonies.

Relations with Germany

Germany was for Britain a more active competitor than Portugal. There was particular concern about the upper Nile region, where recently German explorers had been active. If the region were acquired by Germany, the British position in the Sudan and Egypt would be seriously threatened. Britain was willing to pay a high price to see German influence removed from this area. The price was the small but strategically vital North Sea island of Heligoland, off the

THE GROWTH OF THE BRITISH EMPIRE

ON THE SWOOP!

MARCHEZ! MARCHAND!
GENERAL JOHN BULL (*to* MAJOR MARCHAND). "COME, PROFESSOR, YOU'VE HAD A NICE LITTLE SCIENTIFIC TRIP! I'VE SMASHED THE DERVISHES—LUCKILY FOR *YOU* — AND NOW I'RECOMMEND YOU TO PICK UP YOUR FLAGS, AND GO HOME!!"

Two cartoons of the 1890s that strongly illustrate British concern about imperial rivalry from other European powers. On the left, the German eagle is shown as a sinister competitor for African territory. On the right, John Bull assumes the role of Kitchener in dealing with the French presence at Fashoda.

north-west shores of Germany. Lord Salisbury was quite ruthless in this matter. The clear wish of the islanders on Heligoland to remain under British rule was set aside and the island given to Germany. The way was now open for an understanding over the upper Nile, which was incorporated into the British-held areas of Kenya and Uganda. At the same time, British control over Zanzibar was asserted and boundary adjustments made in the German colonies of the Cameroons and South-West Africa.

Relations with France

France was in many respects Britain's most powerful rival in Africa, with extensive possessions in the north and west of the continent. The third agreement of 1890 was with France. By it Britain recognised the French position in Madagascar and an enlarged area of French Equatorial Africa; for its part, France recognised the British position in Zanzibar and an enlarged area of Nigeria. But the French did not observe the agreement well. With the aid of locally recruited soldiers, they continued to challenge the British position in West Africa and, in particular, to make inroads into the parts of Nigeria which in 1890 they had agreed as British. Largely through the negotiating skills of the British Colonial Secretary, Joseph Chamberlain, a further Anglo-French agreement was signed in June 1898. By this, Britain was assured of most of the Nigerian territories that the earlier agreement had allowed. The agreement also assured France of a dominant position in the interior of west and west-central Africa.

Battle of Omdurman

French concern to develop the position they thus acquired led later in 1898 to a further and more serious breakdown in Anglo-French relations. This breakdown centred on the conflicting claims of the two countries to the upper Nile valley. In September 1898 British and Egyptian forces under the command of Sir Herbert Kitchener had defeated Sudanese forces at the battle of Omdurman, just across the River Nile from Khartoum (see map on page 61). The British victory was decisive. It was a successful conclusion to Kitchener's consolidation of control in the middle Nile valley earlier in the year.

Incident at Fashoda

No sooner had the victory been secured, however, than a French presence in the area was discovered. In the meantime, and against the formidable obstacles of the desert, a French force had been advancing from the French territories in the west. By the autumn of 1898 they had reached the upper Nile valley and had raised the French flag at the remote village of Fashoda. Kitchener's tactful treatment of these Frenchmen prevented the outbreak of hostilities. The dispute was referred for settlement by the governments of Britain and France. In the course of the negotiations that followed, the British government made clear that they were ready to fight to hold the disputed territory. This firm approach worked and by an Anglo-French agreement signed in the following year the French claims were abandoned.

Joseph Chamberlain as Colonial Secretary

When Lord Salisbury formed his third ministry in 1895 he was prepared to offer Joseph Chamberlain a senior post in the cabinet such as that of Chancellor of the Exchequer. But Chamberlain chose the post of Colonial Secretary, generally considered one of lesser importance. As Colonial Secretary during the years 1895–1903, Chamberlain used all his energies to assist the development of the British Empire and to make the people of Britain more fully aware of its value to them. He wanted the British to see the Empire not as a remote, far-off organisation, but as one whose success and wealth they all shared.

Control of epidemics

Settlement in many parts of the Empire was often hindered by epidemics of diseases. Chamberlain gave government encouragement to the research already being conducted into their prevention. Two schools of tropical medicine were set up, in London and Liverpool, financed by government grants as well as by individual donations. The Royal Society was another body whose research was encouraged by the government. Discoveries of great importance were made about the causes of two of the most common and most weakening of epidemics: sleeping sickness and malaria. Further government grants were made available to combat these epidemics in the areas they affected.

The Caribbean

Chamberlain used the term **undeveloped estates** to describe the lands of the Empire in his time. Government grants were needed to draw out the full potential these lands held. His policies in this connection are best illustrated by his work in the Caribbean. Britain's islands there had been acquired long before the late nineteenth-century expansion of the Empire. Yet with the attention given to the imperial expansion in Africa and the Pacific, they had tended to feel that their economic problems were being neglected. Sugar production, the basis of the Caribbean economy since the seventeenth century, was in serious decline; many islands presented a sorry picture of abandoned plantations and workless labourers. Chamberlain was not willing to see this waste of Caribbean resources continued. He appointed a Royal Commission to enquire into the problems of the British Caribbean and he acted on its recommendations. Fruit growing was to be developed as a partial alternative to sugar production; steamer boat communication between the islands was to be improved; encouragement was to be given to allow Caribbean workers to own rather than to rent their land. The result of all this activity was a marked improvement in the Caribbean economy by the time of the First World War.

West Africa

Chamberlain's ambition to make productive the undeveloped estates of West Africa was frustrated by opposition from the Ashanti, in the inland regions of the Gold Coast. They were a particularly warlike people. Already in the early 1870s a British force had battled with them and had at the time subdued them. But in the 1890s, under an ambitious new leader, they had again become troublesome to the British. Chamberlain arranged for a force of locally recruited troops to penetrate the Ashanti territories. A swift campaign followed, in which the Ashanti were once again suppressed and their leader deposed. Chamberlain followed up this action with plans to help develop the economy of West Africa, particularly through the construction of railways.

Free trade increasingly questioned

All that Chamberlain did as Colonial Secretary – progress against epidemics, encouragement of development, suppression of the Ashanti – showed that he saw a more active role for the British government in the British Empire than did most people of his time. As has been shown, the Empire had developed largely as a result of the ambitions of businessmen. Government action had been limited to ensuring that their activities in certain areas were not hampered by European competition. The virtual exclusion of the government from any positive role in bringing out the potential of the Empire, the undeveloped estates, was typical of government attitude towards business in general. It was still the era of **laissez-faire** and of **free trade**, of allowing businesses to be developed and goods to be exchanged without government interference. Chamberlain's development of a stronger government role in the Empire was viewed with suspicion by those who stood firmly by the old ideas of not interfering in these matters.

Imperial preference

Chamberlain took some steps in this direction before the old century was ended. His opportunity came in 1897 when many representatives from throughout the Empire gathered in London for Queen Victoria's Diamond Jubilee. This provided him with the opportunity of discussing how the Empire might be more closely united. There was strong interest in **imperial preference**. This involved the encouragement of trade at favourable terms within the Empire. It had good support from the prime ministers of the self-governing dominions. Such a system would, however, be a serious challenge to accepted free trade principles and it was not accepted by the conference.

The Second Boer War: causes

The Great Trek

The area known today as the Republic of South Africa was at the end of the nineteenth century divided into the two British colonies of Cape Colony and Natal and the two Boer republics of the Transvaal and the Orange Free State.

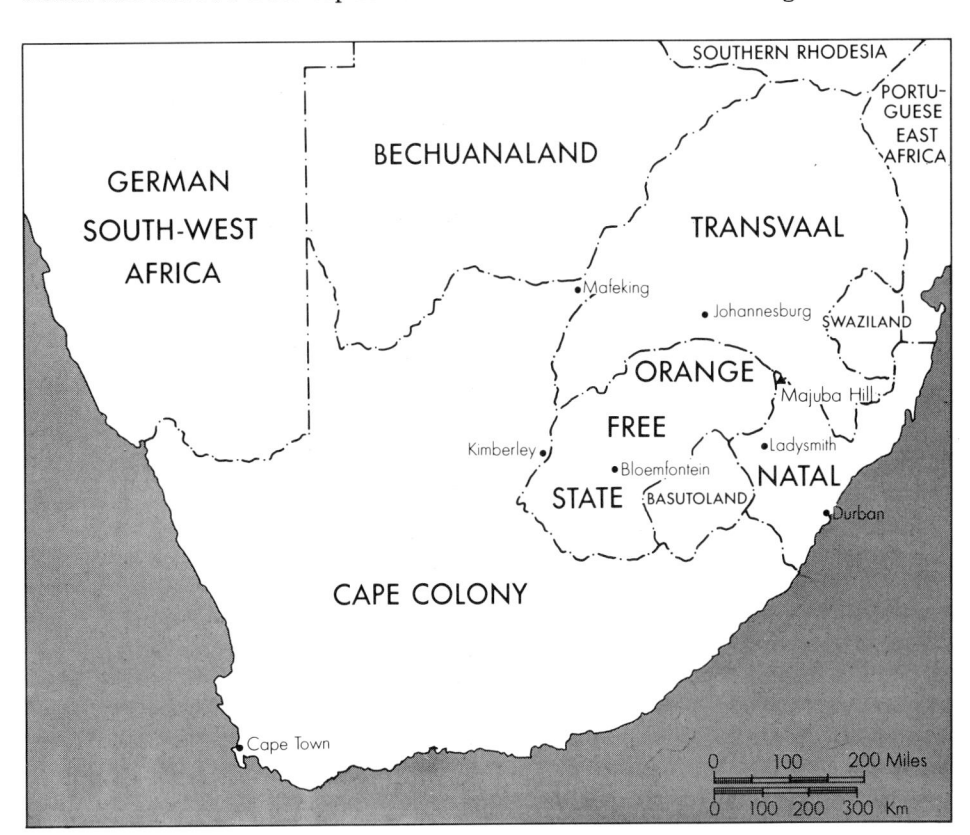

South Africa at the time of the First and Second Boer Wars

White people had settled in this southern part of Africa in larger numbers than they had elsewhere in the continent. The Boers were the descendants of the first European settlers from the Netherlands. They developed successfully the vast farming potential of their new African lands, using the work of blacks – originally as slaves – in doing so. When the British acquired control of South Africa they found difficulty in working in partnership with the already well established Boer communities. This difficulty became most noticeable in 1833 when the British government abolished slavery throughout its Empire. The Boers regarded the blacks not only as valuable slave labour but also as persons who – so their Calvinist religion taught them – were destined by God's design to live in an inferior status to whites. The British abolition of slavery therefore appeared to endanger their economy and to question their religion. Consequently they set up their own independent government in the unexplored lands to the north. Even after their **Great Trek** to these new territories, their independence was not easily defended. They had already in 1880–81 fought a successful war against the British, as shown on page 59.

Uitlanders

By the 1890s the British had come to be seen as even more of a nuisance, threatening both to encircle and to infiltrate the Boers. This is the decade in which the British South Africa Company, under the direction of Cecil Rhodes, was involved in the development of central Africa to the north of the Boer republics. The hopes Rhodes had of discovering valuable minerals in these new areas came to nothing. Meanwhile, however, gold was discovered in the Transvaal and prospectors from the neighbouring British territories were attracted by the immense fortunes that might be made in this Boer republic. These **Uitlanders** (as the Boers termed the new British prospectors) were treated as alien inhabitants within the Boer republic and were denied political rights.

Jameson Raid

The Boers viewed the Uitlanders as a threat placed among them; the British viewed them as persecuted fellow-countrymen. Tensions surrounding the situation of the Uitlanders were vividly demonstrated in December 1895 when some 500 British volunteers, under the leadership of Dr Jameson, raided the Transvaal from the neighbouring Cape Colony. Their purpose was to link with dissatisfied Uitlanders in a rebellion against the Boers. The venture was poorly co-ordinated and the Jameson Raid ended in disaster. Jameson was captured and imprisoned by the Boers before being sent back to Britain for trial. Rhodes, who had become Prime Minister of Cape Colony, was implicated in these events and resigned. In a different connection, the episode made for friction in Britain's relations with Germany, as the German government made public its approval of the success of the Boers in repelling the raid into their territory.

Sir Alfred Milner

Sending Jameson back to Britain in this way was a further means of displaying their own hostility towards what the Boers saw as the increasing hostility of Britain. Most Boers believed that men in high places were responsible for what had happened. Foremost among these, in their opinion, was the Colonial Secretary, Joseph Chamberlain. By contrast, for the British in Cape Colony Joseph Chamberlain was just the type of Colonial Secretary they needed if they were to secure fuller military support from the British government than they could muster themselves. They also felt confidence in their new High Commissioner, Sir Alfred Milner.

Milner was a devoted imperialist who had earlier served the Empire in Egypt and who was determined to prevent any reversal in South Africa. Nor was imperial sentiment the only reason for Milner's increasing commitment to the British cause in South Africa. British businessmen had been looking enviously at the gold resources in the Boer republics. Some of these businessmen asserted strong influence on Milner and persuaded him that a war for this gold would be worthwhile. By the late 1890s Milner was committed to the idea of a war with the Boers. He needed now to create a crisis threatening enough to the British government for it to be persuaded to commit itself to such a war.

THE GROWTH OF THE BRITISH EMPIRE

Paul Kruger — Always a closely knit community, the Boers had become even more so after the Jameson Raid. Their leader, Paul Kruger, was an elderly, autocratic President who in his earlier years had himself taken part in the Great Trek. Dedicated to the Calvinist religion, Kruger had about him something of the appearance and manner of an Old Testament patriarch, often justifying his autocratic policy decisions by biblical references. Since the raid the Boer army had also been extensively re-equipped with German armaments. United, determined and armed, the Boers nevertheless did not seek war and took steps to secure a settlement.

Peace negotiations fail — In June 1899, Kruger and Milner met at Bloemfontein, capital of the Orange Free State, to try to resolve their differences. But the concessions Kruger was prepared to make at Bloemfontein did not satisfy Milner, nor did other modest concessions that Kruger made in the following months. Kruger's actions thus created the crisis for which Milner had hoped. In September, Chamberlain sent out heavy British reinforcements under the command of Sir Redvers Buller. Kruger naturally viewed this as an act of hostility and decided to seize the initiative. In early October 1899, while Buller's troops were still on the sea journey to South Africa, he made a declaration of war against the British.

The Second Boer War: its course

Early Boer successes — The early stages of the fighting turned out well for the Boers. They advanced swiftly into Natal and Cape Colony and laid siege to the towns of Ladysmith, Mafeking and Kimberley. By the time that Buller's troops had arrived, the Boers had strengthened their hold over British territories. It was going to be a hard task to dislodge them. They were fighting in familiar territory and, as earlier in their history, were well aware that they were fighting for their survival.

Black Week — Their British enemies were far less secure. They were in a land whose hot climate and hilly landscape were totally unfamiliar to them and for which their fighting techniques were unsuitable. In addition to this, administration of the army, provision for the injured and even supply of maps of the fighting zones were quite inadequate. These circumstances make it easier to understand the

British troops in action against the Boers in the early twentieth century. The unfamiliar terrain and the determined Boer resistance were the main factors that made the war in South Africa long and difficult.

early British disasters in the war. Though the British concentrated on trying to relieve the besieged towns, by the end of the year this had still not been achieved and British forces had been defeated in a number of encounters with the enemy. Three such defeats in rapid succession took place in what became known as **Black Week** in December 1899. It was difficult for people of a country that held such pride in its Empire to understand that they could suffer defeat. Morale among the troops in South Africa and among the public in Britain could scarcely have reached a lower point.

British successes

The early months of 1900 saw a change in the fortunes of the British forces. They were now under the command of Lord Roberts, a soldier whose heroic reputation in late Victorian times has already been considered (page 59). Roberts concentrated his campaign on the defeat of the Orange Free State and after his success there, the besieged towns were one by one relieved. By mid-1900 the mood of gloom had disappeared and the British government considered the war virtually won. In these favourable conditions a general election – popularly known from its wartime circumstances as the **Khaki Election** – was held. The Conservatives were confirmed in power, though only with a slightly increased majority.

'Methods of barbarism'

British rejoicings were premature, as the war was by no means over. Nor was it to be for the next two years. Its second phase lacked the dramatic reversals and dramatic triumphs of the first. It consisted mainly of a grim campaign to defeat the Boers, who still held out against the British in the countryside. This action brought British troops into direct conflict with the men, women and children of the Boer farming communities as well as with the soldiers of the Boer armies. British troops employed tough methods. Farmhouses were set on fire, the countryside was scorched and the inhabitants of these devastated areas were rounded up into concentration camps. As the number of Boers increased in these camps, their living conditions worsened due to the practical difficulties of keeping the camps properly supplied with food and medicine. The government came under attack for what Liberal politicians termed the 'methods of barbarism' its army was employing, methods which became widely known in Britain through vivid newspaper reports. One writer in South Africa gave this description of what was to be found.

The British defeat at Majuba Hill in 1881 is remembered in the Boer graffiti in this house captured by the British during the Second Boer War some 20 years later. 'Don't forget Majuba, Boys' the Boers have written, to which the British reply 'No fear Boojers' (Boers) 'No fear'.

> **The shelter was totally insufficient. When the eight, ten or twelve persons who occupied a bell-tent were all packed into it, either to escape from the fierceness of the sun or dust or rainstorms, there was no room to move, and the atmosphere was indescribable, even with the duly lifted flap. There was no soap provided. The water supplied would not go round. No bedsteads or mattresses were to be had. Those, and they were the majority, who could not buy these things must go without. Fuel was scanty. The ration was sufficiently small that when the actual amount did not come up to the scale it became a starvation rate.**
>
> E. Hobhouse, *Brunt of War*

Treaty of Vereeniging

These techniques confirmed the fears of a number of Liberal politicians – such as David Lloyd George – who had throughout been doubtful of the value to Britain of fighting this war. The government justified what its army was doing in South Africa on the grounds that only in this way could the Boer resistance be broken down. Eventually that is what happened. In May 1902 the Boers gave in and signed with Britain the Treaty of Vereeniging.

Milner's objective of British dominance in South Africa had been achieved and the Boer republics were brought under British rule by the treaty's terms. But, in defeat, the Boers were given what were considered by those who were involved in the settlement to be generous terms: their language and customs were guaranteed and in compensation for the damage done to their farms in the last two years a grant of three million pounds was made.

The Second Boer War: its importance

Reconstruction and its problems

Attitudes in both Britain and South Africa in the early part of the century made it inevitable that attention would be given to the sufferings of the Boers in the war's closing stages. Milner himself was aware that to create harmony in his new inheritance, he must reconcile the Boers to British rule. Both the initial three million pound grant and later grants helped to achieve this. During the decade after the war ended, efforts were made under Milner's direction to remove the war's physical ravages. The rebuilding of farms, the development of immigration schemes, the construction of railway lines, were all much in evidence in these years. Not all of these policies worked well. Milner unwisely encouraged a scheme for Chinese immigration, to provide a good labour force in the South African mines. The terms of the indentures under which these Chinese were employed were strict and their living and working conditions were appalling. Criticism of Balfour's government for its part in the scheme was widespread and was to contribute to the Conservative failure in the general election of 1906.

Union of South Africa

Throughout the years after the war, progress was made towards a constitutional settlement. In 1906 and 1907 self-government was restored to the two Boer republics of the Transvaal and the Orange Free State. In 1909 the South Africa Act united these two republics with Cape Colony and Natal, in order to form what became known as the **Union of South Africa**. When the new Union came into being in the following year, it had the status of a self-governing dominion within the British Empire, making it similar to Canada, Australia and New Zealand. The areas of Basutoland (today, Lesotho) and Swaziland, within the geographical area of the Union, remained as British protectorates. The Union of South Africa was from the start distinctly different from other dominion countries, as none of the other dominions had within its lands millions of people unrepresented in its parliament. This was to be the situation in South Africa, as the new constitutional arrangements provided for representation in the new parliament at Cape Town only of the British and the Boers.

Blacks in the war

The constitutional arrangements of 1909 therefore worked against the interests of the blacks. Nor during these years had any serious attention been given to their sufferings. The popular view at the time that the Second Boer War was a 'white man's war' and did not involve the blacks was inaccurate. There were large numbers of blacks in the besieged towns in the war's early phase and they were more seriously deprived of food than were the white inhabitants. This was especially so in besieged Kimberley. During the war's later phase they suffered particularly at the hands of the Boers, as is shown in the following account written by a British missionary in the Transvaal in 1901.

> Of all who have suffered by the war, those who have endured most and will receive least sympathy, are the natives in the country places of the Transvaal. They have welcomed British columns and when these columns have marched on they have been compelled to flee from the Boers, abandon most of their cattle and stuff and take refuge in the towns or fortified places, or be killed. I have been asking after my people and this is the account I get of them all. For instance, at Modderfontein, one of my strongest centres of church work in the Transvaal, there was placed a garrison of two hundred white men. The natives – all of whom I knew – were there in their village: the Boers captured this post last month and when afterwards a column visited the place they found the bodies of all the Kaffirs (blacks) murdered and unburied.... I should be sorry to say anything that is unfair about the Boers. They look upon the Kaffirs as dogs and the killing of them as hardly a crime.
>
> Letter of Canon Farmer, 29 March 1901, quoted in Thomas Pakenham, *The Boer War*

Haldane's army reforms

For Britain the war had starkly revealed the shortcomings of its armies. The early disasters and the hard struggle for eventual victory both suggested that the British army was ill prepared for extensive campaigns overseas. A Royal Commission into the conduct of the war underlined the shortcomings of the army and the need for urgent reform. J.R. Haldane, Liberal Minister of War from 1905, put into effect many of the reforms that were needed, generally basing his work on the recent, successful changes in the German Army. His army reforms were extensive and broadly covered three areas. At the highest level, a General Staff was created to have total control. A British Expeditionary Force (BEF) came into being capable of rapid movement overseas. Attention was to be given to the development of a Territorial Army, in which men could serve part-time, and to the Officers' Training Corps at public schools in which boys could be given basic military training. The result of Haldane's work was seen to good effect in August 1914 when the British Army mobilised far more effectively for war than it had in 1899.

EXERCISES

1. (a) Describe the ways in which Britain organised the governing of its Indian Empire in the late nineteenth century.
   (b) Why did Britain give special attention to the governing of India in these years?

2. (a) How do you explain the outbreak of war in South Africa between the British and the Boers in 1899?
   (b) Give an account of the main features of the war in South Africa in the years 1899–1902.
   (c) How do you explain the eventual victory of British forces in this war?

3. Imagine you are a British soldier fighting in the Second Boer War. Write three letters home for any three years of the war, describing your life in South Africa and your attitude towards the war and the way in which it was being fought.

4. Study the two photographs on page 87 and the hymn on page 84 and then answer questions (a) to (e) which follow.
   (a) With reference to the words of the hymn and the features of the top photograph:
      (i) Explain what these two sources suggest to you about British attitudes towards the inhabitants of the Empire.
      (ii) Why was it useful to the British at this time to have references to the Empire contained in a hymn? (5)
   (b) (i) What activity is shown in the lower photograph?
      (ii) What does this photograph suggest to you as one of the motives of the British in extending their Empire? (3)
   (c) Which of these sources do you find helps you most towards an understanding of the British Empire? Give reasons for your choice. (3)
   (d) With reference to your own knowledge and to the evidence in these three sources, indicate to what extent the inhabitants of the Empire benefited from British rule. (5)
   (e) Select one of these men, outline the work that he did for the British Empire and show its importance: Lord Lugard, Lord Cromer, Lord Curzon, Joseph Chamberlain. (4)

8 POLITICS AND REFORM DURING THE EDWARDIAN ERA

As has been shown, the government had taken advantage of the circumstances of the Second Boer War to hold a general election in October 1900. Lord Salisbury was confirmed in office. He was anxious to retire, but a change in the monarchy caused him to continue a little longer. In January 1901, after a reign of 64 years, Queen Victoria died and was succeeded by King Edward VII, her eldest son, a man already in his sixties. So began what became known as the **Edwardian Era**, usually regarded as ending with the outbreak of the First World War in 1914 rather than the death of Edward VII in 1910.

Conservative reforms

Arthur Balfour

After Salisbury's retirement in July 1902 his nephew, Arthur Balfour, succeeded him almost as a matter of course. Balfour's earlier work as Chief Secretary for Ireland during Salisbury's second ministry had shown him capable of tackling a difficult political position at a challenging time (pages 42–3). Since the early 1890s he had been the leader of the Conservatives in the House of Commons and in the last couple of years of his uncle's premiership his influence within the government had increased noticeably. The Conservative party was in need of more forceful leadership than Lord Salisbury had given it in recent years. The party had failed to present the more progressive image that had been developed under the earlier leadership of Disraeli. There had been very little work of reform in the Salisbury years; the Prime Minister had just not seen the need for it. Balfour tried to make up some of the opportunities that his uncle had let slip. Yet during his time as Prime Minister his government met much bad luck and in January 1906 he was to lead the Conservative party to one of the worst electoral defeats it ever experienced.

Education Act

In 1902 a government Education Bill was introduced by R.L. Morant. The bill proposed the abolition of the school boards and the bringing of both the board schools and the voluntary schools under the control of the local county council or

Most children in late Victorian and Edwardian times would have been educated in elementary schools such as this. Notice the disciplined atmosphere and the attractive visual decoration around the walls.

county borough council. These new arrangements were partly designed to make the administration of education more efficient. They were also designed to make improved provision for secondary education, which was beginning to be quite widely developed in the late nineteenth century.

The bill's proposals led to a sharp controversy between Anglicans and Nonconformists. Agreement was reached that religious teaching in the former board schools, now referred to as the **provided** schools, would be undenominational. Nonconformists were prepared to accept this provision but they disliked very strongly the payment of part of the rates for the maintenance of Anglican schools. The Act was roundly denounced by Nonconformists throughout the country, some of whom refused to co-operate with it by refusing to pay their rates. It came under particular attack from Lloyd George in the House of Commons. Balfour, who could see the need for the changes brought about by the Act, was prepared to face the Nonconformist hostility. In this respect he showed much political bravery, as Nonconformist opposition was to the advantage of the Liberal party and was to become a factor in the eventual collapse of his government.

Licensing Act

Combined opposition by the Liberal party and the Nonconformist Churches over the Licensing Act of 1904 was to be similarly troublesome to Balfour's government. There were at that time virtually no restrictions placed on the opening hours of pubs and there was an immense number of them. The temperance societies had for years urged government action to change the situation. The Act of 1904 made provision for compensation to be paid by the brewers to pubs which had to close due to there being too many pubs in the neighbourhood. The Act's opponents considered that the brewery trade benefited too much from the Act, as the closing of some pubs increased the value of those that remained. In an age when drunkenness was a serious problem, many of Balfour's opponents on the Licensing Act would have been satisfied with little other than a wholesale closure of all pubs. In spite of its limitations, the 1904 Act was an important step on the long road towards controlling the problems of drink.

Unemployed Workmen Act

The Unemployed Workmen Act of 1905 was largely a response to a decline in trade and a rise in unemployment in the previous year. The Act permitted local authorities to keep registers of unemployed people and to take steps to help them, by emigration schemes or by the setting up of labour exchanges. These provisions were to form the basis of the labour exchange system that the Liberals were later to establish. The Conservative Act of 1905 merely allowed local authorities to take action along these lines; it did not insist that they did so.

Opposition to Balfour

By 1905 the legislation and policies of Balfour's government had aroused much opposition. Nonconformists were highly critical of the Education Act, the Licensing Act and the treatment in South Africa of Chinese labourers (page 95). Trade unionists were angered by the failure to take steps to amend the Taff Vale judgement (page 54) and felt the Unemployed Workmen Act had little value. Even within the Conservative party there was concern about Balfour's leadership. One issue that caused concern was Ireland, where Wyndham's proposals for devolution of government (page 45) appeared to be moving towards home rule. Of far greater importance was the developing conflict within the Conservative party on the issue of tariff reform.

Tariff reform

Joseph Chamberlain, who had played a major part in splitting the Liberal party over home rule in 1886, was to play a part of even greater importance in splitting the Conservative party over tariff reform. Still Colonial Secretary at the beginning of Balfour's premiership, Chamberlain launched his campaign in

1903. He had become disturbed by the decision of the Chancellor of the Exchequer to abandon a tax on imported corn, which had been temporarily imposed during the Second Boer War.

Chamberlain's proposals

Chamberlain's proposals spelt the end of the accepted system of free trade on which, so it was widely considered, British prosperity was based. Two main reasons led Chamberlain to put forward these proposals. One was rooted in his background as a Midlands industrialist. Already towards the end of the previous century, some manufacturers were noting with concern the building-up of tariff barriers by competitor countries. Other countries, so it seemed, were not prepared to keep so strictly to free trade as Britain was. This was having a damaging effect on British overseas trade. The other was to be found in Chamberlain's experience of the work of a Colonial Secretary during the years since 1895. If the full potential of Britain's **undeveloped estates** was to be realised, it was not enough just to encourage better use of the Empire's resources. The British government should positively encourage trading opportunities with the Empire. His proposals in this respect were really for **imperial preference**, an idea which Chamberlain always linked to that of **tariff reform**. Achieving both would result in Britain protecting its home industries with tariffs, while at the same time applying those tariffs less strictly to goods from the Empire than to goods from other countries.

Political divisions

When Chamberlain launched his tariff reform campaign in a well publicised speech in Birmingham in May 1903 the response was intense. Chamberlain ended with these words.

> **For my part, I believe in a British Empire, in an Empire which, although it should be one of its first duties to cultivate friendship with all the nations of the world, should yet, even if alone, be self-sustaining and self-sufficient, able to maintain itself against the competition of all its rivals. And I do not believe in a little England which shall be separated from all those to whom it should in the natural course look to for support and affection – a little England which shall thus be dependent absolutely on the mercy of those who envy its present prosperity; and who have shown they are ready to do all in their power to prevent the future union of the British race throughout the world.**

Clearly many were doubtful if free trade was still working to Britain's advantage. The issue very quickly became a concern of the government. Balfour tried to steer an even course between the tariff reformers and the free traders, between whom his cabinet very quickly became divided. Chamberlain was dissatisfied with what he considered to be uncertain leadership in this matter by Balfour. In September 1903 he resigned from the government in order to pursue his tariff reform campaign unfettered. He had in the meantime founded the Tariff Reform League, the main means through which his views became popularised.

Economic arguments

It is rarely easy for most people to see their way clearly through arguments about economic matters. At this time the whole issue became confused by the many contributions made by businessmen, academics and politicians. Some idea of the conflict is given by the two political posters overleaf. These posters show the Liberals as critical of Conservative plans for taxation and quote Chamberlain's tariff reform views. Notice how there is a particular reference to **tax on food**. If preferences were to be given to food from the Empire, food from other countries was bound to have some sort of tax placed on it. If that were not done, there could be no 'preference' for Empire products. The Conservative poster points out, in rather exaggerated fashion, the varied dangers that continued free trade will produce.

A HISTORY OF BRITAIN FROM 1867

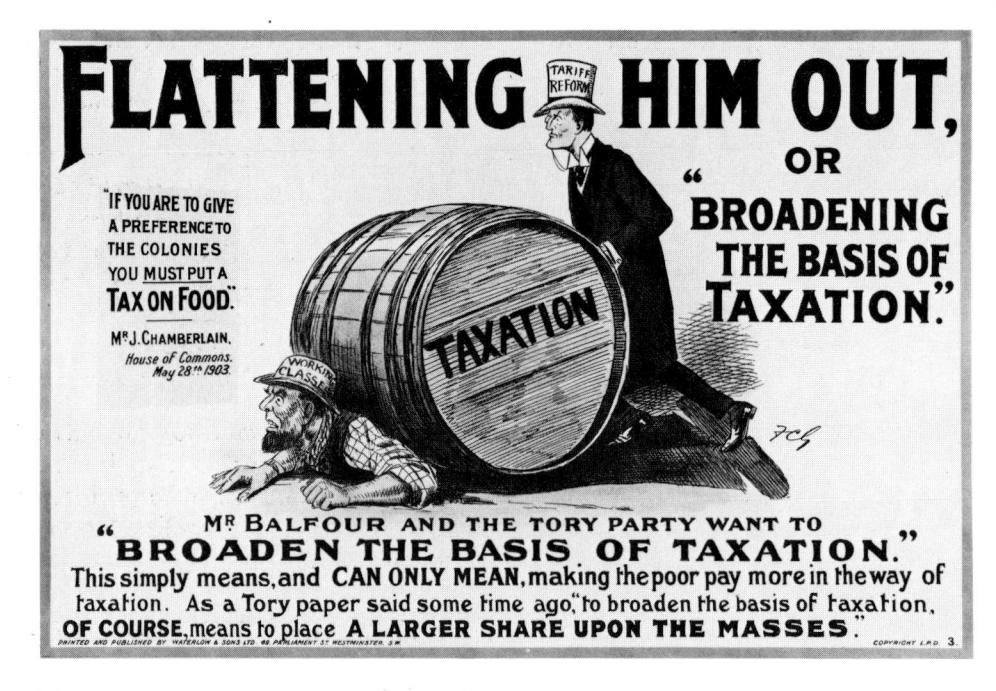

The response of the two parties to the main issues in the 1906 election. The Liberal poster (top) warns of the dangers resulting from tariff reform and imperial preference, while the Conservative poster (below) gives an equally dismal picture of the economic problems which continued pursuit of free trade would bring.

Government resignation

The real difficulty that the issue of tariff reform presented to the Conservatives was that it divided them. Some Conservatives – such as Winston Churchill – left the party and joined the Liberals. The real advantage that it gave to the Liberals was that they became united in defence of their traditional policy of free trade. Both they – and some Conservatives – became critical of Balfour's uncertain leadership. Towards the end of 1905, the Prime Minister attempted to re-assert the strength of his party and his own leadership of it. Taking advantage of what he wrongly judged to be a serious Liberal split on the home rule issue, he resigned, though without dissolving parliament or summoning an election. He did not expect the Liberals to be able to form a ministry. Their recently appointed leader, Sir Henry Campbell-Bannerman, knew that failure on his part to do so would make the Liberals appear feeble. He brought his considerable political skill to bear and a Liberal ministry was formed.

POLITICS AND REFORM DURING THE EDWARDIAN ERA

The 1906 general election

A general election was then summoned for January 1906. The result showed an overwhelming rejection of the Conservative government and it marked the end of the long Conservative dominance in British politics.

General Election: January 1906		
Conservatives	133	157
Liberal Unionists	24	
Irish Nationalists	83	
Labour	30	
Liberals	400	

It was a great triumph for the Liberal party, now confirmed in office by a landslide majority, unequalled in any other general election of the twentieth century. It also marked the beginning of a period of Liberal rule that was to be characterised by extensive legislation, much of it of far-reaching importance in British history.

Liberal reforms: the early stages

Sir Henry Campbell-Bannerman

The reforms for which the pre-war Liberals have become famous got off to a slow start. The party had not entered the election with any overall scheme of reform to offer to the voters. Sir Henry Campbell-Bannerman, the new Prime Minister, was a wealthy Scotsman who had first entered the House of Commons in 1868, the year in which Gladstone had begun his first ministry. Throughout his many years as an MP, Campbell-Bannerman had followed closely the path of reform that earlier Liberal leaders, such as Gladstone and Rosebery, had laid. His political ability and determination had won him many admirers.

Legislation

Much of the early legislation of the Liberals was uncontroversial and tended to continue work begun towards the end of the previous century. The Merchant Shipping Act of 1906 improved working conditions for British seamen and required foreign ships using British ports to conform to the standards defined by the Act. The Workmen's Compensation Act of the same year widened the provisions of the similar Act of 1897 by adding industries and accidents which had not been covered by the more limited earlier Act. Throughout these early years Haldane at the War Office was implementing extensive reforms of the army, described earlier on page 96.

Trade Disputes Act

The new government gave early attention to the issues raised by the Taff Vale judgement of 1901 (page 54). The Trade Disputes Act of 1906 reversed the effects of the judgement. Under the terms of the new Act, it would no longer be possible for a company to sue a trade union for loss of profits during a strike. The Act's importance for the trade unions was that they were again able to use the threat of a strike in their negotiations with employers. The Labour party had pressed more strongly than the Liberals for this change, and the passage of the Trade Disputes Act strengthened the links between the two parties.

Children and young people

Most of the other early legislation by the Liberals was concerned with the young and with the old. At the time of the Second Boer War many recruits had been rejected by the army on account of poor health. A government enquiry into what was termed **Physical Deterioration** followed, and reported in 1904. This gave fuller evidence of the inadequate feeding, health and living conditions of many young people. The report's suggestion that the state should involve itself more fully in these matters was unlikely to be acted upon by the Conservative government of the time.

The Liberals now took up this challenge. From 1906 school meals were to be provided free by local authorities for poor children. From 1907 school medical inspections were to be made, free of charge; the spread of school medical clinics was as a result encouraged so that children needing treatment could receive it. In 1908 followed the wide-ranging Children's Act, sometimes termed the **Children's Charter**. Its main purpose was to emphasise responsibility of parents for the health of their children; the Act contained provision for legal action against parents who neglected or ill-treated their children. It also ensured more appropriate treatment for young offenders, by setting up juvenile courts and by establishing borstal training centres, rather than prison, for young offenders. Among its many other provisions, the Act prohibited smoking by young people under sixteen.

Old age pensions

For many decades there had been abundant evidence of poverty among the elderly. The matter had been brought before the British public in a positive way through the findings of Charles Booth, as shown on page 78. For some decades action on poverty had been urged as essential by Labour politicians. Even those less socially concerned could see that by providing old-age pensions, savings could be made in the cost of administering workhouses, where many elderly people had to be accommodated when they became destitute.

Much discussion had taken place on whether pensions should be available on a **contributory basis**, financed by special contributions made by everyone earlier in life, or on a **non-contributory basis**, financed by government from general taxation. A pension scheme on a non-contributory basis was worked on by Asquith while Chancellor of the Exchequer and was eventually introduced into the House of Commons in 1908 by his successor, Lloyd George, after Asquith had become Prime Minister. The scheme provided for a pension of five shillings (25p) a week for all over the age of 70; the amount was to be progressively reduced for those still receiving a weekly income of some sort. The actual payment of pensions at local post offices was not just a minor feature of the Act. It meant that the whole pensions system had no connection with receiving assistance through the Poor Law. Many old people, not wishing to receive help in that way, had no hesitation in collecting pensions from their local post office.

In her book about English country life at that time, *Lark Rise to Candleford*, Flora Thompson, who was herself a post office worker when pensions were introduced, describes the impact they had on the inhabitants of an English village. In this passage she compares the situation in the 1880s with the situation after 1908.

> There were one or two poorer couples, just holding on to their homes, but in daily fear of the workhouse. The Poor Law authorities allowed old people past work a small weekly sum as outdoor relief; but it was not sufficient to live upon, and, unless they had more than usually prosperous children to help support them, there came a time when the home had to be broken up. When, twenty years later, the Old Age Pensions began, life was transformed for such aged cottagers. They were relieved of anxiety. They were suddenly rich. Independent for life! At first when they went to the post office to draw it, tears of gratitude would run down the cheeks of some, and they would say as they picked up their money, 'God bless that Lord George'; (for they could not believe one so powerful and munificent could be a plain 'Mr') and 'God bless *you*, Miss!' and there were flowers from their gardens and apples from their trees for the girl who merely handed them their money.
>
> Flora Thompson, *Lark Rise to Candleford*

Demand for pensions exceeded earlier estimates. By making pensions available on a non-contributory basis the Liberal government had met what in the case of many elderly people was a desperate need for practical help. Few acts in twentieth-century British history held so great an importance for the people of Britain.

Politics and reform during the Edwardian era

Conditions of work

The scope of reform now widened and attention was given to the conditions of industrial workers. Winston Churchill, President of the Board of Trade, was closely involved in government legislation in this connection. In 1908 the miners' working day was fixed at eight hours. Though acts in the previous century had limited hours of work for women and children, this was the first time that a government had limited the hours for men. It was right that this new step should be first taken in the mining industry, where conditions of work at the turn of the century were exceptionally grim. In 1911 the same principles were used in the Shops Act, which provided for a compulsory early closing day each week.

Another step in the direction of government intervention in industry came in 1909 with the setting up of trade boards. These were to lay down minimum payment standards in those industries where workers were liable to exploitation and where they had no trade union to defend their interests. Such industries, often referred to as **sweated industries**, included tailoring, box-making and lace-spinning. The exploitation of these workers had recently been publicised in a newspaper campaign that had criticised their low piece-rate payments and the slum conditions in which they worked. Nevertheless, the improvements which were provided for by the Trade Boards Act came only slowly.

The grill at the counter and the queues of unemployed men make for a somewhat authoritarian atmosphere in this early labour exchange. But the exchanges quickly proved their value to the unemployed.

Labour exchanges

In the previous year, the government had set up a system of labour exchanges throughout the country. Thus employers and prospective employees were helped in getting in touch with each other. No longer was it necessary for an unemployed person to rely solely on word of mouth or a dreary trudge from factory to factory to find out where employment was available. For the employer, the new system also held advantages as the workers could now be chosen from a wider group of people, and not just from those who happened to call at the factory.

Commons versus Lords: the People's Budget

Opposition of House of Lords

Their first few years in power had therefore shown a developing commitment by the Liberals to widespread reform. But some of the government's reforming policies had failed to get through parliament. As the Liberal majority in the House of Commons was large, they met few problems there. But the House of Lords had an even larger Conservative majority. At that time any piece of legislation had to pass both the Commons and the Lords in order to become law, so the Conservative party had an in-built method of stopping Liberal legislation. Though the Lords had allowed through some earlier Liberal legislation, they had also stopped various bills which the government had considered important. An Education Bill, designed to meet Nonconformist objections to the 1902 Act, had been so much adjusted by the Lords that the government abandoned it. A Plural Voting Bill, to stop wealthy people voting more than once on account of property which they held, and a Licensing Bill, to curb the hours of opening of pubs, were both rejected. Reform of the terms on which land was rented had been an objective among many Liberals while in opposition, but a series of bills designed to bring about such reform in England, Ireland and Scotland were either rejected or severely amended by the Lords. The fact that the Lords did allow through some legislation which they disliked, such as the Trade Disputes Act, had softened the attitude of some Liberals towards this veto which the Lords could employ. There was nevertheless a smouldering feeling of anger within the government at the way in which they were being frustrated from putting their full programme into effect.

Lloyd George

By 1909 feeling within the government was sufficiently strong for them to be ready to challenge the House of Lords over its use of the veto, if the need should arise. The politician who rose to this challenge was the new Chancellor of the Exchequer, David Lloyd George, and the breaking point was the budget of that year. Lloyd George's commitment to the struggle against the privileged position of the aristocracy was rooted in the poor circumstances of his early life in Wales. He was the ideal leader for a full-scale struggle against the House of Lords.

People's Budget

In 1909 the government needed to raise large sums of money. They faced two new and major expenses: old-age pensions and **dreadnought** battleships. In his budget of that year, Lloyd George planned to raise the needed money in novel ways. The method of raising tax was to be adjusted in order to give greater allowance to the less wealthy and extract a higher tax, known as a super tax, from the more wealthy. A tax on land values was introduced for the first time; among its most important features was a 20 per cent tax on profits from the sale of land and a special tax on unused land. Additionally, taxes were heavily increased on tobacco and alcohol and were introduced on motor cars. Lloyd George was by these measures not just raising a large sum of money from taxation, he was also proposing that the main burden of tax would in future fall on the wealthier part of society. The term **People's Budget** was popularly applied to his proposals.

Budget rejected by House of Lords

His proposals were seen as a serious challenge by the House of Lords. Their rejection of earlier Liberal legislation, whilst arousing understandable anger within Liberal circles, could not be regarded as an incorrect use of the traditional powers of their House. But for many decades there had been an unwritten understanding that a money bill (such as a budget) would pass the Lords automatically. In framing his budget, Lloyd George was undoubtedly aware that he was presenting the Lords with a real challenge. If they accepted, their financial interests would be harmed by the budget's provisions. If they rejected, a constitutional crisis would be created. After a difficult passage through the House of Commons the budget went to the House of Lords, where it was decisively rejected in November 1909.

POLITICS AND REFORM DURING THE EDWARDIAN ERA

Crisis develops

Throughout the summer and autumn of 1909 speeches in and out of parliament inflamed the situation. A Budget Protest League was formed to oppose the budget, and a Budget League to advance its fortunes. Lloyd George spoke critically of the Lords on many occasions. The tense atmosphere of these months is well illustrated from this speech of his.

> The question will be asked 'Should five hundred men, ordinary men chosen accidentally from among the unemployed, override the judgement – the deliberate judgement – of millions of people who are engaged in the industry which makes the wealth of the country? That is one question. Another will be, 'Who ordained that a few should have the land of Britain as of right; who made ten thousand people owners of the soil, and the rest of us trespassers in the land of our birth; who is it – who is responsible for the scheme of things whereby one man is engaged through life in grinding labour, to win a bare and uncertain subsistence for himself, and when at the end of his days he claims at the hands of the community he served a poor pension of eight pence a day, he can only get it through a revolution; and another man who does not toil receives every hour of the day, every hour of the night, whilst he slumbers, more than his neighbour receives in a whole year of toil?'

These words of Lloyd George were regarded as very extreme. The King himself expressed concern to the Prime Minister about them. But they show that the controversy was stirring depths of feeling of a type the country had not experienced since the time of the home rule controversy in the previous century.

Commons versus Lords: the Parliament Act

The January 1910 general election

When the House of Lords rejected the budget, Asquith publicly condemned them for acting unconstitutionally. He would now turn to the country at large to see if the government had support among the electorate in its conflict with the Lords. Parliament was dissolved and a general election was called. In the general election of January 1910 the Liberals were returned to power, but with a much reduced majority.

General Election: January 1910	
Conservatives	273
Labour	40
Irish Nationalists	82
Liberals	275

They were now heavily reliant on the support in parliament of the Labour party and the Irish Nationalist party. This reliance was greatly to influence their policies in the following few years. Nevertheless, the immediate issue was the conflict with the Lords and on this issue the Liberals were assured of the support of these two minority parties. Disturbed by what could only be interpreted as a clear vote against them in the general election, the Lords attempted to reach a compromise with the Commons. Shortly after the new parliament met, they passed the controversial budget without more ado. Their compromise came too late however.

Parliament Bill

In the meantime, the government had prepared a Parliament Bill that was designed to limit the power of the House of Lords. This bill had three main clauses:
1. The Lords were to have no power to reject or delay any bill which the Speaker of the House of Commons defined as a **money bill**. Thus a clearer definition was given to the previously unwritten practice, which the Lords had broken by their rejection of the People's Budget of the previous year.

2. The Lords were to have power to delay other bills, but only for a period of two years. This was the key clause of the bill and would prevent in the future the total rejection of laws which the Commons had approved.
3. General elections for the House of Commons were to be held at least every five years (instead of the previous period of seven years). As the importance of the House of Commons was to be increased by the first two clauses it seemed right to make that House more frequently answerable to the electorate.

Crisis deepens

Members of the government were well aware that such a bill was likely to be rejected by the House of Lords. In that event, they hoped to persuade the King to create sufficient Liberal peers to ensure a majority for the passage of the bill. Edward VII, who made no definite commitment to such a course of action, died suddenly in May 1910 and was succeeded by his son, George V. The new King was thrust at once into a complicated constitutional situation, for which his earlier education and training had left him poorly prepared. For the next few months, a constitutional conference provided a means for leading Liberals and Conservatives to discuss the issues involved. By this time there was a good chance that the conference might achieve its goal of a compromise agreement acceptable to both Commons and Lords. But an old problem now re-emerged to prevent this: Ireland. The last time that Irish home rule had been seriously discussed in and accepted by the House of Commons was in 1893; immediately after that acceptance, it had been decisively rejected in the House of Lords. Were the Parliament Bill to be accepted, home rule would certainly follow. The Conservative party at this time still made much of the fact that it was the **Conservative and Unionist party**. Its opposition to home rule was so strong that the constitutional conference broke down on this very point.

Role of King George V

The Liberals were firmly committed to their Parliament Bill and could not turn back even after the failure of the constitutional conference. With reluctance, George V gave the Liberals a secret agreement that if they were successful at another general election, he would create the necessary peers to get the bill through the House of Lords. The result of the second general election of 1910, held in December, was very similar to the first. Once again, the bill was discussed in the Commons, passed there and sent to the Lords.

Eventual passage of the Parliament Act

Though at this stage many peers were willing to give up the struggle, there was a sizeable number, referred to as the **ditchers** (prepared to fight 'to the last ditch' for their aristocratic rights) who were not. They continued the struggle into the stifling heat of the unusually hot summer of 1911. Even when it was made public in July that the King had promised to create the necessary Liberal peers, the opposition of many ditchers continued. But in early August the Lords gave in. They loathed the idea of being swamped by peers created merely in order to humiliate them and most of them now saw that the struggle was hopeless in any case. Even so, the Parliament Bill only passed the Lords by a narrow margin of 141 votes to 131. The low voting figures show that many peers had preferred to abstain.

The government's eventual victory in a crisis that had lasted for more than two years marks another vital stage in the development of democracy in Britain. Meantime other crises – demands for women's political rights, disturbances among industrial workers, and renewed concern over the Irish question – were beginning to develop as further challenges to Asquith's government.

Liberal reforms after the Parliament Act

National Insurance Act

Notwithstanding the further challenges facing them and the tremendous struggle with the Lords, the enthusiasm of the Liberals for reform was by no means exhausted. National Insurance, one of the greatest of the Liberal reforms, was introduced by Lloyd George in 1911. Its origins lay both in Britain

POLITICS AND REFORM DURING THE EDWARDIAN ERA

and in Germany. Within Britain, the Old Age Pensions Act of three years previously had already provided for a state-financed insurance system for the elderly. Within Germany, the system of state insurance created by Bismarck in the 1880s had provided financial security for all German workers. It was studied by Lloyd George as a model on which to base his schemes in Britain.

Health insurance

National Insurance was to be administered in two parts. Part I, to which most attention was given before the First World War, covered insurance against ill health; Part II, which became more significant after the war, covered insurance against unemployment. Both parts differed from the provisions for old-age pensions as, due to the expected high cost of the whole scheme, they were designed on a **contributory basis**. Under Part I, a medical insurance fund was to be built up by a weekly compulsory contribution of four pence from the employee, three pence from the employer and two pence from the state. When ill, the insured person would receive sick pay of ten shillings a week (50p) and free medical attention. The entire scheme was not administered by the government, but by approved insurance companies and friendly societies. The government was to ensure that the scheme was compulsory and to supervise its general administration.

Part I was greeted with much hostility. It had a rough passage through parliament. Many Conservatives disliked the compulsory nature of the contributions and the state interference into the lives of ordinary people that this represented. Rallies of mistresses with their domestic servants, in apparently united opposition to the bill, illustrated this particular type of opposition; a giant rally at London's Albert Hall in the autumn attracted much attention. Many in the Labour party were also critical, though for different reasons. They disapproved of a **flat rate contribution** (an identical contribution by everyone). They held that this was to the disadvantage of the working classes, for whom four pence represented a far higher proportion of their weekly income than the same amount did for the middle classes. Many also felt that money would be better used in improving standards of public health than in aiding the sick.

Lloyd George met this varied opposition with characteristic vigour. In a memorable phrase, he assured the working people of the country that their contribution was in reality 'nine pence for four pence'. He recognised that the Act had one particular defect: it covered only the insured worker and did nothing directly for the family. To him, the value of the Act lay in making a start in the vital area of health.

TOO MANY PIPS.
UITH (to LLOYD GEORGE) "FUNNY THING, MATE: 'E DON'T SEEM TO KNOW S GOOD FOR 'IM. WE SHALL 'AVE TO TRY AGAIN."

In spite of Lloyd George's efforts to popularise the National Insurance Act by suggesting payments represented a generous 'nine pence for four pence', many were doubtful of the Act's value.

Unemployment insurance

The guiding hand in Part II had been that of Churchill at the Board of Trade, who saw provision of unemployment insurance as completing the work he had begun in the setting up of labour exchanges. An unemployment insurance fund was to be built up by a weekly compulsory contribution of two and a half pence from the employee, two and a half pence from the employer and approximately one and two-thirds pence from the state. When unemployed, the insured person would receive pay of seven shillings (35p) a week for a maximum of 15 weeks. Initially the scheme was restricted to men in a limited number of industries. It was expected that the scheme would be extended to more industries once it was seen how effectively it worked. The strong opposition that had greeted the proposals for health insurance was, surprisingly, absent in the case of unemployment insurance. Yet Part II of the Act was a completely new departure in insurance that in no way followed practice abroad, as Part I did. It was only after the war that the issue of unemployment insurance became more intense, as is shown in Chapter 11.

A HISTORY OF BRITAIN FROM 1867

Votes for women

Increasing demand

For many, Britain in the years before 1914 appeared to be visibly breaking down into chaos and violence. The main features of this were the Conservative support for revolt in Ulster, the bitterness of industrial strife, and the activities of the suffragettes in their bid to secure the vote for members of their sex. By the turn of the century, women could look back over half-a-century of notable advance, partly considered in Chapter 6. But women were still not able to vote in parliamentary elections. By the early twentieth century, in spite of other advances in women's rights that had still to be made, attention focused sharply on the one objective of securing the parliamentary vote. There already existed a number of **suffragist** societies, pledged to secure the vote by peaceful persuasion. In 1897 these had amalgamated as the National Union of Women's Suffrage Societies (NUWSS). In 1903 a new organisation was set up: the Women's Social and Political Union (WSPU). From the start it was dominated by the powerful personality of Emmeline Pankhurst and her two daughters, Christabel and Sylvia. From the start also it was pledged to the use of force to secure the vote. Its members became known as **suffragettes** and though their aim was similar to that of the suffragists, their tactics were completely different. When standing in the dock of a magistrates' court, Emmeline Pankhurst justified their use of force.

Mrs Pankhurst arrested at a suffragette demonstration. The tactics of the suffragettes, though initially useful in attracting attention to their cause, tended to lose them the support of the public in the years before 1914.

> **We have tried every way. We have presented larger petitions than were ever presented before for any other reform, we have succeeded in holding greater public meetings than men have ever had for any reform. We have faced hostile mobs at street corners, because we were told that we could not have that representation for our taxes which men have won unless we converted the whole country to our side. Because we have done this we have been misrepresented, we have been ridiculed, we have had contempt poured upon us.**
>
> **... If you had the power to send us to prison, not for six months but for six years, or for the whole of our lives, the Government must not think that they can stop this agitation. It will go on. We are going to win.**
>
> **Well, sir, that is all I have to say to you. We are not here because we are law-breakers, we are here in our efforts to become law-*makers*!**
>
> **Emmeline Pankhurst's speech from the dock, Bow Street, 1908**

Suffragette campaigns

The campaigns of the suffragettes in these years took on many different forms. In the early days, heckling at political meetings became a successful method of attracting attention; other non-violent activities such as the painting of slogans and the holding of demonstrations achieved similar results. Additionally, the violence that was shortly to become a marked feature of suffragette activity was also seen in these early stages: letter-boxes were set on fire, the windows of unsympathetic politicians were smashed, some suffragettes chained themselves to railings in public places. Though many members of the public were angered by these activities, and were critical of the suffragettes, the cause of votes for women was brought before the general public by such action.

Attitudes of the political parties

Yet the Liberal government refused to take any positive steps to meet their demands. Why was a government that had such a fine record of reform unwilling to give justice to women in this matter? One answer to this question lies in the personality of Asquith who, though he had some sympathy with the women's cause, disliked suffragette methods as well as their repeated demands that he should do something for them. Many of his ministers – though not all – shared Asquith's attitude. A more convincing answer is that the Liberals were aware that if women were given the vote, the party that would get most of those new votes would not be their party, but the Conservative party. The Conservative

POLITICS AND REFORM DURING THE EDWARDIAN ERA

party, equally aware of this advantage to themselves, was more sympathetic towards the women. In practice, within all parties there were differences of opinion and in all parties there was concern at the increasing violence which characterised the women's campaigns.

Violence By 1910 suffragette violence was beginning to alienate rather than to attract support. What had earlier been useful in getting their cause known had become an ill-judged tactic. Tragedy overhung the whole movement. There was the suicide of one disturbed suffragette, Emily Davison, who threw herself before the King's horse at the 1913 Derby races. Others continued their protest in prison, where they went on hunger strike and were forcibly fed. Their treatment by the police and by the public was no longer sympathetic or restrained. Rather than continue the force-feeding of those on hunger strike in prison, the government passed what became known as the 'Cat and Mouse' Act in 1913. This allowed for the release and subsequent re-arrest of such women. The movement itself split and was no longer focused so exclusively on the one aim of votes for women. In the years before the First World War progress was minimal and their cause seemed a long way from being achieved.

The Irish question

In August 1914 Britain became involved in the First World War. As will be shown in the following chapter, the issues leading to the war's outbreak had developed over a number of years, yet the actual entry into the war was for most British people sudden and surprising. If they had thought in terms of a crisis during that summer it would not have been one concerning continental Europe, but instead one concerning Ireland. That crisis, coinciding as it did with suffragette violence, and industrial unrest (considered earlier on pages 54–5) had tended to focus attention on Britain's own problems rather than on any problems in Britain's foreign relations.

Renewed demands for home rule The Irish question once again took on an importance in British history after the passage of the Parliament Act in 1911. As can be seen from the figures for the two general elections of 1910, the Liberal party was now maintained in power solely by the votes of the Irish Nationalist MPs. The price of their continued support was a renewed Liberal commitment to home rule. Furthermore, they were aware that this key objective could now be achieved. The previous attempt at home rule, the second attempt of 1893, had been defeated solely by its rejection in the House of Lords, in circumstances described earlier on page 44. Now the power of the Lords had been restricted to a two-year delay of any measure they disliked; they could no longer completely reject such measures.

Third Home Rule Bill The chances for home rule were now therefore very strong. In John Redmond, the Nationalists had one of their best leaders since the time of Parnell. He seized the opportunities that now presented themselves. In April 1912 a Home Rule Bill was introduced into the House of Commons. Like its two unsuccessful predecessors it was moderate. There was to be a reduced number of Irish MPs at Westminster. Although the Irish were to have much control of their own affairs, the British government was still to retain considerable control over them. The proposals were eagerly accepted by the Irish Nationalist party, though the new Sinn Fein party (whose recent beginnings have been considered on page 46) were less enthusiastic.

Sir Edward Carson Sterner opposition emerged in Ulster. Since the time in the late nineteenth century when home rule had become likely, there had been developing among the predominantly Protestant population of this north-eastern province of Ireland a strong sense of **unionism**, of maintaining the union between Ireland and England. By the time of the Third Home Rule Bill, Ulster unionism had acquired a formidable leader in Sir Edward Carson. This eloquent and capable

A HISTORY OF BRITAIN FROM 1867

politician – by birth a Dubliner, not an Ulsterman – strove to maintain the union of the two countries. His hope was that a solid demonstration of Ulster's opposition would be sufficient to compel the government to drop the idea of home rule and preserve the union. Captain James Craig, an Ulsterman, took a similar stand.

Ulster Volunteers

The force of this opposition gathered strength throughout 1912. If home rule came about, the unionists intended to set up an Ulster government of their own, which they would defend by means of a paramilitary force, the **Ulster Volunteers**. In September, at an impressive ceremony in Belfast, the people of Ulster were invited publicly to sign what was known as **Ulster's Solemn League and Covenant**.

> Being convinced in our consciences that Home Rule would be disastrous to the material well-being of Ulster, as well as of the whole of Ireland, subversive of our civil and religious freedom, destructive of our citizenship, and perilous to the unity of the Empire, we, whose names are underwritten, men of Ulster, loyal subjects of His Gracious Majesty King George V, humbly relying on the God Whom our fathers in days of stress and trial confidently trusted, hereby pledge ourselves in solemn Covenant throughout this our time of threatened calamity to stand by one another in defending for ourselves and our children our cherished position of equal citizenship in the United Kingdom, and in using all means which may be found necessary to defeat the present conspiracy to set up a Home Rule Parliament in Ireland; and, in the event of such a Parliament being forced upon us, we further solemnly and mutually pledge ourselves to refuse to recognise its authority. In sure confidence that God will defend the right, we hereto subscribe our names, and, further, we individually declare that we have not already signed this Covenant.
>
> **Ulster's Solemn League and Covenant**

Propaganda from Ulster at the time of the home rule crisis of 1912–14. Craig is shown in a highly patriotic way, giving short shrift to the Prime Minister (held aloft) and to the leader of the Irish Nationalists (trodden down).

Getting people to sign this document was for Carson a useful way to impose some co-ordination and discipline among his followers and to re-emphasise their collective determination to resist home rule.

Conservative attitudes

The Ulster Unionists also became assured, within England, of the support of the Conservative party. Towards the end of 1911, the party had acquired a new leader, Andrew Bonar Law. He came from an Ulster Protestant family and led his party towards a total opposition to home rule. His statements on the subject during 1912 became extravagant and, for a leader of the opposition, dangerous. Among other things he gave a pledge of support to the armed opposition of the Ulster Volunteers in the event of home rule being passed by the British parliament. Naturally such support was a great encouragement to the Ulster Unionists in the stand that they were taking.

Irish Volunteers

At the beginning of 1913 the Third Home Rule Bill eventually passed the House of Commons. On reaching the House of Lords, it was almost immediately rejected. That meant a postponement of two years. The situation in Ireland had by now become so tense that those two years were likely to be troublesome and violent. Civil war was a real prospect. As the Ulster Volunteers were preparing to defend the independence of their province from any home rule government, the situation further south was beginning to slip from Redmond's control. The Ulster Volunteers had provided a model for militant action elsewhere in Ireland.

In the course of 1913 the **Irish Volunteers** emerged, with support from members of the new, more extremist Irish organisations such as Sinn Fein and the Gaelic League. Their objective was not entirely clear. Certainly it was to ensure that Ulster remained a part of Ireland under the new home rule arrangement. But many in the Irish Volunteers were Sinn Fein supporters eager to go further than that and set up an Ireland totally independent of British

POLITICS AND REFORM DURING THE EDWARDIAN ERA

control. So powerful had the Irish Volunteers become by the start of 1914 that Redmond – who had earlier disapproved of their activities – now involved himself with them in the hope of bringing them under his control.

Proposed exclusion of Ulster

In a bid to preserve peace, Asquith's government attempted a compromise. In March 1914 the government proposed that, for a six-year period, Ulster should be excluded from the home rule arrangement. Redmond reluctantly accepted this; but from Carson there was firm rejection. Asquith judged his compromise solution a fair one and now tried to ensure that when the time came home rule would be effectively implemented in Ireland. To do this, he naturally relied on the British army stationed in Ireland. But it shortly became apparent that the loyalty of the British Army in Ireland was doubtful.

The Curragh 'mutiny'

This was shown by an episode at the Curragh barracks near Dublin, an episode often referred to as **the Curragh 'mutiny'**. Here a group of British officers revealed their Unionist sympathies by declaring they would not fight against the Ulster Volunteers if ordered to do so. More serious was the increased activity of both the Ulster Volunteers and the Irish Volunteers in the summer months of 1914. It was therefore not surprising that in the summer of 1914 the British people were expecting war in Ireland rather than war on the Continent. When the First World War broke out in August 1914, the implementation of home rule was postponed. The tensions within Ireland subsided as both sides became involved together in campaigns very far from their homeland.

EXERCISES

1. Show in what ways each of the following groups of people were able to benefit from the work of the Liberal government in the years 1905–14:
   (a) children and young people,
   (b) the elderly,
   (c) the sick and the unemployed, and
   (d) members of trade unions.

2. (a) Explain why so much controversy surrounded the proposals in the People's Budget of 1909.
   (b) Show how this controversy led during the years 1909–11 to a reduction in the power of the House of Lords.
   (c) Why do you think the events associated with the People's Budget and the Parliament Act are regarded as important?

3. Imagine you are a working-class person during the Liberal ministries of 1905–14. Write a survey of these years to show in what ways you feel your life has benefited by government policies and legislation during that time.

4. Study the two posters on page 100 and then answer questions (a) to (d) which follow.
   (a) With reference to the top poster:
      (i) Show how by its use of words and images it attempts to point out the dangers of economic protection.
      (ii) In what ways does the poster appeal both to reasoned arguments and to emotional responses? (4+2)
   (b) With reference to the lower poster:
      (i) Show how by its use of words and images it attempts to point out the dangers of free trade.
      (ii) In what ways does the poster appeal both to reasoned arguments and to emotional responses? (4+2)
   (c) (i) What was the purpose of posters such as these two at the time they were issued?
      (ii) What value do they have as sources for our knowledge of the tariff reform controversy? (4)
   (d) Outline the part played in the tariff reform controversy by Joseph Chamberlain, shown rolling the barrel in the top poster. (4)

9 BRITAIN AND EUROPE IN THE EARLY TWENTIETH CENTURY

The strength and size of the British Empire in the late nineteenth century was such that Britain had felt no need for close relations with any of the powers of continental Europe. Britain had in these years pursued the policy that is usually termed **Splendid Isolation**. Lord Salisbury had been convinced that this was the best policy for a great power such as Britain to pursue. The comparative freedom from serious entanglement with foreign powers during his time as Prime Minister suggested to many that Lord Salisbury was right. Yet some within his cabinet were doubtful. By the time Lord Salisbury's long premiership ended in July 1902, Britain was already beginning to seek closer links with other countries.

The breakdown of Splendid Isolation

Those who wanted a fuller involvement by Britain with other powers expressed concern at the recent experience Britain had of fighting alone in the Second Boer War. Victory had been achieved in South Africa only after prolonged struggle, in which the absence of an ally had been a handicap. There was also concern at the start of the century about the threat posed to Britain by the foreign policies of the Russian Empire. Having failed to expand in the 1870s in the Balkans and in the 1880s in Afghanistan, Russia sought in the 1890s to expand in the Far East. The greater success that Russia had in this area began to imperil Britain's Far Eastern trade, especially its trade with China.

It was this threat from Russia that had prompted a number of politicians – foremost among whom was Joseph Chamberlain – to seek an alliance with Germany in the late 1890s. As Britain's relations with Germany had generally been harmonious for most of the nineteenth century, it was natural for Britain to see Germany as a possible ally. The recent development of German industry and the setting up of a German Empire in Africa showed that Germany was intent upon becoming a major power in the world. Under Kaiser (Emperor) Wilhelm II, who succeeded to the German throne in 1890, this emphasis of Germany's world role was to become even more pronounced. But under Wilhelm II Germany had already begun seriously to challenge Britain and its Empire. Germany had given diplomatic support to the Boers in their recent war with Britain; German plans for a railway through the Middle East to Baghdad led to wrangling with Britain; German businessmen poached on areas of commerce which the British had originally developed. By the early twentieth century, serious hopes for links with Germany were no longer held by the British government.

Anglo-Japanese alliance

Britain looked elsewhere. In the Far East, Japan felt as concerned about Russian activity as Britain did. This mutual concern led to the signature in January 1902 of the Anglo-Japanese alliance. According to its terms, Britain would remain neutral if Japan were at war with one country but would come to Japan's assistance if it were at war with two countries. Thus the era of Splendid Isolation came to an end with Britain allying with a non-European power. The reality of the Russian threat in the Far East was demonstrated in 1904–05 when Japan was at war with Russia and inflicted a severe defeat on Russian forces both on land and at sea.

PARTNERS

At a Christmas day ball in 1901, Russia and France dance together in the background, while Kaiser Wilhelm II looks expectantly towards Britain. Links with the British Empire were one of a number of factors that frustrated hopes for any Anglo-German understanding at the turn of the century.

BRITAIN AND EUROPE IN THE EARLY TWENTIETH CENTURY

The Entente Cordiale

Formation of the entente

Britain's relations with France had been unsteady for a number of years, largely as a result of conflicts over colonial matters. As has been shown on page 90, the two countries had almost engaged in hostilities over the Fashoda incident in 1898. In spite of this unpromising situation, Lord Lansdowne, Foreign Secretary during Balfour's administration, began to forge links with Britain's closest continental neighbour. He formed a good working relationship with the French Foreign Minister, Delcassé. The two men entered into discussions about colonial issues. Edward VII usefully assisted their work by a visit he paid to Paris, a visit which formed part of a general tour of European capitals by the King. His Paris visit was a great success. It helped to remove French suspicion of Britain and to create the right conditions in which the Lansdowne–Delcassé talks could succeed.

Terms

Much discussion was necessary. Only in April 1904, almost a year after the King's visit, was the final agreement signed. It was known as the **Anglo-French entente** and was popularly referred to as the **Entente Cordiale**. The use of the French word **entente** is important, as it suggests a rather loose relationship, one that lacked the firm commitments that might be found in an **alliance**. It was the right word to describe the relationship that now existed between the two countries. Neither side gave any promise of military support if the other were attacked. The entente's terms were designed solely to solve outstanding colonial problems. It was now agreed that Britain would be the dominant European power in Egypt. In return, France was assured that it would be the dominant power in Morocco, where rebels had recently threatened the French position.

The Kaiser in Morocco

The understanding between Britain and France which was established in 1904 was long-lasting and, in spite of some differences from time to time, was to endure throughout the twentieth century. It was strongly challenged almost as soon as it had been signed. Though none of the entente's terms made mention of Germany as a possible enemy, the German government nevertheless viewed the creation of the entente as a hostile act. In March 1905 Kaiser Wilhelm II interrupted a cruise in the Mediterranean in order to land at Tangiers in Morocco. In a well-publicised conversation with the Sultan of Morocco he gave promises of German support for Morocco's independence, thus threatening the recently strengthened French position there. The Kaiser had, in effect, offered a direct German challenge to the Anglo-French entente and there was fear that war might break out. Tension slackened when the German government suggested an international conference to discuss the issue.

The conference met in southern Spain at the town of Algeçiras in January 1906 and, by a large majority among the 12 governments represented there, agreement was reached that France should continue as the dominant power in Morocco. This favourable decision, confirming the terms of the entente by international agreement, strengthened the relationship of Britain and France. Nevertheless, its general effect was to darken international relations. At Algeçiras, Germany had been supported only by its long-standing ally, Austria-Hungary. Germany now felt, more strongly than earlier, a sense of being encircled by hostile powers. The chances of creating harmony among the nations of Europe were now remote.

SOLID.
NY. "DONNERWETTER! IT'S ROCK. I THOUGHT IT WAS GOING TO BE R."

Germany discovers that the Entente Cordiale is stronger than originally thought. This cartoon was produced after the strength of the Entente had been demonstrated at the Algeçiras Conference.

The Triple Entente

Anglo-Russian convention

In this atmosphere of suspicion and hostility, Britain strengthened its position by a further agreement. Since its defeat in the Russo-Japanese War of 1904–05, the Russian Empire had become less of a threat to Britain's trade in the Far East. It was now the obvious choice. For more than a decade Russia had developed friendly relations with Britain's new ally, France. For much of that time there had been the possibility that Russia might ally with Germany, but links with Britain would end any chance of that. An **Anglo-Russian convention** was signed by the two countries in August 1907. Like the agreement with France three years earlier, it was mainly concerned with conflicting interests in different parts of the world. In Persia (today, Iran), Britain was to have influence in the south-east and Russia was to have influence in the north; the remainder of the country was to be regarded as neutral (see map on page 29). Afghanistan was recognised as being under British influence, a situation which Britain held to be essential in order to give proper protection to its Indian Empire. Tibet was recognised as independent.

The Anglo-Russian convention never attracted within Britain the popularity enjoyed by the Anglo-French entente. The Russian Empire was viewed, correctly, as an autocratic power with which Britain had little in common and with which it had been in conflict in quite recent times. In spite of the convention's terms, the Russian threat to Britain's Indian Empire was still a cause of concern.

Triple Entente and Triple Alliance

Nevertheless, the British government maintained a working relationship with Russia up to and including the First World War. What now existed between Britain, France and Russia was termed the **Triple Entente**. Opposed was the older **Triple Alliance** of Germany, Austria-Hungary and Italy. In the years that followed, both these systems became firmer and better armed. From time to time clashes of interests between them led to crises. One of these, in the summer of 1914, resulted in the outbreak of the First World War.

Anglo-German rivalry

Naval rivalry

Rivalry between Britain and Germany intensified during the early twentieth century on issues concerning the navies of each country. As an island power with an extensive overseas empire, Britain had always given a place of importance to its navy. At the end of the nineteenth century Britain's Royal Navy was the largest and most powerful in the world. Successive British governments held to the idea that Britain should maintain in naval matters a two-power standard: the Royal Navy should be equal to or larger than the combined navies of any two other powers. Kaiser Wilhelm II, in the emphasis he gave to Germany's world role, was determined to increase the power of the German navy and break this two-power standard.

Dreadnought battleships

To meet this challenge, Britain perfected a new class of battleship, the **dreadnought**. The first was launched in February 1906, shortly after the Algeçiras conference. The novelty of a dreadnought battleship lay partly in the increased speed that it could use, but mainly in the improved efficiency of its firing power. Unlike earlier battleships, which had guns of narrow bore fixed to fire in one direction, the dreadnought's guns had a 12-inch bore and could be swiftly moved to face the enemy, from whatever angle the enemy might approach. Other countries shortly followed the British example and began to develop their own dreadnoughts. Until the First World War, this type of battleship was regarded as vital for the protection of any sea-going power.

Although the dreadnoughts were an important technical advance in battleship design, they had the effect of destroying all hope of Britain maintaining the two-power standard. All countries now began afresh in the build-up of their navies, so that Britain's earlier lead was no longer so useful. The dreadnought design was quickly applied by Germany, which now had a real opportunity to create a navy that would be a serious challenge to the Royal Navy.

Competition in dreadnoughts

In the years between the launching of the first dreadnought and the outbreak of the First World War, the fierce competition between Britain and Germany in dreadnought production was a continuing source of concern to Britain. During

A British dreadnought of the early twentieth century. The greater destructive potential of this battleship sharpened the naval rivalry between Britain and Germany.

these years, some attempts were made to slacken the intensity of this competition, but none of these had any noticeable success. Britain's Foreign Secretary, Sir Edward Grey, started discussions with the German government on this issue in 1909, but the discussions were slow-moving and broke up two years later, having achieved nothing. Shortly after Winston Churchill became First Lord of the Admiralty in October 1911, he proposed a 'naval holiday', meaning by this expression a pause in the dreadnought production by Britain and Germany, but his proposal met no response from the German government. Similarly in 1912 a visit to Germany by the Secretary for War, Viscount Haldane, to discuss the whole issue of armaments, got nowhere.

Importance of naval rivalry

Why was the British government so concerned about this naval rivalry with Germany? Germany's world-wide commitments, as they then were, made its possession of a large navy less essential than in the case of Britain. Germany had a smaller overseas Empire and was not an island power. The conclusion reached by the British government was that Germany was building up its navy for purposes of prestige, and possibly for purposes of war. There was also concern about Germany's attitude towards the negotiations over naval matters. The British government was never entirely convinced that the German government was genuinely committed in these negotiations to the securing of a reduction of each country's navy. Was Germany perhaps more interested in bringing about a weakening of the Triple Entente by reducing the naval strength of one of its members? It was fear of this latter possibility that made for a slack commitment by Britain to the negotiations of these years.

The Agadir crisis

German demands in Morocco

Events in Morocco in the summer of 1911 led to a further strengthening of Britain's links with the other entente powers. This second crisis over Morocco focused, as had the first one six years earlier, on a German challenge to the French position there. In July 1911 a German gunboat, *Panther*, was sent to the southern Moroccan port of Agadir. The German action was designed to show their disapproval of the steps taken by the French in the Moroccan town of Fez, where French troops had recently put down a rebellion. This action by Germany was followed by a German demand that in return for their recognition of complete French control of Morocco, the French should give the whole of the French Congo to Germany.

Lloyd George's Mansion House speech

Britain became alarmed that Germany intended to set up a naval base at Agadir, and so the issue was seen by Britain as a part of the naval rivalry between the two powers. Britain promised to support its French ally and to resist the German threat. Britain's commitment to a firm line over the Agadir crisis was made not by the Foreign Secretary, but by the Chancellor of the Exchequer, Lloyd George. An added strength was thereby given, as until this time Lloyd George had generally been regarded as a friend of Germany. But there could now be no mistaking the intention of his words at a speech given in London's Mansion House.

> I am also bound to say this – that I believe it is essential in the highest interests, not merely of this country, but of the world, that Britain should at all hazards maintain her place and her prestige amongst the great powers of the world. Her potent influence has many a time been in the past, and may yet be in the future, invaluable to the cause of human liberty. It has more than once in the past redeemed continental nations, who are sometimes too apt to forget that service, from overwhelming disaster, and even from national extinction. I would make great sacrifices to preserve peace. I concede that nothing could justify a disturbance of international good will except questions of the gravest national moment. But if a situation were to be forced upon us in which peace could only be preserved by the surrender of the great position Britain has won by centuries of heroism and achievement, by allowing Britain to be treated, where her interests were vitally affected, as if she were of no account in the Cabinet of Nations, then I say emphatically that peace at that price would be a humiliation intolerable for a great country like ours to endure.

For some months in the late summer and autumn of 1911 there was a definite possibility that war would break out over the Agadir incident. The commitment of Britain and France to the entente was again shown to be firm and as a result of negotiations between all the countries concerned an agreement was reached in November 1911. Germany was compelled to acknowledge the French rights in Morocco in return for a fairly minor transfer of some French land to German control in the Congo.

Importance

The Agadir incident appeared to show that a united and determined policy by Britain and France was sufficient to force Germany to retreat. The governments of both countries therefore felt it advisable to co-operate more closely on military and naval matters. Some military discussions had already been taking place from time to time, but these were now taken further. Agreement was reached on arrangements for the sending of the British Expeditionary Force to France in the event of war and for a division of naval responsibility between the North Sea for Britain and the Mediterranean for France. At the same time, within Britain, better co-ordination was achieved between the Army and the Navy. These various moves show that the governments of Britain and France now viewed the outbreak of war as a very likely event.

Conflicts in the Balkans

Balkan problems

The basic problem in the Balkans was the same in the early twentieth century as it had been in the late nineteenth: the conflicting interests of the Russian Empire and of Austria-Hungary in an area where the rule of the Ottoman Empire was decaying. The tensions between these two powers had reached a crisis in 1908 when Austria-Hungary annexed Bosnia. Russia protested against this annexation, regarding it as a dangerous advance of Austrian power. But as Austria had the firm support of Germany for the annexation, the Russian government felt compelled to accept Austria's action.

First Balkan War The episode had encouraged other subject races of the Ottoman Empire to take advantage of the weakness their rulers were showing. In 1912 the **Balkan League** was formed between Serbia, Bulgaria, Greece and Montenegro with the aim of fighting for the parts of their countries still in Ottoman control. In the closing months of 1912 the Balkan League fought a war against the Ottoman Empire, the result of which was a remarkable victory for them and a substantial reduction of Ottoman power in the Balkans.

The changed fortunes in the Balkans had profound effects on the relations of the great powers. Russian-supported Serbia had been a particular enemy of Austria since the Bosnian annexation of 1908, when many Serbs resident in Bosnia had been taken under Austrian control. Austria was concerned therefore to limit Serbia's expansion and was prepared for war with Russia, should Russian aid be given to Serbia. If in such circumstances France were to come to Russia's support, then Britain as a member of the Triple Entente might find itself with no alternative but to fight.

Role of Sir Edward Grey In the early part of 1913 discussions by the great powers were held in London in an attempt to resolve the various problems which the fighting in the Balkans had produced. The discussions centred mainly on Austria's demand for the creation of the new, independent state of Albania in order to prevent Serbia from having access to the Adriatic Sea. Grey considered that the best way to reduce tension and to avoid war was by supporting this Austrian demand. The terms of the Treaty of London in May 1913, by which the discussions were concluded, provided for the new Albania, as well as for a recognition of most of the territory that the Balkan League powers had seized in their war. Grey had therefore adopted the role of peacemaker, and to good effect. Very largely through his efforts, the Balkan crisis had again been resolved.

Second Balkan War His approach also held dangers, however, as the German government viewed his readiness to agree to the demands of their Austrian ally as a sign of weakness. The German government questioned whether, in the event of war, Britain would come to the support of the other members of the Triple Entente. The terms of the Treaty of London were very shortly broken. In the Second Balkan War (1913), Bulgaria, dissatisfied with its share of the Ottoman spoils, fought against its former allies. Bulgaria's defeat was followed by the loss of most of the gains it had made in the previous year.

Sarajevo and the outbreak of the First World War

Assassination On 28 June 1914 the heir of Austria-Hungary, Franz Ferdinand, paid a visit to Sarajevo, capital of the recently annexed Bosnia. In the course of the visit, he and his wife were shot as they travelled in an open carriage through the streets of what was for them a hostile city. They both died later that day, after some hours of hideous agony in which doctors fought vainly to save their lives. This incident directly provoked the outbreak of the First World War.

Importance for Austria and Serbia Since the two Balkan Wars there had been constant suspicion by Austria that Serbia was encouraging those Serbs who lived in Bosnia to rebel against Austrian control. The events at Sarajevo confirmed just how serious and well-founded those suspicions were. It became known that the assassins of Franz Ferdinand and his wife belonged to a secret society based within Serbia. Towards the end of July, Austria-Hungary sent to Serbia a strongly worded ultimatum, containing humiliating demands. If Serbia refused to accept, war with Austria would follow. To avoid such an outcome, Serbia declared itself ready to support some, but not all, of the demands of the ultimatum. This partial acceptance was not sufficient for Austria which, with the assurance of German support, was now determined to crush Serbia.

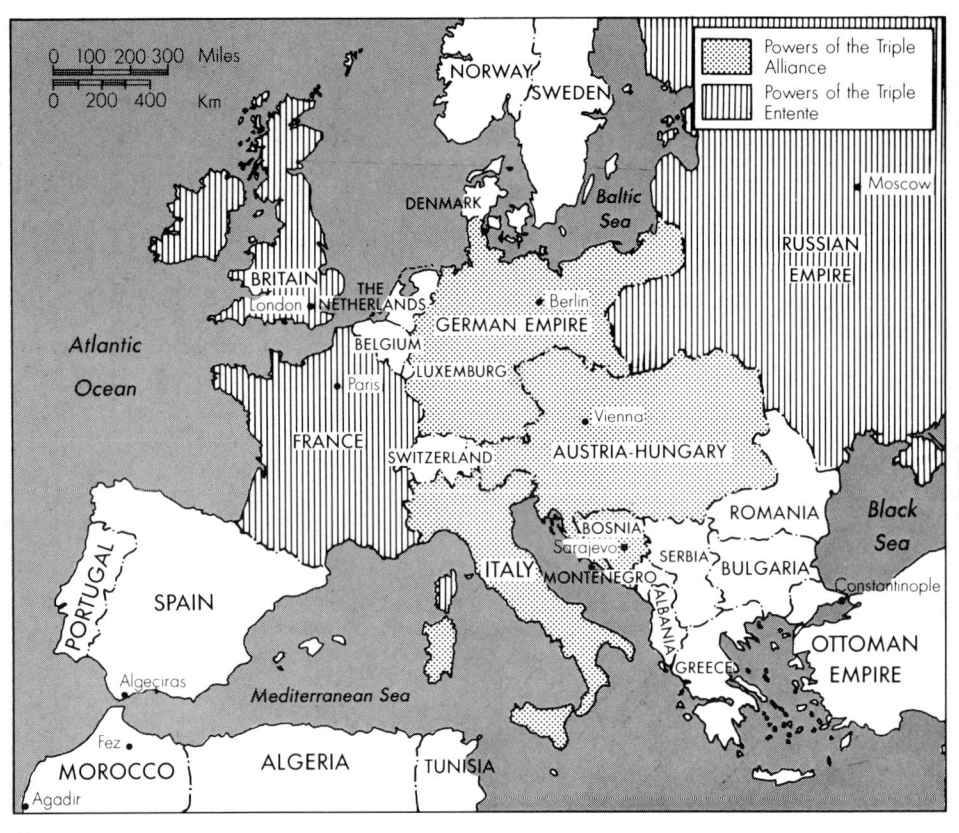

Europe in 1914

International repercussions

So exactly one month after the assassination, on 28 July 1914, Austria and Serbia were at war. It now proved impossible to prevent a widening of this conflict. At this late stage the alliance systems and the fundamental tensions were too strong for peace efforts to have any hope of success. Russia came to the support of its Balkan ally and declared war against Austria; unlike 1908, there was to be no Russian retreat this time. Germany showed its support for Austria by declaring war against Russia and against Russia's ally France.

Response within Britain

The suddenness of these events took the British government and the British people very much by surprise. For the British people the crisis of the summer of 1914 had centred upon Ireland, and the issues of the Balkans appeared to most of them remote and quite unconnected with British interests. Grey hoped to use his services for peace, as he had done at the time of the Balkan Wars. As earlier, this policy held dangers. His attempts to restrain Britain's Russian and French allies in these days of crisis were interpreted by Germany as another sign of British weakness and lack of real intent to wage war. In reality, this was not the case. Grey was quite determined that Britain would give support to France if war broke out.

German invasion of Belgium

Germany appeared, however, to be prepared to risk war with Britain. German war plans were for simultaneous attacks against its enemy to the east, Russia, and its enemy to the west, France. The planned invasion of France involved the passage of German troops through Belgium. Britain would be threatened by enemy control of Belgium, a country so near to its own shores. Furthermore, German action violated the terms of a long-standing British commitment to Belgian independence, given in the 1839 Treaty of London, which the Kaiser now described as 'merely a scrap of paper'. On 4 August 1914 the British government took the fateful decision of declaring war.

Reasons for British involvement in the war

It is doubtful if many within Britain foresaw the appalling bloodshed that the First World War was to bring to those who fought in it. Yet in August 1914 there was within Britain, as in the other countries now at war, an upsurge of patriotic

9 BRITAIN AND EUROPE IN THE EARLY TWENTIETH CENTURY

A popular view of the determination of Britain and its Empire at the outbreak of war in 1914 is shown on this postcard. The extent to which such a stand was really necessary has since been doubted.

"A SCRAP OF PAPER"

willingness to be involved in the forthcoming struggle. British people soon forgot the Balkan issues which had been the war's immediate cause. Instead, the war was seen as one concerned with more immediate British interests. It was to defend Belgium from German bullying. It was to forestall German dominance of the Continent, an event which could follow from France's defeat. It was seen as the only means by which Britain could oppose the increasing arrogance of the Kaiser's Germany, shown through the continuing concern over naval rivalry and the high-handed German actions in the international crises of recent years.

EXERCISES

1. (a) Explain why early in the twentieth century the British government no longer felt it wise to pursue a policy of Splendid Isolation.
   (b) Give the terms of the arrangements made by Britain with Japan in 1902, with France in 1904 and with Russia in 1907.
   (c) What was the importance for Britain of these new links with foreign powers?

2. (a) What factors made for an underlying hostility between Britain and Germany in the early twentieth century?
   (b) By carefully examining the events in the summer of 1914, explain how Britain became involved in war with Germany.

3. Imagine you are an English person with friends in Germany in 1914. Write a letter to your German friends, explaining why the prospect of a German alliance at the turn of the century had eventually resulted in war by 1914.

4. Study the cartoons on pages 112 and 113 and the postcard on this page and then answer questions (a) to (d) which follow.
   (a) With reference to the cartoon on page 112:
       (i) Explain what the cartoon suggests about Britain's foreign relations at the start of the twentieth century.
       (ii) How accurate an impression does this cartoon convey? (3+2)
   (b) With reference to the cartoon on page 113:
       (i) Explain what the cartoon suggests about the Entente Cordiale in the early part of the twentieth century.
       (ii) How accurate an impression does this cartoon convey? (3+2)
   (c) With reference to the postcard on this page:
       (i) Explain in what ways the cartoon suggests reasons for Britain's involvement in war in 1914.
       (ii) What purpose would a postcard such as this be intended to serve at that time? (4+2)
   (d) In your opinion, do these three sources, taken in the order in which they come, help to explain the development of British foreign policy in these years? (4)

10 BRITAIN AND THE FIRST WORLD WAR

Involvement in the First World War was for the British people a wide-reaching experience. It brought changes to British politics and to British society. Its damaging effects on overseas trade marked a major step in the decline of Britain's economy. Of far deeper impact was the human slaughter, in high numbers and in appalling circumstances, which the war brought with it. For the British people, no other war in history had carried with it so much suffering, so widely spread.

Trench warfare

Early enthusiasm

In the emotional atmosphere of patriotism at the war's start there was no difficulty in getting men to recruit for the army. During the first two months of the war, three-quarters of a million men enlisted voluntarily. Few – if any – saw what was ahead of them. The commonly held view was that the war would be over by Christmas. Most therefore thought they were to be involved in a short, swift and successful campaign.

Lord Kitchener

Such was not to be the case. Lord Kitchener, a soldier of successful experience in the Sudan (page 89) and South Africa and one highly popular throughout the country, became the new Secretary for War. His views on strategy went unchallenged by the other members of the government in the war's early stages. In Kitchener's judgement, immense efforts would be needed to stem the German advances in Belgium and France. Britain should involve itself in those efforts by sending across the Channel the British Expeditionary Force (BEF), planned as part of Haldane's pre-war military reforms. It was therefore Kitchener who was mainly responsible for the massive British involvement against Germany along the **Western Front**.

Battle of the Marne

Before the first month of the war had ended, British forces were in combat with German forces at the battle of Mons, in southern Belgium. In contrast with later engagements, Mons was a minor one. After some early British success there, the advance of German reinforcements compelled a retreat southwards. The objective of this German advance was Paris. The French were determined to prevent their capital from falling and made a stand against the enemy on the River Marne in September 1914. British contribution at the battle of the Marne was slight. But the battle was to have a far-reaching importance for the style the war was to take along the Western Front. At the Marne the French turned the German advance into a retreat, and they vigorously pursued the retreating forces. In order to resist this pursuit, the Germans stopped and dug trenches from which to defend the territory they still held in France and Belgium.

Purpose of trenches

Thus began the **trench warfare** for which the years 1914–18 have become so well known. In the late autumn and winter of 1914–15, the Allied forces of Britain and France as well as the German forces dug trenches across the countryside of the Western Front. It was in these trenches that the soldiers of both sides spent their time. The trenches were deeply cut and so provided some safety. That was the only advantage they had. For the soldiers now compelled to inhabit them, the trenches were a constant misery. Efforts made to improve living conditions in the trenches were powerless against bitter weather, mud and vermin. In spite of these degrading conditions, military commanders saw value in the trenches. They afforded quite a secure position from which to defend territory and useful cover for machine-gun fire. They were also a suitable base from which to advance against the enemy, across the **no-man's land** that lay

BRITAIN AND THE FIRST WORLD WAR

between the opposing trench lines. In practice, these advantages were cancelled out by the fact that the trenches resulted in a stalemate situation. Each side defended its position; neither side proved capable of making a decisive breakthrough.

Soldiers fighting in trenches

There is evidence from the memoirs of soldiers involved in trench warfare to suggest that the stalemate situation was one they themselves encouraged. By doing so, they stood a chance of surviving. In this connection, it should be remembered that battles involving massive slaughter were not a constant feature of the war years, nor did they occur throughout the whole length of the 475 miles of trenches along the Western Front. Soldiers at the Front found that by firing in such a way as not seriously to harm the enemy trenches they were unlikely to become the object of any serious attack themselves. One soldier likened this attitude of the men on both sides to that of the Levite in the biblical parable (*St Luke*, Chapter 10, Verse 32).

> **All patrols – English or German – are much averse to the death or glory principle; so, on running up against one another both pretend they are Levites and the other is a Good Samaritan – and pass by on the other side, no word spoken. For either side to bomb the other would be a useless violation of the unwritten laws that govern the relations of combatants permanently within a hundred yards of each other.**
>
> **Quoted in Tony Ashworth, *Trench Warfare, the Live and Let Live System***

Quite obviously such 'unwritten laws' between the two sides were disapproved of by those who commanded the British Army on the Western Front. This other memoir of the time illustrates the attitude of a senior officer, while at the same time suggesting that the troops along this part of the Front knew how to live with their enemies.

> **The Colonel, much to his disgust, discovered that not a shot was being fired at the enemy as they dodged across the gaps in their trench. They in their turn were allowing our men to cross the gaps in our trench without molestation. This was too much for the Colonel. The first sentry he happened to come across received the full blast of his indignation: 'Man alive, what are you here for? Don't you see these Huns?'**
>
> **Quoted in Tony Ashworth, *Trench Warfare, The Live and Let Live System***

Two views of First World War trenches. The photograph on the left illustrates the main purpose of the trenches as a defensive position from which to fire and advance against the enemy. The photograph on the right illustrates the way in which, for much of the war and in many parts of the Western Front, soldiers succeeded in adapting themselves to the squalid environment which trenches provided.

A HISTORY OF BRITAIN FROM 1867

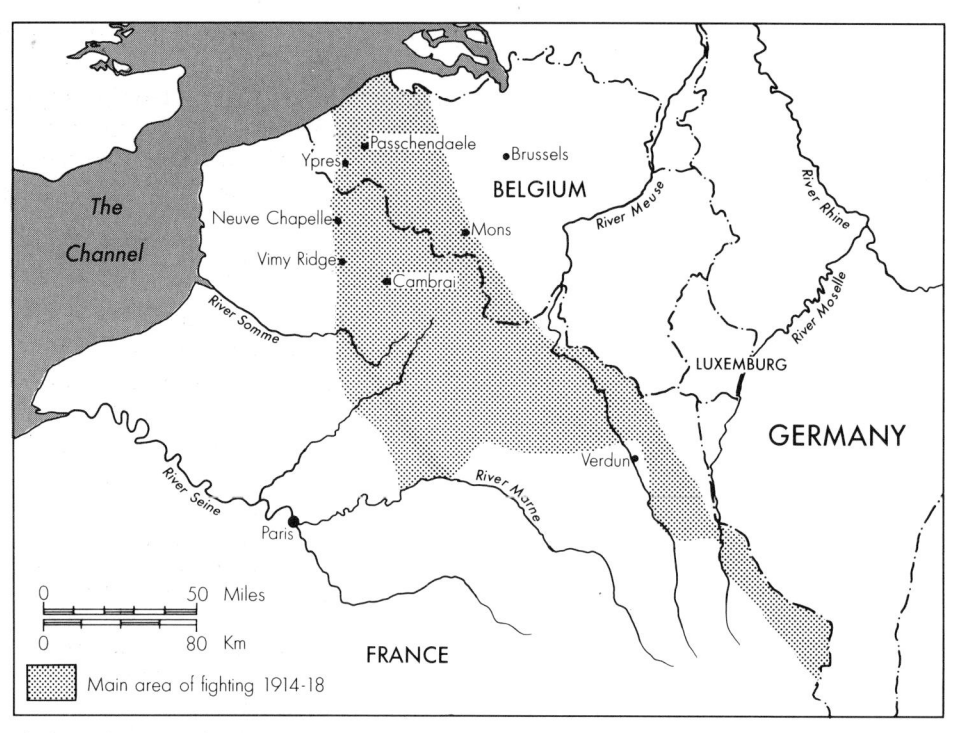

The Western Front in the First World War

Battles launched from trenches

Nevertheless, such situations were completely broken up when there was command for an all-out battle. Determined efforts were made at a breakthrough in the winter and spring of 1914–15. In the first battle of Ypres, in October–November 1914, soldiers fought from trenches, advancing 'over the top' into no-man's land against the enemy. Very high casualty figures accompanied the BEF at this battle and were a foretaste of even higher figures later. Two similar battles occurred in the first few months of 1915. In March some minor British advances were made after a short, bloody campaign at Neuve Chapelle, in France. In May similar minor advances were made after the second battle of Ypres, a battle in which a further element of horror faced the men in the trenches, as for the first time poisoned gas was used by the Germans.

The Dardanelles campaign

Purpose of the campaign

More adventurous members of the government were now seeking other, more promising means of breaking the stalemate of the Western Front by making an opening in the east. Winston Churchill, First Lord of the Admiralty, had put forward such a plan at the end of 1914. What became known as the **Dardanelles campaign** involved an attack on the Ottoman Empire (Turkey), an ally of Germany. This campaign aimed both to defeat the Turks and to open a way through the Dardanelles (see map on page 128) to give assistance to Russia, an ally of both Britain and France. The problem in launching such a campaign was that the men needed for it could not be spared from the Western Front, a zone of fighting to which priority was still given. For this reason the campaign was undertaken mainly by the Navy, with support from the Army.

Its failure

The Dardanelles campaign was a disaster. In March 1915 a combination of poor equipment and inadequate planning resulted in the failure of a naval attempt to breach the Dardanelles straits. Thereafter operations were mainly left to the Army. In the following months a military assault on the western shores of the Gallipoli peninsula was equally ill-fated. Turkish reinforcements had now been sent to the peninsula and put up strong resistance to their enemies, who included Australian and New Zealand troops as well as British. Though landings were made in some parts of the peninsula, the troops were pinned down by enemy attack and made little progress beyond the beaches. To defend themselves they resorted to the digging of trenches. What had been intended as a bold, new venture against the enemy had developed in the same weary way as the fighting on the Western Front. In Britain there was now profound disillusion about the government's conduct of the war.

Wartime politics

Shells scandal

The press gave vent to this sense of disillusion. The disasters, so the press generally argued, were the direct consequence of poor direction of the war by Asquith's Liberal government. Much attention was directed by the newspapers to what they called the **Shells scandal**, the shortage and poor quality of the shells used in the campaigns. *The Times* reported in these terms.

> We are fighting for a cause for which we may have to lay down everything we possess. These things should be said in the great industrial centres, in the factories and in the workshops and the shipyards. The repeated appeals of our military correspondent for more shells are most painful reading. 'We need,' he says, 'more high explosives, more heavy howitzers, and more men.' Another informant has said that a million and a half rounds were fired between Saturday and Tuesday night, and yet this did not suffice. This is a war of artillery, and more and more it is coming to depend upon the supply of armaments. We are told that the new German infantry formations are in many cases inferior to our own, but that their artillery is good and lavishly supplied. British soldiers are dying in vain because more shells are needed. The government, who have so severely failed to organise adequately our national resources, must bear their share of the grave responsibility.
>
> *The Times*, April 1915

There certainly was truth in these criticisms. The Shells scandal was not however the only reason for failure. Though not much commented upon at the time, the poor quality of the military leadership was as important as the poor quality of the shells. Asquith responded in May 1915 by forming the first of the two Coalition governments of the First World War. He continued as Prime Minister of a government that contained Conservatives, Liberals and also Labour members. Arthur Henderson, who had become leader of the Labour party at the outbreak of war, served in the government and was the first Labour politician to hold government office.

Introduction of safeguarding

In the autumn of 1915 the Chancellor of the Exchequer, Reginald McKenna, introduced a budget designed to meet the wartime situation. An excess-profits tax was imposed in an attempt – though not particularly successful – to curb 'profiteering' by businessmen who were taking advantage of wartime circumstances. More significantly, McKenna introduced import duties of one third on various luxury items. The imposing of these fairly limited duties was referred to as a policy of **safeguarding**. In practice, it represented an introduction of the controversial policy of **protection**. Many Liberals were concerned that it was a Chancellor from their own party who had taken this step.

Lloyd George as Minister of Munitions

The most notable appointment of Asquith's Coalition was Lloyd George as Minister of Munitions. Over the following eighteen months, Lloyd George directed his ministry as a highly successful business concern, able to produce the weapons of war efficiently and in large numbers. His growing reputation as a politician determined single-mindedly to achieve victory as soon as possible was shortly to turn to his own advantage.

Lloyd George becomes Prime Minister

DELIVERING THE GOODS.

Lloyd George's skill in directing the two elements essential for wartime munition production was widely praised, as this cartoon of April 1915 suggests. The vigour of the new Minister of Munitions was to lead to his appointment as Prime Minister at the end of the following year.

Defence of the Realm Act

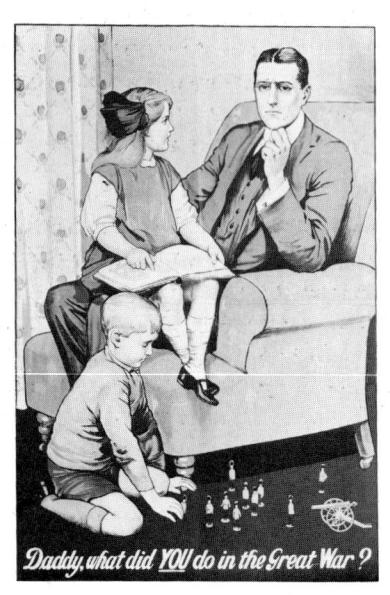

Before conscription was introduced in 1916, posters such as this were considered essential. Notice the appeal that this poster makes to a sense of guilt.

Wartime legislation

Lloyd George's success had meanwhile attracted a personal following among many Liberal MPs. In comparison, Asquith seemed weak and ineffective. Towards the end of 1916, Lloyd George suggested that the war should be directed by a small war committee, within which he – not Asquith – would be the dominant influence. After typical hesitations, Asquith rejected Lloyd George's suggestion; in consequence, Lloyd George resigned. This dramatic step widened his support, as the war's direction would certainly falter without his assertive presence in the government. Labour MPs and some Conservative MPs joined the ranks of his Liberal supporters; and many newspapers urged his appointment as Prime Minister. In these circumstances, Asquith had little option but to resign as Prime Minister in December 1916 and to make way for Lloyd George. The new Prime Minister appointed a much smaller Coalition cabinet, rather similar to the war committee he had suggested. Though more energy and determination were now expected from the government, it was almost another two years before the war came to an end.

Increased government powers

A country's domestic development is always affected by the upheavals that accompany its involvement in a war. In the case of the First World War – and the Second World War later on – the effects were to be profound and, in many cases, long-lasting. Historians have later spoken of the two world wars as **total wars**, ones which affected deeply the lives of everyone in Britain, whether or not they were in the armed forces. Within Britain, some of these effects of the First World War led to severe restrictions on people's liberties; others led to wide extension of people's liberties, often in a permanent way.

The Defence of the Realm Act (DORA) was passed in August 1914 and remained in force throughout the war. It gave to the government stronger powers than it had in peacetime. Provision was made for the censorship of newspapers and for the nationalisation of key industries. In spite of DORA, the government during the early stages of the war encouraged life in Britain to continue as usual. In most respects it did. The war was still generally thought to be something far away, which the volunteer army would quite swiftly win. But victory did not come quickly, and by mid 1915 the number of volunteers was less than earlier.

Pressure for **conscription**, making military service compulsory for all men, was mounting during 1915. The Coalition government gave way to it. Many Liberal and Labour MPs, however, wanted to keep military service voluntary. So at first a compromise known as **Lord Derby's scheme** was suggested, by which men publicly stated their willingness to fight, if called upon to do so. Public opinion was not satisfied by Lord Derby's scheme. Consequently, in January 1916, the government introduced conscription for unmarried men below the age of 41 and extended conscription in May 1916 to married men in the same category. Munition workers and workers in essential industries were to be exempt. **Conscientious objectors**, who refused military service, were treated with little sympathy. Alternative, non-fighting work for the war effort was offered, and accepted by most of them. Those who refused this alternative work were subjected to degrading treatment in prisons, while a few were for a time forcibly sent to the fighting on the Western Front.

The increased power of the government was shown in other less important ways. One concerned licensing hours. A constant complaint in the early months of the war was that soldiers returning from leave and workers in munition factories were often drunk. In Lloyd George's view the country faced three enemies: 'Germany, Austria and drink'. Previously there had been no overall restriction on pub hours, but a series of acts in 1914–15 reduced opening hours and increased tax on drink. Britain's drinking habits were permanently modified by

BRITAIN AND THE FIRST WORLD WAR

this First World War legislation. Of similar permanence was the introduction of summer time, the longer summer evenings being regarded as helpful to the war effort. Only in the last year of the war did the government begin to ration food, a move caused more by panic buying than by any serious shortages. The Fisher Education Act of 1918 was one of the few acts of long-term importance passed during the war. It raised the school-leaving age to 14 and made provision for part-time education between 14 and 18. Unfortunately, post-war financial cuts limited the Act's usefulness.

Women during the First World War

The war brought a great change to the position of women within Britain. By 1915 many of the women employed in munition factories and elsewhere on war work were no longer women who would have been in employment before the war. Partly this was a result of pressure by the women's suffrage societies, most of whose members temporarily dropped their suffrage claims in favour of fuller involvement of women in the war effort. Partly it was the result of the increasing need to get women to fill the places left by the men fighting abroad. By 1916, after conscription had been introduced, the number of women munition workers had increased substantially and women were now involved in many different types of work. Some became nurses; others entered the women's military organisations that came into being during the war, such as the Women's Auxiliary Army Corps (WAACS); women police were recruited for the first time. Women now worked in full public view as conductresses on public transport. Work as bank clerks and shorthand typists attracted others; teaching, which had always employed quite a high proportion of women, now employed more. The only traditional woman's occupation to show a marked decline in its numbers was domestic service, as prospects for employment elsewhere were now so much more attractive. For most women, their new work was quite reasonably paid and gave them a greater degree of independence and freedom than they had previously had. Though it was expected that the women would give up their work to the returning men, the war had nevertheless produced a fundamental change in the position of women in society. After the war it was to prove a permanent change.

The work of a bus conductress was just one of a number of jobs taken on by women during the First World War. Their vital contribution to the war effort resulted in new attitudes towards their role in society.

Votes for women obtained

As the war progressed, it became certain that women would now secure the vote. Their contribution to the war effort coupled, possibly, to the end of the militant protests of the pre-war suffragettes, reduced opposition to their cause. In 1918 the female vote was obtained as part of a general widening of the franchise, for men as well as for women. It seemed wrong that many of the men fighting for their country were unable, simply by not meeting the property requirements of the previous Parliamentary Reform Act of 1884, to cast their vote. In the Representation of the People Act of February 1918, two new changes were made to the British parliamentary system. The old property qualifications were completely removed, so that all men over 21 (though subject to six months residence at their address) were allowed to vote. The vote was now to be allowed to all women over 30. Why was there the difference in voting age between the sexes? Largely because women formed a majority of the population and it was not considered right that their votes should be allowed so suddenly to form a majority. Ten years later few opposed the abolition of this age difference.

The fighting at sea

U-boat campaigns

In the years before 1914, it had been widely imagined that the Royal Navy would play a decisive role in bringing about British victory in a future war. Yet the fighting on land came to have greater importance. For the first two years of the war the German fleet refused to come out of port, preferring not to seek a major engagement. In these years the Royal Navy did, however, play a vital role in two ways: it blockaded the German ports, while at the same time it kept open the sea approaches to Britain. Neither task was easy, and each was made more difficult by the threatening presence of German U-boats (submarines). These were a constant source of trouble for the British, as detection of them was difficult and the torpedoes they launched could sink a ship completely. Much anger was provoked when in May 1915 a German torpedo sank the *Lusitania*, as the ship was known to be carrying passengers who were citizens of the United States, at that time a neutral country.

Battle of Jutland

Early in 1916, German tactics at sea changed. The U-boat campaign became less intense and the German fleet now came out more frequently from its North Sea and Baltic harbours. This gave the British naval commanders the chance for the large naval battle that many felt would decide the war's outcome. But when the two fleets eventually fought at the battle of Jutland in May 1916, the result was far from decisive. It was virtually by accident that the two fleets met. After some brief fighting, the German fleet withdrew to port. Though it had certainly not been destroyed, it did not reappear for the rest of the war. The battle could therefore be said to have been a partial victory for Britain, though far from an overwhelming victory such as that of Nelson at Trafalgar more than a century previously. That was the style of decisive encounter for which many British naval enthusiasts had hoped.

Unrestricted submarine warfare

After the battle of Jutland and the virtual isolation of the German fleet in port, German tactics at sea again changed. Once again they placed their confidence in submarine warfare. This now became more of a threat than it had been earlier. Supplies to Britain began to be badly affected as many ships were sunk. To combat this menace, the **convoy system** was introduced in April 1917. By travelling together in convoys, shipping losses were substantially reduced. German use of submarines was to rebound badly on the Germans themselves. In January 1917 they had begun what was termed **unrestricted warfare**, in which their policy was to attack the ships of neutral countries that appeared to be aiding their enemies. This involved attacking US ships and became one of the most important factors in the US government's decision to enter the war three months later: a fatal decision from Germany's point of view, and one of much value to Britain.

The war on land

Senior command

Meantime, on the Western Front, new men had appeared intent on directing the war more forcefully. Sir William Robertson took overall command as **Chief of the Imperial General Staff**, a position which he insisted should be superior to that of the Secretary for War, Lord Kitchener. In June 1916 Lord Kitchener was drowned when the ship in which he was travelling to Russia was torpedoed. Though he had enjoyed much popularity as a war leader, there were doubts about his ability as Secretary for War. He was succeeded in that post by Lloyd George who, like Kitchener, found relations with Robertson uneasy. Sir Douglas Haig had meantime been appointed British **Commander-in-Chief** in France. Robertson and Haig were to have profound influence on the course of events along the Western Front. It was there, rather than anywhere else, that in their opinion the war would be won.

Battles of Verdun and the Somme

In 1916 there were two formidable battles on the Western Front: Verdun and the Somme. Few British soldiers were involved in the defence of Verdun, which was almost entirely a French operation. The Somme was mainly a British operation, directed by Haig, who was confident of victory due to the large number of men available for the attack. But a breakthrough from the British trenches failed at the beginning of July and the miserable battle dragged on until November. No gain had been made, in spite of vast slaughter, especially in the early days of the struggle. Some 420 000 British lives were lost at the Somme; French and German losses were also very high. A mood of disillusion now set in.

The war poets

There developed an intense sense of the war's futility and of total helplessness in the struggle. The **war poets** such as Edmund Blunden, Wilfred Owen and Siegfried Sassoon sensitively captured the disillusion of the last two years of the First World War. This poem by Sassoon illustrates the mood of these years, and the lack of confidence in the men who were directing the war.

The General

'Good-morning; good-morning!' the General said
When we met him last week on our way to the line.
Now the soldiers he smiled at are most of 'em dead,
And we're cursing his staff for incompetent swine.
'He's a cheery old card,' grunted Harry to Jack
As they slogged up to Arras with rifle and pack.
* * *
But he did for them both by his plan of attack.

Lloyd George's direction of the war

Lloyd George took over as Prime Minister just after the Somme. As we have seen, he intended to bring to the overall direction of the war the type of vigour he had earlier shown as Minister of Munitions. New ministries were created, new men were introduced to oversee the war's direction. His hope of producing better co-ordination among the Allies was never completely fulfilled. He did, however, establish better relations with the French commander, Nivelle, and British troops became a vital part of the Nivelle offensive in April 1917. This was intended as a surprise attack, but the enemy were well aware it was about to be launched and took necessary precautions. Loss of human life was again considerable, though by no means so great as at the Somme. There was one successful feature to the offensive: the capture and defence of Vimy Ridge by Canadian troops, an achievement which emphasised the continuing commitment of the dominion countries to the war effort.

Battle of Passchendaele

Other attempts were made. Haig became convinced of the usefulness of an attack in the Flanders region. Somewhat reluctantly – as they feared a repetition of the Somme disasters of the previous year – the war cabinet gave its approval. Disaster accompanied this attempt to break the enemy line just as much as it had the earlier ones. Conditions for the soldiers became more than usually atrocious in August 1917, as the combined effects of heavy rain and heavy bombardment were to reduce the battlefield – known as Passchendaele – to a sea of mud. Soldiers floundered hopelessly as for three months the battle was relentlessly pursued, again for minimal advantage: on this occasion, four miles.

Tanks

Tanks had been used for the first time at the Somme. It was hoped their weight and manoeuvrability would break the enemy lines. They had failed to do this at the Somme; and at Passchendaele they only made the muddy conditions worse. They did have a success in firmer terrain further south at Cambrai before the end of the year. No real advance was made at Cambrai however, as there were not enough troops there to exploit the initial advantage produced by the tanks.

The final stages

Fighting against the Ottoman Empire

Amidst this desperate situation on the Western Front, there were some signs of hope. Throughout the war, between one and two million British soldiers had been fighting in a series of extensive campaigns against the Ottoman Empire, Germany's ally. The climate made the fighting in these campaigns very far from

The Ottoman Empire at the time of the First World War

the Western Front particularly difficult. The campaigns were marked by serious reversals and slow progress, though nothing comparable with trench warfare was to be found. In Mesopotamia, the siege of Kut-el-Amara had ended in the humiliating surrender of British forces in April 1916. The campaign nevertheless continued and produced some impressive advances; Baghdad had been reached by the end of 1917. In parts of the Ottoman Empire, the British got some advantage by allying with peoples seeking to overthrow Ottoman dominance. The guerrilla campaigns of Colonel T.E. Lawrence in Arabia owed much of their success to the willing co-operation of the Arabs on the British side against the Turks. General Allenby had similar co-operation in the campaigns that resulted in the fall of Jerusalem at the end of 1917 and the persistent though slow advance into Syria during the following year. These successes in the Middle East in 1917 brought the British public some relief from the disastrous events along the Western Front. But their value in the war's overall strategy was limited, as Germany was not seriously harmed by anything that happened in the Middle East.

The entry of the United States

In April 1917 the United States finally decided to enter the war on the Allied side. The German use of unrestricted submarine warfare since early in 1917 had particularly angered them. The final event that persuaded the US government to join the fighting was Germany's offer of assistance to Mexico for an invasion of the United States. It was British intelligence that revealed this offer to the US government. The offer was sent in a coded telegram, known as the **Zimmermann telegram**, which British intelligence experts intercepted and decoded and which the British government revealed to the US government. However, it was not until 1918 that US troops became fully involved in the European fighting.

BRITAIN AND THE FIRST WORLD WAR

The Ludendorff offensive

In the spring of 1918 the Ludendorff offensive was launched, with skill and surprise, by the Germans in the Somme region. The British forces retreated in disorder. It was a rare occasion when substantial gains were swiftly made. In launching the Ludendorff offensive, the Germans were reaping the advantage of no longer needing to fight on their Eastern Front, as the new Communist government in Russia had withdrawn from the war at the end of 1917. There was now a real prospect of total German victory.

The final breakthrough

Lloyd George appealed for full military support from the United States. President Wilson responded and by the summer of 1918 substantial US troops arrived in Europe, supplemented by British troops diverted from the Middle East, and others that had been held in reserve within Britain. By the summer the German troops were finding difficulty in sustaining their recent advances. Events elsewhere were to Germany's disadvantage. By the autumn the other Central Powers – Austria-Hungary, Bulgaria and the Ottoman Empire – had all made peace; the German navy was in mutiny and many German towns were disturbed by revolution. In these circumstances the Allied forces were able to make a series of successful attacks against the Germans, who now themselves faced defeat. In early November 1918 a new German government agreed to an armistice on the basis of the liberal ideals represented by President Wilson's Fourteen Points (page 167) and the fighting at last ceased.

EXERCISES

1. (a) Outline the course of the fighting along the Western Front during the first 12 months of the First World War.
   (b) Explain why the Dardanelles campaign was started in 1915 and why it failed.
   (c) How do you explain the eventual victory of the Allied forces along the Western Front by 1918?

2. (a) Explain the circumstances that led to the formation of:
   (i) Asquith's coalition government in May 1915, and
   (ii) Lloyd George's coalition government in December 1916.
   (b) How successfully did Lloyd George direct the British war effort during the last two years of the First World War?

3. Imagine you are a soldier fighting in the trenches along the Western Front during the First World War. Write three letters home, for any three different years of the war, explaining what your life is like and your thoughts about the war and how it is being fought.

4. Study the poster on page 124 and the two photographs on page 121 and then answer questions (a) and (c) which follow.

   (a) With reference to the poster on page 124:
   (i) What was the purpose of a poster such as this and how did it attempt to achieve this purpose?
   (ii) Explain why posters such as this were necessary in the war's early stages, but unnecessary in the war's later stages. (4+3)
   (b) The two photographs on page 121 give differing impressions of life in the trenches:
   (i) Describe the strict purpose of trench warfare, as illustrated in the photograph on the left. Explain how the photograph helps you to understand this purpose.
   (ii) Describe the atmosphere illustrated in the photograph on the right. Explain why trench warfare sometimes developed in this way. (3+3)
   (c) (i) Describe two attempts made by the Allied forces on the Western Front to break out of the trench warfare situation.
   (ii) Why do you think it was so difficult to do so? (4+3)

1867–1918: Chart of events

A heavy line marks a change of government. Note that the month given for the appointment of a government is not always the same as the month of the general election, as there has sometimes been a short lapse of time between the election and the government's appointment. Remember also that there can be a change of government without a general election having taken place.

Year	Appointment of governments and succession of monarchs	Domestic events — Britain	Domestic events — Ireland	Empire events	Foreign events
1866	Derby-Disraeli, Conservative				
1867		Second Parliamentary Reform Act; Hornby versus Close		Canada a dominion	
1868		TUC first meets			
Dec.	Gladstone (first), Liberal				
1869		Report of Royal Commission on trade unions	Irish Church Act		
1870		Civil service examinations; Forster Education Act; Cardwell army reforms, early 1870s	Land Act; Obstruction by Irish Nationalist MPs, early 1870s		Franco-Prussian War, 1870–71; Russia breaks Black Sea clauses
1871		Universities Tests Act; Trade Union Act; Criminal Law Amendment Act			
1872		Ballot Act; Licensing Act; Crystal Palace speech by Disraeli			*Alabama* award
1873			Irish University Bill		
1874 Feb.	Disraeli (second), Conservative	Public Worship Regulation Act; Factory Act			
1875		Public Health Act; Sale of Food and Drugs Act; River Pollution Act; Conspiracy and Protection of Property Act; Employers and Workmen Act		Purchase of shares in Suez Canal Company	Rebellion in Bosnia
1876		Merchant Shipping Act; Sandon Education Act		Royal Titles Act	Rebellion in Bulgaria
1877				Annexation of the Transvaal	

1867–1918: CHART OF EVENTS

Year	Appointment of governments and succession of monarchs	Domestic events — Britain	Domestic events — Ireland	Empire events	Foreign events
1878		Factory Act		Joint Anglo-French administration of Egypt Roberts's campaigns in Afghanistan, 1878–80	Treaty of San Stefano and Treaty of Berlin
1879		First Midlothian campaign of Gladstone	Land League formed	Zulu War	
1880		Second Midlothian campaign of Gladstone		First Boer War, 1880–81	
April	Gladstone (second), Liberal	Mundella Education Act Randolph Churchill's Fourth Party, early 1880s			
1881		Social Democratic Federation formed	Coercion Act Land (Three Fs) Act		
1882		Married Women's Property Act	Kilmainham Treaty Phoenix Park murders	Battle of Tel-el-Kebir	
1883		Corrupt and Illegal Practices Act			
1884		Third Parliamentary Reform Act Fabian Society formed		Gordon in the Sudan, 1884–85 Berlin Conference, 1884–85	
1885				Pendjeh incident	
June	Salisbury (first), Conservative		Ashbourne Land Act		
1886 Feb.	Gladstone (third), Liberal	Liberal Unionists split from Liberals	First Home Rule Bill	Indian National Congress formed	
Aug.	Salisbury (second), Conservative				
1887			Plan of Campaign by National League, late 1880s		
1888		Local Government Act	Land Purchase Act		
1889		London Dock Strike Technical Instruction Act		British South Africa Company formed	
1890		Housing of the Working Classes Act	O'Shea divorce case		Accession of Kaiser Wilhelm II in Germany
1891		Elementary school fees abolished Newcastle Programme of Liberals	Land Purchase Act		
1892 Aug.	Gladstone (fourth), Liberal				
1893		Independent Labour party formed	Second Home Rule Bill Ulster Defence Union formed Gaelic League formed		

A HISTORY OF BRITAIN FROM 1867

Year	Appointment of governments and succession of monarchs	Domestic events — Britain	Domestic events — Ireland	Empire events	Foreign events
1894 Mar.	Rosebery, Liberal	Local Government Act			
1895		Death duties introduced			
June	Salisbury (third), Conservative			Jameson Raid Joseph Chamberlain, Colonial Secretary, 1895–1903	
1896			Land Purchase Act		
1897		Workmen's Compensation Act			
1898				Battle of Omdurman Fashoda incident	
1899				Second Boer War, 1899–1902	
1900		Labour Representation Committee formed			
1901	Accession of King Edward VII	Taff Vale judgement Rowntree, *Poverty: A Study of Town Life*		Australia a dominion	
1902 July	Balfour, Conservative	Morant Education Act	Sinn Fein party formed	Treaty of Vereeniging	Anglo-Japanese Alliance
1903		Joseph Chamberlain launches tariff reform campaign Women's Social and Political Union formed Charles Booth, *Life and Labour of the London Poor*	Wyndham Land Purchase Act		
1904		Licensing Act	Schemes for Irish devolution		Anglo-French Entente
1905		Unemployed Workmen Act			First Moroccan crisis
Dec.	Campbell-Bannerman, Liberal				
1906		Trade Disputes Act Merchant Shipping Act Workmen's Compensation Act Free school meals begin			Algeçiras Conference Launch of first dreadnought
1907		School medical inspections begin			Anglo-Russian Convention
1908 April	Asquith, Liberal	Children's Charter Old Age Pensions Act Miners' eight-hour day established			Austria-Hungary annexes Bosnia
1909		Osborne judgement Trade Boards Act People's Budget		Morley-Minto reforms in India South Africa Act	
1910	Accession of King George V	Two general elections			

1867–1918: CHART OF EVENTS

Year	Appointment of governments and succession of monarchs	Domestic events — Britain	Domestic events — Ireland	Empire events	Foreign events
1911		Payment of MPs begins Parliament Act National Insurance Act Widespread strikes, 1911–14			Second Moroccan crisis
1912			Third Home Rule Bill Ulster Volunteers formed		
1913		Trade Union Act 'Cat and Mouse' Act	Irish Volunteers formed		
1914		Triple Industrial Alliance formed Defence of the Realm Act	The Curragh 'mutiny'		Assassination of Franz Ferdinand at Sarajevo *First World War, 1914–18*: German invasion of Belgium **Sept:** Battle of the Marne **Oct.–Nov:** First battle of Ypres
1915					**March:** Battle of Neuve Chapelle **March:** Dardanelles campaign starts
May	Asquith, Coalition	McKenna duties Lord Derby's scheme			**May:** Second battle of Ypres
1916		Conscription introduced	Easter Rising in Dublin		**Feb:** German assault on Verdun begins **April:** British surrender at Kut-el-Amara **May:** Battle of Jutland **July–Nov:** Battle of the Somme
Dec.	Lloyd George, wartime Coalition				
1917				Balfour Declaration (on Palestine)	**April:** Nivelle offensive **April:** Convoys introduced **August:** Battle of Passchendaele Revolutions in Russia in February and October
1918		Representation of the People Act Fisher Education Act			**Spring:** Ludendorff offensive **Nov:** German surrender
Dec.	Lloyd George, post-war Coalition				

11 POLITICAL AND ECONOMIC CHANGE IN THE POST-WAR YEARS

Adjustment within Britain to peacetime circumstances after the devastation and upheavals of the First World War would not be easy. Many returned from the fighting with hopes raised that within Britain a fairer society might now develop and poverty might be reduced. Others sought quite definitely to turn the clock back and restore pre-war values. With such diverse views, it is not surprising that the years after the First World War were marked by change and conflict within Britain.

Domestic issues

The Coupon Election

It had been impossible for a general election to be held during the war, so the election of December 1918 was the first for eight years. At the end of the war, it was only to be expected that Lloyd George, the Prime Minister who had successfully led Britain to victory, would be a popular man. So also was his Coalition government. The Liberal party and the Conservative party therefore decided to continue to work together and to fight the election jointly. The leaders of the two parties, Bonar Law for the Conservatives and Lloyd George for the Liberals, showed their acceptance of those parliamentary candidates in both their parties who stood for the Coalition by giving them a letter of approval which became known as the **coupon**. The result of the **Coupon Election** showed that the approach of the Conservative and Liberal leaders had paid off well, and the Coalition government was returned with a very large majority.

Women cast their vote for the first time in the Coupon Election of December 1918. The achievement of this goal was partly a result of suffragette activity, but mainly a result of the contribution of women to the war effort.

General Election: December 1918	
Coalition	478
Conservatives not supporting the Coalition	48
Irish Nationalists	7
Labour	63
Liberals not supporting the Coalition	28
Sinn Fein	73

So the opposition in the House of Commons was small, consisting of some Conservatives who did not support the Coalition, those Liberals who under Asquith's leadership also refused their support, and the Labour party. Additionally there were the Sinn Fein MPs from Ireland.

Housing

At the time of the Coupon Election Lloyd George had promised to provide for the returning soldiers 'homes fit for heroes'. That would be no easy task. In the pre-war years, governments had generally ignored housing problems, while during the war years themselves little attention had been given to house building or repairs. Large parts of many towns had declined into slums. The Coalition government viewed housing as closely linked to health, and set up a Ministry of Health to have responsibility for both.

Christopher Addison

In charge of it was one of the men who had worked successfully with Lloyd George in the wartime Ministry of Munitions: Christopher Addison. His Housing Act of 1919 was to encourage local authorities to construct council

POLITICAL AND ECONOMIC CHANGE IN THE POST-WAR YEARS

houses for rent and to finance this construction by government grant. Addison now brought to house building the dynamism he had earlier shown in munitions manufacture, and as a result of his work at the Ministry of Health more than 200 000 houses were built.

These early council houses were very different in design to those of pre-war years. More attention was given to spacing out the houses so that there was room for the planting of gardens. Tenants on the new estates were therefore less crowded than in the older housing of the previous century. The flaw in Addison's work was the lavish and at times wasteful generosity with which government grants were made. Criticism mounted on this account. In 1921, Addison was as a result forced to resign and the work he had started then received less attention.

Unemployment insurance National Insurance had been the great achievement of the Liberals before the war, but only limited provision had been made, in Part II of the 1911 Act, for insurance against unemployment. During the war the restricted list of workers to whom the Act applied had been extended to munition workers. In 1920 the Unemployment Insurance Act provided insurance against unemployment for almost all workers. Unemployment was not at that time particularly high, and so the Act initially operated without much difficulty. By the beginning of 1921, however, unemployment had increased dramatically and by the middle of that year it had reached two million.

The dole To operate the Act as the **insurance** scheme it was intended to be now proved impossible. The insurance fund to which workers contributed for payment in the event of unemployment just did not contain enough money to cater for so large a number of unemployed people. In spite of this difficulty, the government continued to provide unemployment benefit. The term **uncovenanted benefit** was often applied to the money now received, as it was provided without being 'covenanted for' or 'agreed for' by an earlier contribution to the insurance fund. Another, more common term for it was the **dole**. An allied measure was the Unemployed Workers' Dependants Act which in 1921, for the first time, provided benefit for the members of the family of an unemployed man.

Beginnings of mass unemployment By its actions in the year when mass unemployment first became a serious problem in Britain, the Coalition government set the pattern for government action during the inter-war years. Whatever criticisms might be made – as they often were – that the cash received by the unemployed was too small for their needs, there was always at least some provision made for them by the government of the day. In this respect, unemployed workers in Britain were more fortunate than those in most other countries at that time.

Industrial unrest

Just as the immediate pre-war years had been ones of industrial unrest, so also were the immediate post-war years. A temporary boom during 1919 and most of 1920 helped to reduce tension, though it never entirely disappeared. It became more serious once again with the beginning of the Depression in 1921. But industrial unrest never got out of hand in these years and a general strike planned for 1921 was called off at a late stage.

Industrial relations How did the government manage to avoid the problem that it appeared to face in its relations with industrial workers? Essentially by a policy of compromise. It decreed that minimum wage levels, which had been legally guaranteed during the war, should continue until the autumn of 1920. When serious disruption threatened the coal mining industry in 1919 the government successfully defused a dangerous situation by an act of parliament reducing the miners' working day from eight to seven hours. Similarly, when trouble arose among the dockers in 1920, a government committee of enquiry resulted in improved working conditions.

The miners' strike

The government was lucky to escape the threatened general strike. In the spring of 1921 the mines were again restored to their owners from the temporary government control set up during the war. The policies of the owners – particularly their insistence on lower wages – led to a strike by the miners. Though it appeared likely at one stage that the other members of the Triple Industrial Alliance would support the miners in their struggle, in the event they did not do so. The government may have avoided a most serious industrial dispute, but the miners remained bitter at their treatment in 1921 and their continuing discontent was to lead to the General Strike of 1926, five years later. The whole issue of the mining industry in these years is considered more fully at the start of the next chapter on pages 144–6.

Ireland after the First World War

The Easter Rising

Irish home rule had been postponed by the outbreak of the First World War in 1914. Generally, for the next four years, Irish from both north and south supported the British war effort; some thought that this joint involvement in the fighting might form a useful basis for the home rule that was expected to follow when the war ended. This comparative quietness in Irish affairs had been shattered by events in Dublin during Easter Week of 1916. A group of Irish politicians staged a rebellion, seized control of the city's General Post Office and from it proclaimed an Irish Republic, totally cutting all connections with Britain. Government forces had been taken unawares by the suddenness of this rising, but by the end of the week had managed to suppress it and restore order. The whole episode might well have been forgotten had it not been for the decision of the government to execute 15 of the leading rebels. This action by the government transformed the rebels into martyrs and ensured that the Easter Rising would not be forgotten.

The growth of Sinn Fein

By the end of the war, Sinn Fein was no longer a minority party. Under the leadership of Eamon de Valera, who had been imprisoned for his part in the Easter Rising, Sinn Fein had attracted widespread support. One of de Valera's associates was Michael Collins, shortly to play an important part in directing the fighting needed to bring an independent Ireland into being. Sinn Fein had an opportunity of revealing its strength in the Coupon Election of 1918. As has been shown on page 134, Sinn Fein won an overwhelming victory at the election and virtually put the Irish Nationalist party out of existence. Ireland now asserted its demand for independence, and that independence involved – so far as Sinn Fein was concerned – the inclusion of Ulster.

The Dail

The elected Sinn Fein members refused to go to Westminster. They instead met as a **Dail** (Assembly) at Dublin at the beginning of 1919 and claimed responsibility for the governing of an independent Ireland. There were therefore two governments in Ireland: the official, British government exercising power from Westminster, and the unofficial Dail government exercising power from Dublin. Throughout 1919 these two rival governments existed uneasily together. By 1920 the British government decided to suppress what it regarded as an upstart government.

Warfare in Ireland

By now the pre-war Irish Volunteers had given way to the Irish Republican Army (IRA), an anonymous and secretive army, active in guerrilla attacks against the police. To meet this desperate situation, the British government sent to Ireland a force of volunteer ex-soldiers. They became known, from their wearing of a curious mixture of black hats with khaki uniforms, as the **Black and Tans**. They were assisted in their work by the **Auxis**, the Auxiliary division of the Irish Constabulary. Between them the Black and Tans and the Auxis earned an appalling reputation for violent, often spontaneous reprisals against the Irish, with little enquiry made about the guilt of those whom they

POLITICAL AND ECONOMIC CHANGE IN THE POST-WAR YEARS

attacked. Neither side was getting the better of the other and by 1921 some sort of compromise was the hope of both.

Government of Ireland Act

In all of this turmoil, the old issue of home rule had been all but forgotten. But the British government now went back to it as the best means of resolving the fresh turn which the Irish problem had taken since the end of the war. In December 1920 the Government of Ireland Act was passed at Westminster. Ireland was to be divided into two: six of the nine Ulster counties were to come under their own government at Belfast and the rest of the country, including the three remaining Ulster counties, were to be governed from Dublin. The powers of each separate government were close to those allowed for in the pre-war Third Home Rule Bill. Both parts of Ireland were still to come under the overall control of the Westminster government. By the summer of 1921 these arrangements had been accepted in the north and Sir James Craig had become Prime Minister of a Unionist government there.

The Irish Free State

Further south, the proposals met with total rejection. Sinn Fein opposed both the separation of the northern counties and the setting up of a government in the south that was to come under any form of British control. Nevertheless, Sinn Fein politicians – among whom Griffith and Collins were prominent – negotiated with the British government during the second half of 1921 and in December an agreement was reached. The south of Ireland was to form the **Irish Free State** and was to receive dominion status within the British Empire. Northern Ireland was to be excluded from it; some Irish ports were to remain under British control for defence purposes.

Controversy over the 'treaty'

This agreement represented a triumph for Lloyd George's government. Negotiations had been difficult and the final outcome was to form a satisfactory basis for peace. It nevertheless sparked off fierce controversy among Sinn Fein politicians. Many, including de Valera, held that the negotiators had no right to sign such a 'treaty' and they refused to recognise its contents. For them, continued acceptance of any form of British rule was a denial of the main principles on which Sinn Fein was founded. The negotiators, for their part, argued that what

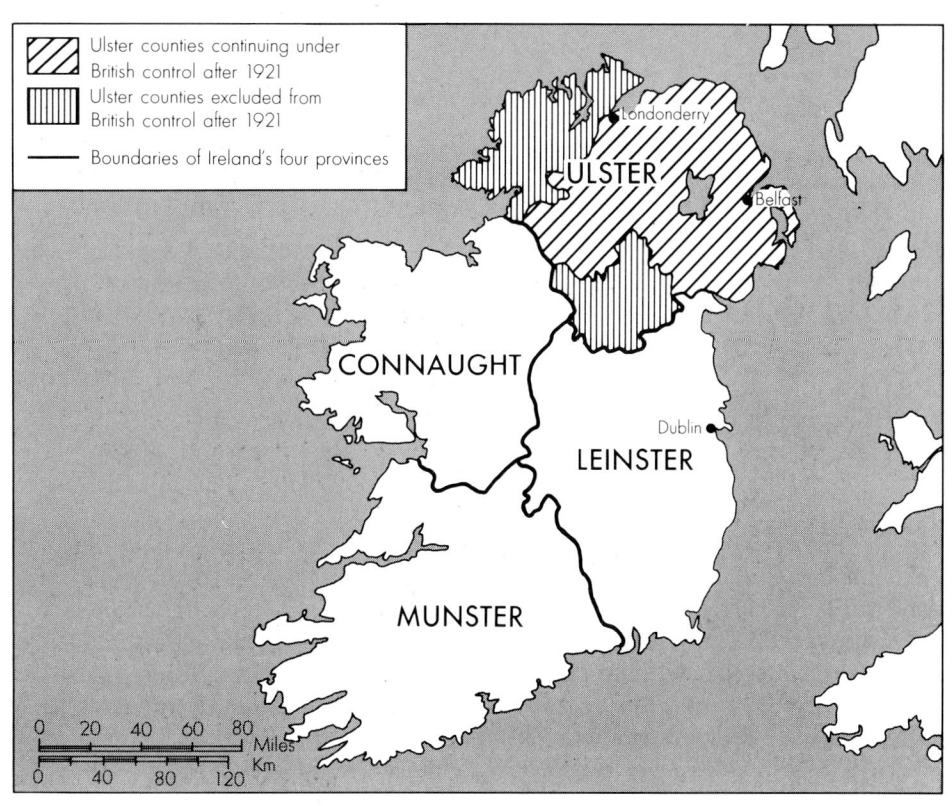

Ireland

the 'treaty' contained was the best they could achieve at that time and was a step towards complete independence. For more than a year after the 'treaty' had been signed, further violence occurred between its supporters and its opponents. By 1923 the fighting had died down and Ireland, though divided, entered upon years of comparative peace.

The fall of the Coalition

Criticisms of the Coalition

Lloyd George's Coalition government collapsed quite suddenly in October 1922. Criticism of the Prime Minister by politicians had been increasing. The selling of honours had attracted much unfavourable attention. Lloyd George had set up a list of the payments expected by those who wanted to receive a political honour and the large sum of money received in this way went into a political fund under his control. Many felt that the whole idea of political honours was devalued by the need to pay for them. It was also suggested that the Prime Minister had failed to give enough attention to solving the difficulties that the Depression of the early 1920s was causing in the lives of many people. The Geddes committee on government expenditure had recommended severe cuts in February 1922. The Fisher Education Act of 1918 was a particular victim of the **Geddes Axe**, the name applied to this policy of reduced spending. Above all, criticism was made of the whole style of Lloyd George's premiership. It was said that he acted more like a US President than a British Prime Minister and that he ignored parliament.

The Chanak incident

His fall from power came over a matter involving the Ottoman Empire. Angered by the ease with which their rulers had agreed to the loss of territory by the terms of the 1920 Treaty of Sèvres, many Turks gave their support to a developing nationalist movement. Under the inspiring leadership of Mustafa Kemal, this movement was by the summer of 1922 threatening to destroy Ottoman rule. In the hope of using Ottoman power as a means of furthering British interests in the Middle East, Lloyd George wished to defend the terms of the Treaty of Sèvres and opposed Mustafa Kemal's further advances. Orders were given for British troops to bar his advance at a place near the Dardanelles, called Chanak. As it was generally considered that Mustafa Kemal would succeed in his aim, no other European power joined Britain in this action, and so British troops at Chanak stood alone. It was only the tact and good sense of the British commander at Chanak that prevented an outbreak of hostilities there.

The Carlton Club meeting

In Britain, events at Chanak rallied those who were distrustful of Lloyd George. The Conservatives held a meeting at the Carlton Club, their headquarters in London's Pall Mall. The leading opponent of Lloyd George at that meeting was Stanley Baldwin, a Conservative MP who had only recently joined the government. His bitter criticism of the Prime Minister was crucial in swaying opinion against Lloyd George.

> I will not beat about the bush but will come right to the root of the whole difficulty, which is the position of the Prime Minister. The Prime Minister was described this morning, in the words of a distinguished aristocrat, as a live wire. He was described to me, and to others, in more stately language, by the Lord Chancellor, as a dynamic force, and I accept those words. He *is* a dynamic force and it is from that very fact that our troubles, in our opinion, arise. A dynamic force is a very terrible thing.
> It is owing to that dynamic force, and that remarkable personality, that the Liberal party to which he formerly belonged, has been smashed to pieces; and it is my firm conviction that in time, the same thing will happen to our party.

Bonar Law becomes Prime Minister

At this meeting, the majority of Conservative MPs decided they would no longer support Lloyd George's government in the House of Commons. With this essential parliamentary support removed, Lloyd George had no alternative but to resign. Bonar Law, the Conservative leader, then formed a government and

POLITICAL AND ECONOMIC CHANGE IN THE POST-WAR YEARS

	General Elections		
	November 1922	December 1923	October 1924
Conservatives	345	258	419
Labour	142	191	151
Liberals	116	159	40

decided to hold a general election straightaway. The election of November 1922 was to be the first of three in three successive years. The figures of these three general elections are shown together in the margin. As can be seen from these figures, in November 1922 Bonar Law's government got the support that it had hoped for. It is also worth noting the figures for the Labour party: by comparing them with those of the previous general election of 1918 (page 134) it can be seen that the 1922 election was an important advance for Labour.

Appointment as Prime Minister

Stanley Baldwin

Six months later a change of Prime Minister took place. Bonar Law had been unwell for some time and in May 1923 he resigned the premiership. The choice of his successor was between two men: Lord Curzon, in the House of Lords, and Stanley Baldwin, in the House of Commons. Though it is usual for a retiring Prime Minister to advise the monarch whom to appoint next, Bonar Law was so ill that on this occasion he was excused from doing so. King George V nevertheless took advice from other leading politicians and as a result decided to ask Baldwin to become Prime Minister.

The King's decision was a bitter disappointment to Lord Curzon, who for years had considered himself destined to become Prime Minister of Britain. But Curzon was an arrogant man and in his long career he had made many enemies, some of whom were in a position to advise against his appointment. A more serious objection was his membership of the House of Lords. The last prime minister to be a member of the House of Lords had been Lord Salisbury, who had retired in 1902. With the recent large extension of the franchise in 1918, great attention now centred on the House of Commons and it was considered essential that a prime minister should be a member of it.

Stanley Baldwin was a comparative newcomer to politics. He came from a west country family that had developed a successful business manufacturing iron; the future Prime Minister's early career had been spent working in the family firm. Though he had entered parliament in a by-election in 1908, he remained almost unknown as a politician for the next ten years. He entered the wartime Coalition towards the end of the war and was a member of Lloyd George's post-war Coalition. After his role in the Carlton Club meeting of October 1922, he served under Bonar Law as Chancellor of the Exchequer. He was destined to be Prime Minister on three occasions: 1923, 1924–29 and 1935–37.

Stanley Baldwin photographed in the garden of 10 Downing Street. Three times Conservative Prime Minister of the country, by his moderate policies he was quietly responsible for adjusting his party to the changed circumstances of the inter-war years.

Baldwin proved himself a most effective leader of the Conservative party. Essentially this was because of his moderation. At a time when the new Labour party was developing and the old Liberal party was declining, Baldwin's moderate leadership was a great benefit to his party and it attracted many voters. He did not present himself in any lofty way, but rather as a country gentleman with a great love of England. He was a most effective speaker, and was the first Prime Minister to use the newly invented radio with success. The fact that his party was to dominate politics during the inter-war years was due to the skill of his leadership.

The 1923 general election

In 1923, however, things did not work out well for him. In December of that year he led his party to a serious electoral defeat. Baldwin wanted the Conservative party to make its mark as the party which lifted Britain out of the Depression, which by 1923 still showed no real sign of coming to an end. He put forward a controversial solution: economic protection. Perhaps his own background in the iron industry was partly responsible for this, as that was an industry that would benefit from protection. Bonar Law had earlier promised that the Conservatives would not adopt economic protection without holding a general election to test the country's feeling on the issue. The Labour party and the Liberal party now both became united around their traditional policy of free trade. The result of the election, given above, shows the clear rejection by the country of Baldwin's proposal.

A HISTORY OF BRITAIN FROM 1867

The first Labour government

A minority government

Study of the election figures on page 139 will show that with Liberal support a Labour government could be formed. Such a government would be a **minority government**, one that depends for survival on the support of another party. The Liberals knew that their support of the Labour government would give them some control over it. If the government were to follow policies which the Liberals disliked, they could withdraw their support and the government would fall. In any case, the Liberals doubted whether Labour would be capable of governing the country properly. If that proved to be so, the Labour party would be seriously discredited and the Liberals could gather up the votes that Labour would lose.

Recent development of the Labour party

The new Labour government was thus restricted in the work that it could do. Nevertheless, the formation of a Labour government was an important milestone in the political history of Britain. For the first time a group of men who had no privilege in their background, who had not been educated in public schools and who did not move among wealthy people had come to power. For the new Labour government and for the Labour party, January 1924 marked a moment of great achievement. One member of the new government expressed his feelings in this way.

> As we stood waiting for His Majesty, amid the gold and crimson of the Palace, I could not help marvelling at the strange turn of Fortune's wheel, which had brought MacDonald the starveling clerk, Thomas the engine-driver, Henderson the foundry labourer, and Clynes the mill-hand, to this pinnacle.
>
> Memoirs of J.R. Clynes

Two views of the first Labour government, before and after its formation. Ramsay MacDonald succeeded in convincing many British people that, despite their fears, the Labour party could exercise power just as responsibly as any other party.

It was an achievement that owed much to the party's progress during the previous ten years. The early development of the Labour movement has been considered in Chapter 4. Progress during the years to 1914 had been steady but slow. During the First World War, the Labour party decided to join the Coalition governments of Asquith and Lloyd George and some of their leaders were thus able to get experience of the work of a minister. Only the emergency of the war had persuaded the Labour party to join a Coalition government; as soon as it was over, they were intent on pursuing their own course once more. In doing so, they were greatly strengthened by a new party constitution, agreed early in 1918. This had created better unity in the party than had existed in the early years and it had emphasised more firmly that the party's aims were fully Socialist. Particular emphasis was given to nationalisation of major industries, maintaining of full employment and the extension of social security. Though less successful than they had hoped to be in the 1918 election, the 1922 election had shown a promising increase in their support among the voters.

Ramsay MacDonald

In 1922 Ramsay MacDonald once again took on the leadership of the party. He had held this position before 1914, but had resigned his leadership during the war, as he was opposed to his party's support for it. He was concerned that Britain's war aims should be for the creation of a permanent peace in Europe once the fighting ceased. He became particularly committed to the ideal of international peace and harmony and was one of the foremost British supporters of the League of Nations (page 170). He lost his parliamentary seat in the 1918 election, but was returned in 1922. Shortly after that he once again became the leader of the Labour party. Rather like Stanley Baldwin, he was a moderate man. He refused to follow the **Clydesiders**, a group of Glasgow Labour MPs, who tried to persuade him to follow extreme left-wing policies. Instead he was concerned to demonstrate that the Labour party was reasonable and respectable, and that it presented no revolutionary threat to the British people.

The government

Once appointed as Prime Minister, this was the course that he followed. His appointments were almost all of moderate men such as Snowden as Chancellor of the Exchequer, Thomas as Colonial Secretary, and Henderson as Home Secretary. The only exception was Wheatley, a Clydesider, who became Minister of Health. As he was so very closely interested in foreign affairs, Ramsay MacDonald decided to take on the post of Foreign Secretary as well as that of Prime Minister.

Wheatley Housing Act For many of its supporters, the government's domestic achievements during its nine months in office were few and disappointing. The one exception was the Wheatley Housing Act, which took up again Addison's earlier work. The government provided increased subsidies for housing, while insisting that the houses were to be available only for rent and not for sale. The Act was not controversial and it won the support of Conservatives as well as of Liberals.

Other policies The Wheatley Housing Act was the only important piece of legislation that the first Labour government produced. In education, attempts to raise the school-leaving age to 15 failed, and attempts to restore the money lost in earlier cuts were not fully successful either. In agriculture, hopes of establishing a minimum wage came to nothing. With the largest problem of all, unemployment, the Labour government made no progress and appeared to have no idea on how to attempt to solve it. All it did in this matter was to make easier the payment of unemployment benefit. In finance, Snowden pursued a very cautious policy. He was anxious not to appear irresponsible by making large grants of money available for government investment. He was more concerned to practise free-trade principles by cutting back the modest **safeguarding** started during the war by McKenna. At all times he insisted that the budget should be **balanced**, that the amount the government spent should equal what the government received.

This portrait of the interior of the House of Commons in the 1920s should be compared with the similar one of the 1890s on page 44. Ramsay MacDonald, as Prime Minister, stands at the despatch box to address the House during a debate.

The fall of the first Labour government

Relations with the Soviet Union

It was an issue in foreign affairs that led eventually to the government's collapse. The first Labour government adopted a less hostile policy towards the Soviet Union than its predecessors and as one of its first actions gave official British recognition to the Communist government there. Having done this, MacDonald then sought to resolve a particular difficulty that had prevented any improvement in Anglo-Soviet relations since the time of the Russian Revolution in 1917. This concerned the payment back to Britain of loans that had been made to the old Tsarist government of Russia, to help in the earlier expansion of Russian industry. The Soviet government now stated that it would be prepared to consider repayment over a long period, but only if an immediate further loan were made by the British government. This was a startling suggestion for the Soviet Union to make. Nevertheless, the Labour government did not at once reject the idea of making a loan, and negotiations on it began.

Red scare

These negotiations were a mistake. Already within Britain there was much hostility towards the Soviet Union. The fact that the government was considering making this loan stirred up fears of Communist influence within the government. The proposed loan helped develop a **Red scare**, a quite unjustified but widespread suspicion that Communist forces were undermining the government of the country. It is against this background that the Campbell case and the Zinoviev letter must be seen. The former led directly to the government's collapse and the latter sealed its fate in the election which followed.

Campbell case

Campbell was editor of a Communist newspaper, *The Workers' Weekly*, which in early August 1924 published an article calling upon British troops not to obey orders to take action against people involved in revolutionary or militant trade union activities. The government regarded the article as encouragement to mutiny, and as such considered it criminal. Government prosecution of Campbell was begun, but was then dropped, as it was thought that perhaps prosecution was in this case extreme and unnecessary. This dropping of prosecution provided the Conservatives with a real opportunity to attack the government, on the grounds that it had interfered in the course of justice. When parliament met in September, the Liberals were persuaded to join with the Conservatives in voting the Labour party out of office.

Zinoviev letter

The election campaign that followed in October 1924 was dominated by the Red scare. Fears that the Labour government, in spite of its apparent moderation, might be in league with Communists were given further support by the publication in a British newspaper, just a few days before the election, of what became known as the **Zinoviev letter**. Though it has subsequently been proved beyond any doubt that the Zinoviev letter was a forgery, it was at the time widely believed to be genuine. Zinoviev was the President of the Communist International, the Soviet organisation whose aim was to spread Communism throughout the world. The letter he was said to have written was addressed to the British Communist party, a small political organisation that had been established in 1920.

> It is indispensable to stir up the masses of the British proletariat, to bring into movement the army of unemployed proletarians. It is imperative that the group in the Labour party sympathising with the treaty should bring increased pressure to bear upon the government and parliamentary circles in favour of ratification of the treaty. . . .
>
> From your last report it is evident that agitation propaganda in the Army is weak, in the Navy a very little better. It would be desirable to have cells in all the units of the troops, particularly among those quartered in the large centres, and also among factories working on munitions and at military store depots.
>
> From the Zinoviev letter

POLITICAL AND ECONOMIC CHANGE IN THE POST-WAR YEARS

As can be seen from a study of these extracts from the letter, the impression was given of active influence by the Communist party within the Labour party, among British workers and among the ranks of the armed forces. For some, it confirmed their worst fears about the Labour government.

Labour loses the general election

Labour now stood little chance of winning the election. Nevertheless, study of the figures on page 139 shows that they did not do too badly by contrast with their performance in the two previous elections. Further study of those election figures will show that the big Conservative majority in this election is really explained by their taking of seats from the Liberal party rather than from the Labour party. The Liberal party entered the election in an unconfident mood, with little to offer the voters. Many who had voted for the Liberals in December 1923 realised that as a result of doing so, a Labour government had come into being. This was not what they had wanted and so in this election they voted for the Conservatives. Among those who in 1924 had moved from the Liberal to the Conservative party was Winston Churchill, who was now elected as a Conservative. The real importance of the October 1924 election lies in this serious blow it gave to the Liberal party.

Baldwin's second government

Nevertheless, the Conservatives now had a large majority and were able to maintain power for almost the full five years. Baldwin formed his second ministry. Austen Chamberlain became Foreign Secretary, Neville Chamberlain (Austen's half-brother) became Minister of Health, Joynson-Hicks became Home Secretary and Winston Churchill became Chancellor of the Exchequer. It was a ministry on which Baldwin wished to place his own stamp of moderation and compromise. It was a ministry which was to have important achievements to its credit. But it also had the misfortune to face the General Strike of 1926, the most serious breakdown in industrial relations that had so far occurred in British history.

EXERCISES

1. (a) How do you explain the success of Lloyd George in the Coupon Election?
   (b) Describe the problems facing Lloyd George's government (1918–22) in Ireland and the way in which the government tackled these problems.
   (c) Describe the problems facing Lloyd George's government (1918–22) from industrial unrest in Britain and the way in which the government tackled these problems.

2. (a) Write an outline history of the Labour party during the years 1914–23.
   (b) How do you account for the success of the Labour party in the general election of 1923?
   (c) How do you account for the failure of the Labour party in the general election of 1924?

3. Imagine you are a political journalist living and working in Britain during the years just after the First World War. Write an article that might be published in a newspaper in the early part of 1924, explaining the developments in the three major political parties during the years since the war ended.

4. Study the extract on page 138, the photograph on page 139 and the cartoon on page 140 and then answer questions (a) to (c) which follow.
   (a) (i) What impression do you gain from the extract and (to a lesser extent) from the photograph about the attitudes of Stanley Baldwin?
   (ii) Explain how Baldwin's attitudes and other factors were helpful to the progress of his party in the years 1922–24. (3+5)
   (b) (i) What impression is the upper part of the cartoon intended to convey?
   (ii) For what reasons might that impression have been quite widely held just before the Labour party took office for the first time?
   (iii) How accurate in practice was the impression given in the lower part of the cartoon? (2+3+3)
   (c) In what respects would you agree that the Conservative party and the Labour party were each well served by Stanley Baldwin and Ramsay MacDonald in the early 1920s? (4)

12 THE GENERAL STRIKE AND THE 1931 CRISIS

The previous two chapters – and the chapter that follows – all emphasise how the years during and after the First World War were ones of important change in the British economy and in British politics. This chapter is principally concerned with two episodes that were of profound importance in this connection. Both the General Strike in the early summer of 1926 and the economic and political crisis in the autumn of 1931 aroused fears at the time that the orderly functioning of government might be disturbed. With the passage of time, it can be seen that such fears were greatly exaggerated. Nevertheless, both episodes form vital parts in the history of Britain during the inter-war years.

The General Strike: causes

The mining industry

The roots of the General Strike lay in the mining industry. Relations in this industry had already been troubled, as has been shown in the previous chapter. The points at dispute had been rates of pay and hours of work. In pressing for improvements, the miners gave loyal support to their union, **The Miners' Federation of Great Britain**. The strong sense of loyalty which the miners showed to their union and to each other in these difficult years is very largely explained by the sharing together of their difficult, dangerous and unpleasant work below ground. Some idea of this is given in George Orwell's book describing the life and work of miners during these years, *The Road to Wigan Pier*.

> **The time to go to a mine is when the machines are roaring and the air is black with coal dust, and when you can actually see what the miners have to do. At those times the place is like hell, or at any rate like my own mental picture of hell. Most of the things one imagines in hell are there – heat, noise, confusion, darkness, foul air, and, above all, unbearably cramped space. . . . The miners are not only shifting monstrous quantities of coal, they are also doing it in a position that doubles or trebles the work. They have got to remain kneeling all the time – they could hardly rise from their knees without hitting the ceiling – and you can easily see by trying it what a tremendous effort this means. Shovelling is comparatively easy when you are standing up, because you can use your knee and thigh to drive the shovel along; kneeling down, the whole of the strain is thrown upon your arm and belly muscles. And the other conditions do not exactly make things easier. There is the heat – it varies, but in some mines it is suffocating – and the coal dust that stuffs up your throat and nostrils and collects along your eyelids, and the unending rattle of the conveyor belt, which in that confined space is rather like the rattle of a machine-gun.**
>
> George Orwell, *The Road to Wigan Pier*

Sankey report

Earlier in the century the formation by the miners, railwaymen and transport workers of the Triple Industrial Alliance had given the miners greater strength in pressing their demands. The nationalisation of the mines during the First World War had been welcomed by the miners and they hoped that there would not after the war be a return to the control by the original owners, whom they distrusted and disliked. Their hopes were to be frustrated. The Sankey report of 1919 had been hopelessly divided about the future of the mines and the government had as a consequence retained its control of them for the time being.

The 1921 miners' strike

The onset of the Depression in the winter of 1920–21 compelled the government to end this control. Many mines were no longer proving profitable and the government was unwilling to take responsibility for their losses. In the spring of

THE GENERAL STRIKE AND THE 1931 CRISIS

1921 they therefore handed back the mines to their owners. The first action of the owners was to insist both on a reduction of wages and on a wage structure based on district agreements rather than on a national agreement. To resist these moves the miners went on strike and called on their fellow members in the Triple Industrial Alliance to join them in support. But on **Black Friday** in April 1921 these workers refused to give their support. The miners continued to strike alone for some months, until compelled to give in. They returned to work with the reduced pay that the owners had originally proposed.

Problems of the mid-1920s

1921 had therefore been a grim year for the miners, memorable to them both for the vicious attitude of the owners and the betrayal by their friends. After that, there was a slight improvement in their situation. Their industry benefited as a result of the problems of the German coal industry during the French occupation of the Ruhr. Though this did not result in any great benefit to the miners' wage packet, it did mean that there was full employment in the industry. By the mid-1920s, however, events both at home and abroad had contributed to a further decline. The ending of the Ruhr occupation and the help given to Germany by the Dawes plan (page 171) led to a revival of the German coal industry. The Germans had regained the markets temporarily lost to the British coal producers and had become serious and damaging competitors.

Gold standard

Meantime, the Chancellor of the Exchequer, Winston Churchill, had in the spring of 1925 re-established the gold standard, abandoned at the time of the First World War. The value of the pound was thereby linked directly to the pre-war value of gold. The move had been urged by the Bank of England as a step towards making the pound more secure and giving it greater prestige. The consequences, however, were unsatisfactory for those who were attempting to export goods from Britain, as the equalling of the value of the pound to the pre-war value of gold had made the pound an expensive currency. As a result, foreign buyers had to pay more for British goods than previously. Coal exports were badly hit. Against this background of declining coal exports must be set the unwillingness of the mine owners to bring about the much needed modernisation of the pits. Mining machinery and mining methods were badly out of date and this in itself further helped to put the British coal industry at a disadvantage with its foreign competitors.

Samuel commission

In the summer of 1925 the mine owners adopted their usual tactic of insistence on a cut in wages as the only way to restore the industry. The miners on their part refused to accept any cuts and, on what became known as **Red Friday** in June 1925, were assured of the support of the General Council of the TUC in their struggle. The government intervened at this stage with two courses of action. It promised a nine-month subsidy to the industry, to give practical help at this difficult time. It also set up a Commission of Enquiry under a Liberal politician, Sir Herbert Samuel. The government's intervention calmed the situation; the cuts in wages did not take place and the miners returned to work.

Preparations for a General Strike

All that this government action did was to postpone the struggle. The spring of 1926 would most probably see it re-emerge. The support the miners now had from the General Council of the TUC meant that it was likely that other workers would be called out in their support. There was a real prospect that a general strike would take place. The government took steps to prepare for this possibility. The Home Secretary, Sir William Joynson-Hicks, made plans for emergency services to be staffed by troops and he divided the country into areas that would each come under the control of a civil commissioner. Additionally, Joynson-Hicks and other ministers encouraged members of the public who wanted to help the government in the event of a general strike to enroll in the Organisation for the Maintenance of Supplies. This was largely run by ex-army officers and a large number of volunteers registered with it in the winter of 1925–26. Its initial letters – OMS – gave it the advantage of sounding like an official government organisation, but it was in fact voluntary.

A HISTORY OF BRITAIN FROM 1867

Impact of Samuel commission report

The Samuel Commission reported in March 1926. Its report had something to offer to both sides. The miners were attracted by its main recommendation of improved working conditions and the amalgamation of smaller pits. All this was to be implemented not immediately, but over a period of years. The mine owners were attracted by its recommendation of a cut in wages that should take place immediately. The owners naturally accepted this idea and at the same time made matters much worse by refusing to agree to the report's longer-term concessions to the miners and by insisting on restoring the eight-hour day. The miners were determined to resist. Their President, Herbert Smith, and Secretary, Arthur Cook, insisted on rejection of what the mine owners now demanded. 'Not a penny off the pay, not a minute on the day' was the slogan the miners adopted, and they stuck by it with courage in the forthcoming struggle.

The lock out of the miners

The General Council attempted with the miners and the government attempted with the mine owners to get the two sides to make concessions that would have led to a compromise solution. But the detailed discussions in the summer of 1926 came to nothing. If the miners would not accept the mine owners' terms by 1 May 1926, they would be **locked out**: prevented from going to their work. The miners put their confidence in the General Council bringing out all trade union members in their support. Further negotiations proved fruitless and the General Strike was called for 4 May.

The General Strike: events

Response of workers

The response of the workers to the strike call was whole-hearted. Some four million people struck and the essential services of the country were severely affected during the nine days that it lasted. There was, however, very little violence or disorder during those nine days. Possibly the fine May weather helped to keep tempers in good control on both sides. The emergency services earlier planned by the government and the OMS worked efficiently and were between them responsible for running the essential services of the country. Such activity could only be regarded by the strikers as blacklegging and it naturally aroused their anger.

This cartoon of the General Strike presents a view widely accepted at the time.

THE LEVER BREAKS.

Attitudes of government and strikers

The lack of disturbance during the strike is in some ways surprising. Even such a moderate man as Baldwin took the view that the strike was intended to 'challenge the existing constitution' of Britain. Other members of his cabinet, particularly Joynson-Hicks and Churchill, took this view further and saw the strike as a threat of revolution, against which the strongest measures should be taken. Churchill's hostility towards the strikers was extreme. He sought

THE GENERAL STRIKE AND THE 1931 CRISIS

government approval for flamboyant displays of military strength, by the parading of armed convoys through the streets. Wisely, Baldwin and most of the cabinet resisted this pressure from Churchill. He was, nevertheless, given the task, while the strike was on, of producing a government newspaper, *The British Gazette*. The General Council itself responded by producing its own newspaper, *The British Worker*. Contrasting the news put out in these two papers a few days after the strike began helps to show how each side saw the struggle they were involved in.

> **The strike is intended as a direct hold-up of the nation to ransom. It is for the nation to stand firm in its determination not to flinch. 'This moment,' as the Prime Minister pointed out in the House of Commons, 'has been chosen to challenge the existing constitution of the country and to substitute the reign of force for that which now exists. I do not believe there has been anything like a thorough going consultation with the rank and file before this despotic power was put into the hands of a small executive in London. I do not think that all the leaders who assented to order a general strike fully realised they were threatening the basis of ordered government and coming nearer to proclaiming civil war, than we have been for centuries past.'**
>
> *British Gazette*, 6 May 1926

> **It is fantastic for the Prime Minister to pretend that the trade unions are engaged in an attack upon the constitution of the country. Every instruction issued by the General Council is evidence of their determination to maintain the struggle strictly on the basis of an industrial dispute. They have ordered every member taking part to be exemplary in his conduct and not to give any cause for police interference. The General Council struggled hard for peace. They are anxious for an honourable peace to be secured as soon as possible. They are not attacking the constitution. They are not fighting the community. They are defending the mine workers against the mine owners.**
>
> *British Worker*, 7 May 1926

Ending of the strike

In practice, the General Council was anxious to bring the strike to an end as soon as it could. Though the strike was generally calm, there was always the possibility that it could get out of control. The General Council did not relish leadership of a revolutionary situation. Many strikers were disturbed by the opinion of Sir John Simon, a Liberal politician and a legal expert, that the General Strike was 'illegal'. This undermined the confidence of many of them and usefully prepared the ground for acceptance of a compromise solution. Samuel once again played a key role. He devised a compromise agreement by which the reduction in miners' wages would take place only after re-organisation of the mining industry had been accepted by the owners. The General Council seized on this formula and the strike was called off on 12 May.

Strike by miners continues

No agreement had been made about the terms on which the strikers were to return to work. Some found that they were victimised when they returned, and consequently further strikes took place. As for the miners, their position was more desperate. They never agreed to the Samuel compromise that brought the strike to an end and they viewed the General Council's agreement to it as just another betrayal which they had to suffer. They managed to keep on with their strike until the late autumn of the year. Then sheer desperation and poverty drove them back to acceptance of the original wage cuts of the owners and to an eight-hour day. Furthermore, the wage agreements were to be worked out on a district rather than a national basis, another backwards step for them. In spite of great courage, firm determination and immense efforts, the miners had gained nothing. In the end, they had turned out to be the real losers in the General Strike.

The General Strike: its importance

Decline in trade unionism

The following figures show the effect of the General Strike on the trade unions.

Year	Total number of trade union members (in millions)	Total number of days lost through strikes (in millions)
1920	7.9	26.5
1921	8.3	85.8
1922	6.6	19.8
1923	5.6	10.6
1924	5.4	8.4
1925	5.5	7.9
1926	5.5	162.2
1927	5.2	1.1
1928	4.9	1.3
1929	4.8	8.2

The first column shows that the decline in trade union membership had begun earlier in the 1920s; experience of the General Strike appears to have given further encouragement to a trend that had already set in. In the second column the industrial unrest of the early 1920s and of 1926 is clearly shown. In that column it is particularly worth noting the large drop in the number of days lost through strikes during the two years following the General Strike. It appears that the experience of 1926 discouraged many workers from taking strike action.

Trade Disputes Act

The strike left its mark on the trade unions in another, more serious way. In May 1927, a year after the strike had taken place, parliament passed the Trade Disputes Act. The clauses of this Act had three damaging effects on the trade union movement. Civil servants were forbidden to join a trade union that was linked to the TUC. Strikes made in sympathy with other workers were to be illegal. Trade union members now had to **contract in** if they wished part of their trade union subscription to go to the support of the Labour party. This last feature reversed the arrangements made under the previous Trade Union Act of 1913. It was thought that trade union members were unlikely to go to the bother of contracting in and Labour party funds would therefore suffer. In effect, the Labour party managed to maintain a reasonable income from trade union subscriptions in spite of the difficulties this Act posed for them.

Mond-Turner conversations

Few trade unionists had welcomed the General Strike. Many, when the strike was over, were anxious to seek closer understanding with management. One of the leading trade unionists who urged such an approach in the late 1920s was Ernest Bevin, leader of the transport workers. He was the main trade union leader involved in the 1928 **Mond-Turner conversations**. These were headed by Sir Alfred Mond, Managing Director of the newly established Imperial Chemical Industries, and Ben Turner, Chairman of the General Council of the TUC.

The conversations were important in cutting new ground in industrial relations. For the first time in British history representatives of management met with representatives of the trade unions to discuss not just wages and working conditions, but the general success of the industry in which they were all concerned. Though much bitterness was created after the General Strike by the victimisation of some strikers, by the treatment of the miners and by the terms of the Trade Disputes Act, the Mond-Turner conversations showed a spirit of understanding between both sides. This spirit did much to make the following years free of the strife that had overwhelmed the early and middle 1920s.

THE GENERAL STRIKE AND THE 1931 CRISIS

The domestic work of Baldwin's second government

Neville Chamberlain as Minister of Health

One of the most active of Baldwin's ministers was Neville Chamberlain. Like Baldwin, he had become an MP somewhat late in life. He had nevertheless earlier had much experience of local politics in Birmingham, where his father, Joseph Chamberlain, had made a great reputation as a reforming Lord Mayor in the 1870s. Social reform was almost a family tradition for the Chamberlains and many of the important pieces of social legislation in the inter-war years were Neville Chamberlain's work. Assisting him closely at this time was Winston Churchill whose earlier commitment to social reform, when a Liberal minister before the First World War, was now given a boost with his appointment as a Conservative Chancellor of the Exchequer.

Pensions Act

The Widows, Orphans and Old Age Contributory Pensions Act, which Neville Chamberlain steered through the House of Commons in 1925, was one of the most important pieces of social legislation of the inter-war years. There were now many more old people for whom provision had to be made. This Act also made provision for the wife and children in the event of the death of the main wage-earner in the family. This was something that the Liberals before the war had never been able to achieve.

Chamberlain's Act built upon both the Old Age Pensions Act of 1908 and the National Insurance Act of 1911. In return for contributions by the employee, the employer and the state – as provided for in the 1911 Act – a pension would be available for the years 65–70; then at 70 the non-contributory pension would be obtained, with additional benefits for those who had contributed to the new scheme. As well as for the elderly, state pensions were available under the new contributory scheme to widows and orphans. Though the amount of the contributions and of the benefits varied, the system Chamberlain set up in 1925 was to survive until after the Second World War.

Local Government Act

His Local Government Act of 1929 was to be even more long-lasting. Recent developments in the social services made it necessary to re-structure local government, so that it could cater for the changes that had taken place. The counties and county boroughs, the bases on which the new Act was to be built, were given wider authority within their areas. The old Poor Law Unions, dating back almost 100 years, were abolished and their work in providing for the poor and destitute was taken on by the Public Assistance Committees of the local councils. These councils also took control of road construction, public health, child welfare and local planning. Some of their responsibilities might be given over to the less important rural district councils and urban district councils.

Churchill was mainly responsible for a further provision of the Act, concerned with de-rating. This relieved agriculture from payment of all of the rates and industry from payment of three-quarters of the rates. To make up for revenue lost in this way, the local authority would receive a grant from the central government. It was hoped that the relief provided by the Act for agriculture and industry would assist their development.

Joynson-Hicks as Home Secretary

The 1928 Equal Franchise Act, which gave the vote to women between the ages of 21 and 30, had been widely expected. It was introduced by the government largely because of a commitment to franchise extension given by Joynson-Hicks at a public meeting. As Home Secretary during these years he was responsible for other and more controversial decisions. A dedicated Anglican Evangelical, he was determined to impose strict standards of morality within Britain. In this respect, he was living in changing times. New fashions in dress, new trends in literature, new forms of entertainment could be seen by those brought up in the Victorian years as evidence not just of change, but of serious moral decline. Joynson-Hicks certainly saw many contemporary trends in this way. He gave strong support to the police, he authorised a number of prosecutions on grounds of morality, and he applied censorship strictly.

He was also among those Conservatives who had a strong suspicion of Communism and of the influence of the Soviet Union within Britain. Acting on rather slender evidence, he authorised a police raid in the spring of 1927 on the London offices of Arcos, a Soviet trading mission, which was said to be a nest of Soviet spies. Though the police found not the slightest evidence of any espionage activity by Arcos, the government nevertheless decided at that time to break off relations with the Soviet Union.

Controversy over the Prayer Book

Joynson-Hicks was also largely responsible for parliament's decision in 1927, and again in 1928, to reject a revised form of the Anglican Prayer Book. This revision, the first for more than 250 years, had been accepted by the Church of England as useful for present-day needs. On account of the established nature of the Church of England it was, however, legally necessary for any revision to be approved by parliament. In a series of spirited debates, in which the voting was free and not along party lines, the revised version of the Prayer Book was rejected. Joynson-Hicks's reason for leading this opposition was his view that the revision permitted Anglo-Catholic members of the Church of England to use

The Prayer Book debates of 1927–28 showed the continuing strong interest of both houses of parliament in the affairs of the Church of England. According to this cartoon, they also tended to concentrate on issues that belonged more to Reformation times than to the twentieth century.

"ADMIT TO STRANGERS' GALLERY."

forms of worship that were similar to forms of worship then used in the Roman Catholic Church. As an Evangelical, he disliked very strongly anything of this kind. Why other MPs, many of whom were not members of the Church of England at all (and one of whom was a Communist), joined him in rejecting the revised Prayer Book, is difficult to say. The whole situation of presenting the Prayer Book for approval by people who would in any case never use it was somewhat ridiculous. Prayer Book revision nevertheless attracted attention from many people in the late 1920s, suggesting that interest in the affairs of the established Church was to be found among many who were not committed members of it.

The 1929 general election

Political campaigns

In the general election of May 1929 all three major parties – Conservative, Labour and Liberal – made determined bids for power. The Conservatives relied on their record of achievement – purposeful reform at home and peaceful relations abroad – as well as on the personality of Baldwin, presented as a moderate man of good common sense. But the programme they offered the electorate was flat. Their use of the slogan *Safety First* was unexciting and depended very much on presenting the Labour party as a danger to the country, something which few people now felt it to be. In fact, the Labour party also

THE GENERAL STRIKE AND THE 1931 CRISIS

Travelling cinemas were a novel feature of the Conservative campaign in the 1929 general election. Here Baldwin is shown undecided between the rival claims of free trade and 'safeguarding' (another name for protection).

THE IMAGE WITH TWO VOICES.

presented a moderate image of itself. Their own policy statement at the election, *Labour and the Nation*, emphasised the goals set out in their 1918 constitution. By this time, the left wing within the party, represented by the Clydesiders, were well under the control of the party leadership.

Liberal proposals

The Liberals had the most far-sighted programme to offer. Lloyd George had again taken control of the party, after Asquith's retirement in 1926. For three years he and his close followers had re-thought the Liberal approach to politics. In 1929 they entered the contest with new policies, determined to regain the position which they had in recent years lost to Labour. The title of their policy document, *We Can Conquer Unemployment*, showed that, alone of the three parties, the Liberals were addressing themselves to what had by the late 1920s become Britain's most serious social problem. Lloyd George's proposals for the conquering of unemployment were revolutionary at that time: massive public works schemes, to be financed by extensive government borrowing. His ideas owed much to the thinking of the leading economist of the time, J.M. Keynes. In the 1930s Keynes's ideas promised a solution to the unemployment situation in many western countries, but were not yet widely accepted. Lloyd George's proposals failed to attract sufficient support and, as can be seen from the figures below, the Liberal party achieved disappointing results. They were nevertheless in a position similar to that of December 1923: their support could put into power either the Conservative party or the Labour party. As Labour had more votes than any other party, the Liberals gave Labour their support.

General Election: May 1929	
Conservatives	260
Labour	288
Liberals	59

Labour again a minority government

Thus, for the second time, the Labour party took power as a **minority government**. Its cabinet was also much the same as it had been five years before. MacDonald was again Prime Minister, but this time the Foreign Secretary was Henderson; Snowden was Chancellor of the Exchequer, and Thomas was appointed to have special responsibility for unemployment. Margaret Bondfield as Minister of Labour was the first woman member of a cabinet. Though the actions of the government were again restricted by its dependence on the Liberals, it seemed unlikely anyway that such a moderate cabinet would have wished to embark on fully Socialist policies.

The domestic work of the second Labour government

Legislation

The government had a number of important domestic achievements to its credit. The Coal Mines Act of 1930 reduced the miners' working day by half an hour to seven and a half hours. It was a compromise measure that was an attempt to show Labour's sympathy for the miners. The Housing Act of 1930, by providing government subsidies, enabled local authorities to take steps to get rid of slums. Slums had been comparatively neglected by the earlier housing acts and this legislation was responsible for the demolition and replacement of many areas of sub-standard housing throughout the 1930s. The Agricultural Marketing Act of 1931 set up boards of producers with power to market and to set prices for agricultural products. Early moves were made during this government by the Minister of Transport, Herbert Morrison, to set up a unified system of transport for London. The many different bus and railway companies were to be brought together under the control of one authority, London Transport. Although it was not until 1933 that the new system came into being, it was the second Labour government that did most of the work that resulted in its creation.

Limitations on legislation

As in the time of the first Labour government, other proposals ran into difficulties either in the Commons or in the Lords. Labour's proposals to raise the school-leaving age came to nothing. Attempts to repeal the hated Trade Disputes Act came up against Liberal opposition. Two reforms of parliamentary practice were proposed. One was to get rid of the additional vote that some electors had as a result of their business address in the city of London or as a result of their education at the universities of Oxford or Cambridge. The other was to make some modest steps towards a system of proportional representation. Both of these proposals were rejected by the House of Lords.

Increasing unemployment

The major problem facing the government, and one which it completely failed to solve, was unemployment. Already a problem when Labour took office, it had by the end of 1930 become much more serious. The effects of the collapse of the US economy at the end of the previous year were much in evidence. Unemployment was about two and a half million by then; in the course of 1931 it was to rise to almost three million. Thomas, who had been appointed to deal with unemployment, was out of his depth in his new task. It was one of his junior ministers, Oswald Mosley, who in 1930 made the most promising suggestions as to how the problem should be tackled.

He proposed that the government should take on the direction of British industry, plan its trade with foreign countries and provide loans for its development. Though much of Mosley's programme was to be the basis for the eventual recovery of industry in Britain and in the United States during the 1930s, it was unacceptable to the Labour government in 1930. Angered by this rejection, Mosley resigned from the government. The Prime Minister himself now took over from Thomas the responsibility of seeking a solution. It was his failure to do so that led to the collapse of the second Labour government in August 1931 and its replacement by the National government.

The economic crisis of 1931

Snowden's financial policies

As the number of unemployed increased, so also did the cost of maintaining them on the dole. The government thus faced a financial as well as a social problem. The Chancellor of the Exchequer, Philip Snowden, had been the leading government opponent of proposals such as those put forward by Mosley in order to reduce unemployment. Snowden was determined to maintain free trade and to curb government spending; above all, he intended to produce balanced budgets, in which the amount the government spent equalled the

THE GENERAL STRIKE AND THE 1931 CRISIS

amount the government received. The increased cost of the dole was thus a threat to his aims. But it had always been the policy of the Labour party that reasonable benefits should be available for the unemployed. As many who had voted Labour into office were among the unemployed, it would be insensitive and unwise for the government to reduce their already meagre benefits.

The May committee

In February 1931 the government appointed an Economy Committee to enquire into how it could deal with the mounting costs of the dole. The committee, under the chairmanship of Sir George May, consisted mainly of men from the business world and it was likely that their report would recommend severe measures. The May Committee met during the spring and summer of 1931. Meanwhile the position of the government was steadily undermined. This can partly be explained by the worsening economic situation abroad, especially in the United States and on the Continent, where during 1931 a number of large banks had collapsed. It was also partly explained by the way the press in Britain helped to create a sense of national crisis which demanded some special kind of solution. The report of the May Committee was anxiously awaited.

Impact of its proposals

The report was published at the very end of July, just as MPs were getting away for their summer holiday. Its recommendations came as no great surprise. A government deficit of £120 million was forecast for the following year. The committee agreed with Snowden's view that the budget should be balanced and went on to recommend how the £120 million should be raised. £24 million was to come from increased taxation; £96 million was to come from government cuts, two-thirds of which were to be found at the expense of the unemployed. It was unlikely that most members of the Labour party would agree with this last recommendation.

Publication of the report heightened the crisis. International financiers began to withdraw their investments from the Bank of England. MacDonald and Snowden were told by the Bank that the cause of these withdrawals was a belief among international financiers that the Labour government would not act upon the May Committee's recommendations. Unless that were done, so these financiers maintained, events would lead to a complete collapse of Britain's currency.

The formation of the National government

MacDonald's policies

MacDonald and Snowden were determined to put the May Committee's recommendations into effect. They sought and got the support of Baldwin and of Samuel, who at that time was leading the Liberals, as Lloyd George was unwell. The support which they failed to get was that of their own Labour cabinet. After a series of lengthy meetings the cabinet became seriously divided. MacDonald therefore felt compelled to resign as Prime Minister of the Labour government. King George V had a high regard for MacDonald and was aware of the support he had from leading Conservatives and Liberals. He therefore asked MacDonald to form a coalition government, with the Conservatives and Liberals. MacDonald had little hesitation in accepting the King's invitation and what was called the **National government** came into being on 24 August 1931. Its cabinet was small, consisting of four Labour members, four Conservative members and two Liberal members.

Controversy over the formation of the National government

There was substantial support in the Conservative and Liberal parties for these moves. But reaction in the Labour party was most unfavourable towards what MacDonald had done. It was even alleged for some years that MacDonald had 'planned' to become Prime Minister of a National government and to get rid of his Labour government. Though this allegation is untrue, MacDonald certainly showed no regret at the ending of the second Labour government and appeared to look forward to his work with men from the two opposition parties.

Few Labour MPs supported what he had done and within the Labour party there was a widespread feeling that they had been betrayed by his actions in August 1931. George Lansbury shortly became leader of the party, which expelled MacDonald and the other politicians who supported the National government. The differing reactions are illustrated by the following newspaper reports of August 1931. The first is favourable to the National government; the second is hostile.

> **All concerned are to be warmly congratulated on this result, so fully in accord with the patriotic spirit which has inspired a week's most anxious negotiations. The Prime Minister and the colleagues of his own party who have followed him deserve in particular unqualified credit, both for the manner in which they took their political lives in their hands by facing and forcing the break-up of the late Cabinet, and for their new decision to translate courage in the Cabinet into courage in the country. Their readiness to share the responsibility – honour is perhaps the better word – of carrying through to the end a policy of retrenchment adds enormously to the prospect of its success. No one will ever henceforth be able to claim that retrenchment is a class or partisan policy, dictated solely by an unsubstantial panic manufactured by industrial and financial interests.**
>
> *The Times*, 25 August 1931

> **Mr MacDonald's decision to form a Cabinet in conjunction with the Liberals and Tories seems to us a mistake, just as it would have been a mistake for him as a pacifist to join a War Cabinet in 1914. For he must inevitably find himself at war with the whole of organised labour, and not only with organised labour, but with all those, in all classes, who believe that the policy of reducing the purchasing power of the consumer to meet a situation of over-production is silly economics. ... An effort is being made to represent the issue as merely one of a 10% reduction in the dole, as if patriotism meant cutting the dole and refusal to cut it could only be based on cowardly subservience to the electorate. We oppose it, because it is only a first step, the crucial beginning of a policy of reductions, disastrous, we believe, alike for England and the rest of the world.**
>
> *New Statesman*, 29 August 1931

Early work of the National government

The immediate benefit of the forming of the National government was the restoration of confidence in Britain's currency. An essential loan from some New York bankers was at once arranged. In September two further measures helped. Snowden introduced a budget which put into effect most of the May Committee's recommendations: increases in taxation, cuts in unemployment benefits and cuts also in the salaries of government employees. This last provision caused sailors at the naval base of Invergordon in Scotland to protest at the pay cuts proposed in the budget.

The press enlarged what was a protest into a 'mutiny'. This exaggerated account further aroused the concern of international financiers and withdrawals of sterling from the Bank of England again took place. To solve the problem the government decided to abandon the gold standard. This move made sterling a worthwhile currency for investment. Withdrawals became fewer. A more important effect of the abandonment of the gold standard was to make British exports cheaper in foreign countries and thus to encourage a much needed expansion of the British economy.

The 1931 general election

A general election was held in October 1931. For the voters, it was a complicated and confusing one. Many felt a need to vote for the candidate who supported the National government, as this was, according to most of the newspapers, a time of 'national' emergency. Among the manifestos put forward, the Conservative one cut new ground. After more than a decade of uncertainty on the issue, the party came down definitely in favour of economic protection as the solution to Britain's long-term economic problems.

General Election: October 1931			
Supporters of the National government		**Opponents of the National government**	
Conservatives	473	Labour	52
Liberals	68	Liberals	4
National Labour	13	Others	5
	554		61

These figures show overwhelming support by the electorate for the National government. They also show that the real victors of the political changes of 1931 were the Conservatives. Baldwin had led his party to another great success and a long-lasting one, as throughout its nine-year life the National government was to be dominated by the Conservative party.

EXERCISES

1. (a) With the exception of its work in connection with the General Strike, what were the main domestic achievements of Baldwin's ministry of 1924–29?
   (b) How do you account for the outcome of the 1929 general election?
   (c) With the exception of its work in connection with the 1931 crisis, what were the main domestic achievements of MacDonald's ministry of 1929–31?

2. (a) Why did the report of the May Committee in 1931 create such controversy?
   (b) Outline the events that led to the creation of the National government and its confirmation in power by the 1931 general election.
   (c) Why did these events create such controversy inside the Labour party?

3. Imagine you are either a striker or a member of the OMS in 1926. Write a diary of your experiences during the strike, explaining why you considered you had supported the right side in the struggle.

4. Study the cartoon on page 146 and the painting on page 141 (in the previous chapter) and then answer questions (a) to (d) which follow.
   (a) (i) Explain what you understand by the two words written on the rock in the cartoon.
   (ii) By reference to details in the painting, explain how it helps to illustrate the meaning of those two words.
   (2+4)
   (b) Show with reference to the causes and events of the General Strike why:
   (i) strikers would regard the cartoon as giving a biased view of their activities, but
   (ii) government supporters would regard it as giving an accurate view.
   (4+4)
   (c) Describe the events that led to the action referred to in the cartoon's caption. (3)
   (d) In what ways is your understanding of the significance of the General Strike assisted by these two sources? (3)

13 BRITISH SOCIETY DURING THE 1930s

The 1930s forms a decade of mixed impressions in British history. While unemployment was a noticeable feature in many areas, the decade also brought to many people in Britain far higher standards of living than they had previously enjoyed. While there certainly was much poverty, it was also a time of increased concern about how to remove the causes of poverty. While there was extremism in politics, it was also a time of stability in government. Though the subject is not the direct concern of this chapter, the 1930s became increasingly a time of concern for the people of Britain about developments on the Continent. Attention will be directed first to what was the main problem facing the country at the start of the decade: unemployment.

The causes of unemployment

Unemployment figures

The following figures show that by 1931 unemployment was neither a new problem, nor one that would quickly disappear. Such high figures were new for Britain. Though unemployment had sometimes been a problem before 1914 it had never become so widespread or so persistent as this.

Average number of unemployed during the inter-war years (in millions)			
1922	1.5	1931	2.6
1923	1.2	1932	2.7
1924	1.1	1933	2.5
1925	1.2	1934	2.1
1926	1.3	1935	2.0
1927	1.0	1936	1.8
1928	1.2	1937	1.5
1929	1.2	1938	1.8
1930	1.9	1939	1.5

British exports slump

Why was unemployment so high during the inter-war years? The level of employment in a country is linked to the sale of what that country produces in industry or in agriculture. In Britain's case, its earlier high level of employment was partly due to good home sales of its own products. But it was mainly due to successful **export** trade, the selling of Britain's goods to foreign countries. When, as happened from time to time, these foreign countries had economic difficulties of their own, they were unable to buy British exports in the usual amounts. As British firms then found their products were not selling, they had to dismiss many of their workers; unemployment consequently rose. This situation of a declining economy and rising unemployment is known as a **slump**. Such a situation was not earlier regarded too seriously, as experience had shown that a slump was shortly followed by a **boom**, a time of reviving economy and increasing employment.

The sharp rise in unemployment within a few years of the end of the First World War was seen by politicians against this background of earlier experience. The temporary slump, they felt, would shortly give way to boom conditions; the problem would disappear of its own accord. The figures show that to an extent this was correct. Unemployment did fall during the middle years of the 1920s as trade improved. Nevertheless, the figures remained high.

BRITISH SOCIETY DURING THE 1930S

Impact of the Wall Street Crash

From 1929 another, more serious, slump affected Britain. A total collapse of the value of business shares sold on the Wall Street stock market in New York led to a widespread decline in the US economy. Britain was no longer able to maintain its previously good level of exports there. But the impact of what became known as the **Wall Street Crash** was more extensive than this. The economies of western European countries were closely linked to the US economy and they also experienced the ill effects of the Crash; thus Britain's exports to western Europe were badly affected. The Crash also had its effects on non-industrialised lands. These supplied the raw materials for the industrialised countries of the United States and western Europe. As the economies of these industrialised countries were declining, they had less need for the raw materials of the non-industrialised countries. There was therefore a fall in the exports of non-industrialised countries, which meant that they themselves had less money with which to buy western European and US products. The fall in trade throughout the world was enormous and in the process Britain's economy was very seriously harmed.

Once again, as the figures at the start of the chapter show, the situation did improve. This was partly due in the 1930s to a changed approach by the government, to be considered later in this chapter. But the figures again show that unemployment remained high. There were, therefore, deeper reasons for unemployment than just the effects of two periods of slump in world trade.

Staple exports less competitive

As shown in the introduction to this book, Britain's economic greatness in the nineteenth century had been based on four major industries: coal, iron and steel, textiles and ship building. Their products dominated the country's exports and they are often referred to as Britain's **staple industries** and **staple exports**. During the short-lived boom following the First World War, much money was invested in these staple industries to help their revival. The money might have been better invested in new forms of industry. The disturbing fact was that the products of Britain's staple industries were no longer in so much demand. The need for goods essential to the war effort in the years 1914–18 had led Britain to abandon most of its export trade.

A highly attractive opportunity was thus presented to Britain's competitors, who now firmly established themselves in the foreign markets where Britain's trade was no longer so strong. Additionally there was general decline in demand for the products of the staple industries. The use of oil and electricity had made coal less valuable as a source of power; the invention of artificial fibres, such as rayon, reduced demand for textiles; improved efficiency and carrying capacity in ships led to a decline in orders for new ones.

Lack of modernisation

Nor in these difficult circumstances were the staple industries much helped by those who managed them. There was a lack of modernisation of equipment and methods. The coal mines continued to use old-fashioned machinery; in the textile mills electrical power and automation techniques were only slowly introduced; too many ships were designed to use the declining power of coal rather than the increasingly important power of oil. As shown in the previous chapter, government economic policies in the 1920s had done little directly to assist British industry. Indeed, the restoration of the gold standard in 1925 could be said to have created even further difficulties for Britain's economy. By increasing the value of the pound, it made more difficult the sale of British goods abroad.

The reality of unemployment

Attitudes of the unemployed

The previous section has shown that the causes of unemployment lie mainly in foreign countries; they were quite beyond the control of workers in Britain. Nevertheless, there attached to the unemployed man in Britain a strong sense of inadequacy; a feeling that his own deficiencies had led to his unemployment.

Unsympathetic attitudes among those fortunate enough to have work tended further to encourage this view of the unemployed. The largest worry of most of the unemployed was how they were to provide for their families while they had no income from work. Apart from seeking work at local factories and attending labour exchanges, there was little else that could be done. Some moved to areas where employment was easier to find, but this was both risky for them and disturbing for their family life. Others emigrated to dominion countries.

The dole

In spite of their difficulties, the unemployed in Britain did have an important benefit which the unemployed in other countries often lacked: the dole. As is shown on pages 107 and 135, a modest start on this had been made by Part II of the National Insurance Act of 1911 and continued by the Unemployment Insurance Act of 1920. Though proposals were made to reduce the amount of the dole, as in 1931 by the May Committee, there was never any serious attempt to abolish it.

The amount of money received on the dole was low. It was fixed by the 1920 Act at less than a pound a week and it did not rise much above a pound throughout the 1920s. Nor was additional benefit for members of the family very much. Surveys among the unemployed showed that a family living off the dole was quite unable to maintain reasonable standards in clothing, food and accommodation, and was additionally very likely to fall seriously into debt.

Means test

The miseries of the unemployed were made worse immediately after the National government had been formed. In making their cuts, the National government both reduced the amount that was paid in dole and also set up a **means test**. The new system hit hardest those who were unemployed for a long time, a category into which most of the unemployed fell.

Those who were still unemployed after receiving the dole for an initial period of 26 weeks had to submit themselves to a means test. This involved a close examination of all the source of income received by the unemployed worker's family. Among the unemployed, the means test was a hated feature of government legislation. For many working-class men the dependence on their wives and children which the means test made necessary was a humiliation that they loathed. In any case, the means test seemed to go against the principle of regarding the receipt of the dole as a natural right. It was particularly disliked for being administered by the local Public Assistance Committee, closely associated with the old Poor Law that had only just come to an end. The following account, written in the early 1930s by an unemployed engineer, shows how the means test made worse the already difficult situation that unemployment had brought to his family.

This Conservative poster, originally designed with the slogan 'Safeguarding will prevent this', was overprinted with a call for National government support. In its appeal, it concentrates on the main problem facing Britain in the early 1930s.

> In the meantime my wife had decided to try and earn a little money so that she might continue to retain our home. She obtained a job as house to house saleswoman, and was able to earn a few shillings to supplement our dole income. It was from this time that the feeling of strain which was beginning to appear in our home life became more marked. I felt a burden on her. Life became more and more strained. There were constant bickerings over money matters, usually culminating in threats to leave from both of us. The final blow came when the means test was put into operation. I realised that if I told the Employment Exchange that my wife was earning a little, they might reduce my benefit. If that happened, home life would become impossible. When, therefore, I was sent a form on which to give details of our total income, I neglected to fill it out. For this I was suspended benefit for six weeks. This was the last straw. Quarrels broke out anew and bitter things were said. Eventually, after the most heartbreaking period of my life, both my wife and son, who had just commenced to earn a few shillings, told me to get out as I was living on them and taking the food they needed.
>
> **Quoted in H.L. Beales, *Memoirs of the Unemployed*, 1934**

13 BRITISH SOCIETY DURING THE 1930S

Unemployment Act

The Unemployment Act of 1934 got rid of the means test in the form set up three years earlier. The merit of the Act, in the eyes of the unemployed, was that the granting of the dole was given to a new Unemployment Assistance Board, organised by the central government. This removed much of their dislike of the means test. The defect of the Act was that the new uniform dole payments which the Unemployment Assistance Board made would result in less dole being paid in areas where local authorities had earlier been generous. The outcry against the Act was so strong that it did not begin to operate until 1937, after it had been amended. It proved its worth however. In the late 1930s the whole issue of the dole was no longer so controversial and the amount of the dole was even increased in these years.

Unemployment: protest by its victims

National Unemployed Workers' Movement

Enforced idleness, biting poverty, and overwhelming desperation at their plight and at the failure of governments to bring any real improvement were the main problems facing the unemployed. Many unemployed therefore sought to put pressure on the government for improvement. The cause of the unemployed was taken up especially by the Labour party and by the trade unions, but an organisation concerned solely with the unemployed also came into being. This was the National Unemployed Workers' Movement (NUWM), set up in the early 1920s. Its main aim was to improve the amount of the dole and to protect the interests of its members. To press its views, the NUWM organised demonstrations of the unemployed. Some of these, especially those directed against the means test and the 1934 Unemployment Act were large and impressive. The government generally was alarmed by the NUWM, which it viewed as a Communist-inspired organisation capable of bringing about revolution. In reality, it was far less dangerous, as only a small proportion of the unemployed were NUWM members.

Hunger marches

One of the most effective forms of demonstration by the unemployed during these years was the **hunger march**. The unemployed would set out on foot from their home areas to march together to London. Attention would be focused on their plight as they made their way through towns and villages while travelling to the capital. Once arrived in London, demonstrations would be held and speeches made. Foremost in organising these marches was the NUWM. As Communist influence was known to exist in the NUWM, many regarded the hunger marches with suspicion. Baldwin, as Prime Minister in the mid-1930s, put this view strongly.

> Ministers have had under consideration the fact that a number of marches on London are in progress or in contemplation. In the opinion of His Majesty's government such marches can do no good to the causes for which they are represented to be undertaken, are liable to cause unnecessary hardship to those taking part in them, and are altogether undesirable in this country, governed by a parliamentary system, where every adult has a vote and every area has its representative in the House of Commons to put forward grievances and suggest remedies. Processions to London cannot claim to have any constitutional influence on policy. Ministers have, therefore, decided that encouragement cannot be given to such marches, whatever their particular purpose, and ministers cannot consent to receive any deputation of marchers, although of course they are always prepared to meet any members of parliament.
>
> Hansard, *Parliamentary Debates*

Jarrow Crusade

Though there were many hunger marches throughout the 1920s and 1930s, one in particular captured more attention than the others. This was the **Jarrow Crusade** of October 1936. It was the only march to be organised by the Labour

The 1936 Jarrow Crusaders, the best known of many 'hunger marchers' during the inter-war years, are shown here on their way to London from a home town devastated by unemployment. Demonstrations such as these made it difficult for the British to forget the human tragedy that unemployment was for its victims.

party and owed its success to the work of the newly elected Labour MP for Jarrow, Ellen Wilkinson. It had a particular message to convey, as Jarrow's shipyards provided one of the country's worst examples of mass unemployment. In Jarrow, few people were not on the dole. The dignity of the Jarrow marchers made a deep impression in the towns and villages they went through on their long journey. But neither the Jarrow Crusade nor any of the other hunger marches can be said directly to have achieved improvement for the unemployed. What they did do was to make it difficult for the country to forget about unemployment. In many areas of the country there was little unemployment. The hunger marchers were determined to make certain that the plight of the unemployed was not forgotten by the country as a whole, and particularly by those who lived in more favoured areas.

Unemployment: the work of the National government

If the unemployed were not to be forgotten, the government would have to take a lead in reviving the country's economy. The National government attempted to create the conditions in which the country's economy would revive. It did not, however, go in for direct state intervention in the economy, as was done by the US government during these years, when President Roosevelt's New Deal programme was put into effect.

Economic protection

The abandonment of the gold standard in September 1931 had been a useful first step by the government. No longer were British goods over-priced in world markets. This was followed a few months later, in February 1932, by the Import Duties Act, a vital piece of legislation in the re-introduction of economic protection and the abandonment of free trade. Its effect was to place taxes of between 10-20 per cent on about half of Britain's imports, though no taxes were placed on imported food. At the same time goods entering Britain from the Empire were allowed to do so without tax payment. This concession was intended as a first step towards the creation of free trade between all the countries of the Empire, a subject which was extensively discussed at a conference of dominion countries held at Ottawa, in Canada, in the summer of 1932. These discussions came to very little, as most dominion countries had economic problems of their own which led them to favour protectionist policies. Nevertheless trade with the dominions did increase during the 1930s.

BRITISH SOCIETY DURING THE 1930S

The old policy of free trade was finally dropped during the early 1930s. Most – though not all – members of the National government show their approval, while Beaverbrook, the arch-enemy of the old policy, takes a parting pot shot.

Cheap money

Another move to create favourable conditions for British industry was government encouragement of low interest rates. For most of the 1930s money could be borrowed from banks at an interest rate of about 2 per cent. This low rate made money more readily available for firms to borrow in order to finance expansion. **Cheap money**, as it was termed, was to be the basis of much expansion during the 1930s, a subject which is considered in the following section.

Special areas

However successful this expansion might be in some parts of the country during the 1930s, unemployment continued to overshadow the areas of the staple industries. The Special Areas Act of 1934 was a direct government attempt to assist these areas. Financial aid was given to what were termed the **special areas** (in reality, the depressed areas) of Scotland, South Wales, West Cumberland and the North-East, and government encouragement was given for industries to move to those parts of the country. The whole scheme was not really successful, partly because the aid was small and partly because of the very serious difficulties that the staple industries were suffering from anyway. Some unemployed gave up all hope of improvement in their home areas and moved to parts of the country where the 1930s had brought prosperity and job opportunity. The government was much criticised for not doing enough to help these depressed areas.

The economic revival of the 1930s

Two distinct pictures can be painted of the British economy during the 1930s. One shows a country plunged into Depression with high unemployment and much suffering among its victims. This gloomy picture has already been looked at. The other picture is of a country with newly developing industries and with an employed population enjoying a far higher standard of living than most of them had previously experienced. What did this more promising picture of Britain look like?

Electricity

New industries were fundamental to this revival and most of these new industries used the new power of electricity. In 1926 the Central Electricity Board was set up to develop a unified system of electrical power for Britain. Over the next few years the grid system for the distribution of electricity was extended. This involved the construction of pylons to carry electricity cables. As a result, in the early 1930s, Britain was better supplied with electricity than any other industrialised country. Electricity was used mainly for two purposes: domestic and industrial. Within the houses of Britain the ready supply of electricity made for many welcome changes. Lighting and heating became simpler, while vacuum cleaners, refrigerators, radios and other electrically powered appliances were beginning to be commonly found in households.

This new factory on the outskirts of London gives evidence of economic development away from the traditional industrial centres. The 1930s were not years of unrelieved economic gloom.

Electricity had an even greater impact in industry. In the past, factories had been set up near to supplies of coal, the main source of power. Electricity distributed by the grid made nearby supplies of coal no longer necessary. Factories could now be set up in other parts of the country, nearer to the people likely to buy their products.

Cars and consumer goods

Many of these factories were employing new techniques of mass production. Conveyor belt methods of production were much used. Particularly important in this respect was the mass-production of cars in the 1930s. What before the First World War and even in the 1920s had been a luxury item individually produced, now had a much larger market. Mass production had helped to make cars cheaper and thus to increase demand for them. Other consumer goods also experienced boom conditions in the 1930s as a result of this technique.

Rationalisation

A solution for the economic troubles of the time was seen in the amalgamation of companies, a process often referred to as **rationalisation**. By bringing together companies engaged on the same kind of work, greater efficiency would result. Though rationalisation often produced difficulties of adjustment and often led to redundancies, the policies certainly assisted the revival of some industries. London Transport, created in 1933, is a good example of rationalisation. Until then, bus, tram and underground transport had been organised in Britain's capital by different companies whose policies often conflicted. These now formed part of one large enterprise. Other schemes of rationalisation led to the creation of such large companies as Imperial Chemical Industries (ICI), Unilever and the Shell Oil Company. These large companies were active in researching new and profitable products. Large stores also tended to displace small shops in the 1930s, a time when many well-known stores became firmly established in the high streets of British towns.

Building industry

The industry that advanced with the greatest success in the 1930s was the building industry. The results of its work at that time are still to be seen in the suburbs of most British towns, as this was a time of extensive building of both private houses and council houses. Much of the development in private house building was a result of building societies lending money to house purchasers. Though the development resulted in the disappearance of country areas as the suburbs advanced even further outwards from the towns, many people were now able to enjoy much better standards of housing with many modern amenities.

Holidays

The various developments in industry, in transport and in housing show that for many the 1930s was a time of improving standards of living. As with the problem of unemployment, there were many regional differences. The improved standards of living were more noticeable in the Midlands and southern England than they were in northern England, Scotland, Wales and Northern Ireland. Those who benefited in these years found new opportunities for the use of leisure. The Holidays with Pay Act of 1938 substantially increased the number of workers who were entitled to take a paid week's holiday each year. Seaside holiday resorts experienced a new lease of life in the late 1930s. Holiday camps, such as Butlin's, were opened in some resorts during these years and provided a different style of holiday for the many to whom a week's freedom from work was a new experience. Throughout Britain, many buildings were adapted into youth hostels, catering for those of all ages who wanted to hike or cycle. Both activities were very popular. Advantage was also taken of the reduction in price of motor cars, and motoring holidays were another innovation of these years.

Radio and cinema

At home, the radio had provided entertainment since the mid-1920s, though comparatively few were able to afford to receive in their homes the new television programmes which began in 1936. The cinema formed the main social activity for most people; by the late 1930s an average of three new cinemas were opening every week. Cinema prices were low and attendance was as popular among the unemployed as it was among the employed.

Fascism and Communism

Oswald Mosley

It was not surprising that Britain was affected by the Fascist movement that made such spectacular advances in a number of continental countries during these years. Some Fascist groups had existed in the 1920s, but they never attracted much support. It was around Oswald Mosley that Fascism in Britain developed in the 1930s. Mosley had earlier been a Conservative MP, had then left the party to join Labour and had been a minister in the second Labour government. After his memorandum on unemployment had been rejected (page 152), he resigned and after attempting to form a political party of his own, was expelled from the Labour party. He became much impressed with Fascism as it had developed in Italy and it was what he saw there that inspired him to lead a similar movement in Britain. In the autumn of 1932 he set up the British Union

Oswald Mosley receives salutes from the black-shirted members of his British Union of Fascists at an East London parade in 1936. Notice the presence of the Italian fascist symbol as well as the Union Jack among the flags, showing Italian fascism and British nationalism as the bases of Mosley's movement.

Fascism

of Fascists, at the same time launching his book, *The Greater Britain*, which put forward the sort of Britain which Mosley hoped his movement would create.

Mosley hoped that the British Union of Fascists would appeal to the unemployed, but it failed to do so. He also hoped that a crisis – comparable to that of August 1931 – would occur in Britain and that in this crisis he would be able to secure power, as Mussolini and Hitler had done in similar circumstances. But the crisis that he hoped for never arrived. The violence that many of his supporters used against hecklers at their meetings – particularly a large meeting at Olympia in June 1934 – turned people away from Fascism. One Conservative present at the meeting recorded the following impression.

> I was appalled by the brutal conduct of the Fascists. ... There seems little doubt that some of the later victims of the Blackshirt stewards were Conservatives endeavouring to make a protest at the unnecessary violence. ... I saw with my own eyes case after case of single interrupters being attacked by ten to twenty Fascists. Again and again, as five or six Blackshirts carried out an interrupter by arms and legs, several other Blackshirts were engaged in kicking and hitting his helpless body.... I saw several respectable-looking people, who merely rose in their places and made no struggle, treated with the unmerciful brutality that I have described. ... I wondered what further violence was inflicted when the Blackshirts had dragged their victims out of public view. It was a deeply shocking scene for an Englishman to see in London. The Blackshirts behaved like bullies and cads.
>
> Letter of Geoffrey Lloyd, MP, to the *Yorkshire Post*

By the late 1930s, when the movement directed much effort into a campaign against Jews in East London, Fascism was a spent force.

Communism

Just as the British gave minimal support to Fascism, so also they gave minimal support to the movement often suggested as its direct opposite, Communism. In fact, Communism could be said to have been rather more successful than Fascism in these years. It had much influence in the NUWM and it produced two MPs in the 1920s and one in the 1930s. Its following was nevertheless slight.

Political developments during the 1930s

Labour party

Most British people were content to give their support to the Liberal, Labour and Conservative parties. Yet all these parties continued to have their own difficulties. The Liberal party was now unlikely to recover the place which the Labour party had taken from it. The Labour party itself was not finding it easy to get over the shock of the events of August 1931. For most of the early part of the 1930s it was under the leadership of George Lansbury, a much respected figure in the party and a committed pacifist. As the international situation became more menacing in the mid-1930s, the party became critical of Lansbury's pacifism. It was trade union influence which was largely responsible for Lansbury's resignation in 1935 and his replacement as party leader by Clement Attlee. By contrast with Labour's earlier leaders, Attlee came from a middle-class background; he had earlier been a university teacher and had done social work in East London. He was to lead his party for the next 20 years, and to bring it to its great success in the 1945 general election.

The 1935 general election

At the time Attlee took on the leadership, electoral success for the Labour party seemed unlikely. The recent divisions in the party were not easily healed, while the Conservatives were free of such troubles. The Conservative position in the National government was now stronger than it had been in 1931. Baldwin took over from MacDonald in the summer of 1935, thus becoming Prime Minister for the third time. The circumstances seemed to him right for the holding of a general election, and this took place in November. The government emphasised the improving state of the economy and the declining figures for unemployment. Baldwin's image as a trustworthy politician was also of value to the government. Their campaign paid off well and the government was confirmed in office.

General Election: November 1935	
Supporters of the National government	**Opponents of the National government**
Conservatives 388 Liberals 35 National Labour 8 others 4 435	Labour 154 Liberals 20 others 6 180

By contrasting these election figures with those for the 1931 general election (page 155) it can be seen that the Liberal party and the Labour supporters of the National government had both declined. The Conservative party remained fairly steady. But the Labour party gained the most seats, while the overall voting figures for the Labour party were higher than these figures alone suggest. As often happens in British general elections, the number of MPs elected for a party on the basis of their constituencies did not reflect the overall support that the party had in the country. In this election, for example, the Conservatives secured 11.8 million votes and the Labour party 8.3 million.

Importance of foreign affairs

It is from this time onwards that foreign affairs became a more important concern for the government than affairs at home. They formed an important part of the government's election campaign in 1935. Baldwin's concern about the Italian aggression then taking place in Abyssinia made him include in the general election campaign a pledge for re-armament. It did not form a major part of the campaign, but it was a sign of the government's concern at the weakening international situation and at the need for strengthened defences. The involvement of the government in foreign affairs during the second half of the 1930s is considered in the following chapter.

The monarchy

George V

Baldwin did, however, face one serious problem at home before he retired. This concerned the British monarchy. In January 1936 King George V had died after a reign of more than 25 years. The country's respect for the King, and for Queen Mary, had been shown during the previous year when many national events had been organised to mark the Silver Jubilee of their reign. George V had reigned during years of much change and difficulty within Britain. His part in the controversy surrounding the House of Lords, his attitude towards the Labour party in power for the first time, his advice for moderation in the General Strike, his role in the 1931 crisis: all show that the monarchy continued to play an important part in a changing Britain.

Edward VIII and Mrs Simpson

The new King, Edward VIII, was a man of different personality. He had already achieved popularity as Prince of Wales and in the early months of his reign the country seemed to enjoy the modern and youthful image that the new King presented. He was an unmarried man, but had already fallen in love with Mrs Wallis Simpson. Baldwin felt it his duty as Prime Minister to warn the King that the attachment was unwise; if he were to marry Mrs Simpson, he would have to abdicate as King. What were the objections to Mrs Simpson? Mainly it

A HISTORY OF BRITAIN FROM 1867

was that she had been twice divorced. However unfair it may seem today, divorce in the mid-1930s was a serious obstacle in any person's career. It would be particularly unsuitable for the King of England to be married to a divorced woman. Additionally, the King of England had the position of Governor of the Church of England. The Archbishop of Canterbury, Cosmo Lang, made plain the Church's opposition to the proposed marriage. Mrs Simpson's US citizenship was regarded as an additional reason for opposition to the marriage, as there was in these years some strong feeling against people from the United States.

Abdication of Edward VIII In December 1936 it became public knowledge that the King intended to marry Mrs Simpson. Baldwin's opposition to the marriage was now shown to be strongly supported by public opinion. Though the King had some supporters in the country – Churchill being a leading politician who felt that the marriage should go ahead – it was not sufficient to be really helpful. So strong was the King's own love for Mrs Simpson that he was willing to abdicate the throne rather than abandon his plans for marriage. On 11 December 1936, after signing a document of abdication, he left the country and was married to Mrs Simpson the next year. He was given the title of Duke of Windsor and both he and his wife continued to live abroad for the rest of their lives.

George VI The new King was his brother, George VI. Neither he nor his wife, Queen Elizabeth, had expected these new burdens to fall to them. There was concern that George VI had not been prepared for the responsibilities he now faced and he was known to be a man of nervous personality. But the new royal family – which included the young princesses Elizabeth and Margaret – soon became well liked. George VI proved a dedicated and conscientious ruler. The example and encouragement that he gave to the British people during the Second World War was to be widely admired. 1936 had been a time of crisis for the monarchy, but in the person of George VI it emerged much strengthened.

Baldwin himself retired just after the new King's coronation in May 1937. Neville Chamberlain, for many years regarded as Baldwin's successor, took over as Prime Minister. As such he was driven to involve himself closely in the affairs of Continental Europe, where in the late 1930s the situation had become dangerously menacing.

EXERCISES

1. 'A country with far higher living standards than most of its inhabitants had previously experienced.'
   (a) How do you account for this important feature of British society in the 1930s?
   (b) In which industries and in which parts of the country was this feature most noticeable?
   (c) Give examples of the effect that higher living standards had in British society in the 1930s.

2. Describe and show the importance of the following in the 1930s:
   (a) the National Unemployed Workers' Movement,
   (b) the British Union of Fascists,
   (c) the general election of 1935, and
   (d) the abdication of Edward VIII.

3. Imagine you are one of the unemployed during the 1930s. Write an explanation of why you and many others are suffering unemployment and how unemployment has affected your way of life.

4. Study the poster on page 158, the photograph on page 160 and the extract on page 159 and then answer questions (a) to (d) which follow.
   (a) (i) How do the words at the top of the poster and the images in the poster help to convey the plight of the unemployed in the 1930s?
   (ii) Why had unemployment become a serious problem within Britain by this time? (3+4)
   (b) (i) Why might the proposal obscured at the foot of the poster have provided a solution for unemployment?
   (ii) To what extent did the National government in the 1930s provide a 'remedy' for unemployment? (2+4)
   (c) Why do you think this poster would have strong appeal at the time of the 1931 general election? (2)
   (d) (i) By reference to your own knowledge and to details shown in the photograph, indicate the type of effect that marches such as this might have.
   (ii) How far do you agree with the view put by Baldwin about such marches in the extract on page 159? (5)

14 BRITISH FOREIGN POLICY DURING THE INTER-WAR YEARS

During the 1920s and the 1930s the conflict of 1914–18 was most usually known as the **Great War**. These two decades were ones in which the British people came to understand – through the publication of novels and historical studies of the war – how pointless and how immense had been the slaughter and the suffering which it had brought. The over-riding aim of British foreign policy was to avoid a repetition. This was no easy aim to achieve. In pursuing it, British politicians followed a variety of courses, yet in the end failed to avert Britain's involvement in the Second World War in 1939.

Britain and the approach to a peace settlement

Self-determination Britain played its part in framing the peace settlement that followed the First World War. The Prime Minister, Lloyd George, held extensive discussions at Paris in 1919, in the company of President Wilson of the United States and the Prime Minister of France, Georges Clemenceau. These men entered the 1919 discussions with fixed ideas on what they hoped to secure. President Wilson struck a highly idealistic note as soon as his country had entered the war in 1917. For him the war and the settlement which followed should create the right circumstances for peace to flourish. He gave expression of his hopes in his **Fourteen Points**, issued in January 1918. It was in this document that he proposed the setting up of the League of Nations. In it he also envisaged a peace settlement based upon the principles of **self-determination**. Why was so much importance given to **self-determination** and what did it involve?

By that stage in the war, many considered that the fundamental cause of its outbreak had been the tensions created by national feelings within different European countries. This led minority racial groups within these countries to dislike the governments that ruled them and to seek help from sympathetic governments elsewhere. If these people were themselves allowed to determine (thus to exercise **self-determination**) to which country they should belong the tensions which could result in war would be removed.

French desire for security When the Paris peace conference opened in January 1919, self-determination was therefore a major issue. It was not the only one. Clemenceau asserted the French need for **security**. Of the main powers represented at Paris, only France had experienced invasion of their territory by German forces. The French search for security involved taking steps to weaken Germany so that the possibility of renewed warfare might be lessened. Lloyd George had a more modest approach to the issue of peace-making than either Wilson or Clemenceau, and showed no strong commitment to either the US desire for self-determination or the French search for security. Lloyd George's approach strongly influenced the terms eventually put into the most important of the various agreements reached at Paris: the Treaty of Versailles. This treaty was reluctantly accepted by Germany in June 1919, and was signed by its representatives at the Palace of Versailles in a carefully arranged ceremony designed to emphasise Germany's defeat and humiliation.

The terms of the peace settlement

War guilt Fundamental to the treaty's terms was a statement that German policies had alone been responsible for the outbreak of the First World War. Though this view was widely accepted at the time, it has since then been regarded as far too

The peace settlement of 1919

sweeping; throughout the inter-war years it was for the German people a particular cause of anger. The provisions of the other clauses were all based on this **war-guilt** clause.

Territorial changes

Former German territory in Europe was lost: Alsace-Lorraine went to France, minor adjustments were made to the Belgian and Danish frontiers, a substantial area in the east was given to the new state of Poland. This was drastic treatment of defeated Germany; nor did it represent justice to Germany or the principle of self-determination, as there were significant numbers of German people in the lost territories, especially those in the east. Yet it was Lloyd George who ensured that German losses were not even more extensive. Clemenceau had hoped to separate the Rhineland from Germany and, in the interests of French security, to set it up as a 'buffer' state separating the two countries. Lloyd George successfully opposed this plan and showed a similar attitude towards suggested changes in the east. There he insisted that Danzig, predominantly German in population, should come under international and not Polish control, and he also insisted that the mixed population of Silesia should be allowed to vote in a referendum on their future with either Germany or Poland.

Colonial changes

Former German colonies were also lost. Many had been occupied by British dominion forces during the war and the Treaty of Versailles merely formalised their changed possession. Self-determination was not entirely put aside in what appeared to be a change that had little regard for the wishes of the inhabitants. These former colonies were now regarded as **mandates**, territories which the new occupants were to hold temporarily until the territories were ready for independence. But that was seen as being a far distant event, so for the foreseeable future the mandates could be regarded as newly acquired colonies. The British dominions and Britain itself did well under the mandates system. The British dominion of South Africa acquired German South-West Africa and the British dominion of Australia acquired New Guinea; Britain itself acquired

Tanganyika, Togoland and part of the Cameroons. As large parts of the Middle Eastern territories of the defeated Ottoman Empire also went to Britain under the mandate system, the entire peace settlement marked an important extension of British power overseas (see maps on pages 81 and 128).

Limitations on arms

Steps were also taken in the treaty to curb Germany's military and economic power for the future. The German army, navy and air force were all to be strictly limited in size and the Rhineland was to be a de-militarised zone, where no fortifications or troops were to be allowed. Before 1914, Britain had mainly been concerned about the challenge which the powerful German Navy had posed to the Royal Navy. Although the terms of the treaty cut down its future size, Britain had at the end of the war already confined the German Navy at Scapa Flow, off northern Scotland. At the time of the signing of the treaty, the German sailors made a defiant gesture of protest. They **scuttled** their own ships, preferring to destroy them rather than to see them controlled by their former enemy.

Reparations

Though the clauses concerning territory, colonies and armaments were much disliked by Germany, the clauses concerning the German economy were the ones that were to create most bitterness in the future. The treaty required that Germany should pay **reparations** (compensation) for the damage that it had done in foreign countries during the war. On this issue also, Lloyd George was more moderate than Clemenceau. His moderation aroused the anger of some 200 Conservative MPs in Britain, who protested at his 'weak' approach towards Germany on reparations. Lloyd George's view was that the future peace of Europe required a prosperous Germany and that excessive reparations would make such prosperity difficult to achieve. The Prime Minister's approach was supported by the economist J.M. Keynes, who in 1919 produced a book called *The Economic Consequences of the Peace*. In this he warned of the dangers for Europe if the German economy was seriously weakened. Due to Lloyd George's influence, the difficult decision on how much reparations Germany should pay was to be considered in detail by a Reparations Commission. Though reparation payments were therefore more carefully considered, the Commission eventually agreed in 1921 the enormous sum of £6600 million.

Austria-Hungary

Peace with Germany was the main British preoccupation at Paris in 1919–20, but it was not the only one. Agreement had also to be reached on the boundaries of the countries that had been set up as the old Austria-Hungary disintegrated after its defeat in the war. These were agreed in the treaties of St Germain and Trianon. Though the British were at the time little interested in countries such as Austria, Hungary, Czechoslovakia, Yugoslavia, Romania and Poland – all of which emerged partly or wholly from the old Austria-Hungary – they were to become areas of important controversy in the late 1930s.

New British involvements abroad

Palestine

Britain was more directly involved in the Treaty of Sèvres, signed with the defeated and decaying Ottoman Empire. By this treaty Britain acquired mandates in Palestine, Transjordan and Iraq (see map on page 128). The British presence in one of these – Palestine – was to become a source of much difficulty during the inter-war years. In 1917 the British Foreign Secretary, Arthur Balfour, had committed the British government to the principles of **Zionism**, to create in Palestine a 'national home' for the dispersed Jewish people. By the 1930s and 1940s conflict between the original Arab inhabitants and the Jewish settlers was to make Palestine one of the most difficult and most violent of Britain's overseas possessions. But these new mandates were considered at the end of the First World War to have distinct advantages for Britain. The Suez Canal could be more readily protected. More usefully, Britain would be concerned in an area where oil was in plentiful supply.

Intervention in Russia

While the peace negotiations were taking place in Paris, British troops were still involved in hostilities in Russia. They had been sent there after the new Communist government, which seized power in the autumn of 1917, had withdrawn from fighting against Germany on the Allied side. The main reason for the sending of troops to Russia was to protect British military equipment that had been sent there earlier in the war. But many of them gave support to the opponents of the Communist government – often referred to as the **Whites** – in what was developing as a widespread civil war within Russia. Their involvement became a matter of controversy within Britain. Some Conservative politicians were anxious to increase British involvement on the White side in order to bring down the Communist government before it was able properly to establish itself. But public opinion did not favour continued involvement of British troops in any further warfare after the First World War had ended. Towards the close of 1919 most of the British forces had been withdrawn from Russia. This British assistance to the enemies of the Communist government, just when it was trying to establish itself, was to embitter Anglo-Soviet relations for a long time to come.

Britain and the League of Nations

Though the creation of the League of Nations is most closely associated with President Wilson, it was British diplomats and politicians who worked out how it was to be organised. In 1920 it began work at Geneva amidst hopes that it would provide – through its widely representative Assembly and its smaller, highly powered Council – a means of preserving the peace of the world. Unfortunately it never secured whole-hearted support and there were significant absentees in its membership: the United States never became a member and, at least at first, the defeated nations of the First World War were kept out.

Geneva Protocol

Britain's approach to the League remained unsteady throughout the 1920s and 1930s. Generally speaking, it was supported with fuller commitment by the Liberal and Labour parties and with rather less commitment by the Conservative party. Ramsay MacDonald gave much attention to the League of Nations when he was Prime Minister and Foreign Secretary in 1924. He worked out an improved method of resolving disputes, known as the **Geneva Protocol**. This pledged League members to accept international arbitration of disputes that might lead to war and to support countries that had suffered an unprovoked attack. The Geneva Protocol was never accepted by the League of Nations. The new government formed by Baldwin in the autumn of 1924 became suspicious of the fuller involvement in the League which the Protocol would require and refused to support it. In any case, during the 1920s, the League did not have to tackle issues that seriously threatened world peace, and none that threatened British overseas interests. When in the 1930s world peace was seriously threatened, the League of Nations proved unequal to the task.

The search for collective security

Idea of collective security

Throughout the inter-war years much attention was given by different British governments to maintaining **collective security** in international relations. It was hoped to maintain peace by means of collective discussions and collective action. If that succeeded, there need be no warfare. The League of Nations provided one means by which collective security might be achieved, and meetings between governments provided another.

British foreign affairs in the early 1920s

The 1920s saw a number of such meetings and Britain played an important part in them. The issues that dominated the early 1920s were all related in one way or another to the First World War and the peace settlement. There was continuing friction with the Soviet Union. Only early in 1924 did Britain's first Labour government recognise the Communist government there, seven years after the Revolution had taken place. The controversy surrounding such issues as the Zinoviev letter (pages 142–3) and the Arcos raid (page 150) caused friction in Anglo-Soviet relations during the 1920s. Relations with the United States were strained as a result of the rigid insistence of the US government that Britain's wartime debts must be repaid in full. Relations with France were also unsteady, troubled especially by the sharpness of the continuing French hostility towards Germany. This became a major issue in 1923, when French forces occupied Germany's industrial Ruhr district due to a temporary German failure to pay its reparations. The British did not fully approve this action, though they could not prevent it. In the following year, Ramsay MacDonald's influence helped to bring about the withdrawal of the French forces and the acceptance by France as well as by Germany of a revised scheme of reparation payments, the Dawes plan, which the United States proposed.

Locarno

The international discussions at the Swiss resort of Locarno in the autumn of 1925 marked a point of greater harmony in European relations. Germany was fully represented in these discussions, which were concerned to remove the bitterness that had characterised Germany's relations with the rest of Europe since the war had ended. The main agreement was an acceptance of the permanence of Germany's western frontiers with France and Belgium. Britain, represented at the conference by its Foreign Secretary, Austen Chamberlain, guaranteed these frontiers. It also supported German membership of the League of Nations, which followed the next year. The Locarno agreements were enthusiastically received in Britain – and elsewhere – as heralding an era of peace. In reality, the agreements contained some distinct weaknesses. There was no comparable British guarantee of the permanence of Germany's eastern frontiers, with Poland and Czechoslovakia. It was issues concerning these frontiers that were to lead to the outbreak of war at the end of the next decade. As for the guarantee of the western frontiers, no steps were taken to ensure that these frontiers would be properly defended if the need should arise.

Kellogg–Briand pact

Britain's rather vague commitments given at Locarno were matched in 1928 by its involvement in the Kellogg–Briand pact. This pact, sponsored by the US Secretary of State and the French Foreign Minister, had as its essential feature the renouncing of war. Britain was among its large number of signatories. It seemed not only right to subscribe to the pact, in view of its noble aim, but also very natural to do so in the late 1920s. These were years which saw little disturbance to the peace of Europe, or to the world. It really did seem that war belonged to history and had no place in the world of that time.

Manchuria and Abyssinia

Strength of pacifism

This peacefulness came to a sudden end in 1931. The Japanese invasion of Chinese-held Manchuria, which took place in September of that year, began a decade of unrest that was to end in the outbreak of the Second World War. For most of these years, the British government's policy on armaments showed poor preparation for the possibility of war. In the early 1930s Britain was gripped by an intense hatred of war. It was well over a decade since the First World War had ended. The pointlessness of the war's slaughter and the incompetence of its direction by both politicians and generals were by then better understood than they had been earlier. This hatred of war had led some in Britain to support the pacifist movement, and totally condemn all wars, even those in self-defence. Among prominent pacifists was the leader of the Labour party in the early 1930s, George Lansbury. A Peace Ballot, organised throughout Britain by League of Nations supporters in 1935 showed that a large majority in the country still favoured disarmament.

Failure in Manchuria

The economic difficulties facing the government in these years were as important in this connection as the strength of public feeling. The government welcomed the opportunity of making major savings in public expenditure. Under the circumstances, it was only to be expected that Britain would respond weakly to aggressive acts by other countries. No positive action was taken against Japan in the early 1930s. Britain and other major powers put their trust in the League of Nations, which sent out a special commission of enquiry under the leadership of an Englishman, Lord Lytton. More than a year passed from the time of the Japanese invasion before Lytton produced his report, at the end of 1932. Though Japanese concern at Chinese mistreatment of some of the

Japan, portrayed as an international gangster, gets lenient treatment from the League of Nations. The weakness of Lord Lytton's report on the invasion of Manchuria gave encouragement to similar acts of aggression later in the 1930s.

property they earlier held in Manchuria was acknowledged as reasonable, their violent actions of the previous year were unreservedly condemned.

But what was to be done about it? Here lies the real weakness of the report, as it made no proposal for any action against Japan, not even the most modest course open to the League of Nations: **economic sanctions**. Such action was designed to put pressure on a country but cutting off its foreign trading links. Britain was the major power to urge acceptance of the report. The whole episode of the Manchurian invasion and the Lytton report had important consequences. Japan secured Manchuria, which became a stepping stone for further Japanese penetration of China later in the 1930s: aggression paid off well for them. The League of Nations was shown as weak and incapable of combating aggression of this kind: collective security appeared no longer to be working.

Failure in Ethiopia

Many of these features were to be found again a few years later when, in an aggressive colonial venture, Italy under Mussolini's leadership invaded Ethiopia in October 1935. The League responded somewhat more briskly to the aggressor on this occasion. Economic sanctions were imposed on Italy, but as these excluded oil, they were not fully effective. Britain supported these partial sanctions. The Foreign Secretary, Sir Samuel Hoare, was anxious to maintain reasonable relations with Italy, in spite of the Ethiopia difficulty. He hoped that Britain might be able to use Italy as an ally against Germany, whose foreign policy was beginning to develop in a far more dangerous way. Concessions to Italy over Ethiopia might help towards the fulfilling of this policy. The French Foreign Minister, Pierre Laval, was also anxious for good relations with Italy. In December 1935 they jointly produced a compromise known as the Hoare-Laval plan, by which Italy was to be allowed to acquire territorial and economic rights in Ethiopia. When details of these proposed concessions were leaked in Britain, protest was surprisingly strong. The plan had to be abandoned, and Hoare had to resign as Foreign Secretary.

British rearmament

All this made little difference to what Mussolini did in Abyssinia. His forces continued to advance into the country which, in May 1936, was incorporated as a part of Italy's overseas empire. The hostility with which Hoare's plans were greeted inside Britain suggested that public opinion was beginning to want a stronger policy towards acts of aggression such as this. This changed mood was of value to the government, which had recently begun rearmament. Its stand on this issue now appeared to be receiving the public support that it needed.

Early responses to German rearmament

Rearmament became a lively issue in the mid-1930s as a result of the open armament pursued by the new government in Germany. In the course of 1933, the same year in which he came to power, Hitler had declared that his country no longer felt committed to the disarmament clauses of the Treaty of Versailles. At the same time, he took Germany out of the League of Nations and began a programme of rearmament which early in 1935 involved the conscription of men for the German armed services. Moves by the British government in 1935 were hesitant and contradictory. In April, Britain joined with France and Italy in the **Stresa Front** to show their concern at the introduction of conscription in Germany and their resolve to combat aggression wherever it should arise. But in June, Britain signed the Anglo-German Naval Treaty, by which Britain agreed that German naval strength could be 35 per cent that of Britain, while the submarine strength might in certain circumstances be equal. Acceptance of this treaty showed that Britain no longer regarded seriously the clauses of the Versailles Treaty which required German disarmament. It also removed any significance from the Stresa Front.

The Rhineland

Government policies towards aggression continued to lack strength. There was virtually no British reaction to Hitler's decision in March 1935 to send German troops into the demilitarised Rhineland zone. The issue was a greater challenge to France than to Britain. As the French took no military action, it was unlikely that Britain would act alone on this issue. In any case, British public opinion saw little amiss in what Hitler had done by walking into what was often called Germany's 'own backyard'.

Spanish Civil War

When in the summer of 1936 a military revolt began the three-year civil war in Spain there was a similar weak reaction by Britain. Together with France, the British government set up the Non-Intervention Committee, in an attempt not to become involved in this troublesome situation and not to permit other countries to involve themselves either. In practice, the Non-Intervention Committee proved quite powerless to stop either Germany or Italy from giving much assistance to the rebel Nationalist side. The government's approach to events in Spain could be seen as another sign of allowing aggression to go unchecked. Some on the left in British politics joined the **International Brigade** that fought for the Republic in Spain. Their involvement emphasised both dissatisfaction with the government's official neutrality on the issue and the movement by the Labour party towards a stronger attitude in foreign policy. Government policy towards events in Spain, as towards events in Manchuria, Ethiopia and the Rhineland, suggested very definitely to the powers concerned that Britain was unlikely to take positive action against any aggressive steps they might take.

The practice of appeasement

Idea of appeasement

Appeasement is most closely associated in Britain with the policies pursued by Neville Chamberlain in the earlier part of his three-year premiership (May 1937–May 1940), when he, rather than the Foreign Secretary, directed the course of Britain's foreign relations. At its best, **appeasement** involved the putting right of justified grievances that Germany might have, especially those arising from the Treaty of Versailles. Men such as Chamberlain and fellow appeasers in the government felt that this was the correct approach to take, as by doing so the threat of war would be removed.

By the late 1930s, the British people were aware that war would mean **total war**, a situation in which civilians at home would be as much involved in hostilities as soldiers abroad. The particular fear of aerial bombardment had been much sharpened by knowledge of recent events in the Spanish Civil War. Surely it was right to avoid total war by removing the grievances of a potential enemy? In any case, with its worldwide imperial commitments and with the effects of the Depression still not entirely ended, the country could ill afford the expense of a war. No real faith could be placed in the League of Nations, so was there really any alternative to direct approaches of this kind?

In practice, appeasement worked out differently. Germany – and Italy to a lesser extent – interpreted appeasement as a sign of weakness. By extending their country's power, international treaties and agreements could be broken at will, as resistance was unlikely. Thus appeasement tended to encourage aggression.

Neville Chamberlain

Chamberlain was, in any case, not well suited to have so strong an influence on the conduct of foreign affairs. Having entered politics comparatively late in life, he had shown distinct ability in tackling the detail of domestic affairs while he had been Minister of Health in Baldwin's second ministry (1924–29) and Chancellor of the Exchequer in the National government (1931–37). The situation and people with whom he had dealt during those years had been familiar and straightforward. There was a great difference between them and those he became concerned with in central Europe during the late 1930s. His assumption that he could solve problems abroad by means of the straightforward, man-to-man meetings that he had employed in tackling domestic problems, was to prove ill founded.

Early examples of appeasement

Though appeasement is most closely associated with Chamberlain's name, it was hardly a policy that began only in his time as Prime Minister. The faltering policies on rearmament and the weak approach to the issues concerning Manchuria, Ethiopia, the Rhineland and Spain have many similarities with Chamberlain's approaches to the problems of the late 1930s. Early in his premiership he showed a determination to pursue appeasement objectives, ignoring the views of those politicians who would have preferred to adopt firmer policies. Conciliatory approaches to Italy over its involvement in Spain brought about a clash between Chamberlain and his Foreign Secretary, Anthony Eden, resulting in the latter's resignation in February 1938. With the appointment of the more amenable Lord Halifax in Eden's place, Chamberlain was able to direct foreign affairs in the way he judged best.

Anschluss

Almost at once a major issue of foreign policy presented itself. Hitler, who had for some years expressed his determination to bring about the **Anschluss** (union) of Germany and Austria, felt strong enough to achieve this in March 1938. He did so with very little trouble either within Austria or from outside. Chamberlain expressed disapproval of Hitler's action but made it clear that Austria was not an issue on which Britain would be prepared to fight. Austria having been secured, Hitler made known that a solution to the Czechoslovak problem was now the priority of his government's foreign policy.

Britain and the problem of Czechoslovakia

Divisions within Czechoslovakia

Czechoslovakia was a new country, a creation of the First World War peace settlement. Its geographical unity and useful economic resources provided the bases for successful development. Unfortunately, there was a lack of harmony between the different peoples within the new country. Relations of the majority Czechs with the Slovaks were tense. So also were Czech relations with the three

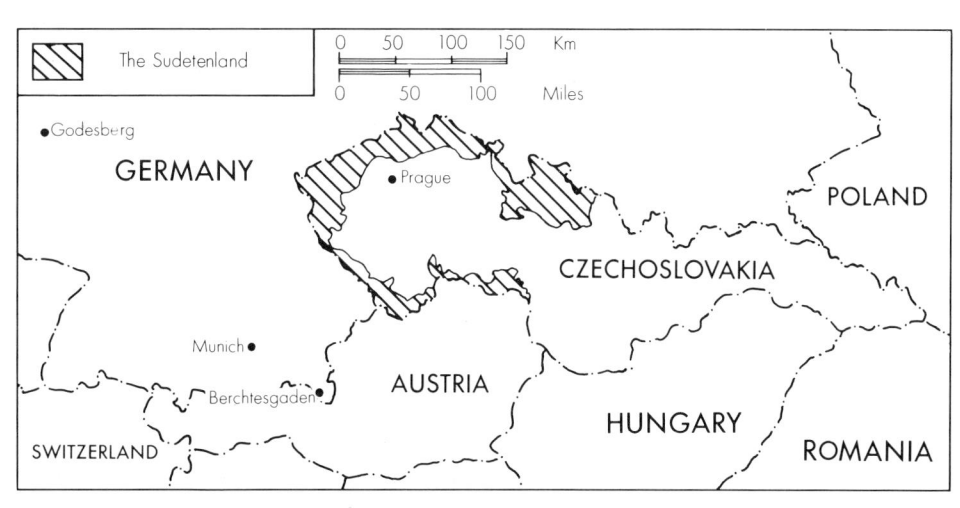

BRITISH FOREIGN POLICY DURING THE INTER-WAR YEARS

Czechoslovakia and Germany at the time of the Munich conference

million Germans who inhabited the mountains of the Sudetenland in the west of the country, bordering on to a Germany now enlarged by the Anschluss with Austria. With Hitler's encouragement, the Germans of the Sudetenland pressed their claims to be incorporated within Germany.

Britain and Czechoslovakia

Britain acted in liaison with France over the Czechoslovak problem. In the Locarno treaties of 1925 France had given a commitment to protect Czechoslovakia from aggression, a commitment which Britain never gave. So from the technical point of view of treaty commitments, Britain had no obligation to go to Czechoslovakia's aid in the event of attack. Chamberlain himself referred to Czechoslovakia as a 'far-away country' and its inhabitants 'people of whom we know nothing'. Why therefore did Britain become so involved with France in this issue? The answer lies partly in Britain's status as a great power. Any adjustment of Czechoslovakia's boundaries would be a matter on which a country such as Britain should give its agreement. If it failed to do so, its reputation as a great power would have been seriously damaged. In addition to this concern about its country's status, the British government considered that by applying the policy of appeasement to the problems of the Sudetenland, it might prevent the situation developing into a war.

Hitler's demands for the Sudetenland

In the summer months of 1938 Hitler increased his demands for 'justice' for the Sudetenland, where the Germans were now loudly demonstrating support for their new-found defender. A real likelihood existed that Germany might invade Czechoslovakia in order to bring the Sudetenland under its control. Such action would almost certainly plunge Europe into war. It was to prevent this immediate threat to peace that Chamberlain decided to involve himself fully in the problem. He did this very largely in a personal way and not always with the full approval of his cabinet.

Berchtesgaden; Godesberg; Munich

Runciman Mission

In August 1938, Chamberlain sent a special team of foreign office officials under the leadership of Lord Runciman to try to mediate between the Sudetenland Germans and the Czechoslovak government. The eventual report of the **Runciman Mission** was very favourable to the claims of these Germans, but other events had overtaken it by the time it was published. In early September violent events in the Sudetenland and violent words by Hitler on the need for a swift solution to the problem prompted Chamberlain to take immediate action himself. On 15 September he went by plane to Hitler's country retreat at Berchtesgaden in the Bavarian Alps.

A HISTORY OF BRITAIN FROM 1867

Berchtesgaden

Here the German dictator and the British Prime Minister held an uneasy meeting. Hitler insisted on the Sudetenland Germans being allowed 'self-determination', words which meant little more than their becoming part of Germany. Chamberlain left Berchtesgaden almost as Hitler's messenger, with the task of securing French and Czech agreement to his demands. Conversations with the leaders of the French and Czech governments followed. Agreement was reached – though very reluctantly by the Czech government – that those Sudetenland territories where more than half the population was German should become a part of Germany.

Godesberg

Chamberlain returned to Germany and at Godesberg in the Rhineland had a second meeting alone with Hitler on 22 September. He was shocked by Hitler's contemptuous attitude towards the agreements he had secured from the French and Czechs. Hitler was now obviously planning an immediate occupation of the whole of the Sudetenland. The only concession Chamberlain could secure was a postponement of this occupation by about a week, until 1 October.

Prospect of German invasion

It had been difficult to get French and Czech agreement to the Berchtesgaden proposals; it would be impossible to get their agreement to the new proposals put forward at Godesberg. In any case, within Britain there was by now much feeling that Hitler should not be allowed to get away with his ever-increasing demands. A German invasion of the Sudetenland now appeared likely, and Britain could only respond to such action by war with Germany. Preparations were made for this, particularly for what people most feared: aerial bombardment. Precautions were taken against incoming aircraft, children were evacuated from towns, bomb shelters were made ready for use. Despair overcame the country as it faced what seemed the inevitable prospect of war.

Summit meeting at Munich

But war was avoided in the autumn of 1938. At the end of September, Mussolini proposed the holding of a four-power summit conference, representing the governments of Britain, France, Germany and Italy, in order to resolve the Czechoslovak problem peacefully. His proposal was seized upon by Chamberlain, and by Daladier, the French Prime Minister. On 30 September they met with Hitler and Mussolini at Munich, and with little discussion accepted the solution to the Czechoslovak problem on which the two continental dictators had already agreed. This solution was little different from what Hitler had demanded at Godesberg, though the occupation of the Sudetenland was to be spread over a period of ten days. It was additionally agreed that Hungarian and

This cartoon of late September 1938 takes a critical view of Chamberlain's pursuit of peace. The words on the pie dish emphasize how humiliating the Prime Minister's policies were. The words of the little bird suggest that very little value was emerging from those policies anyway.

Polish claims to those parts of Czechoslovakia inhabited by Hungarians and Poles were to be satisfied. For Czechoslovakia, which was not represented at Munich, the terms spelt disaster. Valuable economic resources, the defensive protection of the Sudetenland mountains, many of its citizens – all these were lost. Nor, in the light of this experience, did the Czechoslovak government have any confidence in an Anglo-French guarantee for what remained of Czechoslovakia.

Anglo-German agreement

The morning after the Munich agreement on Czechoslovakia had been signed, Chamberlain re-emphasised his determination to avoid war. He persuaded Hitler to sign a joint Anglo-German agreement which presented the Munich settlement as a symbol of 'the desire of our two peoples never to go to war with one another again'. For the British people, peace was the great achievement of Chamberlain at Munich. Apart from that, the country did not feel itself ready for a war for the Sudetenland. It was known that the dominion countries would

This lavish tribute to the Prime Minister, paid by a London florist shop in October 1938, was typical of feeling throughout Britain. As events developed over the next twelve months, the Prime Minister's policies appeared less worthy of praise.

not have been willing to join a British declaration of war on an issue which seemed even more remote for them than it was for people in Britain. It was widely considered that British rearmament had not yet reached a point where Britain could confidently hope to win a war at that time. Rearmament programmes were being increased in 1938. The extra time available would be of great value if war were eventually to come. It must be remembered, however, that the extra time was also of value to Germany.

Churchill and Munich

Amid all the British rejoicings over Munich in 1938, the settlement did have its critics. One cabinet minister resigned; in the House of Commons Labour MPs were generally critical, as were a number of Conservatives. Foremost among these Conservatives was Winston Churchill. While out of office throughout the 1930s, Churchill had often been critical of the National government. In the late 1930s he became, within the House of Commons, Chamberlain's foremost opponent on appeasement. The Munich agreement was seen by him as an appalling, shameful betrayal; in no way did it mark an end of Germany's ambitions. He sternly warned of future dangers.

> **I do not grudge our loyal, brave people, who were ready to do their duty no matter what the cost, who never flinched under the strain of last week – I do not grudge them the natural, spontaneous outburst of joy and relief when they learned that the hard ordeal would no longer be required of them at the moment; but they should know the truth. They should know that we have sustained a defeat without a war, the consequences of which will travel far with us along our road; they should know that we have passed an awful milestone in our history, when the whole balance of Europe has been deranged and that the terrible words have for the time being been pronounced against the Western democracies: 'Thou art weighed in the balance and found wanting.' And do not suppose that this is the end. This is only the beginning of the reckoning. This**

is only the first sip, the first foretaste of a bitter cup which will be offered to us year by year unless by a supreme recovery of moral health and martial vigour, we arise again and take our stand for freedom as in the olden times.

Hansard, *Parliamentary Debates*

Churchill's warnings were fully justified by events over the next 12 months. Meanwhile the government continued appeasement policies. Early in 1939 Chamberlain paid a visit to Mussolini in Rome. Shortly after he acknowledged the government of the military rebels in Spain. The possibility was put to Germany that it might receive back the colonies it had lost after the First World War.

The end of appeasement and the outbreak of war

German invasion of Czechoslovakia

This comparative calm was shattered in March 1939 when German forces marched into what remained of Czechoslovakia. As those who now came under German control were not of German nationality, there could be no justification – as there possibly was in the case of the Sudetenland – for bringing them into Germany on grounds of self-determination. Within Britain, public opinion went strongly against appeasement, which now seemed merely to have encouraged Germany's excessive ambitions. Chamberlain decided that appeasement must be abandoned and announced his decision in a speech at Birmingham.

> Is this the end of an old adventure or is it the beginning of a new? Is this the last attack upon a small state or is it to be followed by others? Is this, in effect, a step in the direction of an attempt to dominate the world by force? While I am not prepared to engage this country by new and unspecified commitments operating under conditions which cannot now be foreseen, yet no greater mistake could be made than to suppose that because it believes war to be a senseless and cruel thing, this nation has so lost its fibre that it will not take part to the utmost of its power in resisting such a challenge if it ever were made.

New commitments

Within the next few weeks, Chamberlain gave positive signs that appeasement really had been abandoned. Britain signed treaties with three European countries which considered themselves under threat of attack: with Poland and Romania (threatened by Germany) and Greece (threatened by Italy). By far the most significant of these alliances was the one with Poland. By the spring of 1939 Hitler had begun to agitate for German control of Danzig and for better German access across the Polish corridor to East Prussia. Though Britain was now committed to help Poland, little was done during the following months to strengthen Britain's links with this state in eastern Europe. Nor was there much prospect of making aid to Poland effective, as Britain had no understanding with the Soviet Union, bordering on Poland's eastern frontier. The government's critics doubted whether it had fully abandoned its pursuit of appeasement, in spite of the treaties signed in the spring of 1939.

Russo-German Non-Aggression pact

Negotiations were begun by Britain to secure an understanding with the Soviet Union, now seen as vital if Poland were to be saved from Germany. But the Soviet Union had been angered by being kept out of the Munich conference. Its government suspected very strongly that Britain and France would stand by in the event of war breaking out and would allow Russia to fight Germany without giving aid. The Soviet Union might therefore best protect its position by coming to an understanding with Germany. While the Soviet Union's negotiations with Britain faltered, secret negotiations with Germany made good progress. On 23 August 1939 a startled world learnt that a Russo-German Non-Aggression pact had been signed. The immediate victim of this would certainly be Poland, sandwiched between the two.

BRITISH FOREIGN POLICY DURING THE INTER-WAR YEARS

Outbreak of war Nothing could now prevent the outbreak of war. With the assurance of the friendly neutrality of the Soviet Union, Hitler's invasion of Poland could be carried through successfully. In these difficult days, Chamberlain repeated the British commitment to Poland and attempted to make clear that there would be no 'Munich' on this issue. Hitler was prepared to risk the possibility of war with Britain: perhaps the British people would fight, perhaps as in the previous year they would back down. When, however, German forces invaded Poland on 1 September, Britain and France demanded their withdrawal. When by 3 September it was clear that no withdrawal would take place, Britain declared war on Germany and was followed later that day by France.

Chamberlain's role In speaking by radio to the British people on 3 September, Chamberlain struck a sad, pathetic note.

> This is a sad day for all of us, and to none is it sadder than to me. Everything that I have worked for, everything that I have believed in during my public life, has crashed into ruins. There is only one thing for me to do: that is, to devote what strength and powers I have to forwarding the victory of the cause for which we have to sacrifice so much. I trust I may live to see the day when Hitlerism has been destroyed and a liberated Europe has been re-established.

Chamberlain never lived to see the destruction of Hitlerism. In circumstances described more fully in the following chapter, he resigned in May 1940 and he died before the end of that year. One of the most important issues in British history in the twentieth century concerns his pursuit of appeasement. How far did his policies – and the similar ones of the French government – encourage Hitler's aggressive acts? How far did he, with the best intentions of preserving peace, in practice bring about war? To deep questions of this kind, no easy answers exist. But among the many events that led to the outbreak of the Second World War, the practice of appeasement by Britain and France has an important place.

--- EXERCISES ---

1. (a) Give an account of the British government's approaches towards:
   (i) the 1919–20 peace settlement,
   (ii) the League of Nations and disarmament in the inter-war years, and
   (iii) aggression in Manchuria and Ethiopia.
   (b) In what respects did the British government's approach to these different issues suggest weakness?

2. (a) What were the main reasons for Neville Chamberlain's pursuit of appeasement policies?
   (b) Show how he pursued appeasement policies in the course of 1938.
   (c) Explain why he abandoned appeasement in the early part of 1939.

3. Imagine you are an MP in the late 1930s. Write your memoirs of these years, explaining why in parliament you either supported or opposed the various approaches that Chamberlain made towards the European dictators.

4. Study the cartoon on page 176, the photograph on page 177 and the extract on pages 177–8 and then answer the questions (a) to (d) which follow.
   (a) (i) The cartoon relates to the Munich conference. Outline the negotiations of the previous few weeks between Chamberlain and Hitler.
   (ii) How does the cartoonist show his general dislike of the Munich settlement?
   (iii) By reference to your knowledge of the Munich settlement, show how the cartoonist's view might be supported. (3+2+3)
   (b) (i) How does the photograph suggest approval of the Munich settlement?
   (ii) By reference to your knowledge of the Munich settlement show how those who approved of it might be supported in their view. (2+3)
   (c) With reference to the extract from Churchill's speech in the House of Commons, show to what extent his fears about the Munich settlement were proved correct. (4)
   (d) Giving reasons for your choice, explain which of these sources you find the most helpful in understanding the events surrounding the Munich crisis. (3)

15 BRITAIN AND THE SECOND WORLD WAR

When the British government had declared war against Germany in August 1914, the public had shown an overwhelming commitment to the struggle. When this sad sequence of events was repeated in September 1939, the public's response was quite different. Few in 1914 had foreseen that the fighting would last for as long as four years. Few had imagined the slaughter and the maiming that those years held for the soldiers caught in trench warfare or the sailors threatened by submarine attack. In 1939 most British people could remember the horror and futility of so much that happened in those years, and they felt therefore no enthusiasm for the renewed conflict with Germany. Yet the Second World War turned out to be quite different from the First. It lasted much longer, the fighting covered wider areas of the world and in the end its slaughter was to reach even vaster proportions.

The Phoney War

Evacuees

For the first six months the war seemed to make very little impact in Britain, or generally in western Europe. There was fear that aerial bombardment would accompany the outbreak of war, and some careful preparations had been made to meet this possibility. These preparations were put into effect in September 1939. The most important feature of them was evacuation of children from the cities of Britain, considered the most likely targets for attack. During the war, there was to be a series of evacuations, coinciding with times of particular danger. The evacuations were well organised; some of the later ones certainly

Four children arrive, with their teacher (left), at the country home to which they have been evacuated at the start of the Second World War. Evacuation was often a disturbing experience for children, as suggested here by the expressions on their faces.

saved the lives of a number of the children involved. Tension was inevitably created by this vast movement of the **evacuees**, as they were termed. The photograph on this page suggests the sort of anxiety that many of them felt on arrival at a strange house in the country. The families accommodating the evacuees often found difficulty in dealing with their young guests, on account of the different town backgrounds from which they came. One useful result of evacuation was to show just how poor many town children brought up in the late 1930s actually were.

BRITAIN AND THE SECOND WORLD WAR

Early wartime precautions

For those left in towns, other preparations had been made. A **black-out** was enforced at night-time: no light should be showing from windows or used on cars or bicycles for fear of alerting enemy aircraft. Gas masks were issued to everyone for protection against the use of poisonous gas, a vile technique of warfare used in the trenches of the First World War and more recently in Ethiopia. Sandbags were used to protect buildings from the effects of bombardment and tape was stuck to windows to minimise danger from flying glass. Air Raid Precaution (ARP) wardens had the task of making sure that the proper precautions were put into effect in their neighbourhood. The Emergency Powers (Defence) Act, passed at the start of the war, gave the government very considerable powers over civilians in its efforts to win the war.

Limited military involvement

Yet much of this immense effort proved in the early stages of the war to be quite unnecessary. Britain suffered virtually no aerial bombardments in the closing months of 1939. By the end of the year most of the evacuees had returned home, and life continued much as it did before war had broken out. Nor were the British armed forces abroad very closely involved in fighting in the early stages. Many served in France with the British Expeditionary Forces, helping in the French defence of the country against the possibility of German attack. Meanwhile the Royal Navy blockaded the German ports in an attempt to weaken the German economy by preventing imports from entering the country.

Action in eastern Europe

This lack of action at home and abroad gave the war an unreal atmosphere in these early months. It became popularly known as the **Phoney War**, the quietness of which encouraged some to hope that it might fizzle out of its own accord. Such hopes were groundless. To the east, during the course of September, the German Army had overrun Poland with amazing speed. The Soviet Union, taking advantage of the terms of the Russo–German pact, had meantime advanced into eastern Poland, the Baltic states and parts of Finand. Hitler had no fear at present of any attack from the east and prepared during the winter of 1939–40 for an all-out attack against western Europe.

Winston Churchill becomes Prime Minister

The attack came suddenly in the spring of 1940. By a series of rapidly deployed **blitzkrieg** assaults, German forces conquered Denmark, Norway, Belgium, the Netherlands and France; in the summer of 1940 it seemed that the conquest of Britain would quickly follow. Meanwhile Britain had become closely involved in the defence of two of these countries: Norway and France.

It had been planned for the Royal Navy to play a crucial part in the defence of Norway. But the resources deployed by the British were not sufficient to prevent Norway's collapse to very strong German forces. Chamberlain's government was already beginning to be criticised for what was considered weak direction of the war. Its failure in Norway provoked such strong opposition in the country and in the House of Commons that Chamberlain had no alternative but to resign in May 1940. Winston Churchill, who had joined Chamberlain's government as First Lord of the Admiralty at the outbreak of war, was appointed Prime Minister. Unlike Chamberlain, he was able to secure support from all parties in the House and he formed a Coalition government in which all parties were represented. For the next five years he was to give firm and widely respected leadership to Britain's war effort. He set out his overall policy in a vivid speech to the House of Commons just after his appointment as Prime Minister.

Prime Minister Winston Churchill and his wife visit towards the end of 1940 a building in the City of London bombed by aerial attack. Visits such as these helped to encourage British morale during the dangers of the Blitz.

> Even though large tracts of Europe and many old and famous states have fallen or may fall into the grip of the Gestapo and all the odious apparatus of Nazi rule, we shall not flag or fail. We shall go on to the end, we shall fight in France, we shall fight in the seas and oceans, we shall fight with growing confidence and growing strength in the air, we shall defend our island, whatever the cost

may be, we shall fight on the beaches, we shall fight on the landing grounds, we shall fight in the fields and in the streets, we shall fight in the hills; we shall never surrender, and even if, which I do not for a moment believe, this island or a large part of it were subjugated and starving, then our Empire beyond the seas, armed and guarded by the British Fleet, would carry on the struggle until, in God's good time, the New World, with all its power and might, steps forth to the rescue and the liberation of the Old.

Hansard, *Parliamentary Debates*

Dunkirk

The first main challenge to confront Churchill as Prime Minister was the plight of British troops in France. They had been forced into retreat towards the north French coast as German forces had swiftly advanced into the eastern parts of France. A successful withdrawal took place from the French coastal town of Dunkirk during the end of May and beginning of June. Almost 350 000 men were withdrawn, of whom about one third belonged to the French Army. It was a superbly conducted rescue operation. Many small private boats assisted the larger naval vessels in ferrying men to Britain, while fighter planes fought off German air attacks on the operation. The value of the operation at Dunkirk was to save the lives of many soldiers. Nevertheless the evacuation marked a serious defeat. Much British equipment had been abandoned to the Germans, for whom Dunkirk was no more than an episode in their swift, spectacular conquest of France. Desperate efforts were made in June by the British government to keep the French in the war. A rather unrealistic offer of common Anglo-French citizenship was a part of these efforts. But the French were faced with an impossible situation. On 22 June 1940 a new French government signed an armistice and the fighting in France ceased for the time being.

The Battle of Britain and the Blitz

Hitler could now direct all his energies towards the defeat of Britain. Ships and landing barges were assembled in the newly conquered French ports and plans were ready for the administration of Britain as a part of the expanding German Empire. If the assault on Britain were to succeed, it was essential that the Royal Air Force (RAF) should be unable to attack the German vessels while crossing the Channel. So the RAF became the first object of German attack. The German planes had the advantage of nearby airfields in France and superiority in numbers. For its part, the RAF had the advantage of the swift, readily manoeuvrable Spitfires and Hurricanes. They also possessed the newly invented radar, which enabled Air-Marshal Dowding, Head of Fighter Command, to deploy his aircraft effectively against the enemy. The contest between the British and German fighter planes in the summer of 1940 has been termed the **Battle of Britain**. As the German air force was unable to defeat the RAF, the invasion force was not launched. The Battle of Britain had effectively saved the country from invasion. It is this that gives a unique importance to the heroism of the British pilots who fought in it.

Frustrated in his initial attempts to invade Britain, Hitler now turned to aerial bombardment of British cities. The **Blitz**, as it was termed by a shortening of the German word **blitzkrieg** (lightning war), began as the Battle of Britain was ending, in September 1940. It continued until May 1941, by which time German air raids on Britain were becoming less frequent. In the meantime the raids had brought devastation to Britain's major cities and had resulted in some 30 000 deaths. It was not easy to combat the raids as they were made at night, when fighter planes and anti-aircraft guns had difficulty in locating the incoming German bombers. A government report described the effect on people in Britain in this way.

An air crew attends a debriefing session at Biggin Hill, Kent. In the Second World War, in both defensive and offensive operations, the Royal Air Force played a crucial role.

BRITAIN AND THE SECOND WORLD WAR

A scene of devastation after a German bomb had been dropped in a built-up area. An Anderson shelter could provide reasonably secure protection in circumstances such as this: notice that there are two in this photograph.

> London people lost much sleep and suffered anxiety and discomfort, but there was no breakdown, no panic and no mass evacuation, except in the small heavily bombed areas. The effect was one very largely of surprise. After a few days the first horror of the raids wore off and people became adjusted to the new conditions of shelter life.
>
> Disorganization was more serious. The complicated network of railways was cut at many places at once. In three weeks, 104 railway bridges were put out of action for periods ranging from a day to a month. Roads were blocked by craters and debris. Thousands of water and gas mains were broken, interrupting supplies over large areas. Telephone exchanges were put out of action and postal deliveries hampered.
>
> **Report by the Home Secretary, 1940**

British response

Evacuation was again organised, though this time (when it was needed) less extensively than the previous year (when it was not). Shelters provided some protection from the raids. The Anderson shelter, made of corrugated iron and set deeply into the garden soil, often proved its value in the raids, as is suggested in the photograph on this page. The Morrison shelter, designed for use inside a house, gave some protection against the effects of blast, but was generally less reliable. Many Londoners took refuge in tube stations, not only in the Blitz of 1940–41 but throughout the entire war. The main aim of these German attacks was to weaken the morale of the British people so that a compromise peace with Britain could be agreed. The British government was determined that they would not succeed. Fire fighting and rescue services worked effectively. Members of the Royal Family or senior government ministers appeared promptly at bombed areas to show concern for the plight of Blitz victims. Certainly the German aim was very far from achieved during the Blitz, and most people showed determination to carry on with the struggle and to support their government in doing so.

Britain and its wartime allies

Britain and the United States

In making its determined stand in 1940–41, Britain stood virtually alone. Continental Europe was now under the domination of Germany and its allies. Though Britain might resist alone, it could not alone bring down the Nazi control of the rest of Europe. Churchill's government was particularly conscious of the need for reliable allies to help in this task. Foremost, he sought the help of

Atlantic Charter

the United States. US assistance was given in the first 18 months of the war through a system known as **cash and carry**: US military supplies would be available if paid for and carried away by Britain. From March 1941 the more generous system of **lend-lease** came into being: supplies were now made available without immediate payment.

In August 1941 the developing spirit of co-operation was taken further when Roosevelt and Churchill, meeting on board a ship off the Newfoundland coast, signed the **Atlantic Charter**. Both countries looked forward to an eventual peace and sketched their plans for a post-war settlement. This would include frontier adjustments acceptable to those living in disputed areas, greater emphasis on democratic government and an efficient system of international security. The Atlantic Charter showed identity in the aims of the two powers, but it did not bring the United States into the war. Later in the year, aggressive Japanese policies did do so. As an essential preliminary to an immense expansion of Japanese power in the Pacific area, the US fleet at Pearl Harbor, Hawaii, was attacked from the air in December 1941.

The United States and the Soviet Union

The attack on Pearl Harbor resulted in the defeat of much, though by no means all, of the US Pacific Fleet. Its importance is, however, greater than that. The United States declared war on Japan and, as Germany and Italy now declared war on the United States in support of their Japanese ally, the United States declared war against them as well. Britain came immediately to the support of the United States by declaring war against Japan, whose sudden expansion now directly threatened British possessions in the Far East and South-East Asia. All these different declarations meant that both Britain and the United States were now committed to fighting in both Europe and the Far East. In this commitment they were joined by the Soviet Union, which for the previous six months had been fighting against an immense German assault launched in June 1941. The term **United Nations** was applied to those powers who now fought against the **Axis** powers of Germany, Italy and Japan. It was from the wartime United Nations powers that the post-war international organisation developed. The scope of military activity had become vastly increased and the fighting could now genuinely be said to form part of a 'world' war.

Reversals in the Far East

Churchill was greatly heartened by the US entry, which he had always judged essential if the war were to be won. The concluding words of his speech shortly after his appointment, reproduced on page 182, show the importance he attached to the involvement of the United States. Yet the early months of 1942 continued to bring defeat for British forces abroad. For Britain the most perilous

British officers carry the white flag of surrender and the Union Jack at the fall of Singapore to the Japanese in February 1942. The fall of this bastion of their power in South-East Asia produced much despondency among the British people.

action of the Japanese was their landing and advance in Malaya. This led to a sustained landward assault on Singapore, which fell in February 1942. It would be difficult to exaggerate the despondency felt by the British at the fall of Singapore. In the 1920s and 1930s much money and effort had been spent in making Singapore impregnable. Its fall to the Japanese was interpreted by many as marking the end of Britain's role in South-East Asia. Nor was its fall the end of the Japanese advance: the neighbouring colony of Burma was swiftly overrun and the Japanese were then able even to threaten Britain's hold on India.

The British in North Africa

Fall of Tobruk In the meantime, British forces elsewhere fared little better. Unable at this stage in the war to establish any secure foothold in Continental Europe, they concentrated attention in North Africa. Egypt provided a sound base for British attacks against Italian-held Libya. Initially the British had scored some impressive successes in Libya, but these ended with the arrival of German reinforcements under Rommel. In May 1942 he was able to force the British to retreat back into Egypt. At Tobruk many British soldiers were left behind the

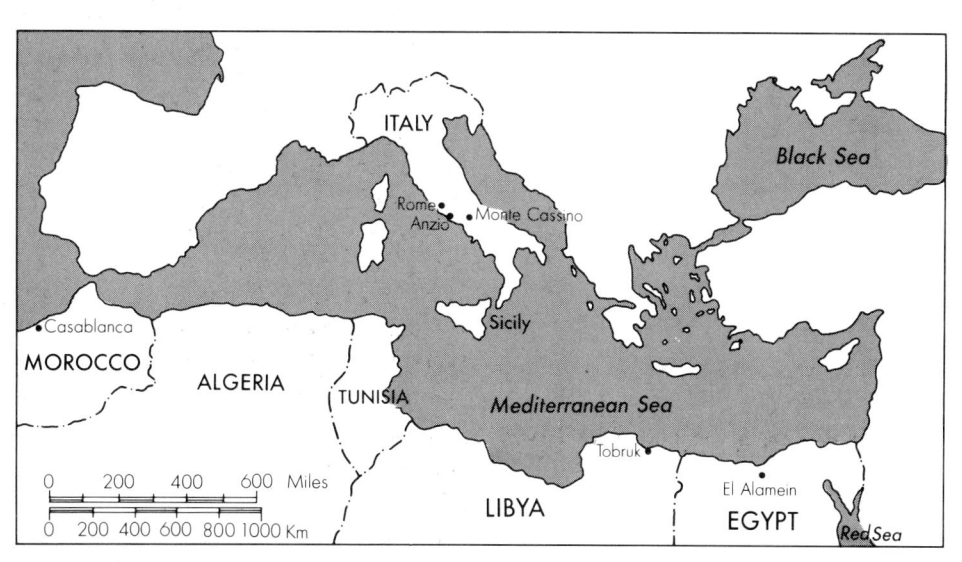

North Africa and Italy during the Second World War

advancing German lines and they attempted unsuccessfully to hold the town against heavy enemy bombardment. The fall of Tobruk in June 1942 produced in British public opinion a despondency similar to that caused by the fall of Singapore four months earlier. Defeat appeared to accompany every step that Churchill's government took in the first half of 1942 and the government was beginning to lose its earlier popularity.

El Alamein The autumn brought better fortune. Back in July Rommel's forces had been halted in their advances into Egypt at what became known as the first battle of El Alamein. Throughout the rest of the summer and autumn the British had held this position. While doing so, heavy reinforcements had been brought in and the Eighth Army, which held the position at El Alamein, acquired a new commander. This was Montgomery, regarded as one of the best British commanders of the Second World War. A strict disciplinarian in military matters, he was able to inspire deep confidence in those he commanded. At the end of October 1942 his reputation was enhanced by his successful direction of the second battle of El Alamein.

This battle began with a sustained artillery barrage which weakened the enemy so seriously that British troops were then able to break through their lines. Fundamental to this early success was the matter of supply: the British were readily supplied via the Suez Canal and the Red Sea, but the German supply lines via the desert and the Mediterranean were less secure. Montgomery's troops now pursued the retreating Germans towards Tunisia. British troops had meanwhile linked with US troops in making swift sea-borne landings in Algeria and Morocco. They also advanced successfully towards Tunisia where the British and US position was consolidated in the early part of 1943 so that the Allied invasion of Italy could be launched in July of that year.

Unconditional surrender

Churchill said of the events of October–November 1942 that 'Before Alamein we never had a victory. After Alamein we never had a defeat.' The British saw it very much in this way: a crucial turning-point for their wartime fortunes. Of greater importance as a turning-point was a lengthy battle begun a little later and fought in the winter months of 1942–43 in the Soviet Union. This was the battle of Stalingrad, in which Soviet forces at last began to turn back the invading Germans.

Stalin, the Soviet leader, was so pre-occupied with the immense struggle then taking place at Stalingrad that he felt unable to join Churchill and Roosevelt at a summit conference in Casablanca in January 1943. They met elated by their recent victories but also conscious of the value of the Soviet fighting. They agreed that in approaching the enemy they would adopt the policy of **unconditional surrender**. This gave some assurance to the Soviet Union that the Western powers would not seek a compromise settlement with the Axis powers to the disadvantage of the Soviet Union. Whether the policy was altogether wise has subsequently been doubted. The last two years of the war were especially bitter and bloody. A more flexible approach towards the enemy countries might have averted some of the horrors that accompanied the war's closing stages.

Life in wartime Britain

The main concern for those living in Britain during wartime was to protect themselves from the effects of aerial attack. How they did this during the Blitz has been shown earlier in this chapter, and similar tactics were used during the later, less frequent raids and during the V1 and V2 raids of 1944 (page 191). Everyday life was affected in other, less dangerous ways. Acute difficulty was experienced in getting usual supplies to Britain during the war, as incoming ships were threatened by German submarines. Almost all goods were therefore in short supply.

Rationing

Public opinion generally supported the idea that the food and goods which the country had should be shared fairly and equally. Rationing was therefore introduced quite early in the war, in January 1940. Everyone was supplied with a ration book for food; shortly afterwards another one was issued for clothing. Points were cut out of these books as purchases were made; without the book and the necessary points purchases were just not possible. As the war went on, supplies became even more difficult. Consequently rationing was even more strictly imposed. At the worst stages, in the middle of the war, about one new set of clothing was allowed each year to each person and the amount of food allowed each week was similar to the amount that might have been eaten in one day before the war. The government helped to offset some of the difficulties the food shortages might have caused by making vitamin supplies, such as orange juice and codliver oil available free of charge to children and expectant mothers. These vitamin supplements helped to make the health of children in wartime much better than it had been during the pre-war Depression.

Home production

Shortages could be relieved by individual efforts to grow food in greater quantity or to use more effectively the scant resources that were available. 'Dig for victory' was a prominent slogan. Encouragement was given to the intensive

BRITAIN AND THE SECOND WORLD WAR

use of allotments, while garden lawns and playing fields were dug up to make room for further home cultivation. The government gave advice on how best to use what was available. Recipes were given by the Ministry of Food on preparing dishes from home-grown vegetables. Enthusiasm and interest was directed in many homes to making things that would almost certainly have been puchased before the war, especially clothes and jam.

Taxation — All of this created a community spirit that helped sustain British morale during the war. It meant that everyone was being treated in the same way. Government taxation policies were a part of this as well. Income tax rose sharply, to as much as ten shillings (50p) in the pound at one stage. But taxation on such purchases as could be made was less steep. In this way the high taxation that wartime circumstances demanded was directly linked with what people could afford to pay. In spite of high taxation, many seemed to have cash to spare to invest quite generously in government defence bonds, for which there was an extensive publicity campaign.

Women — With so many men serving abroad in the armed forces it was inevitable that women would be needed to fill their places at home. In this respect the Second World War was very similar to the First. In the early stages, women contributed in a voluntary way, often by working on the Women's Land Army or the Women's Voluntary Service. In December 1941 conscription for women was introduced. Those who were conscripted served with either the auxiliary military services or in civil defence.

Wartime reconstruction

Forward planning — It was only during the last years of the war that much effort was given to the planning for the type of Britain that should be developed when the war ended. The widespread public support this planning received suggested that many were both aware of and concerned about the social problems Britain had experienced in recent years. Already in the late 1930s attention had been drawn to them by a large number of reports on different social issues; more recently, the evacuees had further highlighted the continuing problems of life in Britain's towns. It was almost as if the people of Britain were now expecting a better Britain in return for the immense sacrifices they were making in the struggle against Germany. The term **reconstruction** was applied to the forward-planning that was getting increasing emphasis.

Beveridge Report — The government appointed a committee under the chairmanship of Sir William Beveridge to enquire into social insurance, improvement of which was considered fundamental to any serious attempt at post-war reconstruction. Beveridge had had a lifetime's experience in social administration and the Report that he published in December 1942 contained a blueprint for extensive future development. It caught much public enthusiasm at the time of publication. Perhaps it was fortunate to be published only a month after the victory at the second battle of El Alamein. The public could therefore feel that far-sighted plans were beginning to emerge at the same time as victory was beginning to come into sight.

Importance — Why was the Beveridge Report so important? It proposed a simplification of the system of social insurance by requiring the payment of one contribution for all categories. It established the principle that benefits would be the same for all who received them. It compelled all to take part in the scheme. Finally, it saw these proposals in the context of a concerted campaign against the **five giants** of Want, Disease, Ignorance, Squalor and Idleness. Thus the implementing of the report would lead to substantial changes in the way in which the social services were administered. Public opinion gave the report a warm welcome, as this account of the time shows.

> Hopes ran high that the Beveridge Plan would be put into operation as soon as possible. Some workers indeed regarded the plan as an enactment. To some women for instance its reality was so actual that they were calculating how much they would be able to draw for their children. One woman, writing to an older one at this time said, 'It's hard lines on you. I arrived at the right time.' Others who had feared wholesale disturbance after the war said, 'This will give us something to fight for and look forward to. The soldiers needn't hang on to their guns after all.'
>
> Soldiers writing home spoke of their pleasure at the scheme, saying, 'This gives us some heart to fight. We know that if something happens to us our wives and children will never want.'
>
> To the critics who enquired 'Can we pay for it?' the impatient reply was given, 'We can always pay for wars, this one costs fifteen million pounds a day. We will just *have* to afford the Beveridge Plan.'
>
> from Janet Beveridge, *Beveridge and his Plan*

Commitment to the Report

Churchill's government – including the Prime Minister himself – showed little wish to implement the report, regarding it as over-ambitious. The Labour party was firmly committed to it and did not allow it to be put aside. The report additionally had the support of a new party of the left, the Common Wealth party, which briefly flourished during the war years. William Temple, the progressive wartime Archbishop of Canterbury, spoke often and strongly in its support. It was therefore political pressure combined with public support which ensured that the Beveridge Report was not forgotten. The last two years of the war were ones that saw the publication of many official and unofficial plans for post-war development. Government white papers were prepared on how best to implement in practical ways the Beveridge Report's proposals on health, unemployment and poverty. A Ministry of Town and Country Planning was set up to implement various wartime reports on the development of the environment, a development which would certainly need strong centralised control. Wartime circumstances made it difficult to give effect to most of the proposals that were produced in these years.

Education Act

R.A. Butler's Education Act of 1944 was an exception. The changes brought about by this Act owed much to wartime evacuation, which among other things revealed the very low educational standards of evacuees. It was also an opportunity to produce an improved and better organised system of education. The old elementary schools were abolished and replaced by a universal system of primary, secondary and further education, for which the newly created office of Minister of Education would have responsibility.

It was within secondary education that the Act had its greatest impact. There were to be three types of secondary school: grammar, technical and modern, each of which was to cater for pupils of different abilities. Additionally, the Act removed grammar school fees, so that the opportunity of an academic education was open to all who were considered suitable for it. Here in fact lay what was to become the main problem connected with the 1944 Act: the way in which the decision on a pupil's suitability for grammar school education was made. The Eleven Plus examination, by which this was done, became increasingly criticised as making too hard a division among pupils at too early a stage in their development. The Act also envisaged the raising of the school-leaving age to 15 (and eventually to 16) but this, like so much else planned during these years, had to be left until the war was won. In 1945, shortly before the war ended, the government acted on one of the Beveridge recommendations when it introduced family allowances.

BRITAIN AND THE SECOND WORLD WAR

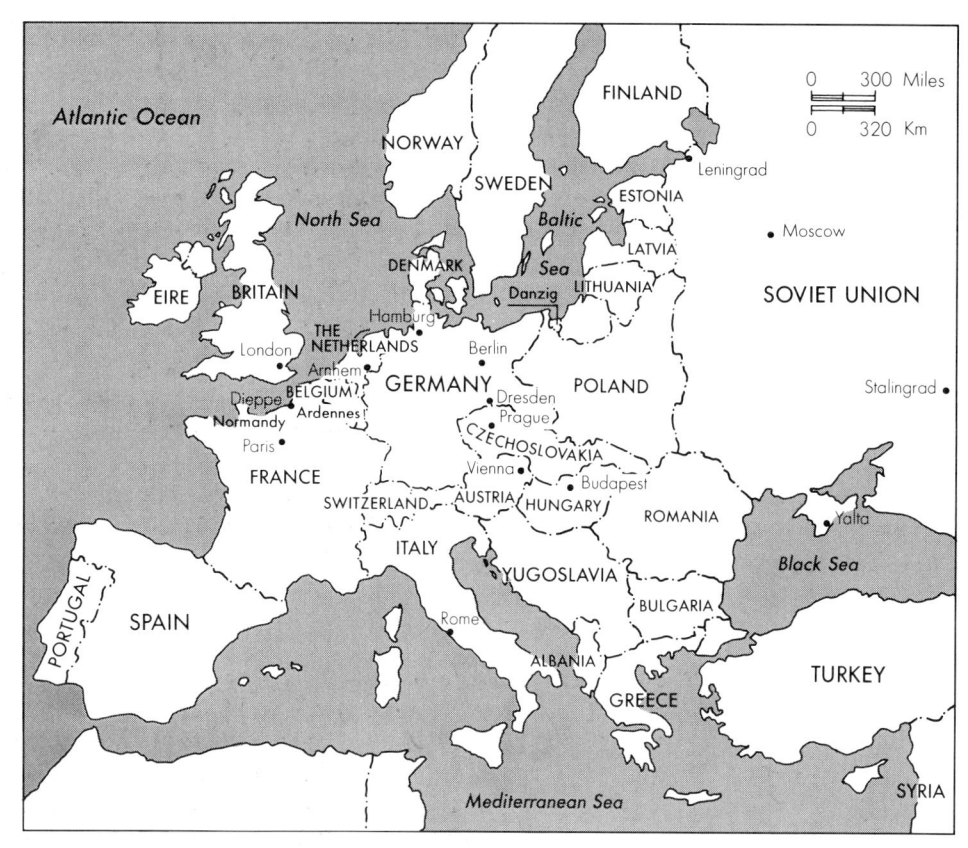

Europe during the Second World War

Allied campaigns in Italy

Slow progress in Italy

In the European war, the events of 1943 marked a positive turn in the fortunes of the two sides. In July 1943, from their North African base, British and US forces attacked Sicily, which fell within the month. Subsequent advance up the Italian peninsula was slowed by the defensive fighting of German troops, who had entered the country in large numbers after Mussolini's government fell at the time of the Sicilian invasion. Major engagements with the enemy failed to clear the way for speedy advance. Early in 1944 sea-borne landings at Anzio, from where it was hoped to launch an attack on Rome, became pinned down on the coastal area by enemy action. A few weeks later a combined Allied assault was launched on Monte Casino, considered to be a vital German command post (see map on page 185). After extensive fighting the Allies secured control of this ancient hill-top monastery, yet little practical advantage came to them as a consequence. Progress was still slow, and many lives were lost as the Allied forces continued northwards. It was not until June 1944 that Rome fell, and even then there was much enemy territory to be conquered. Only in April 1945 did the Allies finally penetrate northern Italy and help to bring about the collapse of the Fascist government there, which with German aid Mussolini had set up during these last two years of the war.

Importance of the Italian campaigns

This slow, uncertain progress in Italy was a disappointment to Churchill. He had hoped Italy might become a base from which to launch aerial raids into the German-held Balkan countries. Nevertheless, many German soldiers who might have been used with dangerous effect elsewhere were needed in Italy to try to combat the Allied advance there. This diversion of German efforts was to help with what the United States regarded as a more important venture: the opening of the Second Front in France.

A HISTORY OF BRITAIN FROM 1867

The Second Front

Need for the Second Front

The United States was not alone in giving priority to the Second Front. Since the battle of Stalingrad in the winter of 1942–43 the Soviet forces had been advancing westwards and removing the German occupying forces from their land. Theirs was a bitter struggle and one in which there was immense loss of life. A successful diversion by their Allies in the west was desperately needed. The campaigns in Italy were not viewed as an adequate diversion, and the Soviet Union waited – rather impatiently – for Allied action in France.

Failure of earlier attempts

The slowness with which the Allies acted in opening the Second Front is partly explained by their determination that it would genuinely mark the beginning of the final, effective thrust to bring down German power in Europe. Already an earlier British attack at Dieppe in August 1942 had failed, due to lack of detailed military planning and lack of sufficient military equipment. These defects had certainly been made good by the time the Second Front was opened in June 1944.

Techniques and methods

The precise area of the landing of the Second Front – on the Normandy beaches – remained a well-guarded secret. By various attacks in the Channel area during the previous few months the Allies managed to persuade the Germans that landings would be made in that area. It was in any case the most obvious area for the landings, due to the comparative shortness of the sea crossing. As Normandy had no harbours capable of taking the 200 000 British, Commonwealth and US soldiers assembled in southern England in the middle of 1944, prefabricated

British troops passing through London on their way to the Second Front in June 1944. The launching of this massive assault against Nazi-occupied Europe was to be a decisive factor in Germany's defeat.

'mulberry' harbours were constructed for floating across the sea with the invasion forces. Fuel for the forces, once landed, was supplied from southern England by pipeline brought under the sea. There was an essential preliminary to the launching of this vast and detailed operation: the Allies must be certain that their landing forces would not be attacked by enemy submarines while crossing between England and France.

Battle of the Atlantic

German submarines had been a serious menace in the early years of the war, when they had disrupted supplies coming to Britain and endangered the lives of men sailing for overseas service. After the US entry into the war, crossing the Atlantic was a perilous experience. The Allied forces were aware that the eventual outcome of the war depended very much on their ability to win the **Battle of the Atlantic**, as these campaigns were called. Atlantic convoys were provided with more effective cover by aircraft, themselves equipped with

BRITAIN AND THE SECOND WORLD WAR

improved radar systems for the detection of enemy submarines. Such techniques brought about a decline in Allied shipping losses, and by the summer of 1943 the Battle of the Atlantic had been won.

Landings The Atlantic menace having been cleared and the plans for the opening of the Second Front having been finalised, the landings were successfully made on the Normandy beaches in June 1944. Not even the appalling weather delayed action now. Within a matter of days, the Allied forces had established firm bases from which to advance. By August they had reached and liberated Paris and by the autumn were at the German frontier. Here their advance halted for a while and it was not until the spring of 1945 that a breakthrough into Germany was made.

Allied differences Major differences on Allied strategy now became troublesome. The overall Allied commander was a US soldier, General Eisenhower. He wanted a **broad front** approach towards Germany. General Montgomery, who commanded the British forces now in Europe and who had won a dazzling reputation by his earlier success at El Alamein, favoured a **direct thrust** towards Germany's industrial heartland. Eisenhower permitted Montgomery to try out the early stages of his plan. Montgomery therefore directed British operations for the crossing of the Rhine in the Netherlands. These operations involved paratroop attacks to secure vital bridgeheads, the most important of which was at Arnhem. Unfortunately the paratroopers landed in areas that were very well controlled by the Germans. Arnhem resulted in the loss of many British lives and no advantage to the Allied cause. Later in the year, a group of young German soldiers made a brief, unsuccessful counter-offensive in the Ardennes region of southern Belgium. Their desperate demonstration of patriotism did little other than show the hopelessness of their country's cause.

Aerial warfare

V1 and V2 attacks The British people were victims of a new campaign in the air launched by Germany in the summer of 1944. The Germans had by then perfected a type of pilotless plane, known as the V1. With their cargo of explosives, these planes were launched from Germany in the direction of Britain and came down in the built-up areas of the south-east as soon as their fuel ran out. The capturing of the launching pads in August 1944 diminished the V1 threat, though it did not entirely remove it. Of greater danger was the V2. This was a rocket, whose silent, swift approach made it particularly difficult to combat. Its effects were even more deadly than those of the V1 pilotless planes. Only when the Netherlands was liberated in the spring of 1945 and Britain was out of the V2 range of flight was the problem removed.

Importance The nature and intensity of the V1 and V2 attacks came as an especially unwelcome surprise to the people of south-east England, as by then victory appeared almost to have been achieved. There were renewed evacuations of children and renewed use of shelters as sirens warned of the approach of the new weapons. Almost 10 000 people, most of them in London, lost their lives as a result of the V1 and V2 attacks.

Bombing of Germany Germany experienced at this time far greater devastation from British aerial bombardment. The British use of aerial warfare changed during the course of the war. In the early stages **strategic bombing** was the objective: selected German targets of economic or strategic importance were attacked. This generally remained the policy of the United States. Throughout the war, for practical reasons, the RAF came to have increasingly less and less confidence in this approach. In day-time raids they could detect their targets, but risked being shot down; in night-time raids the targets could not be properly distinguished.

Consequently, by 1941 **area bombing** became the objective: bombardment should be made indiscriminately in highly populated areas with the purpose of spreading panic and defeatism among the German people. The man responsible for organising the area bombing campaigns was Sir Arthur ('Bomber') Harris. Though Harris was committed to the idea of area bombing, the employment of this policy was of course a government decision. Its scope was never made clear to the British people. They continued to be told that German civilian casualties were accidental and that the raids were directed at economic or strategic targets.

Importance

There were numerous instances of area bombing techniques being put into practice. The two most notable instances were at Hamburg in July–August 1943 and at Dresden in February 1945. In both cities some tens of thousands of German civilians were killed. The whole subject of the British use of aerial warfare in these years has since become one of much controversy. There is no doubt that certain raids were of distinct value, for example the raids that destroyed V1 bases and the raids on German oil supplies as the Second Front was advancing. Beyond that their practical value in hastening the war's end is doubtful. German morale was not destroyed by the attacks, just as British morale had not been destroyed earlier by German attacks in Britain. Nor was the German economy very seriously affected by them.

The war's end

One of the worst features of the aerial bombardment was the indiscriminate waste of human life that it caused. Sadly, similar wastage was much in evidence in many parts of the world in 1945 as the war in Europe and in Asia drew to a close. As the Allied armies advanced into Germany appalling evidence was discovered and filmed of the Nazi extermination camps in which millions had perished. In August the dropping of two US atomic bombs finally brought an end to the war against Japan, at the cost of the deaths of some tens of thousands of Japanese. The use of this weapon was a US decision, but the destructive power that it demonstrated was to be of significance for Britain in its own defences and in its relations with other powers in the years after 1945.

EXERCISES

1. Show how people within Britain were affected by:
   (a) the Phoney War of 1939–40,
   (b) the Blitz of 1940–41,
   (c) the V1 and V2 attacks of 1944, and
   (d) wartime government reports and legislation.

2. Describe the course of British fighting in each of the following and indicate the importance which the fighting had:
   (a) the Battle of Britain,
   (b) North Africa,
   (c) the advances following the D-Day landings, and
   (d) the aerial bombardment of Germany.

3. Imagine you have lived in Britain throughout the Second World War and have kept a diary of events during those years. Give seven extracts for each of the years of the war from 1939 to 1945, describing your experiences in Britain during those years and your hopes for the future.

4. Study the photographs on pages 180, 181, 182 and 183, all of which are concerned with the effects of aerial bombardment, and then answer questions (a) to (d) which follow.
   (a) (i) What evidence is suggested by the photograph on page 180 that this was a disturbing experience for all involved in it?
   (ii) Explain on what specific occasions during the Second World War children were evacuated.
   (iii) What social consequences did evacuation have? (3+2+2)
   (b) Why would a visit such as that shown in the photograph on page 181 have an importance for the people of a devastated region? (3)
   (c) (i) What does the photograph on page 183 suggest about the physical effect of aerial bombardments and the precautions that might be taken to survive them?
   (ii) From the evidence in this photograph and from your own knowledge, indicate the effect that such bombardment had on the morale of town inhabitants. (3+2)
   (d) Explain the importance of the work of airmen such as those shown in the photograph on page 182 either in 1940 or in the years 1942–45. (5)

16 READJUSTMENT WITHIN BRITAIN DURING THE POST-WAR DECADE

1945 marks a turning point in British history. Few in Britain had been able during the previous six years to escape the impact of war. Many had lost their lives in Europe or in Asia or by aerial bombardment in Britain itself. Others emerged from the war shattered by their experiences, their injuries, or by the death of those they had loved. At a less tragic level, the war had had a deep effect on class relations within Britain. In seeking victory, the policy of the wartime government had aimed to create a society in which all were involved equally in the struggle against the country's enemies. The introduction of rationing, the raising of taxes, the conscription of men and women for national service were among the means by which a sense of equal involvement in the war had developed. Once the war was over, it was impossible to go back to the very sharp class distinctions that had been typical of earlier years.

The general election of 1945

Landslide Labour victory

Churchill was convinced that his Conservative party would win the general election of July 1945. This conviction was based on the success of his government's direction of the war and of the inspiring leadership he had given at crucial stages in it. But the result represented a massive defeat for the Conservative party and a landslide victory for the Labour party.

General Election: July 1945	
Conservatives	213
Labour	393
Liberals	12
Common Wealth	1
Communists	2

Reason for Conservative failure

The reason for the Conservative failure lay in the party's out-dated image. Its wartime record was not considered important in peacetime circumstances. The Conservative party was remembered as the party associated with the massive unemployment that had blighted many lives throughout the 1930s. It was also remembered as the party of appeasement, which many now considered to have been a fatal step towards the outbreak of war. Was such a party once again to be entrusted with power? In any case, the Conservatives appeared to have no well thought-out policies for post-war Britain and Churchill did his party no good by making absurd attacks on his political opponents. One of the most insensitive of these was his suggestion that once in power the Labour party would set up a Nazi-style 'Gestapo' to administer the country.

Reason for Labour success

The Labour party's approach to the election was better attuned to the mood of the country. Its manifesto title, *Let Us Face the Future*, in itself suggested the forward-looking thinking that had been developing within the party during the war years. The future that the Labour party promised would be one constructed upon the recent weakening of class divisions. There was a commitment to put the 1942 Beveridge proposals fully into effect, to reconstruct war-damaged houses through centralised planning and, by a policy of nationalisation, to take control of the country's major industries into state hands. All of these commitments were firm and new. All of them suggested that the future for most people

A HISTORY OF BRITAIN FROM 1867

King George VI (centre, in naval uniform) at Buckingham Palace with members of the newly appointed Labour Cabinet in the summer of 1945. The Prime Minister, Clement Attlee, is on the King's right and the Foreign Secretary, Ernest Bevin, is second on his left.

in Britain would be more secure and more prosperous under a Labour government.

New appeal of Labour

A high proportion of those voting in 1945 were doing so for the first time. The previous general election had been held in 1935; due to the war the one legally due five years after that had to be postponed until the fighting had ended. Most of the young people who had become entitled to vote during those ten years voted for the Labour party, whose general popularity among these younger voters was an important reason for the party's success. A number of middle-class people also voted for the Labour party, which was no longer seen as a party solely for the working classes. Those who led the Labour party did much to encourage its image as a progressive party with a wide social appeal. Clement Attlee not only inspired much confidence as party leader, but also had had experience in government. He had been a member of Churchill's wartime Coalition and for the last years of the war had been Deputy Prime Minister. Though he did not possess the dynamic qualities that had assisted Churchill during the war, many judged that Attlee was the man best suited to lead Britain into the post-war years.

Austerity

Economic problems

The end of the war presented the new government with formidable economic problems. The cost of maintaining a large and well supplied army for the previous six years had been so high that by the end of the war Britain was seriously in debt. This debt was increased by the ending of the wartime lend-lease arrangements with the United States. The country had little chance of paying off these debts quickly and in the meantime interest was added to them. To many in Britain the need to rebuild the houses and factories bombed in wartime appeared a more immediate problem than the repayment of foreign debts.

United States loan

The securing of the ready cash needed to solve both of these problems was the main financial task of the government during its early years. In these circumstances the United States, which had not suffered wartime bombing and which had in any case not been in the war for so long as Britain, was the obvious ally to approach. Within a few months of the end of the war a British delegation, headed by the economist J.M. Keynes, negotiated a loan for $3750 million (£1100 million) from the United States repayable at low interest rates. At the same time agreement was reached on easier arrangements for the repayment of

READJUSTMENT WITHIN BRITAIN DURING THE POST-WAR DECADE

the lend-lease debt. The delegates had not achieved such a large loan or such favourable terms as they had originally hoped. There was criticism of the uses to which the government put the loan. Nevertheless, this substantial injection of cash gave much needed help to the British economy at a difficult time.

Marshall Aid

By 1947 the loan had been used up. At the same time other economic problems faced the country. The early months of 1947 had produced some of the bitterest weather of the century, seriously affecting the country's output. The misery of this time is described in these reminiscences.

> In homes and shops electricity was cut off for five hours daily; the streets of London were almost blacked out. It was depressing to walk along the main thoroughfares of London with their glimmering lights and to see the luxury shops showing their wares by candlelight. The prices of candles soared and the shops were exhausted of their stocks. That was the period when the city streets were full of gloomy government posters threatening with want those who would not work. Greyhound racing, all mid-week horse racing and most matinée performances were banned. Gales, fog and snow delayed ships, trains and road transport. Coalships were storm-bound in the Tyne and the transport of coal became a major operation.
>
> Quoted in Herbert and Nancie Matthews, *The Britain We Saw*

Later in the year, mainly as a consequence of the terms of the US loan, much of Britain's gold reserves were transferred abroad. Some measure of Britain's economic difficulties in 1947 is shown by the decision to withdraw British aid to Greece and Turkey in their struggle against Communism (page 234) and to abandon British control of the mandate of Palestine and the Empire of India. But gloom did not entirely dominate the British government in 1947, as in June of that year there came the promise of Marshall Aid. This further assistance from the United States differed from the earlier one as it was a gift of money and not a loan of money. During the years 1948–51 a total of £700 million was received by Britain in Marshall Aid, a figure higher than that received by any other West European country.

Stafford Cripps

Eventually, Marshall Aid was to prove of considerable value to Britain and to be an important reason for the better success of the economy in the 1950s. In 1947, however, this was only a future possibility. A new Chancellor of the Exchequer, Stafford Cripps, took over in November 1947 and pursued a much stricter policy than his predecessor, Hugh Dalton. The term **austerity** is usually applied to the policies that Cripps pursued. He was convinced that Dalton's encouragement of consumer demand and cheap credit should be reversed, so that Britain's exports could grow to be of real value to the country's economy. In pursuing his policy of austerity, Cripps increased taxation, maintained rationing, imposed severe taxes on the most wealthy and urged trade unions not to hinder production by pressing for wage increases or by encouraging strikes. Though his austerity policies were unpopular, Cripps did create among many in Britain a sense of real involvement in bringing about an improvement in the country's economy. Exports also increased and so the policies of austerity could be seen to be working.

Another factor which helped the level of exports was the decision in September 1949 to devalue the pound, so that a pound became equivalent to $2.80 instead of the earlier $4.03. The effect of this **devaluation** was that it became cheaper for those in the United States, and in the many other countries where the currency was linked to that of the United States, to buy British goods. Though this was a distinct benefit of devaluation, the government's critics portrayed this reduction in the value of the pound as a reduction in Britain's international prestige and as another way in which the Labour government was bringing discredit on Britain.

Stafford Cripps displays the Chancellor of the Exchequer's despatch case containing the budget he is to announce in the House of Commons in the spring of 1950. Though his pursuit of policies of 'austerity' may have been necessary, it did little to endear the Labour government to the electors in 1950 and 1951.

Nationalisation

Scope of the policy

Critics were also eager to suggest that Labour's policy of nationalisation was a fundamental cause of the country's economic difficulties. Yet nationalisation was not entirely unknown in Britain. During the inter-war years, concerns such as the BBC, London Transport and electricity generating stations had all come under state control. The experience of temporary government control of much of industry during the war had shown that overall state control could diminish competition and improve output. Labour's nationalisation policies developed from these earlier moves. There were two basic features in the way in which Labour undertook nationalisation. Firstly, full compensation was paid to former owners: nationalisation was therefore done in Britain in a legal way and there was no wholesale seizure of industries by the state, such as had taken place earlier in the Soviet Union. Secondly, once nationalised, public corporations were also set up to supervise the administration of the new industries.

Early examples

Some of the moves were uncontroversial. The nationalisation of the Bank of England in 1946 did little more than put the Bank on the same standing as the nationalised banks of most other European countries. The nationalisation of electricity built upon the earlier nationalisation of the generating stations and re-organised the industry, which now operated through a series of regional boards. Nationalisation resulted in an improvement in the extent of electricity supply and in its quality. The nationalisation of gas in 1948 led to noticeable improvements in an industry that was previously much less well organised than the electricity industry.

Coal mining

Evidence of the poor organisation of the coal industry in recent years had been provided by the report of the wartime Reid Committee. Its recommendation of nationalisation as the best solution for the industry tied in well with the Labour government's approaches. The nationalisation of the coal mines became controversial for two reasons. To the miners, the amount of compensation which the government gave to the mine owners – whom they so much detested – was considered unduly generous. To the public at large, coal nationalisation became linked with the shortages of fuel supplies in general just after it took effect at the beginning of 1947. These shortages were more the result of the severe winter weather on the availability of fuel supplies than of nationalisation, but the blame was widely attributed to the changes that nationalisation brought about. For the miners, however, the taking of the mines into state control was an event of great importance, as this account of the take-over ceremony at a northern coalfield suggests.

> The platform sustained the imposing authority of the Cabinet, of big business, of smaller business, of the powerful unions and of Civic bodies in the district. The band was smart and vigorous.
> But without question, the show belonged to one man – an aged miner in a spotted muffler and a cloth cap. They helped him to the platform. 'I'm ninety-one years old and I've waited all my life for this moment,' said Jim Hawkins. 'There's little time left. Let's cut the cackle and get on with it.' Aided by willing hands, the old man made his way to the flagpole, clutched the cord and ran up a blue flag on which was written in white the letters 'N.C.B.' By his act, Jim Hawkins had translated nationalisation into an accomplished fact.
>
> *Illustrated*, 25 January 1947

Railways and road haulage

Many held similar doubts about the nationalising of the railway system and road haulage in 1947. One of the intended improvements of the nationalisation of transport was better organisation of the various different transport services, but the newly created British Railways continued to receive widespread criticism. Many maintained that rail services after nationalisation were much worse than they had been before.

Controversy over steel

The greatest controversy surrounded the proposal to nationalise steel. This was a successful industry and one in which labour relations were good. Among the steel workers there was little demand for nationalisation. Critics therefore suggested that there was no need to nationalise it and that the government's plans to do so were dictated solely by their overall policy of nationalisation and not by the practical circumstances of the industry itself. In addition to Conservative opposition in the House of Commons, the bill to nationalise steel also came up against opposition in the House of Lords, where Conservative peers were in a majority. Generally the Conservative members of the House of Lords had adopted a co-operative attitude towards the legislation of the Attlee government and had not used their power to delay legislation. They opposed in the autumn of 1948 in the hope that by the time the legislation came into effect a general election would have removed Labour from power. In order to overcome this tactic, the government reduced the veto powers of the House of Lords from two years to one year. The new Parliament Act providing for this became law in 1949. Nevertheless, the Lords used their curtailed power and insisted on amendments to the bill. These reduced its effectiveness by requiring the postponement of steel nationalisation until after the next general election.

Conservative consensus on nationalisation

Steel was the only government failure in its extensive nationalisation programme. In spite of controversy aroused by nationalisation, the work done by the Labour government in these years eventually gained widespread acceptance. Conservative governments in the 1950s and 1960s did not attempt to disturb it in any fundamental way. The identical approach of the two parties to this and to some other issues is referred to as **consensus** and was to become a notable feature of British politics in the immediate post-war years.

The welfare state

Extension of welfare provision

Consensus was also in evidence on the issues concerning welfare. The foundations of the welfare state had been laid during the earlier decades of the twentieth century, particularly by Liberal legislation before the First World War, as shown in Chapter 8. The Attlee government was committed to extend the provision of welfare beyond those earlier foundations. The collective responsibility of society for those of its members who were in need of help due to their age, sickness or unemployment, had always been a basic belief of the Labour party. The wartime Beveridge Report, considered in the previous chapter, had also outlined how this provision could be developed in post-war Britain. The report was taken by the Attlee government as a blueprint in its own furthering of the welfare state.

National Insurance Act

For Beveridge, the extension of the system of national insurance was fundamental to the development of the welfare services. Though it did not entirely implement the Beveridge proposals, the National Insurance Act of 1946 greatly extended the scope of the existing system of national insurance. The new Act went further than this earlier system by insisting that everyone in the country should be insured. Each week the employers and employed bought National Insurance stamps and in times of sickness, unemployment and old age, all were eligible to receive benefit. These came from the National Insurance fund, which was built up by the purchase of the stamps and which was partly assisted by government aid.

Industrial Injuries Act and National Assistance Act

The principle of insurance was taken further by two other acts. The Industrial Injuries Act of 1946 made the state responsible for benefit payments to those injured in industrial accidents or whose health suffered as a result of industrial diseases. It was now no longer necessary for legal action to be taken against the employer. In the past, the expense of such action had often deterred many of those with a good case for compensation. The second Act was the National Assistance Act of 1948, designed to provide assistance to those who were desperately poor and for whom the other provisions of the welfare state were inadequate.

National Health Act

A major step in the development of welfare provision was the National Health Act of 1946. The medical assistance under the 1911 Act had never been fully available; many could not afford a doctor's fees or hospital charges and therefore went without the medical treatment which they needed. Doubts were expressed about the ability of the country itself to afford a national health service. In dealing with such doubts, Attlee emphasised the basic importance of the new service for the country.

> Can we afford it? Supposing the answer is 'No', what does that mean? It really means that the sum total of the goods produced and the services rendered by the people of this country is not sufficient to provide for all our people at all times, in sickness, in health, in youth and in old age, the very modest standard of life that is represented by the sums of money set out in this Bill. I cannot believe that our national productivity is so slow that our willingness to work is so feeble or that we can submit to the world that the masses of our people must be condemned to poverty.

Controversy over National Health

On the introduction of the service in 1948, everyone was to be on the panel of a local doctor and would receive free treatment and free medicine; doctors and chemists would be paid by the state. Most hospitals were nationalised and treatment within them was also to be free. Such major changes did not escape criticism. Doctors held that they were being dictated to by the government, but later most of them accepted the service and worked within it. The high cost of the service was also criticised and it was suggested that much money was being wasted by supplying free medical aids that people did not really need. In spite of these criticisms, the health service came to be accepted by all political parties and further illustrated **consensus** in the politics of post-war Britain.

The legal system

Further steps in this direction were taken by two acts relating to the British legal system. The Criminal Justice Act of 1948 provided for much needed reform of the harsh system of punishment to which criminals could be subjected. The punishments of flogging and of hard labour were abolished. Though an attempt was made to repeal capital punishment, the death sentence continued to be imposed on murderers. Improved scope was given for the probation service, so that young offenders were discouraged from embarking on a life of crime. Apart from moving some way towards a more humane system of punishments, the Act was also concerned with the causes of crime. It marked an important stage in recognising that the solution to the problem of crime lies in treatment as well as in punishment.

The Legal Aid and Advice Act of 1949 dealt with a different aspect of the law. By providing free legal aid and advice to those who had need of it, the Act assisted many whose slender means had earlier prevented them from taking the legal action that was necessary to protect their interests. The Act was of particular value to tenants in rented accommodation, many of whom previously had no way of combating illegal eviction by their landlords.

Political changes in the early 1950s

Mounting criticism of Labour

Its large majority allowed the Labour government to keep hold on power for almost the full five-year term. Towards the end of that time, criticism of the government was widespread. Though Britain's role in foreign affairs during the late 1940s, considered in Chapter 19, and the circumstances surrounding the

British withdrawal from Palestine and India, considered in Chapter 18, were criticised, it was their management of the economy at home that was most strongly attacked. Opponents suggested that nationalisation and the welfare state were too serious a drain on the country's economy. They were particularly critical of the austerity policies of Cripps. They disliked the continued rationing of food and other commodities some five years after the war had ended.

Many hoped for a higher standard of living; others were concerned at the increasing dominance of the state in the lives of individuals. Nationalisation and welfare, whatever their advantages, were often seen in that light. This type of opposition found in the Tanganyikan groundnuts scheme a very useful weapon with which to attack the government. A plan to develop groundnuts on a wide scale in Tanganyika collapsed when it was found that the Tanganyikan soil was unsuited to groundnut cultivation. Much money was wasted on the scheme and the government's opponents did not allow this unsuccessful example of government planning to be readily forgotten.

General Election: February 1950	
Conservatives	298
Labour	315
Liberals	9

Labour difficulties, 1950–51

As shown by the above figures, Labour only narrowly held to power in the general election of February 1950. It would be difficult with so small a majority to pass controversial legislation or to avoid holding another general election in the near future. Further, some senior ministers, serving once again under Attlee's leadership, were in poor health. Cripps, the Chancellor of the Exchequer, died in the autumn of 1950 and Bevin, the Foreign Secretary, in the spring of 1951. They were succeeded respectively by Hugh Gaitskell and Herbert Morrison. Foreign policy issues, especially concerning the Korean War (pages 235–6) and an attempt by the Iran government to nationalise British oil interests in their country demanded much government attention. Morrison was additionally criticised in the course of 1951 by the defection of two senior foreign office officials to the Soviet Union.

The British economy shows signs of strain under the loads placed on it by the post-war Labour government. These particular loads had both increased considerably by the early 1950s.

"ALL I ASK IS THAT YOU GET IT PROPERLY BALANCED"

Labour divisions

In spite of ministers' ill-health and the problems in foreign affairs, the real weakness of the Labour government at this time was to be found in its own internal divisions. The different attitudes of **moderates** and the **left** within the party were not new. These differences were basically a matter of the extent to which Socialist principles were to be put into effect by government legislation.

In the government of 1950–51 these differences became focused on the issue of prescription charges. In the 1951 budget, in order to meet increased military expenditure made necessary by the Korean War, Gaitskell introduced prescription charges in the National Health service. A storm of protest was aroused, leading to the resignation of the service's founder, Aneurin Bevan, and of the then Minister of Trade and future Prime Minister, Harold Wilson. For these politicians and the many who supported them, the government was moving too close to consensus and too far from Socialism. Quite apart from the issues involved in this quarrel, prescription charges were by no means a complete solution to the new expenditure on armaments. It was this that was the most serious factor in keeping the standard of living lower than people expected.

The 1951 general election

The Conservatives were, as widely expected, returned to power in the general election in October 1951.

General Election: October 1951	
Conservatives	321
Labour	295
Liberals	6

As the figures show, the Conservatives had a comparatively narrow overall majority. They promised more wealth and less control under a Conservative government. They were, however, cautious enough not to promise to embark on the task of dismantling Labour's nationalisation and welfare work. They were well aware that public opinion accepted what Labour had done and that few wanted the work of the previous government disturbed in any fundamental way.

Churchill an elderly leader

How far their elderly leader, Churchill, was an asset in 1951 was uncertain. His warlike temperament, which had been so well suited to the situation in the early 1940s, might be less suited to the cold war atmosphere of the early 1950s. Attlee's moderating influence on the US government over their policies towards Korea, as shown in Chapter 19, had been widely admired. On the day of the 1951 general election the arresting headline 'Whose finger on the trigger?' in the *Daily Mirror* was followed by the suggestion that Churchill might be too dangerous as prime minister in a nuclear age.

Britain in mid-century

Festival of Britain

Churchill took power again during the year of the Festival of Britain. This had been organised to commemorate the centenary of the Great Exhibition of 1851 and to mark Britain's emergence from the difficulties of the war and the post-war years. Responsibility for the scheme was in the hands of Herbert Morrison, who was Home Secretary during the late 1940s and who had earlier been closely connected with local government in London. On the unused South Bank of the Thames in central London a series of exhibition halls, brightly and attractively designed, housed a wide variety of recent British inventions and of products from Britain's overseas possessions. In other parts of the country local exhibitions and local celebrations were held as part of the year's festivities. Suggestions were made at the time that the Festival was little more than an expense which the country could ill afford. How far it directly benefited the country's economy by the encouragement of exports is difficult to say. The Festival had a more general importance for the British people. The 1940s had brought severe problems to the people of Britain. Many now enjoyed the opportunity that the Festival gave them of celebrating the end of a difficult decade.

READJUSTMENT WITHIN BRITAIN DURING THE POST-WAR DECADE

A view across the Thames towards the South Bank site of the Festival of Britain in 1951 showing the 'skylon', the Festival's symbol, and the Festival Hall in the background. The Festival provided opportunity for enjoyment by the British, as the years of the war and post-war 'austerity' began to fade.

Town and country

With the exception of the Royal Festival Hall, the various exhibition buildings on the South Bank were all dismantled when the Festival ended. But the design style that had been used on the South Bank was repeated elsewhere. There was a conscious attempt to create newer and brighter designs and to move away from the rather dull, dark designs of the inter-war years. The wartime bomb damage had made extensive re-development and re-building necessary. The New Towns Act of 1946 envisaged the building of some 20 new towns; it involved the re-siting of people in new areas and the encouragement of industry to move to these new centres of population. The building trade continued under the close government control which had been introduced during the war years, and further government control was asserted through the Town and Country Planning Acts of 1944 and 1947. These regulations helped partially to prevent the unplanned, speculative building that had taken place during the inter-war years. The government also used them to encourage the construction of houses for rent, so that provision was made for those who needed accommodation but could not afford to buy it. In spite of much new building, substantial work on the new towns and the brighter designs that became fashionable, many were still living in the unsatisfactory **prefabs** (prefabricated – or pre-built – buildings) put up as temporary accommodation just after the war. Protection of the environment became an issue of importance during these years. This was shown particularly by the use of government powers to protect from further suburban development the **green belt** of rural land around London.

Standards of health

By mid-century the standards of health throughout the country showed much improvement on those of pre-war years. This was the result both of wider availability of treatment under the new National Health Service and of the application of vital discoveries on treatment. The free availability of vitamin supplies for children during the war continued after 1945 and did much to ensure better standards of health among the young. Tuberculosis, a widespread and dreaded disease of pre-war years, was now more effectively controlled by the use of mass radiography to detect its early development and by more effective treatment for its sufferers. Typhoid and diphtheria, also common in pre-war years, could now be treated by immunisation. Many of these improvements, like the better attention given to the health of children, had begun during the war.

Changing society

Society in post-war Britain was changing more rapidly than at any time in its earlier history. The mood for change reflected in the 1945 general election result was not just a temporary swing of opinion. Many wished to turn away from the standards of the inter-war years. Others – mainly among the middle classes – looked back nostalgically to the pre-1939 years, when their position in society appeared more secure, when they could afford servants, when income tax was lower and when the state did not intrude so strongly into their lives. Some who wanted to regain social status of this kind felt that their best chance of doing so was by emigrating to the African colonies, where British rule in mid-century was still untroubled. For many people, however, the greater degree of social equality which the experiences of the war and the legislation of the post-war Labour governments helped to create was a welcome change from the rigid social distinctions and the economic ills of earlier years.

Churchill's government of 1951–55

Conservative ministers

Consensus in politics was much in evidence during Churchill's second ministry. Anthony Eden, clearly marked out as Churchill's successor, served as Foreign Secretary. Major domestic appointments were given to moderate Conservative politicians. The new Chancellor of the Exchequer was R.A. Butler and the new Minister of Housing was Harold Macmillan. Both had separated themselves from the more rigid Conservative policies of the 1930s and were to play major parts in forming a popular image for their party during the early 1950s. The appointment of Walter Monckton as Minister of Labour was designed to encourage good relations with the trade unions. There was, however, criticism of one feature of Churchill's appointments. Experience as a wartime Prime Minister had impressed on Churchill the value of linking together government departments under one minister. He now repeated this method in peacetime. But the ministers he appointed – all men who had worked with him in government during the war – were members of the House of Lords and so not able to answer questions directly in the House of Commons. There was much criticism of these **overlords**, as they became known, and by 1953 this particular feature of government was abandoned.

Consensus

As shown earlier in this chapter, the legislation of the Labour government of 1945–51 had produced fundamental changes. The Conservatives now did little to disturb those changes. The welfare state that Labour had constructed remained intact. Only one serious adjustment was made to the nationalised industries; that concerned the de-nationalisation in 1953 of iron and steel, the most controversial feature of Labour's nationalisation policies. No package of domestic legislation comparable with that of their predecessors was produced by the Conservatives under Churchill. Yet by the 1955 general election the Conservatives had so gained in popularity that they were confirmed in office by a larger majority than they had secured in 1951.

The beginnings of affluence

Increasing consumer expenditure

The explanation of Conservative popularity by the mid-1950s is to be found within the British economy. These were years when **austerity** was declining and when **affluence** was increasing. The term **affluence** refers to improved standards of living becoming available to larger numbers of people. Its develop-

READJUSTMENT WITHIN BRITAIN DURING THE POST-WAR DECADE

The newly crowned Queen Elizabeth II on the balcony of Buckingham Palace shortly after her coronation in June 1953, with the young Prince Charles and Princess Anne in the centre. Coinciding as it did with the beginning of affluence, the coronation was held by many to mark the dawn of a new 'Elizabethan Age' of British greatness.

ment is one of the most notable features of British history during the 1950s. It is worth looking at some of the different ways in which affluence showed itself. Its basis was in the increased amount received in wages during these years. Between 1951 and 1958 average wages rose by 20 per cent and between 1958 and 1964 they rose by a further 30 per cent. As these two figures take account of the inflation of these years, they show that many people now had more opportunity than earlier to spend money. Figures of **consumer expenditure**, how money was spent, give further indication of increasing standards of living.

Consumer Expenditure in Millions of Pounds	1951	1955	1959	1964
Cars and motorcycles	90	354	522	910
Furniture, electrical and other household goods	526	664	888	975
Alcohol	843			1195
Tobacco	898			1055

Affluence unequally spread

The general increase in wages is not the sole explanation of the increase in consumer expenditure. Much of it is explained by a substantial increase in **hire purchase**. What had in the inter-war years been regarded as a somewhat shameful way of buying goods became widespread throughout the 1950s; and it has become even more widespread since then. Nor should it be thought that this affluence was evenly spread among all social classes. Those who did best in these years were those who were already reasonably wealthy. Large profits were to be made on the London stock market during the early 1950s, and again during the late 1950s. In these years stock market investors were able to double the value of the money they invested.

Changes in transport

As can be seen from the above figures, the items on which expenditure during the 1950s and 1960s most increased were cars and motorcycles. A virtual revolution in methods of transport took place during these two decades, as private transport on the roads increased at the expense of public transport on railways. Motorways were constructed to cater for the substantial increase in road traffic. Meanwhile, the railways abandoned the use of steam and many small branch lines were closed. Particularly severe adjustments were made in the 1960s to Britain's railway network through the application of the Beeching Report, which recommended rationalisation of the railway system and a concentration on the development of main-line routes. In view of the popularity of motor travel, such rationalisation of the railways was inevitable. The motor car had become one of the most noticeable features of the affluence of these years.

Butler as Chancellor of the Exchequer

Affluence was obviously a great boost to the government's popularity. It was closely associated with the work of R.A. Butler as Chancellor of the Exchequer. One of the fundamental reasons for his apparent success was the devaluation of 1949, which by the early 1950s had produced good export figures. Butler took steps to reduce both controls on the economy and rationing of goods and food. This was part of the 'freedom' which, while in opposition, the Conservatives had promised they would implement once in power. For most people, the ending of rationing was the most obvious way in which this was shown. It was reduced gradually and in 1954 ended completely. No longer were there so many restrictions on overseas investments, hire purchase or on building licences within Britain. In the budget of 1955 – just one month before the general election – there was a spectacular reduction in income tax by six pence ($2\frac{1}{2}$p) in each pound.

House building

In opposition the Conservatives had been particularly critical of Labour's poor achievements in house building. Harold Macmillan as Minister of Housing had therefore to prove that under the Conservatives better success could be achieved. In his approach to this demanding task, encouragement was given to private builders, both by improved government subsidies and by readier granting of building licences. He ably co-ordinated the work of different departments in working towards his goals. In both 1953 and 1954 well over 300 000 houses were built each year. The housing figures represented the major domestic achievement of the Conservatives in the early 1950s and were particularly useful to Macmillan in furthering his own political career.

EXERCISES

1. (a) Explain what you understand by the term *nationalisation* and show in what ways the Labour governments of 1945–51 pursued this policy.
   (b) Explain what you understand by the term *welfare state* and show in what ways the Labour governments of 1945–51 tried to create a welfare state in Britain.
   (c) What advantages and disadvantages did nationalisation and the welfare state produce in Britain in these years?

2. (a) How do you account for the outcome of the general elections of 1950 and 1951?
   (b) In what respects would you agree that the domestic policies of Churchill's government of 1951–55 marked the change from 'austerity' to 'affluence'?

3. Imagine you are a working-class person during the time of the Attlee governments and with childhood memories of the 1930s. Write an account to show in what ways and for what reasons life in the 1940s has been an improvement on life in the 1930s.

4. Study the extracts on page 195 and page 198 and the cartoon on page 199, all of which refer to the Labour governments of 1945–51, and then answer questions (a) to (d) which follow.
   (a) (i) In what respects does the extract on page 195 give a critical view of the government?
   (ii) By reference to details in the extract and to your own knowledge, indicate to what extent you feel this critical view to be justified. (3+3)
   (b) (i) What do you understand from the extract on page 198 about the priorities of the government?
   (ii) By reference to details in the extract and to your own knowledge, indicate in what ways the government acted on these priorities. (3+3)
   (c) How accurate a view of the domestic work of the Labour government is conveyed by these two sources? (3)
   (d) (i) With reference to various events of the years 1945–51, explain in what respects the cartoon gives a useful summary of government problems.
   (ii) What particular difficulties had the situation shown in this cartoon created for the Labour government by the early 1950s? (3+2)

17 CONSERVATIVE AND LABOUR POLICIES 1955–70

The Conservative party was to win the next two general elections after their victory in 1951. In 1955 and again in 1959 increased majorities were secured and the Conservatives held power for 13 years (1951–64). The party continued to pride itself on the affluence which many sections of society now enjoyed. Members of the Labour party, despite consensus on many issues, saw the work of the Conservatives in a different way. They became critical of the policies that were pursued during what they later dubbed the '13 wasted years' of Conservative rule. When again in power later in the 1960s, the Labour party sought to give more dynamic direction to the governing of Britain. Like their political opponents, they also found that the task of governing Britain in these changing years was no easy one.

Eden's government 1955–57

Churchill's retirement

In April 1955, the elderly Churchill finally retired. Eden, whose claims to succeed Churchill had never been seriously challenged, followed his appointment as Prime Minister by immediately summoning a general election for May. The timing could not have been more fortunate for the Conservative party nor more disastrous for the Labour party. The success of Macmillan in housing, the success of Butler in the economy and the prosperity that affluence was bringing for many all suggested that the country's prospects would be better under continued Conservative government. Eden's achievements in foreign affairs – particularly his success at the 1954 Geneva Conference on Indochina (page 237) – also helped the Conservatives in the election. Eden's interests and his strength had always lain in foreign affairs. Yet as the new Prime Minister he was conscious of the importance of domestic issues for the British electorate. He focused particularly on affluence, and made much in his election speeches of his wish to develop in Britain 'a property-owning democracy'.

The 1955 general election

By contrast, the opposition was weakened by serious splits. There was much bitterness between the supporters of Aneurin Bevan and the party leadership under Attlee. Bevan, the leader of the left-wing of the party, was eager for Britain to shed some of its commitments to the United States. He therefore urged the Labour party to dissociate itself from the Conservatives on this important issue of foreign policy. Apart from this troublesome division, there was little certainty as to what the Labour party had to offer the voters in domestic matters. As for the Liberal party, it played only a slight political role in these years. Under these circumstances, it was not surprising that the Conservatives won the election with little difficulty.

General Election: May 1955	
Conservatives	344
Labour	277
Liberals	6

Weakness of the Eden government

Despite this success, Conservative fortunes were to decline sharply and seriously during Eden's short premiership. When ill-health caused his premature retirement in January 1957, he departed from 10 Downing Street as one of the least successful of Conservative prime ministers in the twentieth century. The 1956 Suez crisis, considered more fully on pages 238–42, is the main reason for Eden's poor reputation. His abilities as Prime Minister, however, had begun to be seriously questioned even before the Suez crisis developed. He seemed incapable of giving his government the forthright leadership expected of a Prime Minister. He was further hampered by his own rather nervous personality and periods of illness. The weakness of his position was seized upon by the press, which became highly critical of him.

Economic difficulties

In the summer of 1955 Butler's economic policies began to show weakness. The economic expansion that had been so evident recently had produced such financial uncertainty that there were rumours of a further devaluation of the pound. Though this course of action proved unnecessary, Butler nevertheless had to introduce a further budget in the autumn, which increased taxation. This took out of the economy the money which his pre-election budget had put in. The opposition became highly critical of the uncertain and changeable way in which the economy was being directed. Before the end of the year, Macmillan had replaced Butler as Chancellor. During the following year, he continued the trend set by Butler's autumn budget.

Stop-Go

The uncertainties of 1955–56 illustrate a fundamental problem that was to disturb the British economy for many years to come. Economic expansion (typified by such features as tax cuts, low interest rates and freedom in hire purchase agreements) alternated – often very speedily – with economic contraction (typified by such opposite features as tax increases, high interest rates and restrictions on hire purchase agreements). This variable approach to the economy became known as **Stop-Go** and was much criticised by the Labour opposition. In their view, firmer, more far-sighted **planning** of Britain's economy would avoid these uncertainties.

Macmillan and the 1959 general election

Macmillan succeeds Eden

Whoever succeeded Anthony Eden on his retirement in January 1957 faced a difficult task in reviving Conservative fortunes. There were two contenders: Butler and Macmillan. The choice of those Conservatives who were consulted about it was for Macmillan. His earlier success as Minister of Housing, his loyalty to Eden during the Suez crisis, his commanding style and effectiveness as a popular speaker, all combined to make him the more suitable. He fully justified his party's confidence by leading them two and a half years later, in October 1959, to their third sucessive general election victory, with a majority impressively larger than the one obtained in 1955.

Macmillan and affluence

The key to his success once again lay in the economy. Four chancellors of the exchequer served during Macmillan's time. He kept a closer watch on their work than either Churchill or Eden had done with their chancellors. His overriding concern was not to lose the affluence that had begun to develop in the early 1950s. His pre-war experience as an MP for the northern town of Stockton had given him a close insight into the effects of the Depression on the lives of many of his constituents. Quite early in his premiership he put his views on the matter in this way in a speech in the House of Commons.

> I find it a strange experience to sit here day after day and listen to the arguments presented by high prices and over-full employment. When I first stood for the House of Commons in 1923 and for the next fifteen years, one problem only held the political field. The problem of rapidly falling prices and massive unemployment. We debated it week by week. We put forward all kinds of rival views as to how it should be solved.
> Today it has solved itself. Every MP knows that for the mass of the people there has never been such a good time or such a high standard of living. I repeat what I said in a speech at Bedford, they have 'never had it so good'. I have been glad to see the change. I believe that all of us in the house, certainly the older members, feel grateful that there has been this great change.
>
> Hansard, *Parliamentary Debates*

Macmillan was determined that the conditions he knew when he was a young MP should not return while he was Prime Minister.

CONSERVATIVE AND LABOUR POLICIES 1955-70

Economic policies

His first Chancellor, Peter Thorneycroft, after some initial moves in the direction of expansion, reverted by the end of 1957 to a quite severe policy of contraction. His policies were regarded as **monetarist**, involving the strict accounting of the country's finances. Interest rates were increased; government spending was decreased. His policies were likely to lead to unemployment and resulted in poor relations with the trade unions. Macmillan became worried by this unpromising trend in the economy and at the beginning of 1958 he appointed Derick Heathcote Amory in Thorneycroft's place. The **Stop** that had typified Thorneycroft's policies as Chancellor changed gradually to **Go**. Interest rates were reduced, cuts were made in both income tax and purchase tax; the budget of 1959 was particularly generous. These policies paid off well for the Conservatives in the general election of October 1959.

General Election: October 1959	
Conservatives	365
Labour	258
Liberals	6

The 1959 general election

This was a great Conservative success and a great triumph for Macmillan personally. The Conservative success in 1959 was even more remarkable on account of the fuller unity then existing in the Labour party under the new leadership of Hugh Gaitskell. Labour promises of improvement in social services and increases in government spending were seen during the campaign to have some appeal to the voters. Nor had the government's record in foreign and colonial affairs been particularly good. The issues surrounding Suez three years earlier were still by no means dead, while British policies in Cyprus (page 226), Kenya (pages 225-6) and Nyasaland (page 229) were lively and controversial issues in 1959. In these circumstances, the spectacular Conservative victory can

The Prime Minister greets the allies that had proved so useful to him in the general election of 1959. The bases of his success, as suggested in this cartoon, posed severe problems for the opposition.

'Well, gentlemen, I think we all fought a good fight ...'

be attributed to nothing other than the general affluence of the 1950s, which had benefited particularly from Heathcote Amory's recent Go policies. The Labour party was plunged into profound disillusion by the election results. Its main appeal to the voters had always been that it would bring about improvement in living conditions and a fairer society for all. Many now doubted whether such an appeal had relevance for working-class voters. The living standards of many of them had risen noticeably during the 1950s as a result of the affluence that they enjoyed under successive Conservative governments.

The economy 1959–64

Further economic difficulties

The successful economic expansion under Heathcote Amory was not to survive the general election of October 1959 for very long. Early in 1960 a Stop policy had to be initiated. This was a consequence of the over-expansion of the economy towards the end of 1959. Heathcote Amory was replaced in the summer of 1960 by Selwyn Lloyd. Only shortly after his appointment, figures were published showing a serious decline in Britain's balance of payments. To counteract the economic problems that this produced, Stop policies were more assertively pursued. In addition to the usual package of measures, Selwyn Lloyd introduced a six-month pay pause, involving a complete freeze on pay increases to government employees and discouragement of pay increases to other workers. Though these severe measures helped solve the immediate financial crisis they created severe tensions between the government and the trade unions, tensions which the Conservatives had generally avoided during the 1950s.

Planning

It was in Selwyn Lloyd's time, however, that the government decided to involve itself more fully in the kind of long-term planning of the economy which the Labour party and the trade unions were advocating. In 1961 the National Economic Development Council (NEDC) was set up, modelled on a similar French organisation that had recently proved successful. Its function was to collect information from different industries and to attempt to encourage a consistent growth rate so that Stop-Go policies would be a thing of the past. But it never secured full commitment from the Conservative government, nor were its powers as extensive as those of its continental counterpart.

Unemployment

In any case, another change of Chancellor in the summer of 1962 led to further changes in the direction of the country's economy. Change was certainly shown to be necessary. In the bitterly cold winter of 1962–63, unemployment figures reached what was by the standards of the time the very high figure of 800 000. It was this problem, rather than any other, that persuaded Maudling, the new Chancellor, to initiate yet another Go policy. His hope was that business confidence would thus be renewed, and the problem of unemployment would diminish. Though he achieved some success as Chancellor, the British economy was by no means set on a consistent or a satisfactory course when the Conservatives left office in October 1964.

The Chancellor of the Exchequer

In the twentieth century the office of Chancellor of the Exchequer has developed as one of the most senior appointments in the Cabinet. Recent chapters have shown how vital economic matters had become in British history: Depression in the inter-war years, austerity in the immediate post-war years, affluence and its problems in the 1950s and the 1960s. Controlling and directing the economy had now become a matter of over-riding importance for the government of the day. No government could now fail to give it priority. It had become the vital issue for any party at a general election. Voters were themselves aware that their standards of living were directly affected, for good or for ill, by the economic policies pursued by the government.

But an understanding of the workings of the economy is not easy to achieve. Technical terms and difficult concepts are involved; even an expert knowledge of these matters by a Chancellor and those who advise the Chancellor is no guarantee that success will result. The details of economic policies given so far in this chapter are a simplified version of a complicated and difficult subject. They do not always make for very interesting reading. Yet in view of the direct effect of the economy on the lives of the people of Britain, they form an essential part of any study of British history in these and later years.

Political changes of 1963–64

Liberal revival

In the early 1960s political opposition to Macmillan's Conservative government became more effective. The background to this development was a general sense of disillusion with the government's handling of the economy and with its lack of positive policies. There was little legislation of any importance and the government appeared to have no real sense of purpose or direction. The Liberal party was the first to get advantage from Conservative misfortune. After a number of years in which they had played only a minimal role in British politics, Liberal fortunes began to revive. This was shown by Liberal success in local elections and in parliamentary by-elections. A spectacular Liberal victory was achieved in March 1962 at a by-election at Orpington in Kent. Opinion polls confirmed the general popularity of the Liberal party. Heady predictions began to be made that the Liberals would form the next government of the country.

Hugh Gaitskell

The Labour party was now more effectively united than it had been for some years. In the immediate aftermath of the 1959 general election the party had to consider what was the best way in which to show that it still had a place in British political life. Gaitskell tended to adopt what his critics considered a 'right-wing' approach to major issues. The party's long-standing commitment to nationalisation (Clause Four of the party's 1918 constitution) seemed to him unwise amidst the affluence of these years. He therefore attempted to advance the idea of a **mixed economy**, an economy based both on state-owned and on privately-owned industries. Gaitskell himself put it in this way when speaking about Clause Four:

> **It implies that common ownership is an end, whereas in fact, it is a means. It implies that the only precise object we have is nationalisation, whereas in fact we have many other Socialist objectives. It implies that we propose to nationalise everything, but do we? Everything? – the whole of light industry, the whole of agriculture, all the shops – every little pub and garage? Of course not. We have long ago come to accept, we know very well, for the foreseeable future, at least in some form, a mixed economy.**

So intense were the internal wranglings which this idea evoked that he abandoned the attempt to get it accepted by the party. He ran into similar difficulties from those Labour party members who were also members of the Campaign for Nuclear Disarmament (CND) considered more fully later, on pages 237–8. Their attempt to get the Labour party committed to their cause was strenuously opposed by Gaitskell.

Harold Wilson

After the premature death of Gaitskell in January 1963 the party leadership was taken over by Harold Wilson. He was a skilled economist, who had served, at a young age, as a junior minister in Attlee's government. His political position on the left of the Labour party enabled him to get the support of many who had opposed his predecessor. His skill as a politician ensured that he did not at the same time alienate more moderate members of the party.

Government disasters

In parliament, Wilson quickly revealed himself as a formidable opponent of the Conservatives, whose declining fortunes he readily seized upon. Further disasters befell the government in the summer of 1963. The Profumo scandal caught much public attention. It became known that the Minister of War, John Profumo, had had a liaison with a prostitute who had among her other clients a Soviet diplomat resident in London. Though the seriousness of this scandal was grossly exaggerated, it was seen as a potential threat to the country's security. **Rachmanism** was a more serious issue that Wilson took up. Rachman was an unscrupulous landlord in East London who exploited to his own financial advantage large numbers of tenants in the slum dwellings that he owned. Wilson attributed the ease with which Rachman had been able to operate to the Rent Act, passed by the Conservatives in 1957. This Act had been opposed by the

Labour party on the grounds that it gave too great a freedom to landlords to do as they wished in respect of their tenants. The revelations of Rachmanism appeared to confirm that their fears were justified.

Retirement of Macmillan

An unexpected internal crisis broke within the Conservative party in the autumn of 1963. Just before the annual party conference was to be held at Blackpool in October, Macmillan became ill, suddenly and seriously. An operation was necessary. Knowing he would be unable to carry out a prime minister's work for some considerable time, he decided to retire. The Blackpool Conference was obviously dominated by discussion on the right person to succeed him. This was an issue of intense importance to the party, as their fortunes were beginning to decline and a general election would have to take place within the next 12 months.

A decision about Macmillan's successor was not, however, something that would be resolved at Blackpool. It was reached instead through what were loosely described as the 'customary processes' for electing a Conservative leader, processes which involved consultation among various important members of the party. From among a number of contenders, the choice fell on the Foreign Secretary, Lord Home. Membership of the House of Lords was not considered appropriate for a prime minister in the twentieth century, but that problem – which had earlier been so important in Lord Curzon's failure to secure the premiership in 1923 – could in 1963 be overcome. By the Peerage Act of the same year, it was possible for a member of the House of Lords to renounce his title and seek membership of the House of Commons. This Lord Home did, taking the name of Sir Alec Douglas-Home and becoming elected for a Scottish constituency at a by-election before the end of the year.

Sir Alec Douglas-Home

Much controversy surrounded both the man chosen by the party as leader and also the old-fashioned way in which that choice had been reached. Douglas-Home had sound qualities as a statesman, but some in the Conservative party doubted if he was the right man to lead the party at that time. Certainly the new Prime Minister was a poor match to Wilson. The leader of the opposition – both in the House of Commons and outside – made much of Douglas-Home's aristocratic background. He claimed that a government headed by Douglas-Home was inappropriate for Britain in the 1960s and belonged to a former age. Wilson did much in the following 12 months to give Labour the image of a dynamic, forward-looking party. Modern science and modern technology were to be more effectively harnessed to the needs of British industry which, Wilson claimed, had been allowed to stagnate during the 13 years of Conservative rule.

The 1964 general election

The general election was eventually called for October 1964. Conservative political fortunes had to a certain extent revived earlier in the year, particularly as a result of Maudling's work as Chancellor. But the Labour party under Wilson presented a serious threat. Its election manifesto, *The New Britain*, continued the party's emphasis on the image that Wilson had been carefully cultivating. It presented itself as capable of forming an attractive alternative government, well suited to the times. Their long period in office was a disadvantage to the Conservatives, who tended to give the image of a tired government, incapable of providing direction to the nation's business.

The Wilson governments, 1964–70

Labour's small majority

Labour's victory in October 1964 was a very narrow one.

General Election: October 1964	
Conservatives	304
Labour	317
Liberals	9

CONSERVATIVE AND LABOUR POLICIES 1955–70

Labour had an exceptionally small overall majority of only four. Such circumstances created uncertainty for the government in the House of Commons, as illness or unfavourable by-election results might well deprive them of a majority there. Wilson sought to get a more secure basis in the House of Commons by holding a further election whenever the chance of success looked promising. He judged the moment right some 18 months later, in March 1966.

Edward Heath Meanwhile Edward Heath had become leader of the Conservative party. Conservatives had become critical of Douglas-Home's leadership at the time of the previous election and his poor subsequent showing as leader of the opposition. In the summer of 1965 Heath was the first leader of the Conservative party to attain the position as a result of election by Conservative MPs. The party had discarded the 'customary processes' which had become much criticised since Douglas-Home's appointment two years previously. Heath's appointment was novel in another way, as he was the first leader of the Conservative party not to come from a privileged, wealthy background. The Conservative choice had therefore been for a man whose leadership would suggest a closer identity of their party with the electorate. In spite of the qualities their new leader possessed, the general election of March 1966 confirmed the Labour government in power, with a substantially increased majority.

General Election: March 1966	
Conservatives	253
Labour	363
Liberals	12

Labour planning The state of the economy was the most troublesome of the problems that Labour inherited. Now was an opportunity for the Labour party to put into effect the planning of the economy that it had recommended and to make an end to the Stop-Go policies that it had so roundly condemned. A new government department, the Department of Economic Affairs, was set up under the direction of the Deputy Leader of the Labour party, George Brown. Its first concern was to arrive at an agreement on prices and incomes. Brown managed to secure an agreement from the TUC and from the Confederation of British Industry (CBI) – the organisation which represented the employers – to link any increases in prices and incomes to increases in productivity. Operation of this agreement was voluntary, but the reaching of the agreement was regarded as an important step towards a better organised economy for Britain. It was also seen as an important step towards the formulation of the National Plan to which Brown gave much emphasis. This was published in December 1965, having been based upon careful analysis of economic statistics and trends. A rate of growth for the British economy of 4 per cent each year was the Plan's main content. Such a rate was to prove over-ambitious and by the late 1960s the Plan was no longer regarded as meaningful.

Sterling crisis In any case, the Labour governments of these years encountered obstacles that made it difficult to carry through any purposeful economic planning at all. In an autumn budget in 1964 many election promises were fulfilled. Pensions and national insurance benefits were increased and prescription charges were abolished. But income tax, company tax and capital gains tax (a tax mainly applicable to profits made by dealings in shares on the stock market) were all increased. Such measures were to be typical of Labour's years in power during the 1960s. They proved unwelcome to international financiers who, as a consequence, sold their holdings in Britain's currency (sterling). They did so in such large bulk that the value of sterling on the international money markets declined dramatically, thus creating a series of sterling crises.

Wilson's emphasis on the dynamic appeal of Labour did much to win success for his party in the 1964 election. But it was not long before the practical problems of governing the country held back the progress that he promised.

Devaluation or deflation

Though the Labour governments faced sterling crises from the very start, the most serious occurred just after the election of March 1966. By July, the international value of sterling had slipped dramatically. Events in Britain after the election had contributed to this. A lengthy strike by seamen had reduced the level of exports. Trade union opposition to the government had been further aroused by the government's proposed Prices and Incomes Bill, which attempted to give legal force to the restrictions that earlier had been voluntary.

In one of the most serious financial crises of recent times, the government considered it had two choices. One was **devaluation**, the lowering of the value of sterling against other currencies in order to make British goods cheap abroad, boost exports and thus help the economy. The other was **deflation**, the cutting back of demand by tax increases and restrictions, the type of Stop on the economy which Labour had so strongly criticised only a few years earlier. Wilson persuaded his Cabinet that **deflation** was the course they should follow. The package of cuts which he announced in July was exceptionally severe. Purchase tax was increased, hire-purchase facilities were curbed, the amount of money that could be taken out of the country was restricted, a six-month 'freeze' was imposed on prices and incomes. Nor was it expected that financial circumstances would be much easier in the following year.

Decision for devaluation

Even these drastic measures failed to produce the desired results. Sterling continued to be a weak international currency, while unemployment reached half a million by the summer of 1967. The situation was not helped by the effects of the Six Day War between Israel and its Arab neighbours nor by technicalities in negotiations for Britain's entry into the European Economic Community. Wilson decided on firmer measures and, after having himself taken on the direction of the Department of Economic Affairs, he announced a **devaluation** of sterling in November 1967. The pound was now to be exchanged at the rate of $2.40 instead of the previous $2.80. Callaghan, as Chancellor of the Exchequer, had always taken the view – to which the Labour government had anyway earlier pledged itself – that there would be no devaluation. He now felt compelled to resign and was replaced by Roy Jenkins, who held the office until the Labour government fell from power in 1970. Jenkins continued to pursue policies of economic restraint, in spite of vocal opposition in the House of Commons from members of his own party. Towards the end of the 1960s, some degree of stability in economic affairs had been restored.

Developments in education

Comprehensive education

It was not until the mid-1960s that serious government attention was given to changes in the organisation of the education provided by schools. For about 20 years the system set up by the 1944 Butler Act had been practised. Serious doubts had been voiced about the manner in which pupils were categorised by means of an examination at the fairly early age of 11. Some local authorities had taken the opportunity – available to them under the terms of the 1944 Act – of setting up **comprehensive** schools, to cater for all pupils of secondary school age. By the time the Labour party was returned to power in 1964, it had a commitment to the extension of comprehensive education throughout the country. In 1965 all local authorities in England and Wales were required to change the secondary schooling they provided to the comprehensive system. Though there was some resistance and delay by Conservative-dominated local authorities, by the end of the 1960s about one third of all secondary school pupils were being educated in comprehensive schools.

CSE and GCE

It was during these years that the new Certificate of Secondary Education (CSE) examination, set up in 1965, was increasingly taken by school pupils. The intention of this new examination was to provide a leaving certificate for those pupils considered best suited to the CSE rather than to the Ordinary Level of the General Certificate of Education (GCE), which had been set up in 1951 as a successor to the old School Certificate.

Standards in schools

Such fundamental changes in the organisation of schools and examinations did not take place without fears being expressed on declining standards. Such doubts focused both on what was taught in the schools and on the effectiveness of discipline within them. The raising of the school leaving age to 16 in 1973 only tended to heighten this continuing debate about educational standards.

Universities and higher education

The 1960s was also a time of development in higher education. Towards the end of the Conservatives' 13 years, a number of new universities had been set up. In 1963 the Robbins Report into higher education recommended further expansion, of universities and of polytechnics. By the end of the 1960s there had been a substantial expansion in student numbers. Instead of being a small, privileged and quiet section of the community, students were now more numerous and more vocal. In 1968 student 'sit-ins' and even riots in a number of universities and polytechnics suggested some kind of breakdown in staff-student relations, which may partly have been caused by the rapid expansion of recent years. One of the most novel and most successful innovations of these years was the setting up in 1969 of the Open University. It was intended to cater for those who were older than most students, who had the ability to engage in higher education and yet had lacked the opportunity of doing so earlier in life. Teaching was largely by means of correspondence, linked to programmes on the television and radio.

Crime and punishment

Capital punishment

Whether it was right to hang murderers had become an issue of much controversy within Britain during the 1950s. The controversy had been stimulated during these years by a number of murder cases in which the circumstances made the justice of the death penalty doubtful. A Labour MP, Sidney Silverman, took up the cause of abolition, voting on which in the House of Commons was on the basis of a **free vote**, one not on party lines. Progress towards abolition was gradual. The Homicide Act of 1957 provided for imprisonment rather than death for certain categories of murder, though for others the death penalty could still be imposed. After the Act's passage, there were fewer executions in the late 1950s and early 1960s. The new Labour government was committed to abolition, but it was again a free vote that allowed the passage of the Murder

(Abolition of Death Penalty) Act in 1965. This abolished the death penalty for an experimental five-year period which parliament extended indefinitely at the end of that time. The last occasion on which the death penalty was imposed in Britain was in 1964.

Changing nature of crime

Law and order continued to be a troublesome matter. Affluence, so it was often said, far from discouraging crimes of theft and violence, seemed almost to act as an encouragement to them. More time continued to be devoted by the police, welfare workers and probation officers in attempts to prevent crime and to eliminate its root causes, but the struggle in doing so was a hard one. There was particular concern about crime among young people, which became the subject of important government legislation. The Children and Young Persons Act of 1969 was the most significant of a number of acts attempting to deal with this problem. It was concerned with the working of the juvenile courts and with more effective provision in community homes for young offenders. Other steps were taken in attempting to deal with adult offenders. The Criminal Justice Act of 1967 introduced suspended sentences and allowed acceptance of majority rather than unanimous verdicts by juries.

Immigration

The West Indies and the Indian sub-continent

Few topics in post-war Britain evoked more varying views than immigration from Commonwealth countries. Part of the original process of the Empire's expansion had been the granting of British citizenship to all who came under the Empire's rule. Such a right conferred another right automatically: the right to settle in Britain. Until after the Second World War, few responded to such an opportunity. In 1948, immigration from the West Indies began on a large scale and continued throughout the 1950s, when immigrants also came in large numbers from the Indian sub-continent. The immigration had been partly encouraged by statements from the British government that more workers were needed in Britain during the post-war years. So far as the West Indies were concerned, poor living conditions and restrictions imposed on immigration into the United States in the early 1950s had made immigration to the mother country of Britain seem an obvious and sensible step to take.

Effects of immigration

While the economy of Britain benefited from this much needed new labour supply, some distinct social problems emerged in the urban areas where the new immigrants settled. Many immigrants found themselves the victims of discrimination and poor housing; many became disillusioned with life in the Commonwealth's mother country. White people often complained that the presence of immigrants in their neighbourhood was a disturbance to their established way of life. The tensions which continued immigration was producing during the 1950s became starkly revealed in the summer of 1958 when racial disturbances broke out in London's Notting Hill district. Marked increases in immigration levels in the following few years drew further public concern to what was now regarded by many as a very serious problem.

Annual rate of immigration	
1959	20 000
1960	58 000
1961	115 150

Curbing of immigration

The Commonwealth Immigration Act of 1962 was an attempt to curb what the government viewed as a dangerous situation arising from continued immigration. Under the terms of the Act, immigration was restricted to those who secured the necessary **voucher** in their home country. This voucher signified that a person either had been accepted for a specific job in Britain or had a skill or qualification that would be of value in Britain. The Act encountered stormy opposition in the House of Commons from Labour MPs.

Yet once in power, the Labour government continued along the lines laid down by the 1962 Act. The leaders of the Labour party and Labour MPs were aware by that time that though they might not like the 1962 Act it nevertheless had much support from working-class people in Britain. When they tackled the issue in 1965, they did so by means of a White Paper which in practice took further the principles of the 1962 Act.

Race relations The Labour government did tackle in a more positive way the problems which immigrants and their descendants faced in Britain. A Race Relations Act of 1965, an attempt to prevent racial discrimination, set up a Race Relations Board to enquire into allegations of discrimination of this kind. Its powers were extended by the terms of a similar Act of 1968, which made more specific the ban on all forms of discrimination in employment, housing and other aspects of life.

EXERCISES

1. (a) Describe the main changes that took place in Britain during the 1950s and 1960s in:
   (i) provision for education,
   (ii) treatment of criminal offenders, and
   (iii) legislation affecting immigrants and their descendants.
   (b) Why do you think these various changes were important?

2. (a) Why do you think the direction of Britain's economy has become a matter of such importance in the second half of the twentieth century?
   (b) Outline the main features of Conservative economic policies in the years 1955–64.
   (c) Outline the main features of Labour economic policies in the years 1964–70, showing in what ways these policies differed from those of the Conservatives.

3. Imagine you have lived throughout the 25 years from the end of the Second World War in 1945 to the formation of the Heath government in 1970. Write your memoirs of those years, showing in what ways your standard of living changed during this quarter-century.

4. Study the cartoons on pages 207 and 212 and then answer questions (a) to (c) which follow.
   (a) (i) Show, by reference to its details, how the cartoon on page 207 suggests reasons for the Conservative victory in the 1959 general election.
   (ii) By reference to your knowledge of the policies of the Conservative and Labour parties at that time, indicate how accurate you feel the cartoon to be. (3+4)
   (b) (i) Why, by the time of the 1964 general election, was the poster on the left of the cartoon on page 212 likely to have an appeal?
   (ii) In what ways does the poster on the right of this cartoon give a generally accurate impression of the Labour government during the two years (not just the hundred days) following the election? (4+4)
   (c) (i) How useful do you find these cartoons as sources for your knowledge of Conservative and Labour attitudes at this time?
   (ii) What other sources might help to further such knowledge? (5)

18 THE BRITISH EMPIRE AND COMMONWEALTH IN THE TWENTIETH CENTURY

Britain's status as a great power had been constructed upon its earlier industrial and commercial achievements. At the turn of the century it was, however, Britain's overseas possessions that were regarded by many in Britain as showing their country's greatness to the rest of the world. Additions to these possessions were still being made. This sense of pride was well expressed in the Anthem set to the rousing music of Elgar's Pomp and Circumstance march.

> Land of hope and glory, mother of the free.
> How shall we extol thee, who are born of thee?
> Wider still and wider shall thy bounds be set;
> God who made thee mighty, make thee mightier yet.

As shown in Chapter 7, much of the British Empire – especially in Africa – had been built up in a quite short space of time towards the end of the nineteenth century. Few foresaw that the new century would see an equally rapid decline in Britain's authority overseas.

The British Commonwealth

Empire to Commonwealth

As the lands of the Empire secured independence from British rule in the twentieth century, most did not entirely abandon links with their former rulers. After independence, they continued to be members of what was termed the **British Commonwealth**. In the course of the twentieth century the idea of a British Commonwealth gradually came to replace that of a British Empire. In the later nineteenth century, the Liberal party was showing a preference for the word **Commonwealth**, a word which suggested some kind of equality between its members. For much of the first half of the twentieth century, Conservatives still tended to prefer the word **Empire**, which emphasised British rule rather more strongly. By the middle of the twentieth century it was less and less in use.

Dominion countries

The countries to which in the early twentieth century the idea of the Commonwealth had greater significance were the **dominion** countries: Canada, Australia, New Zealand and South Africa. All were lands to which British people had emigrated in large numbers. Such emigration was to continue well into the twentieth century. The arrangements made for Canada in the British North America Act of 1867 were to set a pattern for the others. The various different Canadian colonies were brought together into a federation, which was to have its own elected parliament and Prime Minister with responsibility for what was termed the **dominion of Canada**. The new dominion was loyal to the British Monarch, who was represented in the country by the Governor-General. For all practical purposes, the 1867 Act gave Canada the right to govern itself.

Other colonies where there had been considerable British settlement hoped to achieve a similar **dominion status** for themselves. In 1900 the Commonwealth of Australia Act federated the Australian colonies and provided for an Australian parliament. New Zealand, which had been self-governing since 1856, was declared a dominion in 1907. The arrangements made for South Africa in 1909 represented in large measure an attempt to heal some of the wounds of the Second Boer War. The British and the Boer territories were united as the **Union of South Africa** and granted dominion status. South Africa differed from the other dominions in having whites as a minority of the total population, yet the arrangements of 1909 placed voting rights in the newly

THE BRITISH EMPIRE AND COMMONWEALTH IN THE TWENTIETH CENTURY

created Union almost entirely in the hands of white settlers. The idea of **majority rule** had no place in most of Britain's overseas possessions in the early twentieth century.

Changing role of dominions

Though granted much freedom of government, the dominions were not permitted control of their foreign and defence policies. These were still decided upon by the British government. August 1914 was a time of particular importance in this respect. When Britain declared war on Germany, the declaration automatically involved the dominion countries. Their soldiers were much in evidence in the fighting, for example the Australian and New Zealand troops at Gallipoli (page 122) and Canadian troops at Vimy Ridge (page 127). Supplies of essential raw materials from dominion countries increased during the war. The successful wartime co-operation of the dominions was seen by some to promise closer co-operation when the war was over.

A constant supporter throughout the inter-war years of the importance of their overseas possessions for the people of Britain was Leopold Amery, a Conservative MP. In the dominions themselves, similar emphasis on the

Leopold Amery was a tireless advocate of trade links with the dominion countries and the colonies. Here – in a setting modelled on a famous portait of Tudor times – he is shown attempting to persuade fellow politicians that the solution to Britain's economic ills in the inter-war years lies in the adoption of his policies.

TALES OF THE DOMINIONS.

importance of Commonwealth links was made by General Smuts of South Africa, who had been a member of Britain's wartime Coalition government. Yet these men and others were to be disappointed by the unwillingness shown by the dominions to collaborate with the policies of British governments once the war was over. There was instead much wrangling between the dominion governments and the British government as to what exactly their relationship was.

The Balfour Definition

In 1926 a partial solution to this was arrived at by Lord Balfour, the former Prime Minister. He produced what became known as the **Balfour Definition** of dominion status (not to be confused with the 1917 **Balfour Declaration** on Palestine). According to the Balfour Definition, Britain and the Dominions were

> **Autonomous communities within the British Empire, equal in status, in no way subordinate one to another in any aspect of their domestic or external affairs, though united by a common allegiance to the Crown, and freely associated as members of the British Commonwealth of Nations.**

It is interesting to notice how the Balfour Definition contains the two words **Empire** and **Commonwealth**, at a time when no one was really certain which was the more appropriate word to use. In 1931 the Statute of Westminster was another attempt at readjusting Commonwealth relations. Dominion parliaments were now free to control their own foreign and defence policies; legal appeals to Britain were to be limited; the Governor-General in a dominion was in future to represent the Monarch rather than the British government of the day.

Trade links

The Depression that so troubled Britain in the 1930s had also a particular importance for the dominions. As shown in Chapter 13, the passage of the Import Duties Act in February 1932 marked Britain's abandonment of free trade. Later that year an Imperial Economic Conference was held at Ottawa, where preferential arrangements for Commonwealth trade were agreed upon. The result during the 1930s was an increase in Commonwealth trade. It was in this way that while the constitutional links within the Commonwealth became weaker, commercial links grew stronger. The fundamental loyalty of the Commonwealth to Britain was well illustrated in 1939. With the exception of the Irish Free State, all the dominion countries entered the war in support of Britain, though there was by then no obligation on them to do so.

India

The First World War

Dominion status had by the early twentieth century become the goal of the Indian National Congress, whose origins have been considered in Chapter 7 (page 88). The British government's resistance to this demand made the Indian sub-continent particularly difficult to control during the inter-war years. During the First World War, however, Indian troops had fought alongside dominion troops on the Western Front and in Mesopotamia. As a result of more sensitive government by Britain, the disorders that had been aroused earlier in the century by the partition of Bengal (page 88) had died down.

Montagu-Chelmsford reforms

Towards the end of the war, and partly as a reward for Indian loyalty during the war, reform was taken further. The Viceroy, Lord Chelmsford, and the Secretary of State for India, Edwin Montagu, proposed a reform package, the **Montagu-Chelmsford reforms**, sometimes known as the **Montford reforms**. The basic principle of these reforms, as implemented in the Government of India Act of 1919, was **dyarchy**, the sharing of government with Indians in a limited way. This was to have greatest impact in the local government of India, where in each province there were now to be two governments. One came under the control of the Governor of the province and the other was responsible to a locally elected assembly. In central government, an elected assembly was to be created and Indians were to be represented on the Viceroy's Council. Elections for both local government and central government were on the basis of a very limited franchise, so that only the more wealthy Indians were able to vote. The Montagu-Chelmsford reforms – like the more limited Morley-Minto reforms earlier in the century – represented a bold attempt by the British government to win over the Indian middle classes to the idea of a very gradual progress towards dominion status for India.

Amritsar massacre

This promising course came to nothing. India once again became seriously disturbed in the years just after the war. An upsurge of national feeling led to riots and terrorism. Emergency government measures such as the interning of suspects without trial appeared only to encourage further disorders. Mishandling by the British authorities of events in the northern city of Amritsar in April 1919 was to have a decisive impact on the course of Anglo-Indian relations.

The military commander at Amritsar, General Dyer, issued instructions forbidding the holding of public meetings in the city. When his instructions were disobeyed, he ordered his men to open fire on a defenceless crowd of thousands packed into an enclosed space within the city. More than 500 Indians were killed and many more than that injured. Dyer's actions were not untypical of the way in which British officers had tackled the problem of rebellious Indians some half a century previously at the time of the Indian Mutiny, but such approaches were badly out of date by 1919. When called to account for what he had done, Dyer asserted that only by firm action such as he had taken could the British be certain of continuing to control India and the Indians. This excuse for what became known as the **Amritsar massacre** was not accepted. Dyer was

Mahatma Gandhi and the British

Satyagraha The man who was to channel this hostility towards the British into a positive force of opposition which was eventually to result in independence within the sub-continent, was Mahatma Gandhi. He was born into a prosperous Hindu family and embarked on a career as a lawyer. He practised in South Africa during the years before the First World War. There he undertook work on behalf of many Indians who lived in South Africa and in attempting to defend their interests he developed the approach known as **satyagraha**. This involved passive resistance against the authorities and it was to be developed very successfully by Gandhi in India after his return there at the end of the war.

British response The British found Gandhi's tactics difficult to handle. He succeeded in getting mass support by boycotting British goods and British authority; British taxes remained unpaid. Both he and many of his followers were sent to prison, where overcrowding then became a problem. He encouraged his followers to practise the hand-spinning of cotton, a simple method of production that identified Gandhi's movement with the mass of the Indian population. So widespread was his following that some violence was inevitably associated with the movement, though for Gandhi, non-violence was at the very heart of the practice of satyagraha.

A cynical view of Gandhi's non-violence is taken in this cartoon. Though there were excesses among some of his followers, Gandhi's message of non-violence was crucial in the achievement of independence in the Indian sub-continent.

This emphasis was illustrated in the way he encouraged his followers to break the complete control which the government had over the sale of salt within India. In a well-publicised demonstration, Gandhi led his followers to the sea at Dandi in southern India, where he dramatically condensed sea water into a lump of salt. Technically, his action broke the law in British India, yet it seemed an innocent thing to do. The British authorities were now put in the ridiculous position of having to imprison Indians for offences which were very minor indeed. By the late 1920s satyagraha was getting the results that Gandhi wanted: a mass movement of protest against a government which he was successfully ridiculing.

Round-table conferences While trying to deal in India with Gandhi's movement as best it could, the British government continued to pursue policies in the spirit of the Montagu-Chelmsford reforms. In 1927 Baldwin's government appointed the Simon

Commission to enquire into the working of these reforms and to suggest further developments for India. Indian opinion was angered by the exclusion of Indian representatives from the Commission. Nevertheless, Gandhi was able to establish good relations with the new Viceroy, Lord Irwin. The two men held deep religious feeling in common, Gandhi as a Hindu and Irwin as a high church Anglican.

Irwin became convinced that India should get dominion status eventually, but hoped it would be implemented gradually. After 1929, his view coincided with that of Ramsay MacDonald's second Labour government. Irwin therefore committed the British government to the achievement of dominion status. To work out how that was to be achieved, a series of **round-table conferences** were to be held in London, in which Indians and British could take part. The first round-table conference towards the end of 1930 was able to consider the report of the Simon Commission which had been issued in the meantime. But the conference made little progress as, due to a further imprisonment, Gandhi was not present at it. He attended the second round-table conference in the autumn of 1931, but it made only slight progress, as did a third in 1932.

Opposition within Britain

The National government was less enthusiastic than the second Labour government had been about the achievement of dominion status, though it took the view that there was little other course open for India eventually. Within Britain there had developed a quite strong spirit of resistance to Indian demands. Fear had been expressed in 1919 that the modest Montagu-Chelmsford reforms heralded the end of British rule in India. Although General Dyer had been relieved of his command after the Amritsar massacre, there was much public support in Britain for what he had done. A newspaper fund was launched for 'The Man who saved India' and raised £26 000 as a personal gift for Dyer on his return to Britain. Foremost in opposing British concessions to India in the 1930s was Winston Churchill. He had a contempt for Gandhi and in one of his most vivid passages gave vent to his anger at Gandhi's meetings with Irwin.

> It is alarming and also nauseating to see Mr Gandhi, a seditious Middle Temple lawyer, now posing as a fakir of a type well-known in the east, striding half-naked up the steps of the Viceregal palace, while he is still organising and conducting a defiant campaign of civil disobedience, to parley on equal terms with the representative of the King-Emperor.
>
> Hansard, *Parliamentary Debates*

Though Churchill was sincere in his views about a continuing role for Britain in India, there were other motives that led him to take up the imperial cause so strongly in the early 1930s. Having been angered by his exclusion from the government, he hoped to rally support within the Conservative party and unseat the moderate Baldwin as its leader. Most Conservatives preferred Baldwin's moderation and mistrusted Churchill on this issue.

Government of India Act

In the meantime, as a long-term result of the Simon Commission's report and the various round-table conferences, another Government of India Act was passed in 1935. This was an Act of particular importance and was eventually to be the basis of independence 12 years later. In the provinces, the elected assemblies were now to have fuller responsibilities than the governor. A two-chamber parliament was established, one chamber representing the provinces and the other representing the princely states. The franchise was extended, to include one-sixth of the total population. The Viceroy nevertheless still retained substantial powers. In Britain, for Churchill and a number of Conservatives, the Act represented a serious step towards the abandonment of India. In India, Gandhi's followers were angered at the limitations on Indian freedom which was implied by the reserving of particular powers to the Viceroy. Nevertheless, the terms were generous and independence could not now be far off.

THE BRITISH EMPIRE AND COMMONWEALTH IN THE TWENTIETH CENTURY

Independence and partition

Moslems in India

As the 1935 Act was put into practice in the late 1930s, a new problem emerged. The Moslem minority in India became concerned at the domineering and unco-operative attitude adopted by the Hindus. The Moslem League, founded in 1906, had generally worked closely with the Congress party until this time. Its present leader, Ali Jinnah, now developed the demand that at the time of independence the sub-continent should be partitioned, so that Moslems could have their own state of Pakistan. During the Second World War the Moslem League tended to be favoured by the British, as under Jinnah's lead the Moslem League gave stronger support to the British war effort than the Hindus did.

Quit India campaign

In India, the British government responded to these events by making a generous offer in 1942 of complete independence when the war ended. They also committed themselves to the creation of Pakistan. But Gandhi opposed the British concessions and rallied the Congress behind him. He launched a new campaign in 1942: **Quit India**. Immediate British withdrawal was demanded and passive resistance was organised on a particularly wide scale. Gandhi was imprisoned for the rest of the war as were many of his followers. The Moslem League had not taken part in these campaigns, whose timing during the war the British regarded as particularly underhand. The cause of the League therefore continued to gain favour among the British.

Wartime circumstances

The Second World War had profoundly affected the situation in India, just as it had the situation in Britain's other overseas possessions. In view of the difficulties of the struggle with Germany, Britain was compelled to make promises for the future in order to secure the co-operation at this dangerous time of the inhabitants of the lands which it ruled. Furthermore, the experience of war showed Britain that at a time of danger the Empire was more of a liability than a help, as many British troops had to be sent to parts of the world that were

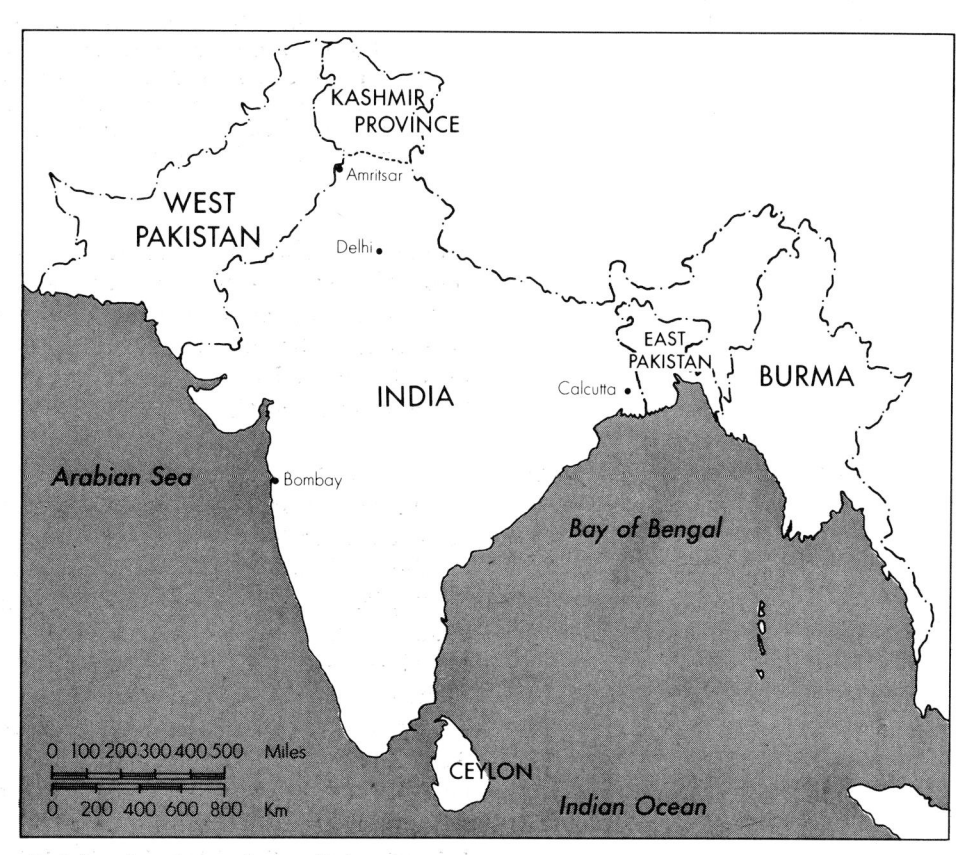

The Indian sub-continent at the time of independence

Jawaharlal Nehru, the first Prime Minister of an independent India, in conversation with Lord Louis Mountbatten, the last Viceroy of Britain's Indian Empire. Lord Louis Mountbatten's actions led to a swifter granting of independence than originally planned.

threatened by enemy forces. The British failure in the early stages to combat Japanese expansion in the Far East damaged the prestige of Britain as a great power. Those who in different parts of the Empire hoped to bring about the end of British control were much encouraged by these wartime difficulties of Britain.

Demands for partition

After 1945 the real problem facing Attlee's government in India was not when independence would be secured, but how bloodshed between the Congress party and the Moslem League could be avoided. To reach a compromise between them was almost impossible. The Moslem League insisted on partition and the creation of Pakistan. The Congress party insisted on the creation of one country containing Moslems and Hindus. Riots in Calcutta in August 1946 led to the slaughter of thousands of Hindus and Moslems. These illustrated the tensions that existed in the sub-continent and were a sad foretaste of what was to come.

Lord Louis Mountbatten

Attlee decided to face the people of India with a strict timetable. In February 1947 the British government made clear their intention of withdrawing from India by June 1948. A new Viceroy was appointed with the task of supervising this delicate operation. He was Lord Louis Mountbatten, a man sympathetic to the aims of the Attlee government and related to the Royal Family. He was able to persuade Nehru, whose influence in the Congress party was now greater than that of the aged Gandhi, that partition was essential. By the summer of 1947 the situation was so tense that Mountbatten decided on an earlier withdrawal, and fixed August 1947 as the date.

Problems of partition

Controversy still surrounds this decision. Did it allow sufficient time for the borders between India and Pakistan to be properly drawn? The drawing of these borders to mark exactly the religious differences within the sub-continent was an exceptionally difficult task. However carefully it was done, the borders would still be imperfect. Additionally, the borders made for a divided Pakistan. The new country consisted of a large area approximately in the western Punjab and a smaller area roughly in eastern Bengal; between them lay Indian territory. Communal strife in the northern province of Kashmir was so intense that it was impossible in 1947 to allocate it to either India or Pakistan. In the summer months of 1947 desperate attempts were made by the inhabitants of the sub-continent to reach the area where their religion predominated and where they felt their lives would be safe. Hundreds of thousands of lives were in fact lost in these attempts. All this was a dismal end to British rule and it created a long-lasting bitterness within the sub-continent.

THE BRITISH EMPIRE AND COMMONWEALTH IN THE TWENTIETH CENTURY

Dominion status achieved

Nevertheless dominion status had now been achieved by the new India and the new Pakistan. Both countries were willing to maintain links with Britain by remaining members of the Commonwealth. Gandhi had played little part in the final events leading to independence. In these years he had devoted much effort to attempts to soften the rigidity of the Hindu caste system and it was these attempts that led to his death at the hands of a Hindu fanatic in January 1948.

Ceylon and Burma

Independence now having been granted within the sub-continent, it would be difficult to deny independence to neighbouring British territories. Ceylon (today, Sri Lanka) and Burma achieved their independence at the start of 1948. Ceylon remained within the Commonwealth, but Burma did not; it wanted to sever its connections with Britain completely. The events of 1947 and 1948 in the Indian sub-continent and these neighbouring lands were of great importance in British history. The pride with which the British had held India in the past has been strongly emphasised both in this chapter and earlier in Chapter 7. It was the most significant retreat that British power overseas had yet made in the twentieth century, and it showed the type of development that might shortly follow in Britain's colonies in Africa, the West Indies and elsewhere.

The British in Palestine

McMahon correspondence

Communal violence was to be a problem for Britain elsewhere. In Palestine conflict between Jews and Arabs was to be just as intense in these years as had been the conflict between Hindus and Moslems in the Indian sub-continent. Palestine had been one of the three Middle Eastern mandates that the British acquired at the end of the First World War, for motives and in circumstances more fully considered in Chapter 14. The opposing claims of Jews and Arabs in Palestine were almost incapable of resolution. Nor had British policy in the area at the time of the First World War made the prospect of resolution any easier. In order to get the support of Arabs within the Ottoman Empire for their war effort against the Turks, the British had made promises to the Arabs. In what is known as the **McMahon correspondence** between Sir Henry McMahon, British High Commissioner in Egypt, and the Sharif Husain of Mecca, the most prominent of the Arab leaders, the British expressed support both for Arab independence from the Turks and for Arab control of Palestine.

> As for the regions lying within the proposed frontiers, in which Great Britain is free to act without detriment to the interests of her ally, France, I am authorised to give you the following pledges on behalf of the government of Great Britain, and to reply as follows to their note: That, subject to the modifications stated above, Great Britain is prepared to recognise and uphold the independence of the Arabs in all the regions lying within the frontiers proposed by the Sharif of Mecca.
>
> **Letter of Sir Henry McMahon**

Balfour Declaration

Yet a contrary wartime commitment was also made to the Jews. In November 1917, the British Foreign Secretary, Arthur Balfour, issued what became known as the Balfour Declaration. In this, some support was expressed for the recently developed idea of **Zionism**, which urged the return of the Jews to their historic homeland in Palestine and the creation there of a Jewish state.

> His Majesty's government view with favour the establishment in Palestine of a national home for the Jewish people and will use their best endeavours to facilitate the achievement of this object, it being clearly understood that nothing shall be done which may prejudice the civil and religious rights of existing non-Jewish communities in Palestine, or the rights and political status enjoyed by Jews in any other country.
>
> **Balfour Declaration**

It should, however, be noted that the British commitment to Zionism was not wholehearted. The Balfour Declaration speaks of a **national home** for the Jews and not a **national state**, which was the real objective of the Zionists and which involved the exclusion of Arabs. The British hoped that Palestine might be a 'home' for Arabs as well as for Jews. It was in this spirit that Sir Herbert Samuel, the first British High Commissioner for the mandate of Palestine, attempted to administer the country. Though violence was not so serious a problem in the 1920s as it was to become in the 1930s and 1940s the seeds of the later strife were sown at that time.

Jewish immigration

This was done mainly through land purchases. Arab land was purchased by Jews, who then excluded Arabs from that land and established a close-knit Jewish community on it. By the early 1930s certain parts of Palestine – especially in the north west and in the city of Tel Aviv – were almost exclusively Jewish. A new menace also existed in the 1930s. In Germany, Hitler was now in power and was beginning his anti-semitic campaigns; consequently, Jewish immigration from Germany increased considerably. Land purchases and increased immigration aroused widespread Arab fears that their interests in Palestine were being ignored.

Restrictions on Jewish immigration

British concern at the increasing friction within Palestine led them to issue a White Paper in 1930 which severely restricted Jewish immigration. The restrictions were not thoroughly applied and antagonism between Jews and Arabs continued to make Palestine a troubled land. An Arab general strike in April 1936 developed into a widespread rebellion. The British appointed a Royal Commission under Lord Peel to suggest a solution. When the Peel Commission reported in July 1937, it recommended partition of Palestine between Jews and Arabs. Within Palestine this recommendation was poorly received and violence continued at an increased level. The British then resorted to the device they had attempted at the beginning of the 1930s. In a White Paper of May 1939, Jewish immigration was restricted to 75 000 over the next five years.

Increasing Zionist pressure

The fact that Britain was fighting against Germany in the Second World War was good reason for the Jews in Palestine to co-operate more closely with the British during the early years of the war. When it was becoming clear that Germany would lose the war, Jewish resistance to Britain began to stiffen once again. The Palestinian Jews now had in David Ben Gurion a more forceful leader. In May 1942 he presided at a Zionist conference at the Biltmore Hotel, New York. At the Biltmore Conference, the Zionist claim to a Jewish state was reasserted in the strongest terms; and it was also clear that this reassertion now had substantial support within the United States. When the Second World War ended, Palestine was one of the most severe problems facing the Attlee government.

The abandonment of the mandate of Palestine

Wartime circumstances

The problem at that time was made worse by knowledge of the hideous sufferings of Jewish people in Nazi-dominated Europe during the previous few years. Those Jews who had managed to survive this time now sought to enter Palestine in increased numbers. Conscious of the need to protect Arab interests in Palestine, the British continued to restrict Jewish immigration. Given the sad circumstances of the Jewish people in these years, British policies in this respect were judged unfavourably by most world opinion.

Abandonment of the mandate

Within Palestine it was not surprising that it was now Jewish opposition rather than Arab opposition that was more troublesome to the British. A Jewish underground army, the Haganah, organised acts of terrorism of which the most notable was the blowing up of the British military headquarters in Palestine at the King David Hotel in Jerusalem. A situation which had always been difficult

THE BRITISH EMPIRE AND COMMONWEALTH IN THE TWENTIETH CENTURY

Illegal Jewish immigrants at sea near Palestine in 1947 make a desperate appeal to the consciences of the British authorities. The turning back of such would-be immigrants caused much world opinion to turn against Britain on the Palestinian issue.

to handle had now reached impossibility. As Palestine was a **mandate**, British rule would not continue there for ever. After Ernest Bevin, the Foreign Secretary, and Creech Jones, the Colonial Secretary, had entered into further negotiations on a compromise solution, the British government decided to abandon the mandate and pass its problem to the United Nations.

Arab-Israeli War This decision was taken in February 1947. British troops continued to police Palestine while the United Nations decided on what action to take. Towards the end of 1947 the United Nations adopted the idea first put forward in the Royal Commission's report (and, incidentally, an idea put into effect in India only a few months previously): partition. The idea was generally acceptable to the Jews, who felt they stood to gain from such an arrangement. By contrast, the Arabs opposed partition and in the winter of 1947–48 much violence occurred, which the British did little to curb. Bevin had become much embittered by the Palestinian situation and made little secret of his pleasure at getting rid of it. When British troops left in May 1948, the Jews at once proclaimed their own state of Israel in the areas allocated to them. In fighting against an Arab invasion, they extended these areas during the Arab-Israeli war of 1948–49. There was never any question of Israel becoming a member of the Commonwealth after the unpleasantness of the final years of the mandate.

Three colonial wars: Malaya, Kenya and Cyprus

Malaya In the 1940s and 1950s violence marked Britain's withdrawal from other colonial possessions. A rubber-growing industry had developed in the Federation of Malay States earlier in the century. By astute arrangements with local rulers – rather similar to the arrangements made in India with the princes – this had become highly profitable. It was not an investment which the British wanted totally to abandon. When therefore in 1948 a Communist rebellion began in the jungles of Malaya, British troops were sent to suppress it. The campaigns against the rebels, involving difficult jungle warfare, lasted until the mid-1950s, by which time the Communist rebellion had been successfully suppressed. Arrangements were made for the transfer of power in 1957 to a local ruler, entitled the **Tunku**, whose government continued to favour British interests. Neighbouring Singapore, North Borneo and Sarawak became independent in 1963 and joined with Malaya to form **Malaysia**.

Kenya It was to suppress what appeared to be an even more serious rebellion that British troops were sent in the mid-1950s to Kenya. Nationalist sentiment had already gathered some support in this East African colony, but had not been particularly troublesome until this time. A movement known as the **Mau Mau** developed among the Kikuyu people, who earlier in the century had been deprived of much of their land by white settlers. Mau Mau was a distinctly African movement of protest. The physical mutilations that its members inflicted on their victims, who were not usually British settlers, caused widespread revulsion in Britain against the movement. Military action and stern punishment of convicted terrorists brought the movement under control by the late 1950s. It was, however, during the Mau Mau emergency that Jomo Kenyatta increased his standing within Kenya, apparently unharmed or even assisted, by the suggestion that he was associated with the movement.

Cyprus

As pressure for independence was developing within various overseas territories, the government took the view that at least one territory – the island of Cyprus – must continue to remain under British control. A statement by a member of the British government in 1954 made this clear.

> **It has always been understood and agreed that there are certain territories in the Commonwealth which, owing to their particular circumstances, can never expect to be fully independent. Nothing less than continued sovereignty over this island can enable Britain to carry out her strategic obligations to Europe, the Mediterranean and the Middle East.**
>
> Hansard, *Parliamentary Debates*

The 'strategic obligations' referred to Britain's role in the cold war, in particular the need to maintain a base in the eastern Mediterranean, near to the Middle East and the Soviet Union. After the Suez episode of 1956 (considered in more detail on pages 238–42), it appeared to many in Britain to be even more important to hold on to this base. Anyway, controlling Cyprus was not considered to be difficult. But the very strong statement of the government in 1954 encouraged opposition within Cyprus to British rule. The **Enosis** movement quickly developed as a formidable force of opposition. Its support was based among the majority Greek population of Cyprus and it aimed to create a union between Cyprus and Greece. Archbishop Makarios provided powerful and skilful leadership to this movement. Terrorism also played an important part in opposition to the British, organised by the Eoka movement headed by a former Greek soldier, George Grivas.

Independence of Cyprus

Encouraged by their recent suppression of the Communist rebels in Malaya, the British felt confident of being able to suppress the Eoka rebels in Cyprus. They hoped to get moderate opinion on their side, and also that of the minority Turks in the island. But the Turks were not numerous enough to be of importance and the concessions that the British offered were not sufficient to win over moderate opinion. The imprisonment of Archbishop Makarios only made worse an already difficult situation.

Shortly after becoming Prime Minister, and in spite of some strong opposition within the Conservative party, Macmillan ordered the release of Makarios from prison and negotiations began on granting the island independence. This was achieved in 1960, when Makarios became the island's President and the island's Turkish leader became its Vice President. From the British point of view the outcome was not entirely unsatisfactory, as the British were able to keep their military bases on the island, which itself continued as a part of the British Commonwealth. Unhappily, friction between Greeks and Turks continued to trouble the island of Cyprus.

The wind of change

Macmillan's speech

In the first two months of 1960 Macmillan went on an extensive tour of Britain's African colonies. While in South Africa, at the end of the tour, he made what was interpreted as a positive commitment to withdrawal by Britain from its African colonies.

THE BRITISH EMPIRE AND COMMONWEALTH IN THE TWENTIETH CENTURY

> In the twentieth century, and especially since the end of the war, the processes which gave birth to the nation-states of Europe have been repeated all over the world. We have seen the awakening of national consciousness in peoples who have lived for centuries in dependence on some other power.
>
> Fifteen years ago this movement spread through Asia. Many countries there of different races and civilisations pressed their claims for an independent national life. Today the same thing is happening in Africa. The most striking of all the impressions I have formed since I left London a month ago is the strength of this African consciousness. In different places it may take different forms, but it is happening everywhere.
>
> The wind of change is blowing through the continent.

Importance In making this commitment, Macmillan was facing the realities of a changing world. He recognised that the increasing strength of nationalist feeling in Africa made it unwise for Britain to continue to maintain its colonial control there. He was also conscious that opinion at the United Nations and within the government of the United States favoured a swift and peaceful withdrawal by the British from Africa. During the next few years, under the direction of his able Colonial Secretary, Iain Macleod, independence came rapidly for colonies in Africa and elsewhere.

African nationalism In Africa, this process had already begun. At the end of the Second World War, nationalism was already an important factor in Britain's West African colonies. The development of national feeling had been closely linked with the growth of towns. As Africans were brought together in the towns, they were able to discuss grievances and to join the developing trade unions. It was then only a short step to the emergence of movements demanding independence. African nationalism in these immediate post-war years owed much to the abilities of its new leaders. It owed something also to the generally sympathetic policies of the post-war Labour government towards the colonies. Under the guidance of Creech Jones, Labour's Colonial Secretary, the government made useful grants for the economic development of the colonies through a series of Colonial Development Acts. The ill-fated groundnuts scheme (page 199) is an example of such a policy, in that case one that got out of hand.

In British Africa, nationalism first made major impact in the Gold Coast. What was for an African colony at that time a very progressive constitution had been put into practice in the Gold Coast in 1946. It provided for an African parliament, though elected on a limited franchise. Kwame Nkrumah was determined that Africans should take as full advantage as they could of this constitution and his United Gold Coast Convention quickly came to dominate the new parliament. In February 1948 continuing opposition to the British was shown by widespread riots.

The British government decided to make further concessions and under a new constitution of 1951 Gold Coast elections were to be held on the basis of universal suffrage. Nkrumah's party – which in the meantime had changed its name to the Convention People's party and had widened its appeal – won a resounding victory and Nkrumah became Prime Minister. The Gold Coast was not yet independent. For the next six years there was a period of transition, during which Nkrumah worked closely with the British Governor. Independence was secured in March 1957, when the new country adopted the ancient West African name of **Ghana**.

"AS YE SOW, SO SHALL YE REAP"

The Colonial Secretary in Labour's post-war government made generous – though not always wise – grants for the development of the colonies. Creech Jones also began some early encouragement of independence in Africa.

Majority rule The emergence of Ghana was important in the history of Britain's African possessions in a number of respects. It was the first British African colony to secure independence. More significantly, it provided a blueprint for the granting of independence to the other African colonies. Power was to be on the basis of **majority rule**: elections were to be held to determine the wishes of the people of the country. The structure of the government in the country was to be based on the structure of the government at Westminster, though in practice it was doubtful whether this type of government suited the African situation very well. Many African countries were subsequently to depart from it and to become one-party states. Most important of all, independence was not to be rushed. A fairly lengthy transition period was expected so that the politicians and civil servants of the new country were given a good understanding of the responsibilities involved in governing a country.

Britain's continuing role in Africa

The Ghana blueprint for independence was not repeated so successfully elsewhere in Africa. It owed much of its sucess in the early stages to the support provided by the post-war Labour government and to the orderly achievement of independence. The new Conservative government was pledged to a similar approach, but their commitment to it was less wholehearted. In Conservative eyes, there still was an imperial role for Britain to play. The Suez crisis of 1956, considered in the next chapter, provided a forceful illustration of this.

For most of the 1950s they were therefore unwilling to follow with either speed or enthusiasm along the road towards African independence that Labour had marked out. Attempts were made to ensure that British interests would not be jeopardised as demands for independence became more vocal. Additionally, they were concerned that the interests of white settlers – who in Kenya and Southern Rhodesia were quite numerous – should not be entirely neglected by the British government.

Federations within the Commonwealth

Partnership

The Conservative policy in Africa by which they hoped to achieve these objectives became known as **partnership**. Oliver Lyttleton, the Colonial Secretary in Churchill's Conservative government of 1951–55, judged that this would be best achieved through a policy of **federating** colonies together into larger units. He proposed two federations in Africa, the East Africa Federation (Kenya, Uganda and Tanganyika) and the Central Africa Federation (Northern Rhodesia, Southern Rhodesia and Nyasaland), and one in Britain's West Indian islands.

West Indies

As there was no significant settler population in the West Indies, its Federation was designed solely in order to further the economic interests of the islands. Discussion on its creation was lengthy and difficult. At the end of the war, Britain's Colonial Secretary put the case for federation in this way.

> Under modern conditions it has become more difficult for very small units ... to maintain full and complete independence in all aspects of Government.... Indeed the trend of post-war development, under the stimulus of greatly improved air communications, may well show a marked impulse towards a closer political and other association of those smaller territorial units which, through proximity or a common language, have mutual interests. I consider it important, therefore, that the more immediate purpose of developing self-governing institutions in the individual British Caribbean Colonies should keep in view the larger project of their political federation.
>
> **Despatch of the Colonial Secretary to Britain's West Indian Colonies, March 1945**

Only in 1958 did the West Indies Federation come into being, yet by 1962 friction between its members had resulted in its break-up. In the same year, its most prominent members – Jamaica, Trinidad and Tobago – achieved independence. Most other British West Indian islands – such as Barbados and the Leeward and Windward islands – became independent later in the 1960s.

Central African Federation

The federations in Africa were designed not just to further the economic interests of their members, but also to defend the interests – at least for the near future – of the white settlers. The Federation of East Africa never came into being. The Central African Federation did, and was supported for the ten years of its existence (1953–63) by British governments and by the white settlers in its member colonies. It failed to attract support from the majority population within the Federation.

Lyttleton, who before entering politics had been a successful businessman, saw this Federation as a tidy and useful business operation. Nyasaland would supply a large black population as a workforce, Northern Rhodesia had the valuable mineral resources of its copper belt and Southern Rhodesia had a stable white government already. Since the time of Rhodes's pioneering work (page 83) Southern Rhodesia had developed in a unique way for a British African colony. When in 1923 the British South Africa Company had handed over control of the colony to the British government, a large white settler population already existed and managed to reserve considerable powers for themselves in the way in which Southern Rhodesia was to be governed. In the years since then they had firmly established their supremacy.

Work of the Federation

When the Central African Federation was set up in 1953, the new federal government was based on the Southern Rhodesian capital of Salisbury. The Southern Rhodesian Prime Minister, Godfrey Huggins, became the first Prime Minister of the Federation and was followed by Roy Welensky from Northern Rhodesia. Under both men the position of the white settlers – many of whom had emigrated to these parts of Africa only since the end of the Second World War – was given every support. The Federation had useful economic achievements to its credit, such as the building of the Kariba Dam on the Zambezi River.

Opposition nevertheless developed within the Federation, led particularly by Kenneth Kaunda in Northern Rhodesia, Hastings Banda in Nyasaland, and Joshua Nkomo in Southern Rhodesia. Most forceful among these men was Kaunda. He demanded that universal suffrage should be set up in place of the restricted franchise on which the federal parliament was elected. The refusal of the federal government, or the British government, to heed this request – which was considered by them as wholly irresponsible – stimulated disorder. So serious did this become in Nyasaland in 1959 that a state of emergency had to be declared there.

Criticisms of the Federation

By the late 1950s the Conservative government in Britain was beginning to question the wisdom of continuing to support the Federation. This new thinking accorded with the consistent view of the Labour party, which had opposed the Central African Federation ever since it had been set up. In 1959 a commission led by Patrick Devlin, a British High Court judge, was sent to enquire into the situation in Nyasaland. His unfavourable report described the administration of Nyasaland as being that of a 'police state'.

Independence in other African colonies

Macmillan's **wind of change** speech came shortly after this. The speed with which Macleod conducted the withdrawal from other African colonies in the early 1960s came as a shock to some members of the Conservative party and to some within the old dominion countries. Even some African politicians doubted if the process was carefully thought out. One put his doubts thus.

> I have had the impression about several Colonial Secretaries... that they would have come forward with more positive programmes, but hesitated because of their own back-benchers. Colonial issues only became hot matters in the House of Commons when settlers went over and talked to Tory back-benchers, and then the Ministers were subjected to heavy pressure. It became evident that the face of East and Central Africa depended more on the atmosphere inside the Conservative party than on any logical analysis of the African case as such. The number of contradictions – the way British Somaliland was handed independence almost overnight, the way a liberal franchise was provided for Uganda, a country almost without settlers – shows that the only consistent factor in the Conservatives' colonial policy was a yielding to the greatest pressure.
>
> Tom Mboya, *Freedom and After*

As noted earlier, West Africa had been in the forefront of African nationalism. Outside Ghana, Nkrumah's achievement had most immediate effect in Nigeria, the largest of Britain's colonies. Though there were fears that the colony's economic, religious and regional differences might make for particular difficulties after independence, nationalists within Nigeria pressed strongly for it. Independence was achieved in 1960, though the fears about the consequences of the country's division were shown to be justified when civil war broke out in the late 1960s. Sierra Leone became independent in 1961 and the small colony of Gambia in 1965. In 1961 Britain also relinquished control of the Cameroons, which it had originally held – jointly with France – under League of Nations supervision as a mandate and latterly under United Nations supervision as a trust territory. Part of it joined with neighbouring Nigeria, while most became independent as Cameroun.

East Africa

In East Africa the most difficult to handle was Kenya. Here there was a substantial white settler population, though it was not so numerous or so powerful as were the settlers in Southern Rhodesia. Both they and the British government were alarmed by the popularity of Jomo Kenyatta in the late 1950s. With an eye to the future, the British feared he would be an unco-operative leader of a country where they hoped they would still be able to maintain some influence. Elections were held in 1961 and, as expected, Kenyatta's Kenya Africa National Union won a large majority. In negotiations Kenyatta proved more amenable than had been thought. When independence came in 1963 there was good prospect that blacks and whites would work together in the type of harmony that the British government had hoped to encourage.

Tanganyika, another British mandate, achieved independence at the end of 1961 and was joined in 1963 with the island of Zanzibar to form Tanzania. Julius Nyerere, the nationalist leader, had been given every encouragement by the United Nations in his bid for independence and had received little opposition from the British government. Uganda achieved its independence in 1962, though its later history was to be marred by civil strife and dictatorship.

End of the Central African Federation

In the light of these developments elsewhere in Africa, there was no prospect that the Central African Federation with its white domination would be permitted to continue. In December 1962 R.A. Butler, who had recently been appointed by the British government as head of a Central African office, announced the dissolution of the Federation. Arrangements were made for independence in Northern Rhodesia, which took the name of Zambia in 1964, and in Nyasaland, which took the name of Malawi in the same year. Neighbouring Bechuanaland became independent, as Botswana, in 1966. These events were regarded by the white settlers in Southern Rhodesia as a 'betrayal' and were greeted with intense anger. In the aftermath of the Federation's dissolution, no progress was made towards the achievement of independence on the basis of majority rule in Southern Rhodesia.

The problem of Rhodesia

The government of Ian Smith

A situation now existed in Southern Rhodesia which would not be readily solved. Within Southern Rhodesia in the early 1960s, settler opinion turned against those of their politicians who had supported the Federation. A new party, the Rhodesia Front, now sought to emphasise their interests. It was led by Ian Smith, a Southern Rhodesian farmer who had earlier served as an RAF pilot in the war. In 1963 Smith became Prime Minister of Southern Rhodesia. His main object was to secure independence for Southern Rhodesia on terms that would protect settler interests. As majority rule had been the principle on which all the recent grants of independence had been made, there was little prospect that the British government would make an exception in this case. Negotiations

THE BRITISH EMPIRE AND COMMONWEALTH IN THE TWENTIETH CENTURY

with the Conservative government of Douglas-Home and the new Labour government of Harold Wilson made no progress.

Unilateral Declaration of Independence

Smith therefore decided on bold action. In November 1965, with his government's approval, he issued a **Unilateral** (one-sided) **Declaration of Independence (UDI)** for what he now simply termed **Rhodesia**. His action was one of rebellion against the British government. Yet successive British governments found it very difficult to deal with this particular rebellion. Swift military action might have brought down the Smith government. Such a campaign might have become protracted and many lives might have been lost. Nor was public opinion within Britain united in hostility to Smith; in certain

Ian Smith, Prime Minister of Southern Rhodesia, speaks with reporters in October 1965 after one of his many discussions with the British government. Smith's illegal seizure of power a month after this photograph was taken provided the Commonwealth with one of its most serious challenges in the twentieth century.

sections of the press and the Conservative party there was a tendency to sympathise with a group of settlers seen to be defending their traditional position. There was even some doubt whether the British Army would remain loyal if ordered to take action against white Rhodesians. The Wilson government decided therefore on a policy of economic sanctions. These were not consistently applied. Though they affected the Rhodesian economy, they were a negligible factor in leading to the eventual fall of the Smith government. Crucial to Smith's survival was the favourable attitude of the Portuguese government in the neighbouring colonies of Angola and Mozambique.

South Africa

Of even greater value to him was the help and encouragement of the government of South Africa. Britain's own relations with South Africa had deteriorated badly in recent years. The South African government, controlled by the National party of the Afrikaners since 1948, had pursued a policy of **apartheid** (separate racial development) that ran contrary to what Britain was trying to do elsewhere in Africa. In 1961 South Africa left the Commonwealth and ceased to be a dominion country. Nevertheless, on many issues – not least racial ones – there was similarity of outlook between the South African government and the Smith government on its northern borders.

Negotiations over Rhodesia

Attempts were made to break the deadlock between Britain and Rhodesia. On two occasions, Wilson and Smith met for discussions on the neutral territory of a ship in the Mediterranean Sea: *Tiger* in December 1966 and *Fearless* in October 1968. Neither set of conversations produced a result. After the failure of the

A critical view of the ineffectiveness of British sanctions on Rhodesia. In spite of Wilson's efforts, Smith appears secure, with no major problems of imports or exports.

Tiger conversations Wilson was able to secure UN co-operation for more extensive sanctions. In spite of Wilson's assurances that sanctions would now bring down the Smith government, they appeared still to have only slight impact. In November 1971, Douglas-Home, then the Foreign Minister in Heath's Conservative government produced a settlement formula with Smith. The Labour party criticised the settlement as giving inadequate guarantees of majority rule, and it was in any case rejected by the people of Rhodesia in a referendum. Military action was in fact needed to bring down the Smith government, which eventually fell in 1976, mainly as a result of guerrilla activity within Rhodesia. Negotiations for independence were protracted and the independent country of Zimbabwe did not emerge until 1980.

EXERCISES

1. (a) What do you understand by the idea and practice of *satyagraha*, as advocated by Gandhi during the inter-war years?
   (b) Trace the course of relations between Britain and its Indian Empire during the inter-war years, showing the importance of satyagraha at that time.
   (c) What events in the 1940s led to independence in the Indian sub-continent?

2. (a) Describe the events in the 1940s and 1950s that led to the independence of the British colony of the Gold Coast.
   (b) Describe the Mau Mau emergency in Kenya during the 1950s and explain why it was considered to be so serious for British rule in Africa.

3. Imagine that in the mid-twentieth century you are a well established British resident in Southern Rhodesia. Write a letter to a friend in Britain explaining your reasons why in the 1960s and 1970s you either supported the government of Ian Smith or wished to return to Britain because you opposed it.

4. Study the photograph on page 225, the speech on page 227 and the cartoon on this page and then answer questions (a) to (c) which follow.
   (a) (i) What evidence does the photograph contain of both the desperation of those sailing on the boat and of the attitude of Britain towards their plight?
   (ii) By examining the events concerning Palestine in the 1940s, indicate whether you feel the impression conveyed by the photograph correctly interprets the situation at that time.
   (3+4)
   (b) (i) Why do you think that the speech on page 227 was regarded as so important?
   (ii) What events in Africa during the 1950s suggest that the 'wind of change' had already begun to blow through the continent?
   (iii) Why do you think Macmillan's 'wind of change' policies in Africa in the early 1960s caused some controversy? (2+3+2)
   (c) (i) By reference to details in the cartoon, indicate how accurately the situation in Rhodesia in the late 1960s is portrayed.
   (ii) Why did the Rhodesian situation become so troublesome in Britain's process of decolonisation? (6)

19 BRITAIN AND THE WORLD 1945–73

The introduction to this book emphasised that in the late 1860s Britain was among the great powers of the world. By the mid-twentieth century much of the greatness had faded. The effects of two world wars, in spite of Britain's victory in them, had produced a changed position for Britain in relation to other powers. The achievement of independence by so many of Britain's overseas possessions was one of the most important features of that change. For Britain it was part of a general adjustment to a changed world role.

Britain in the post-war world

Wartime conferences

Towards the end of the Second World War, Britain was involved as a key participant in the conferences of the Allied powers. Planning for the post-war world was a matter of crucial discussion at them. The two conferences of 1945 were at Yalta (in Russia) in February, which Churchill attended, and at Potsdam (in Germany) in July, at which Attlee replaced Churchill as Britain's representative. The course of the fighting during the previous couple of years had shown that Britain's military contribution in the last part of the war was not so important as it had been in the war's opening stages. Consequently Britain had at these conferences a junior role to play in conversations with the leaders of the United States and the Soviet Union.

Soviet threat

Without doubt, it was the Soviet Union which secured most advantage from the discussions at Yalta and Potsdam. Agreements favourable to the Soviet Union were reached both on Poland's frontiers and on the division of Germany into zones of occupation. As much of Eastern Europe was already occupied by their forces, the Soviet Union was in a position further to consolidate control not just in Poland and East Germany, but in Hungary, Romania and Bulgaria as well. To a certain extent, Britain was prepared to accept a Soviet dominance in much of Eastern Europe. In October 1944 Churchill and Stalin had a private meeting in Moscow in which certain **spheres of influence** in Eastern Europe were agreed between them. Many features of this agreement were kept to quite faithfully by the Soviet Union.

But by 1946 British governments were concerned particularly by the forceful policies of the Soviet Union in much of Eastern Europe and in other parts of the world. Soon after the war had ended, much concern was expressed by Britain about Soviet intentions in the Middle East and the eastern Mediterranean. The Soviet forces which had occupied Iran and Turkey in the course of the war were showing no readiness to depart, while civil war had broken out in Greece between Communist and non-Communist forces.

Ernest Bevin

The Foreign Secretary in Attlee's government during these years was Ernest Bevin. He had risen within the Labour party through his earlier work in the trade union movement. In the years before the war he had firmly urged rearmament. As Foreign Secretary he adopted a similarly strong approach to what he judged to be menacing Soviet policies. His concern in the years just after the war – a concern which Churchill had also felt just before the war ended – was the lack of urgency with which the government of the United States approached this problem. Until 1947, the United States appeared to view Soviet policies without a great deal of concern. At the same time it adopted a critical approach towards Britain over its continued possession of colonies and, in particular, its role in Palestine. Bevin wanted to make the United States a firmer, more reliable partner for Britain in combating the Soviet threat.

The Iron Curtain

He was able to do this in 1947. Already the dangers of the European situation had been spelt out to the people of the United States by Churchill. As leader of the opposition he had given a well-publicised speech in the United States, at Fulton, in the spring of 1946.

> **A shadow has fallen upon the scenes so lately lightened by the Allied victory. Nobody knows what Soviet Russia and its Communist international organisation intends to do in the immediate future, or what are the limits, if any, to their expansive tendencies. I have a strong admiration and regard for the valiant Russian people and for my wartime comrade, Marshal Stalin. There is deep sympathy and good will in Britain towards the peoples of all the Russias, and a resolve to persevere through many differences and rebuffs in establishing lasting relationships. It is my duty, however, to place before you certain facts about the present situation in Europe.**
>
> **From Stettin in the Baltic to Trieste in the Adriatic, an iron curtain has descended across the Continent. Behind that line lie all the capitals of the ancient states of central and eastern Europe. Warsaw, Berlin, Prague, Vienna, Budapest, Belgrade, Bucharest and Sofia, all these famous cities and populations around them lie in what I must call the Soviet sphere, and all are subject in one form or another, not only to Soviet influence but to a very high, and in many cases, increasing measure of control from Moscow.**
>
> **Whatever conclusions may be drawn from these facts, this is certainly not the Liberated Europe we fought to build. Nor is it one which contains the essentials of permanent peace.**

Churchill's Fulton speech, by its vivid description of the nature of the problem, formed a useful basis on which Bevin could build.

Truman Doctrine

At that time Britain's closest involvement in opposition to Soviet designs was in Greece. Since 1946 Britain had been giving active help – in arms, men and money – to the Greek forces fighting against Communism in their country. The winter of 1946–47 was, as has been shown in Chapter 16, a time of financial crisis for Britain and, in view of this, Bevin announced in February 1947 the ending of British support for the non-Communist forces there. Combined with closer US awareness of the problems that a Communist-dominated Greece would pose, this announcement produced action from the US President, Harry Truman. In March 1947, in a speech of far-reaching importance for the foreign policy of the United States, he asked the US Congress for the money with which to defend Greece (and Turkey) from Communism. What he said on that occasion is usually referred to as the **Truman Doctrine**. It was to be applied more widely than Greece and was in practice a commitment by the United States to defend any country likely to fall to Communism by force rather than by properly conducted elections.

Marshall Aid

Three months later, in June 1947, the US government went further. George Marshall, US Secretary of State (the US equivalent of Foreign Secretary) announced a programme of financial aid for Europe, a programme that became known as **Marshall Aid**. Its underlying purpose was the creation of good living standards in European countries, so that Communism would stand little chance of success. Bevin saw the Truman Doctrine and Marshall Aid as providing the US involvement in Europe which he had always judged essential.

He now took a leading role in co-ordinating the response of the governments of Western Europe which, by the following year, were linked together in the Organization for European Economic Co-operation (OEEC) whose purpose was to administer this new US aid. Marshall Aid was a generous gesture by the government of the United States. Receipt of the Marshall Aid nevertheless carried with it an obligation to approach foreign affairs from a similar viewpoint as the United States.

Britain and the cold war in Europe

The Berlin blockade

This identity of view between the Western European recipients of Marshall Aid and the government of the United States sharpened the sense of division in Europe between Communist and non-Communist countries. The Soviet Union disliked the idea of Marshall Aid and would not permit Eastern European countries – to whom Marshall Aid was offered – to receive it. By this time there existed between the Soviet Union and the Western powers, now under the very positive leadership of the United States, a situation of acute tension to which the term **cold war** is usually applied. The tensions increased in 1948 when, in February, a Communist coup was carried out in Czechoslovakia and, in June, a Soviet blockade was imposed on Berlin.

The latter crisis was regarded by Britain, the United States and the other powers of Western Europe as being particularly serious. The Soviet Union had become angered by the steps taken by the United States, Britain and France to develop close links, in administration and finance, between the two western zones in divided Germany. By blockading Berlin it showed its opposition to these recent developments. All land contact between the western zones of Germany and the western zones of Berlin, located within the Soviet eastern zone of Germany, were cut. So West Berlin was virtually besieged. Yet the Western powers overcame what was a serious threat to the peace of Europe by supplying West Berlin by air. Britain became fully involved in these costly and difficult manoeuvres, which the Western powers continued to mount for as long as the blockade lasted. In May 1949, the Soviet forces abandoned their tactics. The policy of Britain and its allies had succeeded. Supplies for West Berlin had been assured, without recourse to war.

North Atlantic Treaty Organisation

These events suggested to the Western powers that in response to the Soviet threat there should be better military co-ordination between them. Under the initiative of the US government, negotiations took place on the formation of a military alliance between the countries of Western Europe and the United States, together with Canada. These negotiations led to the setting up in April 1949 of the North Atlantic Treaty Organisation (NATO). Member countries contributed forces to serve under the command of the Supreme Headquarters of the Allied Powers in Europe (SHAPE). The key feature of NATO was acceptance of the principle that an attack against one NATO member should be regarded as an attack against them all. It would therefore produce the response of a co-ordinated, collective counter-attack against the Soviet Union.

Britain and the cold war in the Far East and South-East Asia

Korean War

With the ending of the Berlin Blockade and the creation of NATO, Western Europe for a while was no longer the focus of cold war tension. In 1950 these tensions emerged most strongly in the Korean peninsula. After being a Japanese possession for most of the century, the peninsula had been divided along the thirty-eighth parallel in 1945. A Communist government supported by the Soviet Union developed in the North and a democratic government supported by the United States developed in the South. In June 1950 North Korean forces invaded the South. A decision was quickly reached by the United Nations Organisation to commit troops of member countries to the defence of South Korea.

The British government regarded what was happening in Korea as vitally important for Britain. It was considered that the Soviet Union, whose attempts at aggression in Western Europe had recently been repelled, had now turned its attention to the Far East. Furthermore, the British government was acutely suspicious of the new Communist government in China, which had secured

Infantry and tank action by the British in the Korean War, after a spotter aircraft (right) had located enemy positions. Involvement in Korea in the early 1950s showed both Britain's support for its US allies and its readiness to follow UN initiatives.

power in 1949 after lengthy civil war. They were aware that the rebel forces against whom they were currently fighting in Malaya (page 225) were gaining aid from this new, powerful government in the Far East.

British involvement in Korea

Britain made a distinct contribution to the fighting though it was of less importance than that of the United States. The stand made by the Gloucestershire regiment under difficult circumstances at the Imjin River was a heroic episode. Generally, the British co-operated well in the overall UN strategy. A crisis in relations had been faced in the autumn of 1950 when there appeared to be a prospect of US use of the atomic bomb. Any differences existing between Britain and the United States were resolved in a visit of Attlee to Truman. Until his dismissal by Truman in the spring of 1951, the extravagantly aggressive attitudes of the US Commander in Korea, General Douglas MacArthur, caused further concern. Peace negotiations began in the summer of 1951 and were concluded in the summer of 1953. When the war was over, the situation in Korea went back almost to what it had been three years earlier: a Communist-supported North Korea and a Western-supported South Korea, though the border between the two ran slightly differently.

Britain and Indochina

Nevertheless, Britain had taken part in a military campaign which prevented Communism from expanding by force. In the judgement of many, Britain's role was fully justified by this successful outcome. Soon after the Korean War was ended Anthony Eden, Foreign Secretary in Churchill's post-war government, was concerned to achieve a similar result in another part of South-East Asia, but without committing Britain to war. This issue concerned the French withdrawal from their colony of Indochina.

Virtually since the end of the Second World War the French had been fighting to keep hold of this colony. Their particular enemies were the Communist Vietminh forces, located mainly in northern Vietnam, a part of the French colony of Indochina. As by 1954 the fighting was going badly for the French, who were decisively defeated at the battle of Dien Bien Phu in the spring of that year, the US government suggested joint action by Britain, France and the United States. Britain rejected this suggestion. It would certainly have been inappropriate to fight to preserve a colony for France only a few years after Britain had granted independence to the inhabitants of the neighbouring sub-continent of India.

BRITAIN AND THE WORLD 1945-73

Geneva conference on Indochina

Instead a conference on Indochina was held at Geneva in May 1954, while the battle of Dien Bien Phu was raging many thousands of miles away. The decision was reached to partition the French colony into four: Laos, Cambodia, North Vietnam and South Vietnam. Communist forces remained in control of North Vietnam. In view of this and other difficulties, no decision was reached on the future status of Vietnam, which was held over until elections were completed at a later date. The US government considered this to be an unsatisfactory agreement, giving away too much to the Communists. As a result, they later took steps to ensure that the elections it provided for were never held. In spite of the US objections, Eden – whose influence in reaching the agreement had been crucial – received much credit for his work. But the US opposition to him was not to be forgotten two years later, at the time of the Suez crisis.

Britain and atomic warfare

Development of British atomic bomb

The atomic bombs that had been used with such horrific effect at Hiroshima and Nagasaki in August 1945 had been manufactured in the United States and were on those occasions used specifically by the United States. For some years, no other country possessed atomic weapons. It became known in 1949 that the Soviet Union by that time possessed such weapons. In the late 1940s Britain began to manufacture atomic weapons, but the process was kept a well-guarded secret by the government. Such secrecy meant that atomic weapons attracted little attention until it became known that Britain had successfully exploded an atomic bomb in a test explosion. This happened in 1952.

Reasons

As the two powers which previously alone had atomic weapons undoubtedly also possessed great power status, it was argued the possession of such weapons gave the same status to Britain. It was also maintained that Britain's role in international negotiations was strengthened by knowledge that it possessed such power. Eden, so it was said, would not have been so successful at Geneva in 1954 if Britain had not by then become a nuclear power. Recent friction and recent hostilities with the Soviet Union only emphasised further the need to be defended in the most effective way, so the argument continued to run. In 1955 the government became committed to the manufacture of the even more destructive hydrogen bomb. Further defence white papers in the 1950s and 1960s made fuller commitment to even more destructive forms of atomic weaponry.

Campaign for Nuclear Disarmament

From the 1950s onwards no British government of either political party felt it right to abandon nuclear weapons. In taking this view, they were never opposed by a majority of the British people. Most people within the country, either from conviction of the value of these weapons or apathy about the whole issue, allowed the government of the day to do as it wished in this matter. Nevertheless, opposition to the possession of nuclear weapons did develop. In the early 1950s this was confined to the left wing of the Labour party. In 1957, the Campaign for Nuclear Disarmament (CND) was formed, to act as a pressure group for those of any political party or none to press for the abandonment of Britain's nuclear weapons. Their aim was for **unilateral** (one-sided) nuclear disarmament, involving Britain's abandonment of nuclear weapons, regardless of what hostile or allied powers might be doing in this respect.

Arguments of CND

Many of the arguments put forward by CND were based on moral principles. The movement emphasised particularly the indiscriminate, widespread killing and maiming that accompanied the use of such weapons. They sought to distinguish between the effects of nuclear weapons and the effects of conventional weapons of war. In this respect, they alerted the public to the long-term effects on human life of the radioactive fallout. Passive resistance, organised campaign marches, non-violent demonstrations all became features of CND activity in the late 1950s and early 1960s. They also attempted to get a

A HISTORY OF BRITAIN FROM 1867

commitment to unilateral disarmament from the Labour party, but until the 1980s continued to meet opposition from the Labour leadership and from a majority of Labour party members.

Multilateral disarmament

Opponents of CND – and successive British governments – generally asserted a complete readiness for **multilateral** (many-sided) disarmament. This would involve disarmament in agreed proportions by all nuclear powers. Governments became anxious to bring about a reduction in nuclear arms, for reason of their immense cost if for no other. Yet progress by British governments – or any other governments – was very limited. In August 1963 the Test Ban Treaty was signed by Britain, the United States and the Soviet Union, by which nuclear tests were no longer to be conducted in the atmosphere. This really did nothing to cut down on the amount of the world's nuclear weaponry, but it did diminish the problem of radioactive fallout from tests, which had become particularly frequent in the late 1950s and early 1960s. Later in the 1960s Wilson set up a Ministry of Disarmament, but it achieved little. Severe cuts in Britain's defences during the Wilson governments made no impact on Britain's nuclear power, nor were they intended to. Meanwhile, some of the early enthusiasm of CND disappeared and its membership declined.

Further alliances

Britain's commitment to nuclear weapons – like so many other topics of recent history considered in this book – is a subject of great importance, to which only brief treatment is possible in these pages. Yet the commitment illustrates the theme suggested at the start of this chapter: a desire by Britain to retain great power status. Commitment to other alliances in the early 1950s was another way in which this concern was shown. In 1954 Britain joined the South-East Asia Treaty Organisation (SEATO), to defend that area from further Communist expansion. It was seen as an equivalent of NATO but it lacked the strength of the earlier alliance. In 1955 Britain joined the Central Treaty Organisation (CENTO) which by the end of the year included Turkey, Iraq, Iran and Pakistan, though not the United States. Britain's membership was motivated by a desire to defend its interests in the Middle East. The refusal of the United States to join is partly explained by continuing US suspicion of Britain's intentions in the Middle East. It was in this part of the world in 1956 that Britain's great power status was to receive a formidable rebuff.

The Suez crisis

Britain and Egypt

When the Suez Canal was constructed in the 1860s it was regarded as an outstanding engineering achievement of its time. It also had a vital importance for the British, who could now abandon the lengthy Cape route to India. They could instead travel far more directly, via the Mediterranean Sea, the new canal and the Indian Ocean. As shown earlier in this book, the British government under Disraeli had taken an opportunity to acquire a majority of the shares in the Suez Canal Company (page 28). Soon after that, in Gladstone's time as Prime Minister, the British took control of the government of Egypt and under the direction of Lord Cromer in the late nineteenth century had reformed its administration (pages 59–60 and 84). Nationalist opposition within Egypt during the inter-war years had resulted in the signature in 1936 of an Anglo-Egyptian Treaty providing for an eventual withdrawal of Britain from most of Egypt, though the area around the Suez Canal, known as the **Suez Canal zone**, would continue to be garrisoned by British forces. The Second World War – during which (as shown on pages 185–6) Egypt proved an invaluable base for British operations in North Africa – caused delay in the British departure. By the early 1950s, nationalist feeling in Egypt had become strong once again. There was also dissatisfaction with the corrupt and decadent monarchy of King Farouk. In July 1952 a military coup d'état brought about the end of the Egyptian

BRITAIN AND THE WORLD 1945-73

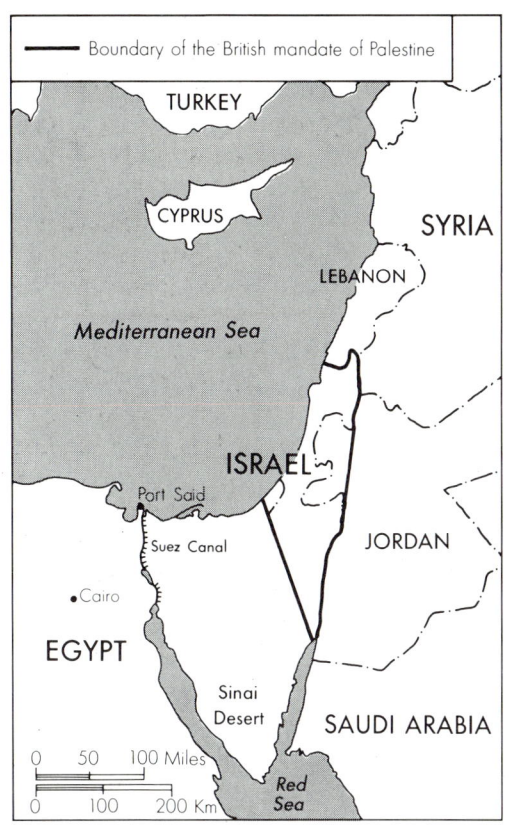

The Middle East in the 1940s and 1950s

monarchy; a republic was created in its place and shortly became dominated by one of the soldiers prominent in the earlier coup, Colonel Abdul Nasser.

Colonel Nasser

Nasser's ambition was to construct an Egypt that was modernised and independent. In seeking to achieve this ambition, he entered into negotiations about the continued presence of British forces in the southern area of the Sudan and in the Suez Canal zone. An early agreement was also reached on withdrawal of British forces from the Suez Canal zone, to be completed over the following 20 months. This did not involve any abandonment of the Suez Canal Company, nor did it hinder the passage of ships through the canal. A number of Conservative MPs nevertheless regarded it as an unacceptable retreat for British power in the Middle East. They formed what became known as the **Suez group** and were active in criticism of their own government for its weak policies towards the new government of Egypt. As events turned out in 1956, they were to consider their opposition well-justified.

Concern in Western Europe

Nasser's policies continued to cause concern to the government of Britain, and to those of other Western powers. The French disliked his support for the rebels against their rule in neighbouring Algeria. The British felt that it was he who had caused the dismissal in March 1956 of General Glubb, a long-standing and highly respected British military adviser to the government of Jordan. The governments of all Western powers became concerned at the way in which Nasser aggressively asserted Egypt's non-aligned role, showing willingness to take aid from the Soviet bloc as well as from Western countries. It was to be his pursuit of this policy, linked to his concern for Egypt's modernisation, that led directly to the Suez crisis.

Nationalisation of the Suez Canal

The planned Aswan Dam on the River Nile was viewed by Nasser as crucial for Egypt's modernisation; its construction became a virtual symbol of his country's rebirth. When he failed to get sufficient Western aid for the dam, he suggested that the Soviet Union might assist. This so angered the US Secretary of State, Foster Dulles, that in July 1956 he cancelled the US loan. Britain and France

A HISTORY OF BRITAIN FROM 1867

did likewise. Nasser responded by nationalising the Suez Canal Company, claiming that the revenue received by the company was now needed for the construction of the dam.

British politicians of both parties responded initially with outrage and, in doing so, reflected public opinion in the early stage of the crisis. Why was there such strong reaction to what Nasser had done? There was, after all, no direct threat posed to the passage of ships through the canal. In any case the vital links which the canal provided between Britain and India were no longer as important as they had been before Indian independence. Nasser's action was viewed as that of an international law-breaker. If he were allowed to get away with this, where would he stop? In this respect, he began to be compared with Hitler; there were demands that no 'appeasement' should be adopted in this case. Though British overseas trade and British supplies of oil were not directly affected by what had happened, there were fears that both would not now be so secure for the future.

The Suez crisis: the British response

Eden's initial policies

Eden became convinced that military action against Egypt would become necessary and he instructed the armed forces to make plans accordingly. In the meantime he felt it advisable to support the conciliatory policies of the US government, in the hope that these might lead to an eventual settlement. Dulles proposed a Suez Canal Users Association to provide joint control of the canal by its users and the Egyptian government. The scheme came to nothing, as it was rejected by Nasser. Attempts by Britain and France to get action by the United Nations were frustrated by the opposition of other world powers, who regarded this issue as one of less vital importance.

Collusion

Increasingly Britain and France moved closer to each other in their plans to oppose Nasser. Both had reasons to dislike the Egyptian leader; both had direct interests in the Suez Canal Company. In mid-October they began to concert their policies very closely and at the same time to become involved with the government of Israel, also an enemy of Nasser. A cabinet minister – Anthony Nutting, later to resign on account of his opposition to the British government's policies over Suez – gave an account of the secretive origins of the plans at the British Prime Minister's country residence of Chequers. Two representatives of the French Socialist government of Mollet arrived for discussions.

> I asked what, if any, information he had that Israel was contemplating an attack on Egypt. For a moment or two he did not answer, but sat looking nervously at the Private Secretary, who was busy taking notes in the background. When Eden told his Secretary to stop, the representative then proceeded to outline what he termed a possible plan of action for Britain and France to gain physical control of the Suez Canal. The plan, as he put it to us, was that Israel should be invited to attack Egypt across the Sinai Peninsula and that France and Britain, having given the Israeli forces enough time to seize all or most of Sinai, should then order 'both sides' to withdraw their forces from the Suez Canal, in order to permit an Anglo-French force to intervene and occupy the Canal on the pretext of saving it from damage by fighting. Thus the two powers would be able to claim to be 'separating the combatants' and 'extinguishing a dangerous fire', while actually seizing control of the entire waterway. . . . Doing his best to conceal his excitement, Eden replied noncommittally that he would give these suggestions very careful thought and would convey his reactions to Mollet early that week, after he had had an opportunity to discuss them with certain of his colleagues.
>
> Anthony Nutting, *No End of a Lesson*

Discussions between the French and British continued during the next fortnight. They included a highly secretive meeting of the British Foreign

BRITAIN AND THE WORLD 1945-73

A demonstration in London's Trafalgar Square at the height of the Suez crisis in November 1956. Both the size of the crowd and the tone of the banners suggest the anxiety that many felt about the government's actions at this time.

Secretary, Selwyn Lloyd, at the Parisian suburb of Sèvres later in the month. Here he met with Mollet, the French Prime Minister, and also with Ben Gurion, the Israeli Prime Minister. Details of the operation were finalised, based essentially on the original proposals made at Chequers.

Attacks on Egypt

Accordingly on 29 October Israeli forces launched an attack against Egypt across the Sinai desert. They very rapidly reached the Suez Canal and Egyptian forces had no option but to fight the invaders. A joint Anglo-French ultimatum was given that both sides should withdraw ten miles from either side of the Suez Canal. As this involved an Egyptian withdrawal within their own country, Nasser not unnaturally refused to abide by what he regarded as arrogant foreign dictation. The excuse was then provided for an Anglo-French invasion of Egypt, which followed rapidly and successfully in early November. Yet just when it seemed possible that the entire canal would come under Anglo-French control, the British government decided to accept UN intervention.

Reasons for British withdrawal

The events of late October and early November 1956 encountered much opposition within Britain and from outside. The Conservative party was divided

On leaving Egypt at the end of 1956, British troops greet the United Nations force taking over from them. The arrival of these troops (notice the UN emblem at the front of the train) provided some sort of solution to Britain's most controversial foreign intervention in the twentieth century.

A HISTORY OF BRITAIN FROM 1867

on the issue, while those who supported the government's action were dismayed at its eventual decision to retreat. The Labour party, under the slogan *Law not War*, was forthright in its opposition both inside parliament and outside. The government of the United States both opposed the British action and was angered by it, especially by its timing in the middle of a US presidential election. World hostility towards Britain's actions was measured particularly by the substantial sale of sterling on the international money markets and its declining value. It was probably this rather than anything else which persuaded the government to withdraw. Before the end of 1956, British troops had been replaced by those of the United Nations; at the same time the Israeli invasion forces were persuaded to withdraw.

Controversy over collusion

Eden always maintained that his had been the right course of action to take. 'We make no apology and shall make no apology for the action that we and our French allies took together' was a view expressed by him later in 1956 and which he never revised. Others took a very different view. Apart from any other consideration, there was dislike of the government's **collusion** over Suez. This expression referred to the secretive discussions with Israel that led to the Israeli invasion and to the excuse for British action with the French. This seemed an underhand way of approaching the problem. For many years there was dislike and contempt for the ways in which leading British politicians tried to conceal the fact that collusion had taken place. When questioned about it in the House of Commons, Selwyn Lloyd chose his words very carefully in his reply.

> The Right Honourable Gentleman asked whether there had been collusion with regard to this matter. Every time an incident has happened on the frontiers of Israel and the Arab states we have been accused of being in collusion with the Israelis about it. That allegation has been broadcast from Radio Cairo every time. It is quite wrong to state that Israel was incited to this action by Her Majesty's Government. There was no prior agreement between us about it. It is, of course, true that the Israeli mobilisation gave some advance warning and we urged restraint upon the Israeli government and in particular drew attention to the serious consequences of any attack upon Jordan.
>
> Hansard, *Parliamentary Debates*

Britain and the world after Suez

Britain's relations with other powers were damaged. The sterling crisis was a sign of widespread feeling against Britain. The United States had been particularly opposed to the British action, which thus created a rift with Britain's major ally at a time of continuing cold war tensions. The whole Western world was so distracted by the events of Suez that they were unable to respond to the Soviet invasion of Hungary that took place at the same time. Third world countries saw Britain's actions as those of an outdated colonial power. In future they might prefer to accept Communist aid rather than seek continuing links with Britain. Nasser himself did well from these events. Though his forces had been defeated and though the United Nations forces stayed for more than a decade to help preserve peace, there was much sympathy for him in the way in which he had been treated. Many saw the episode as a failed attempt by Britain to show that it was still a great power.

Britain and Europe

Changing circumstances

Britain's changed status in world affairs was more sharply illustrated in the Suez crisis than in any other single episode. The achievement of independence by Britain's overseas possessions also showed this change in a more gradual way. In many international conflicts and conferences of these years, the British role was no longer so vital as it had been before the Second World War. Britain was represented at world summit conferences at Geneva in 1955 and Paris in

1960, but did not play a major role in the discussions or in such decisions as were reached.

Relations with the United States improved again after the damage done to them by the Suez crisis. Successive British governments continued to assert that the Anglo-US **special relationship** formed a sound basic link between the two countries. Yet British support for the United States in world affairs was not shown by active involvement. The British government supported the stand made by their allies in the autumn of 1962 when the United States successfully insisted on the removal of Soviet offensive missiles from neighbouring Cuba. In the 1960s and early 1970s, the increasingly extensive and damaging involvement of the United States in Vietnam was supported by Britain, yet there was never any suggestion that British troops might be sent there. In the 1960s, for financial rather than any other reasons, Britain became increasingly dependent on the United States for its nuclear defence. During the Wilson years there were many troop reductions **east of Suez**, symbolic of a further diminishing of Britain's world role. In 1967 the British withdrawal from Aden – originally a coaling station on the sea route to India – was a particular feature of this process.

The treaties of Dunkirk and Brussels

In seeking to adjust to changed circumstances, the British looked with a curious mixture of interest and doubt at events in Western Europe generally. Britain had already become fully involved in OEEC and NATO, respectively concerned with economic co-operation and military co-operation (pages 234 and 235). Earlier, other more direct links had been established with continental countries, such as the Dunkirk Treaty of 1947, signed between Britain and France, and the Brussels Treaty of 1948, when the Benelux countries joined the Anglo-French agreement of the previous year. Both agreements aimed to strengthen and unify Western Europe. Although it was stated that the Brussels Treaty was designed to combat any renewal of German aggression, it was clearly the Soviet Union that the signatories most feared.

Council of Europe

Encouraged by what had so far been achieved, Britain participated in the discussions that led to the creation in 1950 of the Council of Europe. Its headquarters at Strasbourg were to become a forum for discussion by the Western European governments and parliaments on matters of common concern. It possessed no authority and had no clear idea of any positive role that it might play in Western Europe. It had been the influence of Attlee's government which had contributed to the vagueness which surrounded the Council of Europe. The government continued to view developments of this type as ones with which Britain as a great power in its own right should not become too closely involved. Meanwhile, in opposition, Churchill was one of the strongest supporters of the idea of closer unity in Western Europe.

European Defence Community

Yet as Prime Minister in the early 1950s, Churchill did not take the British any further into Europe. The main issue for Britain in this connection during these years was the possibility of involvement in a new military organisation, the European Defence Community (EDC). After much discussion it became clear by 1954 that continued disagreements – especially over technical problems raised by France in relation to West Germany – were such that the EDC would not come into being. Throughout, Britain showed a lack of enthusiasm for the EDC. More successful within continental Europe in these years was the European Coal and Steel Community – France, Italy, West Germany, Belgium, the Netherlands and Luxemburg – who entered negotiations to form a more broadly based community. The result was the emergence of the European Economic Community (EEC) in March 1957, by the terms of the Treaty of Rome.

European Economic Community

The European Economic Community was a powerful organisation. The main principle on which it was based was that of a common external tariff for all the member countries. It also had an administrative structure carefully designed on a **supra-national** basis. It was therefore intended to develop the interests of the

A HISTORY OF BRITAIN FROM 1867

Community as a whole and not specifically those of its individual member countries. Britain refused to involve itself with the EEC in its early stages. The common tariff would be to the disadvantage of its Commonwealth countries. The administrative structure might imperil Britain's freedom to take independent action.

European Free Trade Association

Nevertheless, Britain saw a need to co-operate with fellow-countries in Europe. It therefore proposed a European Free Trade Association (EFTA). Member countries could not operate a common external tariff, but would practise free trade policies between themselves; the whole organisation would have a looser structure and administration than the EEC. When initiated in January 1960, EFTA had seven member-countries: Austria, Britain, Denmark, Norway, Portugal, Sweden and Switzerland. The United States, with a view to cold war tensions, was concerned at the way in which the EEC and EFTA suggested division rather than unity in Western Europe. Its government therefore put pressure on Macmillan's government in Britain to involve itself fully with its neighbours in Western Europe by seeking membership of the EEC.

Britain's applications for EEC membership

Britain's first application

In July 1961 Macmillan announced that Britain was to apply for membership of the EEC. The government's decision to do this aroused little enthusiasm in the country. Many in the Labour party and some in the Conservative party were opposed. Within the Commonwealth countries and the EFTA countries there was a general feeling of unease about their future trading prospects with Britain. Edward Heath had charge of the protracted and difficult negotiations that developed; in these he endeavoured to protect Britain's existing trading interests as best he could. Much of the discussion concentrated on the length of the transitional period of adjustment from the old ways to the new.

The negotiations came to nothing. Throughout, President de Gaulle of France had shown a lack of sympathy for the British application. He considered that Commonwealth commitments and close US connections made a full and wholehearted involvement by Britain in Europe unlikely. In January 1963 he put his main objection to British membership in this way.

> The question arises as to how far it is possible for Great Britain at the present time to accept a truly common tariff, for this would involve giving up all Commonwealth preferences. Can she do this? That is the question....
> It is possible that one day Britain might manage to transform herself sufficiently to become part of the European Community. In this case, the Six would open the door to her and France would raise no obstacle, although Britain's simple participation in the community would considerably change its nature and its volume.

Quoted from *The Annual Register for 1963*

"She'll never make it with all that lot."

Harold Wilson's bid for Common Market entry in the late 1960s is weighed down by Britain's commitments. Nor on the other side of the Channel does there seem to be much encouragement for his venture.

Whatever the hopes for the future might be, de Gaulle's words effectively imposed a veto on any further negotiations at that time. Though British enthusiasts for entry were dismayed at de Gaulle's actions, the circumstances of the application in the early 1960s suggest that his approach may well at that time have been a wise one. The British government's decision to apply for membership had its origins more in Britain's changed international circumstances than in a genuine commitment to Europe. Those in favour of membership refused to allow the matter to rest, though clearly the application could not be renewed immediately.

Britain's second application

In the late 1960s, in spite of Labour's earlier opposition to the EEC, Wilson's government took up the cause of British entry for a second time. Changes within the Commonwealth and within the EEC led Wilson to consider that membership was now in Britain's interests. Negotiations were renewed in 1967. They

BRITAIN AND THE WORLD 1945-73

were briefer than the Heath negotiations but came up against the same obstacle: the veto of President de Gaulle, which he imposed in May 1967 for reasons similar to those which had prompted his earlier decision.

Britain's third application

By the time of the 1970 general election, all three political parties were committed to EEC entry. The fact that the rejected application of 1967 had not been withdrawn showed that de Gaulle's veto was not regarded by Britain as the final word on entry. De Gaulle had in any case retired in 1969 and the French government of Pompidou in the early 1970s was more sympathetic towards the British cause. In addition to Britain, there were now other applicants for entry: Denmark, Ireland and Norway. As Prime Minister, Heath was determined that the goal towards which he had worked in the Macmillan government some ten years previously should now be achieved. Geoffrey Rippon had immediate charge of the negotiations, but Heath himself was closely involved. He played a vital role at different times, especially by a direct meeting with Pompidou in May 1971, at a time when negotiations were proving difficult.

By the summer of 1971 negotiations had been satisfactorily concluded between Britain and the EEC countries. The terms of entry represented a compromise. Rippon had not been able to secure all the concessions on the transitional arrangements that he had hoped for. The government now faced the very considerable problem of getting the terms accepted by parliament and by the British people. The Labour party insisted that the terms were unsatisfactory; even within the Conservative party there was quite open discontent. Parliament debated the issue at length in the winter of 1971–72 and the terms were eventually accepted in the spring. Doubts about the wisdom of Britain's decision were to continue as a disturbing feature in British politics in the years ahead. At a ceremony held at the EEC headquarters in Brussels on 1 January 1973, Edward Heath signed the Treaty of Accession that marked the formal entry of Britain into the EEC.

The British Prime Minister, Edward Heath, signs the treaty by which his country entered the European Economic Community. Britain's closer involvement with its Continental neighbours marked one of the most important post-war developments in foreign relations.

EXERCISES

1. Show in what ways Britain aligned its foreign policies with the United States in respect of each of the following:
   (a) the Berlin crisis of the late 1940s,
   (b) the Korean War of the early 1950s, and
   (c) the development of nuclear weapons during the 1940s and 1950s.

2. (a) Why did British governments remain suspicious of the value of EEC membership during the 1950s?
   (b) Trace the course of events that led to British membership of the EEC by 1973.
   (c) Why did it take so long for Britain to become a member of the EEC?

3. Imagine you are living in Britain at the time of the Suez crisis of 1956. Write a letter to a friend of yours abroad who has asked you to explain the approaches of the Eden government towards the crisis. In the course of your letter give reasons for either supporting or opposing Eden at this time.

4. Study the two photographs on page 241 and then answer questions (a) to (c) which follow.
   (a) (i) What evidence does the top photograph contain of the concern of many people at the course of events in the early stages of the Suez crisis?
       (ii) How justified do you feel this concern was? (3+4)
   (b) (i) How does the lower photograph suggest that the aim of those in the earlier photograph was achieved?
       (ii) Outline the course of events in the area of the Suez Canal that led to the events shown in this second photograph. (2+4)
   (c) (i) What reasons account for the withdrawal of Britain from its Suez involvement in 1956?
       (ii) Why do you think the Suez crisis of 1956 has been regarded as so important in recent British history? (3+4)

20 BRITAIN IN THE 1970s AND 1980s

British involvement in the **European Community** (as it came to be termed) was almost as controversial after the securing of membership as it had been before. A referendum of 1975 showed a majority of British people in favour of continued membership, but the majority was not large and complaints of a variety of difficulties arising from membership continued to be heard in the 1970s and 1980s. In those two decades Britain continued to adopt in world affairs the more modest role established in the post-war years. Within Britain, however, these were years of important development and of new directions.

The Heath government, 1970–74

The 1970 general election

The Conservatives entered the general election of June 1970 with a distinctly more right-wing approach than the party had adopted for some years. This new approach had been formulated at a meeting of senior Conservative politicians at the Selsdon Park Hotel, near London, at the start of 1970. The intention of the **Selsdon policies** was to reduce the role of government and increase the role of private enterprise. Part of these policies was strong action against excessive trade union power. Conservative victory had been by no means certain during the course of the election campaign, yet Heath in fact achieved a sound result that provided a good parliamentary base for his new government.

General Election: June 1970	
Conservatives	330
Labour	287
Liberals	6

Heath's domestic policies

In domestic affairs the Heath government gave particular attention to the economy and the trade unions. Yet the government's poor record in both was to be a major factor in its fall from power in February 1974. **Monetarist** policies were pursued, involving cuts in both government expenditure and in income and company taxation. Industry was to be given the opportunity to fend for itself, and was not to expect the government to help it in difficult times. Such policies did not work. By 1972, in the face of increasing unemployment and increasing inflation a change of policy was felt necessary. The government now reverted to the more cautious strategies of Jenkins, strategies that the Conservatives had condemned in the late 1960s.

Industrial Relations Act

The government had no easier time in its relations with the trade unions. The Industrial Relations Act of 1971 gave many concessions to the trade unions, but it aroused their anger by removing others and by imposing the Act's terms with considerable force. Provision was made for a ballot of trade union members before a strike was held and for a 'cooling off' period to delay and, it was hoped, avert a threatened strike. It banned what was known as the **closed shop**, the right of a trade union to insist that all workers in a company should belong to a trade union. A new National Industrial Relations Court was to be set up to ensure that the terms of the Act were not infringed. It was this Court that became the object of much trade union anger and the Court found difficulty in dealing with the cases that came before it. A climax to the hostility was reached in August 1972 when the brief imprisonment of five dockers under the direction

The Industrial Relations Act of 1970 was a bold measure by the Heath government to control the power of the trade unions. But the Act proved unworkable and resulted in a worsening in industrial relations.

of the Court produced much protest throughout the country. This led to the release of the dockers and the virtual abandonment of the Act.

Downfall of the Heath government

Issues concerning industrial relations made an important contribution to the downfall of the Heath government. As part of its new economic strategy in 1972, the government imposed restrictions on income. Towards the end of the following year, when these restrictions were still in force, the miners struck for increases substantially above the level allowed by the government. The cause of the miners was strengthened by vast increases in oil prices that occurred at the same time, increases which made the country heavily reliant on the coal which the miners produced. Heath made a stand for the government's pay policy. To conserve fuel supplies the country was placed on a three-day week in the winter of 1973–74. Yet the miners stuck to their course and in February 1974 Heath summoned a general election in an attempt to secure the country's support for his policies and to decide whether the country was to be run by the miners or by the elected government of the day.

The Labour governments of 1974–79

General elections of 1974

There were two general elections in the course of 1974.

General Elections: 1974	February	October
Labour	301	319
Conservatives	296	276
Liberals	14	13
Others (mainly nationalist parties)	24	27

By studying the figures for the first of these elections, it can be seen that Heath was denied the support he had sought from the country. At the same time, the Labour party had not secured an overall majority. Heath held some hope that a Conservative–Liberal coalition might be formed, but nothing came of this. Wilson therefore became Prime Minister for a second time.

The Social contract

Wilson set himself and his government the immediate task of restoring harmony in industrial relations. A negotiated settlement was made to the miners' strike and the Industrial Relations Act was repealed. The government intended to replace recent conflicts by harmony in the approach of both government and trade unions to industrial relations. The **social contract**, of which the government made much in the summer months of 1974, was to be the basis of this harmony. On the union side there was to be less frequent use of strikes; on the government side there was to be greater readiness to resolve acceptably the claims of the unions.

Callaghan succeeds Wilson

Though the social contract never secured full commitment on either side, it helped to improve industrial relations. By the autumn the improvement was sufficient to persuade Wilson to hold a further general election in which – as can be seen from the figures on the previous page – he secured the overall majority which his government required. Some 18 months later James Callaghan succeeded Wilson on his retirement as Prime Minister in the spring of 1976. Callaghan was a moderate politician whose earlier trade union links helped him to work reasonably well with the unions throughout much of the remaining time of the government. No general election was held until May 1979, by which time the Labour government had run almost its full five-year course.

Unemployment and inflation

Increasing unemployment

By the mid-1970s unemployment was once again a serious problem within Britain. In the immediate post-war years it had been thought that this scourge of the 1930s had been banished for ever. By the beginning of the 1970s the number of unemployed stood at more than half a million; by 1976 it had risen to 1.3 million and for the rest of the 1970s it remained at about that figure. In the 1980s it was to increase to over three million.

The unemployment of these years was different from that of the 1930s in many respects. In the absence of the means test and with greater generosity in the payment of benefits, the plight of the unemployed in the 1970s and 1980s was less serious than earlier. The causes of unemployment – a feature of life in other European countries as well as in Britain – were not as easy to detect as they had been in the inter-war years. Advances in computer technology, increased attention to modernisation, the trend towards amalgamating companies involved in similar work: these were all among the many reasons for this new wave of unemployment.

Government policies

To solve the problem there was to be less reliance on government aid to stimulate the economy, less reliance therefore on the Keynsian economics that had brought relief in the past. This had been the policy in both Britain and other countries in the 1930s and more recently. By the mid-1970s the Labour government took the view that government spending did not necessarily create more jobs and tended instead to increase the already serious problem of inflation. The Labour view was quite close to the Selsdon policies of the Conservatives earlier in the 1970s, and also the Conservative policies as developed in their governments during the 1980s.

Inflation

Inflation certainly had developed into a serious problem. Like unemployment, its causes are difficult to disentangle. Certainly the vast increases in oil prices and high wage settlements were among them. Some in Britain felt that inflation was a result of membership of the European Community and there were suggestions that the change to a decimalised currency in 1971 had also had an effect. By the mid-1970s inflation had reached an annual rate of 25 per cent and it continued at a high rate until the early 1980s. In order to cater for soaring prices, large wage increases were essential; yet prices continued to race ahead. Inflation made for financial uncertainty all round as everyone was affected by it. By the late 1970s it was regarded as the most important problem facing the government.

BRITAIN IN THE 1970S AND 1980S

Margaret Thatcher and the general election of 1979

Thatcherism

Margaret Thatcher became leader of the Conservative party in 1975. Four years later she led her party to the first of three victories in successive general elections. This was an outstanding political achievement, unmatched by any prime minister in the period covered by this book. The term **Thatcherism** came increasingly to be applied to the direction of Conservative policies under her leadership.

In its essentials Thatcherism involved a return to the earlier Selsdon principles. There should be less involvement by the government in the country's economy. In that way business would learn to be competitive and strong. Trade union power was to be curbed, so that industry could develop untroubled by the prospect of strikes and industrial disorder. Pay increases should equal only what could be afforded. Government grants to nationalised industries or to local government were similarly restricted to what the government could afford. Direct taxation (such as income tax) was to be reduced, so that people were given incentive to work harder by being allowed to keep more of what they earned. In all of these policies, encouragement was to be given to private enterprise and to individual initiative. Those who would do well under this system were those able and willing to work with success. As Thatcherism developed in practice in the 1980s, critics increasingly complained that lack of government funds meant that such services as the state provided – for example, welfare services and education – were much damaged.

The 1979 general election

Mrs Thatcher's success in the general election of May 1979 was a narrow one.

General Elections			
	May 1979	June 1983	June 1987
Conservatives	339	397	374
Labour	268	209	227
Liberals	11	—	—
Alliance	—	23	22
Others (mainly nationalist parties)	17	21	27

Her victory in 1979 may have been partly due to the policies she promised. Certainly of much importance in that victory was the experience the country underwent in the winter of 1978–79, the 'winter of discontent' as it became known. Widespread strikes occurred, particularly in the public services. These strikes could be seen as a natural consequence, in a time of continuing high inflation, to the ending of some years of government restraint in pay. The government tended to be blamed for the chaos that resulted from these strikes in the coldest months of the year. Callaghan did not help the fortunes of his party by suggesting that the crisis was less serious than many held it to be. On the other hand, Mrs Thatcher's policies – and particularly her promise to curb what was seen by many as excessive trade union power – were viewed by many as increasingly attractive.

However narrow her victory was, the election of a Conservative government in May 1979 was an event of much significance in modern British history. For the first time a woman had become Prime Minister of Britain. The many developments of women in society during the previous 100 years had made it possible for a woman to occupy the highest position in the land. This was a very prominent example of the types of advance that women had made during the 1970s. May 1979 also marked a new direction for government policy, based on the principles of Thatcherism and held to firmly by the new Prime Minister in subsequent years. Only a minority of Conservatives, sometimes referred to as

Margaret Thatcher with a group of soldiers. Her premiership – that of the first woman prime minister – was notable for new and often controversial directions.

A HISTORY OF BRITAIN FROM 1867

'wets', lacked sympathy with the party's new direction. May 1979 signified therefore an important shift to the political right.

Economic policies A budget passed shortly after the election victory gave an early indication of the government's determination to implement its promised policies. There were substantial reductions in direct taxation, such as income tax, with corresponding increases in indirect taxation, such as Value Added Tax (VAT). It would take time, however, for the government's monetarist approach to show good results. In the early 1980s, with unemployment rising and little improvement in the inflation rate, the government's popularity waned. By 1982 the electorate was beginning to show greater confidence in the value of Thatcherism and their confidence increased sharply as a result of the government's handling of the Falklands issue.

The Falklands

Argentine claims The Falkland islands, situated some 700 kilometres from the coast of Argentina, were among the most distant of Britain's overseas possessions. Their inhabitants were less than 2000 in number and as other parts of the Commonwealth achieved independence, the Falkland islanders showed no wish to follow them. Maintaining loyalty to Britain seemed the best way to ensure that the long-standing Argentine claim to possession of the islands remained unfulfilled. Until the events of 1982, most British people knew little about the Falklands; a good many very probably did not even know where they were.

Argentine attack In 1982 the Falkland issue became one that attracted worldwide attention and became of much importance for the British people. In April of that year Argentine troops were sent by their government to take over the islands in the name of Argentina. They did this successfully and speedily, the few British troops on the islands being unready for surprise attack. The reasons that prompted the Argentine dictator, General Galtieri, to take such action at that time are

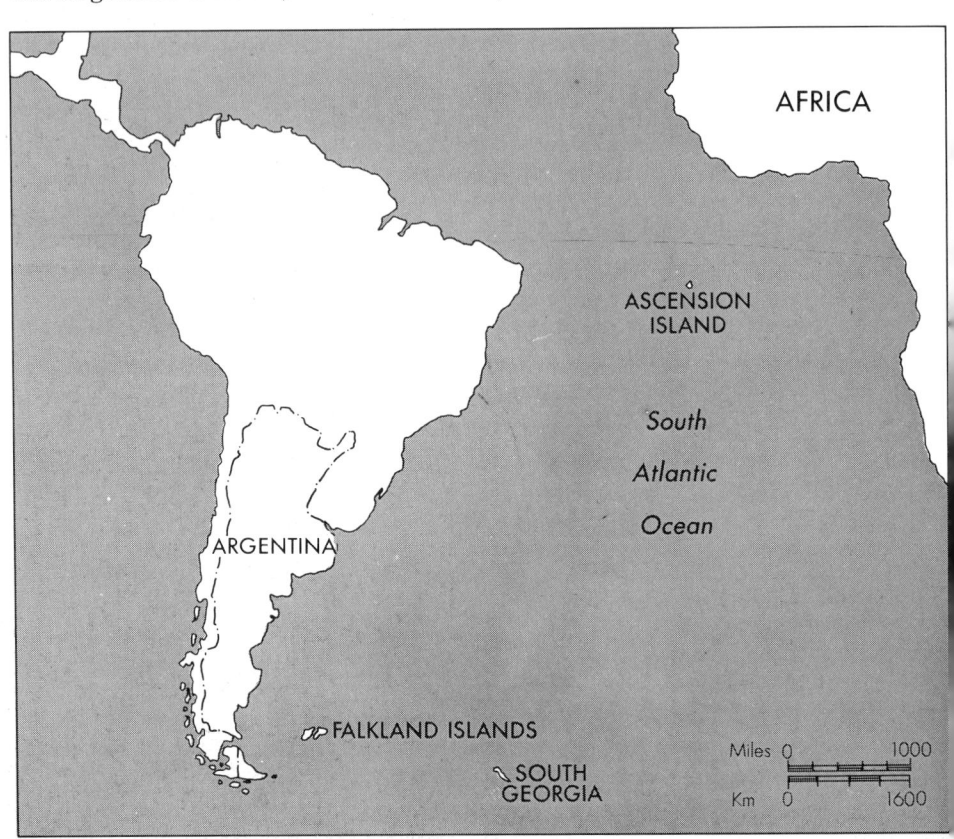

The Falklands campaign of 1982

BRITAIN IN THE 1970S AND 1980S

not easy to detect. It may be that he wanted to revive his government's fortunes by a spectacular move abroad. The recent British decision to withdraw HMS *Endurance*, the British patrol vessel in the South Atlantic, may have suggested to Galtieri that Britain might not fight to defend its possession of the islands.

Response in Britain

Reaction in Britain was one of outrage at the Argentine action. All political parties united in support of the government's decision to send a task force of ships on the immense 13 000 kilometre journey to the South Atlantic. This task force developed to a considerable size, consisting of merchant ships and cruise liners as well as the ships of the Royal Navy. British possession of Ascension Island, almost at the mid-way point, was of great value in the conduct of the exercise. Meantime, attempts to resolve the issue by peaceful negotiations made slow and uncertain progress. In all of this, Britain was assisted by the decision of the European Community to place economic sanctions on Argentina and by the support of the UN Security Council for the British cause.

Controversy over the *General Belgrano*

In late April action began in the South Atlantic against Argentine ships. Some of the smaller islands taken by Argentina, such as South Georgia, were re-secured. What was to develop as one of the most controversial engagements of this war occurred in early May, when the Argentine ship *General Belgrano* was sunk, with many casualties. The British sinking of the *General Belgrano* had taken place outside what was termed the **exclusion zone**. This term referred to a defined area around the Falklands in which attacks on Argentine ships might take place. It was not therefore expected that an attack would take place outside that zone. The government maintained that the *General Belgrano*, in spite of its position, was a threat to the British forces and had to be eliminated. For some years after, this issue remained one of much controversy.

British victory

Events in and around the Falklands became more violent in May. In spite of the loss of some ships from aerial attack by Argentine aircraft flying from the mainland, a successful foothold was secured in the Falklands. Though outnumbered by Argentinians, British troops continued their advance towards the capital, Port Stanley, which was liberated in mid-June. The British commander sent the following message to the Prime Minister.

> In Port Stanley at 9 p.m. Falkland Islands time tonight, 14 June 1982, Major-General Menendez surrendered to me all the Argentine armed forces in East and West Falkland, together with their impediments. Arrangements are in hand to assemble the men for return to Argentina, to gather in their arms and equipment, and to mark and make safe their munitions. The Falkland Islands are once more under the Government desired by their inhabitants. God save the Queen.

The return to England of HMS Invincible, the leading ship of the task force sent to re-secure the Falklands in 1982. This photograph captures the strong sense of patriotism that surrounded the successful conclusion of the campaign.

Importance The liberation of the Falklands had been secured at the cost of 255 British lives, and a much higher figure than that in Argentine lives. Only a minority questioned whether this had been too high a price to pay to maintain the rights of a very small number of people in a very distant part of the world from Britain. In the moment of victory there was much rejoicing and much praise of the government's determination in seeing its policies through to so successful a conclusion.

Politics in the 1980s

British industry The direction of the Falklands campaign had shown that Britain had a government capable of deciding on a policy and carrying it through to success. In certain respects, there had been a similar approach to domestic issues. There had been a reduction in the number of strikes and, by 1983 in the rate of inflation also, both of which had been matters of much concern in the late 1970s. Though unemployment had increased in excess of three million, the government claimed that British industry was now on a firmer base due to the encouragement given to private initiative and to technical advance and modernisation. As the figures on page 247 show, Mrs Thatcher's government was returned in 1983 with a substantially increased majority and was able therefore to continue its policies for the foreseeable future.

The Labour party A major element in the government's success both in the 1983 election and that of 1987 was the division of the opposition. Internal differences within the Labour party have been noted at many points in this book; they have been a continuing feature ever since the party's foundation at the start of the century. On Callaghan's retirement as leader of the party shortly after the loss of the 1979 election, the left-wing came to dominate. One of their number, Michael Foot, was elected as party leader. It seemed therefore that Labour was moving further to the left, just as the Conservatives had moved further to the right. The 'centre' ground of politics, attractive to people of more moderate opinions, had no adequate representation.

Social Democratic party Some members of the Labour party were much disturbed by the leftward trend in their party. In 1981, under the leadership of Roy Jenkins, a former Labour Home Secretary and Chancellor of the Exchequer, they left the Labour party in order to form the Social Democratic party. In doing this, they claimed that they were continuing to represent the more moderate Socialist policies of the 1960s and 1970s. Some members of the Labour party and even some members of the Conservative party joined them in their new venture. The central position occupied by the Social Democrats was similar to that occupied by the Liberals. It seemed that each party would benefit by some kind of linkage between them. Thus it was that the **Alliance** was formed. By this the Social Democratic party and the Liberal party agreed to act jointly in politics, while still retaining their separate identities as political parties.

Political fortunes of the Alliance At various by-elections throughout the 1980s, results suggested that the more moderate position of the Alliance had for the electorate an attraction which the Conservative and Labour parties lacked. Some spectacular gains by the Alliance were made. Hopes were raised that the Alliance might after a general election come to form the government or at least hold the balance between the two other parties. But at the general elections of 1983 and 1987 the Alliance secured very few seats. Such poor results did not mean that the Alliance lacked support among the electorate. For example, in the 1983 general election in spite of gaining only 23 of the 650 seats in the House of Commons, the Alliance had in fact attracted more than a quarter of all the votes cast in the election. The Alliance naturally urged strongly a change to a system of **proportional representation**, but the major parties stood to lose from such a system and no

… such change was likely. For the Alliance their fortunes (and particularly the Social Democrat fortunes) in the 1987 election were even less satisfactory than in 1983. Many within the Alliance asserted the need to forge one party from the Social Democrats and the Liberals and before the end of 1987 moves had begun to do that.

Neil Kinnock

The Conservatives were greatly advantaged by the division of the opposition which the emergence of the Alliance had produced. It was a fundamental factor in their continuing electoral success. The Labour party's 1983 campaign had emphasised the evils of unemployment. This issue, however, had little appeal to the many whose jobs were secure. Immediately after the election, Foot resigned as party leader. He was succeeded by Neil Kinnock, a younger politician and a highly effective speaker, who occupied a more central position within the party. As the next general election approached, Kinnock endeavoured to guide the Labour party to a more moderate political position and to give it a more attractive image. In spite of such efforts, the party did poorly in the 1987 election. Labour did nevertheless secure a distinct level of support in Scotland and in the north of England, areas where the monetarist policies of the Conservative government had had their harshest impact.

Proposals for devolution

The figures on pages 247 and 249 show that the nationalist parties (the Scottish Nationalists, Plaid Cymru in Wales and the Ulster Unionists) had attracted an increased popularity, especially in the 1970s. Their popularity suggested some dissatisfaction with dominance of government from Westminster. In the case of Scotland, the discovery of North Sea oil off the Scottish coast was another factor. The Scottish Nationalists complained of the injustice in not allowing the revenues from this highly valuable resource to go directly to Scotland. In both Scotland and Wales there were demands for **devolution** of government. This would involve, among other things, the setting up of national assemblies in Edinburgh and Cardiff. But when definite proposals along these lines were put to the Scottish and Welsh peoples in 1979, they were rejected. The force of Scottish and Welsh nationalism declined thereafter. In Northern Ireland however, a very different situation existed, linked to the continuing difficulties of the Irish situation.

Problems in Northern Ireland

Disturbances in the late 1960s

Little has been written in this book about Northern Ireland since the events of the early 1920s, considered in Chapter 11. In 1969 the problems of this part of the United Kingdom had surfaced once again, and in violent form. In the intervening years many problems had existed and had passed, generally, unnoticed. Back in the 1930s the unemployment rate in Northern Ireland was among the worst for the whole of the United Kingdom. The Protestant majority, who held political control in the Northern Ireland parliament at Stormont, continued to practise discrimination against Roman Catholics in matters of jobs and housing.

In the mid-1960s, encouraged by the Wilson government, some limited steps began to be taken to diminish this discrimination. By 1968 a Civil Rights Association had emerged in Northern Ireland to press more strenuously for improvements. Disturbances took place at the end of 1968 and in 1969, when members of the association clashed violently with the 'B' specials, part of the armed police force of Northern Ireland. By August 1969 the situation had become so serious that the British army was sent to maintain order between the Protestant and Roman Catholic communities. At the same time the 'B' specials were disbanded and attempts made by the British government to resolve some of the difficulties within the province.

Increasingly a new element emerged in the situation. The Irish Republican Army (IRA), which had not in recent years been a force of much importance,

Direct rule

In March 1972 the British government decided that Stormont was no longer capable of performing its function of governing Northern Ireland. The province now came under the direct rule of Westminster. Protestants in Northern Ireland were appalled at this step, as they were also by the British government's proposals for the future of Northern Ireland, published in March 1973. A power-sharing Executive was to be set up, on which all political parties in the province were to be represented. Opposition to this Executive on the part of the majority in Northern Ireland – led particularly by the trade unions – was so strong that the experiment was abandoned in the following years.

Government policies

Violence in Northern Ireland – and occasionally in mainland Britain – continued to take place. The most famous such episode was the attempt to assassinate the Prime Minister at the 1984 Conservative conference, in the course of which five people were killed. Protest took other forms, such as the hunger strikes of imprisoned IRA members in the early 1980s. The government continued to support the right of the majority in Northern Ireland to maintain the province as a part of the United Kingdom for as long as they wished. In the meantime, the government also sought to improve relations with the Republic of Ireland and to suggest that a long-term solution might be the incorporation of Northern Ireland into the Republic. Such an event was viewed as very far off and it would be the people of Northern Ireland who would decide.

Trade unions and the miners' strike of 1984–85

Decline in importance of trade unions

Given the increased strike activity in the 1970s and the excesses of the 'winter of discontent' it was not surprising that the electorate felt, on the eve of the 1979 general election, that trade union power was a major issue facing the government. Throughout the 1980s – though not consistently – the number of days lost through strike action was noticeably reduced. By the time of the third Thatcher victory in 1987 the trade unions were, by their own admission, facing a crisis situation. Their membership and their influence were both in decline and the unions themselves were uncertain of the part they should play in the society that had developed under successive Thatcher governments.

Trade Union Act

In the early stages, legislation had been passed to prevent the recently developed practice of **secondary picketing**. This involved picketing at the site of a strike not just by those normally employed there, but by others who came from elsewhere to support the strikers' cause. Secondary picketing led to some violent confrontations and Mrs Thatcher had earlier been committed to its abolition. Of greater importance was the Trade Union Act of 1984. Among its many far-reaching provisions two were of particular importance. There was provision for secret election of union officials and for a secret ballot on whether or not a strike should be called. The government maintained that the Act was allowing greater rights in trade unions to trade union members. The trade union leadership maintained that the Act prevented them from taking industrial action to further the interests of their members. The result was a slackening of industrial unrest, though not without a major challenge to the government from within a part of the trade union movement. This challenge was presented by the miners' strike of 1984–85, possibly the most important industrial action in Britain since the General Strike of 1926.

Origins of the miners' strike

There always had been much sympathy in Britain for the miners, on account very largely of the hard and demanding nature of their work. This point has already been made and illustrated in connection with the General Strike in

BRITAIN IN THE 1970S AND 1980S

Chapter 12, though conditions in the mines were much harder in those days. Strikes by miners had in the post-war years very often secured their aims. The origins of the 1984–85 strike lay in the competition provided to coal by the recent exploitation of North Sea oil. For the government this was an immensely more profitable source of power than coal, which had tended in recent years to decline anyway. The government therefore decided – in accord with monetarist principles – that a number of unprofitable pits should no longer be supported by the government and should close. The leadership of the National Union of Mineworkers (NUM) determined not to hold a national ballot on the issue of whether or not to strike; instead regional ballots were held. The results of these regional ballots were varied. While Scotland, Yorkshire and Kent were solidly in favour of strike action, Nottingham was much against it and other coalfields were divided in their attitudes.

Collapse of the strike

The strike never therefore secured the full support of the miners throughout the country and its uncertain start was the main reason for its eventual failure. Picketing – some of it secondary – was mounted on a large scale in order to help intensify the strike, especially in such areas as Nottingham, where support was weak. Police action was needed to ensure reasonable order at picket lines and to give safe conduct through the picket lines to those miners who wished to continue working. As the months passed, the strike became violent and bitter. In the early months of 1985 the solidarity of the strikers – which to that time had been impressive – began to collapse, and the NUM leadership called off the strike in March.

Importance

There had been no settlement to the strike and the miners had therefore to accept the pit closures that were part of the government's plans. The Nottinghamshire miners, many of whom had been angered by an attempt to coerce them into a strike they had not sought, founded a break-away union, the Union of Democratic Mineworkers. The mining community had been seriously split. The Labour party had also been disadvantaged by the strike. The NUM had criticised the weak support given to them by the Labour leadership, while the government had criticised the Labour leadership for lack of vigour in condemning the violence caused by pickets. The government emerged with much political advantage. There were elements within the NUM that had hoped the strike action would unseat the Thatcher government, just as the miners' strike of 1973–74 had been a factor leading to the collapse of the Heath government. This had not happened. Nor had the government wavered in its intent to support those miners who wished to continue working and also to ensure that trade union law was upheld.

British society in the 1980s

Violence in society

Unhappily, violence in society was not confined to events concerning Northern Ireland or the lengthy miners' strike. In the spring and summer of 1981 riots occurred in the streets of the London suburb of Brixton and in the Liverpool district of Toxteth and in some other inner city areas. The violence caused by the rioters was serious and it was only with difficulty that the police contained it. Both the government and the public in general were shocked by what was a form of violent protest unparalleled in twentieth-century British history. In 1985 other street riots took place, some of them in the same areas as those four years earlier.

Hooliganism

Much attention focused on the causes of these events. There was little doubt that hooliganism was one element. Such behaviour – involving verbal or physical abuse launched from the apparent security of a gang of like-minded individuals – developed as a disturbing feature of British life in the 1980s. It was capable of transforming a young person who on his or her own might be thoughtful and sensitive into one filled with aggression. Hooligan behaviour was in evidence

Street violence in Brixton in the spring of 1981. Conflict such as this was a disturbing feature of inner-city life in 1981 and 1985.

among some British holidaymakers abroad, at football matches and, most tragically, at the European Cup Final in Brussels in 1985, when 39 Italian spectators were killed. No firm answer could be given as to why some young people behaved in a hooligan way, though many suggestions were made. Certainly alcohol abuse was one factor. A breakdown in respect for authority and lack of guidance by parents in the home and teachers in the school were also points of discussion in this respect.

Riots

Nevertheless, the social circumstances in the riot areas suggested that there were underlying reasons for discontent. Unemployment tended to be higher than average, housing conditions tended to be worse and there was suggestion of earlier insensitivity by some police in their relations with young people. There was little evidence that racial tension was a major element in the riots, though there was much discussion on this point. In his official report on the Brixton riots, Lord Scarman tackled the issue of ethnic minorities in this connection with these words.

> Unemployment and poor housing bear on them very heavily; and the educational system has not adjusted itself satisfactorily to their needs. Their difficulties are intensified by the sense they have of a concealed discrimination against them, particularly in relation to job opportunities and housing.... In addition, they do not feel politically secure. Their sense of rejection is not eased by the low level of black representation in our elective political institutions.
> None of these features can perhaps be usefully described as a *cause* of the disorders, either in Brixton or elsewhere.... But taken together they provide a set of *conditions* which create a predisposition towards violent protest.

Ethnic minorities

By the 1980s approximately 6 per cent of the British population were from the ethnic minorities. Almost half of these were not actually immigrants themselves, but were the children or grandchildren of immigrants. They tended still to concentrate in urban areas and to retain distinctive features of the life-style of the West Indies or the Indian sub-continent. The government held to the view that members of the ethnic minority groups in Britain were as much British as were those of long-standing descent in the British Isles. Consequently the government, while protecting the rights of all under the Race Relations Act, did not consider it their task to give **positive discrimination** in favour of members of the ethnic minorities, as some urged them to do. Many did make noticeable advances, both professionally and financially, during the 1980s. Many became prominent in local government and in the 1987 general election four black MPs were elected.

BRITAIN IN THE 1970S AND 1980S

Educational standards

In the autumn of 1976, James Callaghan as Prime Minister had given an important speech in which he expressed concern about the state of education in the country. After a decade of development of the comprehensive schools this had become a highly topical issue, with much comment directed at declining standards of work and discipline. The Prime Minister urged a review of teaching methods and the creation of a core curriculum of basic subjects. Much discussion followed to try to work through the Prime Minister's suggestions in a practical way.

Progress was slow. In any case, education at all levels soon became subject to financial cuts. These began under Labour in the late 1970s and continued under the Conservatives in the early 1980s. Relations between government and teachers were generally poor. Nevertheless the Callaghan initiative was not lost. There were attempts to make the education in schools more closely related to later work. A major education bill was promised after the 1987 election to allow for greater parental choice in schools and a core curriculum, first projected a decade earlier.

Prosperity

The government's opponents were strong in denouncing Britain in the 1980s as a divided society, between rich and poor, between employed and unemployed, between South and North. For many, however, the years of Mrs Thatcher's government had brought a new prosperity which they enjoyed and for which they were willing to give her government support by their votes. Council tenants had been allowed to buy instead of rent their houses. Many nationalised industries were sold to the public, a process known as **privatisation**. The general public could therefore buy shares in them. Many more people became share-holders and throughout the mid-1980s the value of shares on the London stock market rose impressively. By the second half of the 1980s inflation had ceased to be a major problem and there were signs of reduction in the high unemployment figures. Individual freedom and individual responsibility within the framework of a lawful and democratic society continued to be given emphasis.

EXERCISES

1. Examine the main features of each of the following in British life during the 1970s and 1980s:
   (a) Northern Ireland,
   (b) race relations,
   (c) education, and
   (d) economic prosperity.

2. (a) Why had the issue of trade unionism in Britain come to be one of much controversy by the time of the 1979 general election?
   (b) Describe the course of the miners' strike of 1984–85 and explain why it failed.
   (c) In what ways was trade union power curbed during the course of the 1980s?

3. Imagine you are a political journalist living and working in Britain during the 1980s. Write an article that might be published in a British newspaper at the time of the 1987 election explaining, with reference to the events of the 1980s, why you would encourage your readers either to support or oppose the Conservative government at that election.

4. Study the photographs on pages 256, 251 and 249 and then answer questions (a) to (d) which follow.
   (a) (i) What evidence does the photograph on page 256 contain of violence and disorder on the streets?
   (ii) What circumstances in the first half of the 1980s might have contributed to the causes of the events shown in the photograph? (2+4)
   (b) (i) What evidence does the photograph on page 251 contain of a sense of patriotism?
   (ii) By reference to the events of the Falklands crisis, indicate to what extent you feel this sense of patriotism was justified. (2+5)
   (c) In what respects was the role of the Prime Minister important in resolving the two issues referred to in (a) and (b)? To what extent is her portrayal in the photograph on page 249 a suitable one? (3)
   (d) Indicate what are the strengths and weaknesses of these three photographs in helping towards an understanding of British history during the 1980s. (4)

1919–1987: Chart of events

A heavy line marks a change of government. Note that the month given for the appointment of a government is not always the same as the month of the general election, as there has sometimes been a short lapse of time between the election and the government's appointment. Remember also that there can be a change of government without a general election having taken place.

Year	Appointment of governments and succession of monarchs	Domestic events	Empire and Commonwealth events	Foreign events
1919		Addison Housing Act Sankey Commission reports	Government of India Act, based on Montagu-Chelmsford reforms Amritsar massacre	Paris peace conference Treaty of Versailles Treaty of St Germain
1920		Unemployment Insurance Act Conflict of Black and Tans with IRA Government of Ireland Act	Satyagraha campaigns in India begin, early 1920s	
1921		'Black Friday' Anglo-Irish 'treaty'		
1922				Chanak incident
Oct.	Bonar Law, Conservative			
1923 May	Baldwin (first), Conservative			
1924 Jan.	Ramsay MacDonald (first), Labour	Wheatley Housing Act Campbell case Zinoviev letter		Geneva Protocol
Nov.	Baldwin (second), Conservative			
1925		Restoration of the gold standard 'Red Friday' Widows, Orphans and Old Age Contributory Pensions Act		Locarno treaties
1926		Samuel Commission reports General Strike	Balfour Definition (on dominion status)	
1927		Trade Disputes Act Revised Prayer Book rejected, 1927–28	Simon Commission on India, 1927–30	
1928		Equal Franchise Act Mond-Turner conversations		Kellogg-Briand pact
1929		Local Government Act		
June	Ramsay MacDonald (second), Labour			Wall Street Crash
1930		Coal Mines Act Housing Act		

1919–1987: CHART OF EVENTS

Year	Appointment of governments and succession of monarchs	Domestic events	Empire and Commonwealth events	Foreign events
1931		Agricultural Marketing Act May Committee reports		
Aug.	Ramsay MacDonald, National	Abandonment of the gold standard Means test 1931–34		Japanese invasion of Manchuria
1932		Import Duties Act British Union of Fascists formed		
1933		London Transport formed		Hitler becomes Chancellor of Germany
1934		Unemployment Act Special Areas Act		
1935				Stresa Front formed
June	Baldwin, National	Peace Ballot results announced	Government of India Act	Anglo-German Naval Treaty Italian invasion of Ethiopia Hoare-Laval plan
1936 Jan. Dec.	Accession of King Edward VIII Accession of King George VI	Jarrow Crusade Abdication controversy		German remilitarisation of Rhineland Spanish Civil War, 1936–39
1937 May	Neville Chamberlain, National		Report of Peel Commission on Palestine	
1938		Holidays with Pay Act		Anschluss of Austria with Germany Meetings at Berchtesgaden and Godesberg Summit conference at Munich
1939				British treaties with Poland, Romania and Greece *Second World War, 1939–45*: Phoney War, 1939–40
1940		Wartime rationing introduced		
May	Churchill, Coalition			**May–June:** Dunkirk evacuation **Summer:** Battle of Britain **Autumn–winter:** The Blitz
1941				**Aug:** Atlantic Charter **Dec:** Japanese attack on Pearl Harbor
1942		Beveridge Report published	Gandhi's Quit India campaign begins	**Feb:** Fall of Singapore **June:** Fall of Tobruk **July and Oct:** two battles of El Alamein
1943				**Jan:** Casablanca Conference **July:** Allied attack on Sicily **July–Aug:** Allied bombardment of Hamburg

A HISTORY OF BRITAIN FROM 1867

Year	Appointment of governments and succession of monarchs	Domestic events	Empire and Commonwealth events	Foreign events
1944		Butler Education Act		**June:** Second Front opened **Oct:** Churchill and Stalin define spheres of influence **Autumn–winter:** V1 and V2 attacks on England
1945				**Feb:** Allied bombardment of Dresden **Feb:** Yalta conference **May:** German surrender
July	Attlee, Labour	Loan from United States		**July:** Potsdam conference **Sept:** Japanese surrender
1946		Bank of England nationalised Coal mines nationalised National Insurance Act National Health Act New Towns Act		Fulton speech by Churchill
1947		Railways nationalised Austerity policies of Cripps, 1947–50	Independence of India and Pakistan	Dunkirk Treaty British aid to Greece and Turkey ends Truman Doctrine Marshall Plan
1948		National Assistance Act Criminal Justice Act Increased immigration from the West Indies begins	Independence of Ceylon and Burma British withdrawal from Palestine Suppression of Communism in Malaya, 1948–57	Coup in Czechoslovakia Brussels Treaty Berlin Blockade, 1948–49
1949		Parliament Act Devaluation of the pound Legal Aid and Advice Act		Formation of NATO
1950 Feb.	Attlee, Labour	Beginnings of affluence, early 1950s		Korean War, 1950–53
1951		Festival of Britain		
Oct.	Churchill, Conservative			
1952	Accession of Queen Elizabeth II			Britain experimentally detonates an atomic bomb for the first time
1953			Central African Federation formed	
1954			Suppression of Mau Mau in Kenya, mid-1950s	Formation of SEATO Geneva conference on Indo-china Formation of CENTO
1955 May	Eden, Conservative			
1956				Suez crisis

1919–1987: CHART OF EVENTS

Year	Appointment of governments and succession of monarchs	Domestic events	Empire and Commonwealth events	Foreign events
1957 Jan.	Macmillan, Conservative	Rent Act Homicide Act CND formed	Independence of Gold Coast (renamed Ghana)	Treaty of Rome establishes EEC
1958		Peerage Act		
1959 Oct.	Macmillan, Conservative		Devlin Commission on Nyasaland	
1960			'Wind of Change' speech by Macmillan Independence of Cyprus, and of Nigeria	Formation of EFTA
1961		National Economic Development Council formed	Independence of Sierra Leone, and Tanganyika (joined in 1963 with Zanzibar to form Tanzania) Relinquishment of British control in the Cameroons	Britain applies for EEC membership
1962		Commonwealth Immigration Act	Independence of Uganda, and in the West Indies of Jamaica, Trinidad and Tobago	
1963			Central African Federation disbanded Malaysia formed Independence of Kenya	First British application for EEC membership rejected
Oct.	Douglas-Home, Conservative			
1964 Oct.	Wilson, Labour		Independence of Northern Rhodesia (renamed Zambia), and of Nyasaland (renamed Malawi)	
1965		Murder (Abolition of Death Penalty) Act Race Relations Act Comprehensive education to be introduced throughout England and Wales National Plan	Independence of Gambia Unilateral Declaration of Independence in Rhodesia	
1966 Mar.	Wilson, Labour	Severe measures of deflation	Independence of Bechuanaland (renamed Botswana)	
1967		Devaluation of the pound Criminal Justice Act	Relinquishment of British control of Aden	Second British application for EEC membership rejected
1968		Widespread student demonstrations		
1969		Children and Young Persons Act British Army deployed in Northern Ireland		
1970		Conservative politicians meet at Selsdon		
June	Heath, Conservative			
1971		Industrial Relations Act Decimalisation of currency		
1972		Direct rule by Westminster in Northern Ireland		

A HISTORY OF BRITAIN FROM 1867

Year	Appointment of governments and succession of monarchs	Domestic events	Empire and Commonwealth events	Foreign events
1973		School leaving age raised to 16 Power sharing executive in Northern Ireland fails Miners' strike, 1973–74		Britain joins the EEC
1974 Feb. and Oct.	Wilson, Labour	*Social contract* between government and trade unions		
1975		Referendum on EEC membership Margaret Thatcher leader of the Conservative party		
1976 Mar.	Callaghan, Labour	Callaghan speech on education		
1977				
1978		'Winter of discontent', 1978–79		
1979 May	Thatcher, Conservative	Rejection in Scotland and Wales of devolution proposals		
1980			Independence of Zimbabwe	
1981		Formation of Social Democratic party Street riots in Brixton, Toxteth and elsewhere		
1982			**Falklands crisis**	
1983 June	Thatcher, Conservative	Kinnock leader of the Labour party		
1984		Trade Union Act Miners' strike, 1984–85		
1985		Further street riots		
1986				
1987 June	Thatcher, Conservative	Proposals to amalgamate Social Democratic and Liberal parties Proposed Education Bill		

GLOSSARY

affluence   Availability to an increasing number of people of improved living standards, essentially in such matters as incomes and housing.
Anglican   A member of the Church of England.
Anglo-Catholic   An Anglican who emphasises the Catholic nature of the Church of England.
anti-semitic   Dislike of or hostility towards Jews.
artisans   Members of the working classes who are involved in skilled work.
austerity   A government policy of severe economic restraint, typified by increased taxation and reduced government expenditure.
balance of payments   The difference between the value of a country's imports and the value of its exports.
balanced budget   A government budget in which the amount that the government receives in taxation equals the amount it is prepared to spend.
blacklegs   Those who are prepared to work during a strike, thus undermining the value the strike might have.
(The) Blitz   A shortened version of **blitzkrieg**, applied to the German aerial bombardment of British towns in 1940–41.
blitzkrieg   Translated literally from German it means *lightning war*. It refers to the swift and successful assaults made by the German army in the opening stages of the Second World War.
by-election   A constituency election held between general elections, after the death or sudden retirement of the previous MP.
collective bargaining   Discussion between trade unionists and employers so that collectively they can bargain to produce agreement on wages, hours or conditions of work.
collective security   The maintaining of international peace by means of collective discussions and collective action. The policy was much supported during the inter-war years.
collusion   The term usually applied to the secretive Anglo-French discussions with Israel in 1956 that created circumstances favourable for the joint invasion of Egypt.
commission of enquiry   An official body set up by the government to enquire into a particular problem and to make recommendations for government action on it.
conscription   Compulsory military or national service.
consensus politics   A political situation in which members of different parties are in general agreement on the issues they face.
constitution/constitutional   A reference to the ways in which the governing of a country is organised.
coup d'état   Translated literally from French it means a **blow of state**. It refers to a sudden and illegal change of government.
denominational teaching   The teaching of Christianity according to the doctrines and ideas of a particular Christian denomination.
depression   A decline in the country's economy. The term **Depression** alone is often applied to the British economy during the 1930s; the term **Great Depression** is often applied to the British economy in the late nineteenth century.
devaluation   The lowering of the value of a country's currency in relation to the currency of other countries, thus making exports cheaper.
devolution   The placing of certain powers of government under regional control.
disestablishment   The cutting of the historical and constitutional links between an established church and the state.
Evangelical   An Anglican who emphasises the Protestant nature of the Church of England.
federation   The grouping together of different regions, states or countries for the purpose of common government.
flat-rate contribution   A financial contribution that is identical for everyone making it. It has particular reference to the terms of the National Insurance Act of 1911.
franchise   The right to vote in elections. The term **suffrage** has an identical meaning.
free trade   The absence of protective tariffs on goods entering a country.
friendly society   A society which, in return for regular contributions, provides benefit in the event of sickness, injury or death. Such societies had a particular importance before the passage of the National Insurance Act in 1911.
habeas corpus   The right not to be imprisoned without a trial.
home rule   The internal government of a country under the overall control of another country. In this book the term refers particularly to Irish demands in the late nineteenth and early twentieth centuries.
hustings   The place where votes were made in public before the introduction of the secret ballot in 1872.
inflation   Increases in prices and wages. In such circumstances the value of a unit of money decreases, as it is unable to purchase as much as it previously did.
isolationism   A foreign policy on non-involvement with other states, either as enemies or as allies.

GLOSSARY

jingoism A strong expression of British patriotism and of determination to take action against foreign powers that have challenged British authority abroad.

laissez-faire A policy permitting trade to be carried on between countries without any restrictions or taxes.

left (wing) A political attitude that generally favours radical change. In practice the term often lacks a precise meaning, as it is applied to a wide range of different views.

Liberal Unionists Those Liberals who in the late nineteenth century wanted to maintain the union with Ireland and who split from their party when it first proposed home rule in 1886.

majority rule A constitutional system in which the government is elected by a majority of the adult population, regardless of colour or belief.

mandates Colonies of countries defeated in the First World War which, subject to the supervision of the League of Nations, were to be administered by countries victorious in the war, referred to in this connection as **mandatories**.

means test An examination of all incomes received within a family, in order to decide the correct amount of unemployment benefit allowed to the head of the family.

minority government A government whose continuance in power depends on the support in parliament of political parties other than its own.

monetarist An economic policy in which the finances of the country are managed in the same way as anyone might manage personal finances. In such a system, the country spends only what it receives; and it tries to avoid borrowing.

parliamentary government A government whose decisions are subject to approval by an elected parliament.

patronage The securing of a post of employment as a result purely of personal recommendation.

Peelite A follower of the Conservative Prime Minister Robert Peel, after the political crisis of 1846. Most Peelites had become absorbed into the Liberal party 20 years later.

picketing Persuasion asserted by strikers on fellow-workers in order to get them to co-operate in the strike action.

plural voting The right to cast more than one vote in an election.

proportional representation A system of election in which the number of elected politicians is directly linked to the number of votes cast for their party in the election.

protection The economic policy of placing tariffs on imports, in order to provide economic 'protection' for home-produced goods.

rationalisation Improved organisation of an industry. Usually rationalisation involves the amalgamation of different firms and can often result in loss of jobs.

reparations Payments of money after a war by a defeated power to a victorious power, in order to cover the cost of war damage.

right (wing) A political attitude which generally represents property and status, which is reluctant to introduce change and seeks to defend the country's traditions. In practice the term often lacks a precise meaning, as it is applied to a wide range of different views.

safeguarding Another term for **protection**. Use of this term had some popularity during the inter-war years, when the term *protection* was associated with the increased cost of goods.

sanctions (economic/military) Action, of either an economic or military kind, taken in an attempt to compel a country to change its policies.

satyagraha Passive resistance tactics employed by the followers of Gandhi in their campaigns against British rule in India.

scuttle Destruction of ships, undertaken in preference to allowing them to fall into the possession of the enemy.

Speaker The chairman who presides over the debates in the House of Commons.

staple industries Industries on which the main wealth of the country is based. In Britain, until the early twentieth century, they were coal mining, iron and steel, textiles and ship building.

suffrage The right to vote in an election. The term **franchise** has an identical meaning.

supra-national Concern with the overall interests of an international organisation, rather than with the interests of any one national group within it.

suzerainty The right to govern and administer a particular territory.

tariffs Taxes imposed on goods entering the country. The policy for imposing tariffs is referred to as **protection** or **safeguarding**.

temperance (society) A movement urging people to abstain from alcohol and urging governments to impose stricter controls on alcohol consumption.

Tory Democracy A term applied by some historians to the social legislation of the Conservative party in the late nineteenth century.

Uitlanders Translated literally from Afrikaans it means *outsiders*. It refers to the British who were attracted to settle in the Boer republics during the 1890s in the hope of successfully mining gold.

veto Power given to a country or organisation to prevent, in certain circumstances, action to which others have agreed.

white paper An official statement of government policy, subsequently to be debated in parliament.

INDEX

Pages shown in italic type refer to a map or illustration.

abdication (of Edward VIII), 165–6.
Addison, Christopher, 134–5, 141; Housing Act of, 134–5. **Aden,** 243.
Adullamites, 12–3. **adulteration** (of food), 27. **aerial warfare,** fear of, 174, 176, 180–1; in Second World War, *181, 182–3, 183,* 191–2. **affluence,** 202–4, 205, 206, *207,* 208, 209, 214.
Afghanistan, 23, and Anglo-Russian convention, 114; and campaigns (1878–79), 29, *30,* (1879–80), 29, 58–9; and Pendjeh incident, 62. **Africa,** early settlement in, 80, 216; emigration to, 202; and Germany, 112; independence in, 223, 227–32, *227;* national feeling in, 227; stability of British rule in, 202; and trade, 80. **Agadir crisis,** 115–6, *118.* **agnostics,** 70. **agriculture,** 7, 141, 149, 152; labourers in, 49–50; ...al Marketing Act, 152. **Air Raid Precaution wardens,** 181.
Alabama settlement, 23, 24. **Albania,** 117, *118.* **alcohol** (*see also* drink), abuse of, 256; expenditure on, 203; tax on, 104.
Alexandria, bombardment of, 59, *60, 61.* **Algeçiras conference,** 113, *113,* 114. **Algeria,** 81, 185, 186. **Allenby, General,** 128. **Alliance, Liberal and Social Democratic,** 252–3. **allotments and small holdings,** 64, 65, 187.
Alsace-Lorraine, 168, *168.*
Amalgamated Society of Carpenters and Joiners, 47, 48; of Engineers, 47; of Railway Servants, 50, 54. **America,** *see* United States. **Amery, Leopold,** 217, *217.* **Amritsar massacre,** 218–9, 220, *221.* **Anderson shelters,** 183, *183.*
Anglo-Catholic (members of the Church of England), 67, 68, 77, 150. **Anglo-French entente,** *see* Entente Cordiale. **Anglo-German agreement** (at Munich), 177. **Anglo-German Naval Treaty,** 173. **Anglo-Japanese alliance,** 112. **Anglo-Russian convention,** 113–4.
Anschluss, 174–5, 175. **Anzio,** *185,* 189. **appeasement,** 173–9; and Anschluss, 174; and Chamberlain, 174, *176, 177;* and Conservative party, 193; discussion of, 179; idea of, 173; and Suez crisis, 240. **Applegarth, William,** 48.
Arab-Israeli War, 225. **Arabi Pasha,** 59. **Arabs,** 169, 212, 223–5. **Arch, Joseph,** 50. **Archbishop of Canterbury,** 68, *68,* 166, 188. **Arcos Raid,** 150, 171. **Ardennes,** *189,* 191. **area bombing,** 191–2. **Argentina,** 7, 250–2, *250.* **Army,** British, 19, 21–2, *22,* 96; and Campbell case and Zinoviev letter, 142–3; at Chanak, 138; and 'Curragh mutiny', 111; and First World War, 120–9; and Rhodesia, 231; and Second World War, 180–6, 189–92. **Arnhem,** *189,* 191. **artisans,** 11, 13, 47, 77; ... Dwellings Act, 27, 64. **Ashanti,** 90–1. **Ashbourne Land Act,** 40. **Asquith, H.H.,** as Chancellor of the Exchequer, 102; and Parliament Act, 105–6; as Prime Minister, 102–11, 123–4; retirement of, 151; and suffragettes, 108–9; and Third Home Rule

Bill, 111; and wartime Coalition, 123–4, 140. **atheists,** 70. **Atlantic,** battle of the, 190–1; ... Charter, 184. **atomic bombs,** and Britain, 192, 236, 237–8; use of, 192, 237. **Attlee, Clement,** and Europe, 243; and moderation in foreign affairs, 200; and National Health Service, 198; becomes party leader, 164; personality of, 194; as Prime Minister, 193–200, *194;* retirement of, 205.
austerity, 194–5, *195,* 202, 208.
Australia, as a dominion, 216; emigration to, 7, 50; and First World War, *119,* 122, 217; government system of, 12; and Great Dock Strike, 51; relationship to Britain, 80; as trade competitor, 7; and Versailles, Treaty of, 168. **Austria,** 168, 169, 174, *175,* 244. **Austria-Hungary,** *118;* and Balkans (before 1914), 116–9; collapse of, 129, 169; and Eastern Question, 31, 33; and Germany, 113, 117, 118; and Paris peace settlement, *168,* 169; and Serbia, 117–9. **automation techniques,** 157.
Axis powers, 184.

balance of payments, 208. **Baldwin, Stanley,** *139;* and abdication of Edward VIII, 165–6; background and attitudes, 139; and Carlton Club meeting, 138; and 1929 general election, 150, *151;* and General Strike, 146–7; and hunger marches, 159; and India, 220; and National government formation, 153, 155; becomes Prime Minister (1923), 139, (1935), 165; as Prime Minister (1923–24), 139, (1924–29), 143, 144–50, (1935–37), 164–6. **Balfour, Arthur,** background and attitudes, 97; dominion status, Definition of, 217; and Education Act (1902), 98; and Ireland, 42–3, 97; opposition to, 69, 98–9; Palestine, Declaration on, 169, 217, 223–4; as Prime Minister, 62, 95, 97–100; and tariff reform, 98–101, *100.* **Balkans,** and conflict (during 1870s), 31–4, 72, (before 1914), 116–9; ... League, 117; and Russia, 23, 31; and Second World War, 189; ... Wars, 117. **Ballot Act,** 14, 19–20, *20,* 24, 37.
Banda, Hastings, 229. **Bank of England,** 145, 153, 154, 196.
Barbados, 228. **Baring, Sir Evelyn,** *see* Cromer, Lord. **Barnardo, Dr,** homes of, 77. **Basutoland,** 91, 95. **Battle of Britain,** 182. **BBC,** 196.
Beaconsfield, Lord, *see* Disraeli, Benjamin. **Beale, Miss Dorothea,** 75. **Bechuanaland,** 81, *91,* 230. **Beckton gas workers strike,** 50. **Beeching Report,** 203–4. **Belfast,** 137, *137.* **Belgium,** *118;* and Africa, 80, 81, *81;* and EEC, 243; and First World War, 118, 120; and frontier adjustments, 168, *168,* 171; neutrality of, 22–3, 118; and Second World War, 181, 191. **Bengal,** partition of, 88, 218. **Berchtesgaden,** meeting at, 175–6, *175.* **Berlin,** *118;* Blockade of, 235; Conference of (1884–85), 88; Congress and Treaty of (1878), 33–4, *33,* 62. **Besant, Annie,** 50. **Bevan, Aneurin,** 200, 205. **Beveridge, Sir William,** 187; report of, 187–8, 193, 197. **Bevin, Ernest,** as Foreign Secretary, *194,* 199, 233–5; and Palestine, 225; as trade union leader, 148. **Bible, The,** 12, 18, 70, 93. **bicycle,** 74–5, *74,* 163. **Biltmore Hotel,**

conference at, 224. **Birmingham,** 26, 99, 178. **Black Friday,** 145. **Black Sea clauses,** 23. **Black and Tans,** 136. **Black Week,** 94–5. **black-out,** 181. **Blackpool,** Conservative Conference at, 210. **blacks** (*see also* immigration, Race Relations Act), in Britain, 256; in South Africa, 30, 95. **Blitz, the,** *181,* 182–3, 186. **blitzkrieg** (warfare), 181, 182. **blockade** (of Germany), 126, 181.
Blunden, Edmund, 127. **board schools,** 18–9, 97–8. **Boer War,** First (1881), 30, 59, *91,* 94; Boer War, Second (1899–1902), *91;* causes of, 59, 91–3; course of, 93–4, *93, 94;* effects of, in Britain, 72, 96, 99, 101, 112; and Germany, 112; importance of, 95–6, 216. **Boers,** 30, 59; and Second Boer War, 92–6, *93, 94.* **Boilermaker's Society,** 47.
Bonar Law, Andrew, and Lloyd George, 134; as Prime Minister, 138–9; and Ulster, 110. **Bondfield, Margaret,** 151.
boom, 156, (after 1918), 135, 156, 157.
Booth, Charles, 78–9, 102. **Booth, 'General' William,** 77. **Borneo, North,** 81, *82,* 225. **borough representation** (in parliament), 10, 13–4, 58.
borrowing (by government, *see also* debts, wartime), 151. **borstal training centres,** 102. **Bosnia,** 31, *32,* 116, 117, *118.* **Botswana,** 230. **boycotting** (in Ireland), 38. **Bradford,** 47.
Bradlaugh, Charles, 70. **bribery,** 19, 58. **British Expeditionary Forces,** in First World War, 96, 116, 120, 122; in Second World War, 181. **British and Foreign Society,** 17. *British Gazette, The,* 147. **British North America Act,** 216. **British South Africa Company,** 82–3, 92, 229. **British Union of Fascists,** 163–4, *163. British Worker, The,* 147. **Brixton,** riots in, 255–5, *256.* **Brown, George,** 211. **Bruce, H. A.,** 24. **Brussels,** *122;* European Cup Final tragedy at, 256; Treaty of, 243. **building industry,** 162, 201, 204; ... societies, 162. **Bulgaria,** 31–4, *32, 33,* 117, *118,* 129, *168,* 233. **Buller, Sir Redvers,** 93. **Burma,** 81, *82,* 185, *221,* 223. **Burns, John,** 51, *51.* **Buss, Miss Frances,** 75. **Butler, R. A.,** and Central African Federation, 230; as Chancellor of the Exchequer, 202, 204, 205, 206; and Education Act (1944), 188, 213. **Butlin's holiday camps,** 163. **Butt, Isaac,** 37.

Calcutta riots, 222. **Callaghan, James,** as Chancellor of the Exchequer, 212, 248; as Prime Minister, 248–9, 257.
Cambrai, battle at, *122,* 127.
Cambridge, Duke of, 21; university of, 20, 21, 24, 75, 152. **Cameroons,** *81,* 89, *168,* 230. **Campaign for Nuclear Disarmament,** 209, 237. **Campbell case,** 142. **Campbell-Bannerman,** Sir Henry, 100–1. **Canada,** as a dominion, 216; emigration to, 7, 50; and First World War, *119,* 127, 217; and NATO, 235; and Ottawa conference, 160; relationship with Britain, 37, 80; trade competition with, 7. **Cape Colony,** 80, *91, 91, 92, 93.* **capital punishment,** 198, 213–4.
capitalist system, 52. **Cardwell, Edward,** 21–2, *22.* **Caribbean, the** (*see also* West Indies), 90. **Carlton Club**

meeting, 138. **cars,** *see* motor cars.
Carson, Sir Edward, 109–11.
Casablanca conference, *185,* 186.
cash and carry, 184. **'Cat and Mouse' Act,** 109. **Catholic Church,** *see* Roman Catholic Church. **Cavendish, Lord Frederick,** 99. **CBI,** *see* Confederation of British Industry. **Cecil family,** 62.
censorship, 124, 149. **census,** 8.
CENTO, *see* Central Treaty Organisation. **Central African Federation,** 228–30. **Central Electricity Board,** 161. **Central Treaty Organisation,** 238. **Cetewayo,** 31. **Ceylon,** 223. **Chamberlain, Austen,** 143, 171. **Chamberlain, Joseph,** and Boer War, 92–3; and Caribbean, 90; and Churchill, Lord Randolph, 63; as Colonial Secretary, 64, 89, 90–1, 98, 99; and epidemics, 90; and German alliance (proposed), 112; and home rule, *40,* 41; and imperial preference, 91; and Jameson Raid, 92; as Mayor of Birmingham, 26, 149; and ministry of 1880–85, 57–8; and tariff reform, 98–100; and West Africa, 90–1. **Chamberlain, Neville,** abandons appeasement, 178; and appeasement, 173–8, *176, 177;* becomes Prime Minister, 166; as Chancellor of the Exchequer, 174; as Minister of Health, 143, 149, 174; resignation of, 179, 181.
Chanak incident, 138. **chancellor of the exchequer,** importance of office, 208. **chartered companies,** 82–3.
cheap money, 161. **Cheltenham Ladies College,** 75. **chemical industry,** 7. **children and young persons,** 101–2, 149, 180, 201–2, 214; —— Act, 214. **Children's Act/Charter,** 102. **China,** 80, *82,* 112, 171–2.
Chinese immigration (in South Africa), 95, 98. **Christianity** (*see also* references to individual churches), 15, 70, 85–6.
church building, 67. **Church of England,** and abdication of Edward VIII, 166; and ancient universities, 21; and Education Act (1870), 17–19, (1902), 98; and Gladstone, 15; and Nonconformist Churches, 69; and Prayer Book controversy, 150, *150;* and ritualism, 67–8, *67;* and Tory/Conservative party, 16, 69; and trade unions, 50. **Church of Ireland,** 36. **Church of Scotland,** 69.
Church of Wales, 65, 69. **Churchill, Lord Randolph,** 63, *63.* **Churchill, Winston,** 43; and Baldwin, 220; becomes Prime Minister (1940), 181–2; and Beveridge Report, 188; as Chancellor of the Exchequer, 143, 149; and cold war, 234–7; and Dardanelles campaign, 122–3; and Edward VIII, 166; and El Alamein, 186; and Europe, 243; as First Lord of the Admiralty, 115, 122, 181; and general election (1945), 193; and General Strike, 146–7; and gold standard, 145; and India, 220; joins Liberal party, 100; and Munich settlement, 177–8; as President of the Board of Trade, 103, 107; as Prime Minister (1951–55), 200–4 (*see also* as war leader); retirement of, 205; as war leader, 181–92, *181,* 193, 194, 233, and warlike temperament, 181–2, 200; and US involvement in Second World War, 183–4, 186. **cinemas,** 72, 163. **Civil Rights Association,** Northern Ireland, 254.

civil servants, 148; —— service, 19, 20–1, 24. **class distinctions,** 193, 202.
Clause Four (of Labour party constitution), 209. **Clemenceau, Georges,** 167–9. **closed shop,** 246.
Clydesiders, 140, 141, 151. **CND,** *see* Campaign for Nuclear Disarmament.
Coal Mines Act, 152. **coal mining industry,** conditions of workers in, 144; developments in (after 1918), 135; exports of, 145; importance of, 5, 157; nationalisation of, 196. **Coalition government,** of Asquith, 123–4, 140; of Churchill, 181, 181–8; of Lloyd George (1916–18), 124, 126, 127, 129, 140, (1918–22), 134–8; called National government, 153–5, 160–1. **Coercion Acts** (in Ireland), 39, 42. **cold war,** 226, 235–7.
collective bargaining, 49; —— security, 170–1. **Collins, Michael,** 136, 137.
collusion (in Suez crisis), 240–2.
Colonial Development Acts, 227.
Commander-in-Chief (of Army), 22.
commerce (*see also* trade), 17, 23.
commissions, purchase of, 21–2.
Common Market, *see* European Economic Community. **Common Wealth party,** 188. **Commons, House of,** and Bradlaugh, 70; free vote in, 213; functions of, 9–10; illustrations of interior, *44, 141.* **Commonwealth, British** (*see also* dominions, and references to individual Commonwealth countries), —— of Australia Act, 214; and EEC, 243–5; —— Immigration Act, 214; immigration from, 214; nature of, 216; trade within, *217,* 218; in twentieth century, 216–32. **Communist party,** British, 150, 164; influence of, 159; and Zinoviev letter, 142.
comprehensive education, 213, 257.
computer technology, 248.
concentration camps (in Boer War), 94. **Confederation of British Industry,** 211. **Congested Districts Board,** 43. **Congo, the,** 88, 89, 115.
Congregationalists (Church of), 69.
Congress, Indian National, 88, 221–3.
conscientious objectors, 124.
conscription, in First World War, 124, *124,* 125; in Second World War, 187, 193. **consensus,** 197, 198, 200, 202, 205. **Conservative party,** and Asquith Coalition, 123–4; Baldwin as leader of, 139; and British Empire, 216, 229; and Carlton Club meeting, 138; and Church of England, 69; and death duty, 66; and Disraeli, 25–6; and EEC membership, 244; and first Labour government, 141; and Fourth party, 63; and general election (1929), 150, (1945), 193–4; and House of Lords, 104–6; and Ireland, 38–46; and League of Nations, 170; and Lloyd George Coalition (1916–18), 124–5, (1918–22), 134–8; and National government, 153–5, 164–5; and new image (1950s), 202; and newspapers, 71; and poverty, 79; and Russian Civil War, 170; and Second Reform Act, 11–4; and succession to Macmillan, 210; and Suez crisis, 244; and suffragettes, 108–9; and tariff reform, 98–101; and Ulster, 108, 109–11; and Versailles, Treaty of, 169; and working classes, 52. **Conspiracy and Protection of Property Act,** 28, 48, 54.
Constantinople, 31, 32, *32, 33, 128.*

consumer expenditure, 203.
contracting in, 148. **contributory/non-contributory** (basis for pensions and insurance), 102, 107. **convoy system,** 126, 190. **Cook, Arthur,** 146. **Co-operative Movement,** 49. **Corrupt and Illegal Practices Act,** 14, 58. **cotton industry,** 87. **Council of Europe,** 243. **council houses,** 135. **county representation** (in parliament), 10, 13–4, 58. **Coupon Election,** 134, *134,* 136.
Cowper-Temple clause (of Education Act, 1902), 18. **Craig, Captain James,** 110, *110,* 137. **Crimean War,** 21, 23.
crime, 17, 213–14. **Criminal Justice Act** (1948), 198, (1967), 214. **Criminal Law Amendment Act,** 24, 48. **Cripps, Stafford,** 195, *195,* 199. **crisis of 1931,** 144, 152–5, 164. **Cromer, Lord,** 60, 84–5, 238 **Cross, Richard,** 26–7, 48.
crown colonies, 82. **Crystal Palace,** *5,* 25; —— speech (of Disraeli), 25–6. **Cuba,** missiles crisis of, 243. **Cumberland,** 161. **Cup Final, European,** tragedy at, 256. **Curragh 'mutiny',** 111. **Curzon, Lord,** 88, 139. **Cyprus,** 33, *33,* 207, 226. **Czechoslovakia,** and Britain, 175; and Communist coup, 235; German invasion of, 178; and international problems, 174–5; *175;* and Locarno treaties, 171; and Paris peace conference, *168,* 169, 174.

Dail, the, 136. *Daily Herald,* 53; —— *Mail,* 71; —— *Mirror,* 71, 200; —— *News,* 71; —— *Telegraph,* 71. **Daladier,** 176.
Dalton, Hugh, 195. **Dandi,** Gandhi's demonstration at, 219. **Danzig,** 168, *168,* 178–9. **Dardanelles,** 31, 122–3, *128.* **Darwin, Charles,** 69–70.
Davison, Emily, 109. **Davitt, Michael,** 37. **Dawes plan,** 145, 171. **death duty,** 66. **debts,** wartime, 171, 194.
decimalised currency, 248. **Defence of the Realm Act,** 124. **Definition of Time Act,** 73. **deflation,** 212.
Delcassé, 113. **Denmark,** *118,* 168, *168,* 181, 244, 245. **depressed areas,** *see* special areas. **Depression,** and foreign policy, 172, 174; Great ——, 6–7, 34, 43, 53; of inter-war years, 135, 138, 139, 156–61, 206, 208; and miners' strike (1921), 144.
de-rating, 149. **Derby, Lord,** 12–4; First World War scheme of, 124.
Descent of Man, The, 69–70.
devaluation (of pound, 1949), 195, 204, 206, (1967), 212. **Devlin commission,** 229. **devolution,** proposals for, 45, 98, 254. **Dickens, Charles,** 78. **Dien Bien Phu,** battle of, 236. **Dieppe,** attack on, *189,* 190. **diphtheria,** 202.
direct rule (in Northern Ireland), 255.
disarmament (*see also* multilateral ——, unilateral ——), 171, 238. **disease,** 26–7. **disestablishment,** of Church of Ireland, 36, 69; of Church of Scotland (proposed), 65; of Church of Wales, 65, 69; Nonconformist goal for Church of England 69. **Disraeli, Benjamin,** 15; and Afghanistan, 58; background and attitudes, 25, 63; and Conservative party, 25–6, 97; and Eastern Question, 31–4; and Ireland, 42; as Prime Minister (1874–80), 25–35, *28;* and ritualism, 68; and Second Reform Act, 12–4, *13;* and Suez Canal, 28;

and trade unions, 48; as writer, 78.
district officers (in colonies), 86.
divorce, 42, 76, 166. **Dock Strike, Great,** 50–2, *51.* **dockers,** 51–2, 54–5, 135. **doctors,** 75, 198. **dole, the** 135, 153, 158–9. **domestic service,** 75, 125. **dominions, the** (*see also* Commonwealth, British), and African independence, 229; emigration to, 158; and First World War, 122, 127; and imperial preference, 91; and Munich settlement, 177; nature of, 80, 216–7; and Second World War, 190; South Africa as a, 95, 231; and trade, 160; and Versailles, Treaty of, 168–9. **DORA,** *see* Defence of the Realm Act. **Douglas-Home, Sir Alec,** leader of the Conservative party and Prime Minister, 210; and Rhodesia, 231, 232. **Dowding, Air-Marshal,** 182. **dreadnought battleships,** 104, 114–5, *115.* **Dresden,** bombardment of, *189, 192.* **drink,** and music halls, 71; problem of, 24, 77–8, *78,* 98. **dual mandate,** 85. **Dublin,** 36, 39, 136, *137.* **Dulles, Foster,** 239–40. **Dunkirk, Treaty of,** 243; withdrawal from, 182. **dyarchy,** 218. **Dyer, General,** 218–9, 220.

East African Federation, 228–9. **east of Suez,** 243. **Easter Rising,** 136. **Eastern Question,** 31–4, *32. Echo, The,* 71. *Economic Consequences of the Peace, The,* 169. **Eden, Anthony,** and Chamberlain, 174; as Foreign Secretary, 202, 236–7; and Indochina, 236–7; as Prime Minister, 205–6, 239–42; and Suez crisis, 239–42. **education,** and comprehensive schools, 213; and CSE and GCE examinations, 213; lack of, among prospective voters, 11; and raising of school-leaving age, 141 188; and standards in schools, 213, 257; steps towards being compulsory, 19, 28, 57; towards being free, 19, 28, 64, 188; and universities and higher education, 213. **Education Act** (1870), 17, 19, 71, 75, (1876), 28, (1902), 97–8, (1918), 125, 138, (1944), 188, 213. **Edward VII,** 97, 105, 106. **Edward VIII,** 165–6. **EEC,** *see* European Economic Community. **EFTA,** *see* European Free Trade Association. **Egypt,** and Anglo-Egyptian Treaty, 238; British control of, 28, *30,* 81, *81;* Cromer's administration in, 60, 84; and Entente Cordiale, 113; and German threat, 88; and Gladstone, 57, 59–60; and purchase of shares in Suez Canal Company, 28; and Second World War, 185–6, *185;* and Suez crisis, 238–42. **Eighth Army,** 185–6. **Eisenhower, General,** 191. **El Alamein,** 185–6, *185,* 187. **electricity,** 7, 157; and economic revival (1930s), 161–2; motive power for underground, 74; nationalisation of, 196. **elementary schools,** 17, 19, 188. **Eleven Plus examination,** 188, 213. **Elgar,** 216. **Elizabeth, Queen,** Consort of George VI, 166. **Elizabeth II, Queen,** 166, *203.* **Emergency Powers (Defence) Act,** 181. **emigration from Britain,** 7, 77, 158, 202, 229. **Empire, British,** and British citizenship, 214; and British Commonwealth, 216–8; and British greatness, 80, 216; and Chamberlain, Joseph, 90–1; development (to 1914), 80–

96; and Disraeli, 26; and First World War, *119;* and imperial preference, 99; and Ireland, 41; and other European powers, 88–90, *89, 112;* and Splendid Isolation, 112; and Versailles, Treaty of, 168–9. **Employers and Workmen Act,** 28, 48. *Endurance, HMS,* 251. **Enosis,** 226. **Entente Cordiale,** 113, *113,* 114, 116. **entertainment,** 71–2, 149, 163. **environment,** concern for, 188, 201. **Eoka,** 226. **epidemics,** 90, 91. **Equal Franchise Act,** 14, 149. **Estonia** (*see also* Baltic states), *189.* **Ethiopia,** *81,* 165, 172, 173, 174. **ethnic minorities** (in Britain), 256. **European Community,** *see* European Economic Community. **European Defence Community,** 243. **European Economic Community,** 212, 246, 248; British entry into, 242–5, *244, 245;* and Falklands, 251. **European Free Trade Association,** 244. **evacuation** (in wartime), 176, 180–1, *180,* 183, 187, 188. **Evangelical** (members of the Church of England), 61, 68, 75, 149, 150. **evolution,** theory of, 69–70. **examinations,** civil service, 21; CSE and GCE, 213; School Certificate, 213. **exclusion zone,** Falklands, 251. **exports,** and Conservative governments (1951–64), 204; and gold standard, 145, 154; importance of, 5, 7; inter-war slump in, 156–7; and Labour governments (1945–51), 195–200, (1964–70), 212. **extermination camps,** Nazi, 192.

Fabian Society, 52, 53. **factories,** work in, 75. **Factory Acts** (1874, 1878), 27. **Falklands, the,** 250–2, *250, 251.* **family allowances,** 188. **Far East,** cold war in, 235–7; Second World War in, 184–5, 192. **Farouk, King,** 238–9. **fascism** (in Britain), 163–4, *163.* **Fashoda,** incident at, *61,* 90, *89.* *Fearless* **negotiations** (on Rhodesia), 231. **federations** (within the Commonwealth), 228–30. **Festival of Britain,** 200–1, *201.* **Fighter Command,** 182. **Finland,** 181. **Fisher Education Act** (1918), 125, 138. **flogging,** 22, 198. **food,** 27, 125, 186–7. **Foot, Michael,** 252, 253. **football matches,** violence at, 256. **Forster Education Act** (1870), 17–9, *18.* **Fourteen Points,** 167. **Fourth party,** 63, 70. **France,** *118;* and Africa, 80, *81,* 88, 89–90, *89,* and Agadir crisis, 115–6; and Algeria, 239; and Arabi Pasha rebellion, 59–60; and British entry into EEC, 243–5; and Czechoslovakia, 175–7; and Entente Cordiale, 113; fall of (1940), 181–2; and First World War, 118, 120–2, 126–7, 128–9; and Franco-Prussian War, 22–3; and Indochina, 236–7; and Munich summit meeting, 176–7; relations with (during inter-war years), 171; and Rhineland, 173; and Ruhr occupation, 145; and Second World War, 181, 190–1; and security, 167, 171; and Spanish Civil War, 173; and Stresa Front, 173; and Suez Canal, 28, ... crisis, 239–42; system of government in, 10; trade competition with, 6. **franchise,** 10–4, 58, 125, 149. **Franco-Prussian War,** 21, 22–3. **Franz Ferdinand,** 117. **free trade,** 5–7, *6,* 15; abandoned, 160, *162;* and British Empire,

160; and Labour party, 141; questioned, 91, 99; and tariff reform, 99–100, *100.* **free vote** (in parliament), 213. **Frere, Sir Bartle,** 31. **Fulton speech** (of Churchill), 234.

Gaelic League, 46, 110. **Gaitskell, Hugh,** 199, 200, 209. **Gallipoli peninsula,** 122–3, *128,* 217. **Galtieri, General,** 250–1. **Gambia,** 81, *81,* 230. **Gandhi, Mahatma,** 219–23, *219.* **gas,** nationalisation of, 196; warfare with, 122, 181. **Gaskell, Elizabeth,** 78. **Gaulle, President de,** 244–5. **Geddes Axe,** 138. *General Belgrano,* 251. **General Council** (of TUC), 145–7, 148. **general election** (1868), 16–7, 19, 25; (1874), 23–4, 25, 26; (1880), 31, 34–5, 38, 57; (1885), 40, (1886), 42; (1892), 43, 64; (1895), 45, 65; (1900), 94, 97, (1906), 46, 53, 95, 97, 101; (January 1910), 105, 109; (December 1910), 106, 109; (1918), 134, 140; (1922), 239, 140; (1923), 139; (1924), 139, 143; (1929), 150–1, *151;* (1931), 155, *157,* 165; (1935), 164–5, 194; (1945), 193–4, 202; (1950), 199; (1951), 200; (1955), 202, 205; (1959), 205, 206, 207, *207,* 209; (1964), 210–1, *212;* (1966), 211; (1970), 245, 246; (two in 1974), 247; (1979), 248, 249, 254; (1983), 249, 252–3; (1987), 249, 252–3, 256; ___s and economic issues, 210; every five years, 106; not an accurate reflection of party support, 165, 252–3. **General Strike** (1926), 143, causes of, 136, 144–6, events of, 146–7, *146,* importance of, 148, 254–5; idea of a, 55; projected (1921), 135, 136. **Geneva,** Conference on Indochina, 205, 237; ___ Protocol, 170; summit conference at, 242. **George V,** and choice of Baldwin as Prime Minister, 139; and General Strike, 165; and India, 86; and Labour party, 165; and National government, 153, 165; and Parliament Act, 106, 165; Silver Jubilee and death, 165. **George VI,** 166, *194.* **Germany,** *118;* aerial bombardment, of, 174, *175;* and Africa, 80, 88, *89,* 92, 93, 112; and appeasement, 174, *175;* and coal industry, 145; and divisions of (1945), 233; and Entente Cordiale, 113; and First World War, 120–2, 125–9; and Fourteen Points, 129; and Locarno treaties, 171; and Munich summit meeting, 176–7; and its navy, 114, 169; and Paris peace settlement, 167–9, *168;* and rearmament (1930s), 173; relations with Britain (before 1914), *112, 113,* 114–9, (before 1939), 173–9; and Ruhr occupation, 145; and Second World War, 180–93; and Socialism, 52; and South Africa, 92, 93; and Spanish Civil War, 173; trade competition with, 6, 112; and world role, 112, 114. **Ghana,** 227–8. **Gladstone, William Ewart,** and Afghanistan, 58–9; background, attitudes and personality, 15–6; and Eastern Question, 31–4; and Egypt, 59–60; and First Boer War, 59; and imperialism, 60; and Ireland, 17, 36–41; *39, 40,* 43–4; and Liberal party, 16; and Midlothian campaigns, 34, *34;* opponents of, 16; as Prime Minister (1868–74), 16–24, (1880–85), 57–62, (1886), 40–1, *44,* 62, (1892–94), 64, 65; retirement of, 64; and Roman Catholicism, 68; and Second Reform Act,

11–2; and the Sudan, 60–2, *62;* and Suez Canal, 28; and trade unions, 48, 52. **Glasgow,** 140. **Gloucestershire regiment,** 236. **Glubb, General,** 239. **Godesberg,** meeting at, *175,* 176. **Gold Coast,** *81;* and Ashanti, 90–1; British settlement in, 81; development of, 90–1; independence of, 227–8. **gold standard,** 145, 154, 157, 160. **Gordon, General,** 61–2, *62.* **Government of India Act** (1919), 218, (1935), 220–1. **Government of Ireland Act,** 137, *137.* **grammar schools,** 188. **Great** Depression, *see* Depression; ‑‑‑ Exhibition, 25, 200; ‑‑‑ War (*see also* First World War), 167. **Greece,** *33,* 117, *118,* 178, 195, 226, 233, 234. **green belt,** 201. **Grey, Sir Edward,** 115, 117. **Griffith, Arthur,** 46, 137. **Grivas, George,** 226. **groundnuts scheme,** 199, 227. **Gurion, David Ben,** 224, 240.

habeas corpus, 39. **Haganah,** 224–5. **Haig, Sir Douglas,** 126–7. **Haldane, J.R.,** later Viscount, 96, 101, 115, 120. **Halifax, Lord,** earlier Lord Irwin (*see also*), 174. **Hamburg,** bombardment of, *189,* 192. **Harcourt, Sir William,** 66. **Hardie, Keir,** 53, *53.* **Harmsworth, Alfred,** 71. **Harris, Sir Arthur ('Bomber'),** 192. **Hartington, Lord,** 41. **Hawarden,** 15. **health** (*see also* poverty), and Beveridge Report, 187, 188; and Local Government Act (1929), 149; Ministry of, 134; and National Health Service, 198; and National Insurance, 107, 197; and Public Health Act, 26; standards of, 201–2. **Heath, Edward,** becomes leader of Conservative party, 211; and EEC membership, 244–5, *245;* as Prime Minister, 246–7, 255. **Heathcote Amory, Derick,** 207–8. **Heligoland,** 88–9. **Henderson, Arthur,** 123, 141. **Hicks, Colonel,** 60. **high church** (members of the Church of England), 15, 21, *67,* 68, 220. **higher education,** 213. **Highlands, Scottish,** 8, 73. **Hindu religion,** 220, 223. **hire purchase,** 203, 204, 206, 212. **Hiroshima** (*see also* atomic bombs, use of), 237. **Hitler,** 164, 224, 240. **Hoare, Sir Samuel,** 172–3. **holidays,** 163; ‑‑‑ with Pay Act, 163. **Home, Lord,** *see* Douglas-Home, Sir Alec. **home rule,** Irish, 36–46, 98, 100, 109–11; ‑‑‑ Bill, first (1886), 40–1, *40,* second (1893), 43–4, third (1912), 109–11, *110,* 137; issue of (after 1918), 136–7; and Newcastle Programme, 65; and Parliament Act, 106; ‑‑‑ party, *see* Irish Nationalist party; and Ulster, 109–11. **Homicide Act,** 213. **honours,** sale of, 138. **hooliganism,** 255–6. **Hornby versus Close,** 47, 48. **hospitals,** 198. **House of Comons,** *see* Commons, House of; ‑‑‑ of Lords, *see* Lords, House of. **housing,** and electricity, 161; legislation concerning, 27, *27,* 64, 134–5, 141, 152, 201, 204, 257; private ‑‑‑, 162, 163, 257; standards of, 27, 64, 134–5, 152, 201, 256. **Huggins, Godfrey,** 229. **Hungary,** *168,* 169, 176–7, 233, 242. **hunger marches** (*see also* Jarrow Crusade), 159–60. **Hurricanes** (fighter aircraft), 182. **Husain of Mecca, Sharif,** 223. **hustings,** 19. **Hyde Park riots,** 13. **hydrogen bomb,** 237. **Hyndman, H.M.,** 52.

Imjin River, battle of, 236. **immigration,** 214–5. **Imperial British East Africa Company,** 82. **Imperial Chemical Industries,** 148, 162. **imperial preference,** 91, 99. **imperialism** (*see also* Empire, British; Commonwealth, British; dominions), development (to 1914), 80–96. **imperialist,** Cromer as an, 84; Curzon as an, 88; Lugard as an, 84; Milner as an, 92; Rhodes as an, 83; Rosebery as an, 65. **imports,** 7; ‑‑‑ Duties Act, 160, 218. **Independent Labour party,** 53. **India,** administration of, 86–7, *87;* and Afghanistan, 29, 58–9, 114; Civil Service in, 86–7; early British settlement in, 80; economy of, 87–8, *87;* and First World War, 218; immigration from, 214; importance of, for Britain, 80, 223; independence of, 195, 199, 219–23, *219, 221, 222,* 236; and Mutiny, 86, 218; and princes, 87, *87;* and Royal Titles Act, 28, *28;* and Russian Empire, 23, *29,* 31; and Second World War, 185; and Suez Canal, 28, 59, 238. **indirect rule,** 84. **Indochina,** *82,* 205, 236–7. **industrial relations** (*see also* industrial unrest), and Mond-Turner conversations, 148; ‑‑‑ Act, 246–7, *247.* **industrial revival in 1930s,** *see* revival, industrial, in 1930s. **industrial unrest** (before 1914), 54–5, 106, 108, (after 1918), 135–6, 148, (in 1970s and 1980s), 246–7, 254–5; and General Strike, 143, 148. **industry,** 5–7; and education, 17; and protection, 139; and rates, 149. **inflation,** 248–50, 252, 257. **interest rates,** 161, 206, 207. **international arbitration,** and *Alabama* settlement, 23. **International Brigade** (in Spanish Civil War), 173. **Invergordon 'mutiny',** 154. **IRA,** *see* Irish Republican Army. **Iran,** 199, 233, 238. **Iraq,** *128,* 169, 238. **Ireland,** *137;* and EEC, 245; and famine (1840s), 15; and First World War, 136; after First World War, 136–8; and Gladstone, 17, 36–41, 43–4, 57; and home rule, 36–41, 43–4, 45–6; and land problems, 36, *38;* population of, 8; relations with Britain, in the nineteenth century, 8, 35, 36, 43; and Second Reform Act, 13; and Third Home Rule Bill, 109–11; and Third Reform Act, 58. **Irish,** British contempt for, 68; ‑‑‑ Church Act, 24, 36; ‑‑‑ famine (1840s), 36; ‑‑‑ Free State, 8, 137, 218; ‑‑‑ Land Act (1870), 24, 36, (1881), 39, *39,* 42; ‑‑‑ Nationalist Party (after 1918), 136, and Ballot Act, 20, and home rule, 37–46, and Liberals, 105, and Third Home Rule Bill, 109, and Third Reform Act, 58; ‑‑‑ Republican Army, 136, 254–5; ‑‑‑ Republican Brotherhood, 46; ‑‑‑ University Bill, 36; ‑‑‑ Volunteers, 110–1, 136. **Iron Curtain,** 234. **iron and steel** (*see also* steel), 5, 157. **Irwin, Lord,** later Lord Halifax (*see also*), 220. **Isandhlwana,** battle of, 31. **Islam,** 60. **Israel,** 212, 225, 240–2. **Italy,** *168;* and appeasement, 174; and EEC, 243; and Ethiopia, 172; and Munich meeting, 176–7; and Second World War, 184, 185, 189, 190; and Spanish Civil War, 173; and Stresa Front, 173.

Jamaica, 228. **Jameson Raid,** 92–3. **Japan,** and Anglo-Japanese alliance, 112; attack on Pearl Harbor, 184; and British Empire, 185, 222; and Korea, 235; and Manchuria, 171–2, *172;* and Russo-Japanese War, 112; and Second World War, 184–5, *184,* 192. **Jarrow Crusade,** 159–60, *160.* **Jenkins, Roy,** 212, 246, 252. **Jerusalem,** 128, *128.* **Jews,** and British Union of Fascists, 164; and Palestine, 169, 223–5. **jingoism,** 33, 72. **Jinnah, Ali,** 221. **Jones, Creech,** 225, 227, *227.* **Jordan,** 230, 239. **Joynson-Hicks, Sir William,** and Equal Franchise Act, 149; and General Strike, 145, 146; as Home Secretary, 143, 149; and Prayer Book controversy, 150. **Jubilees** (of Queen Victoria), 9, 91. **judicial system** (of Britain), 47. **juries,** majority verdicts by, 214. **Jutland,** battle of, 126. **juvenile courts,** 102.

Kabul, 29, *29,* 59. **Kaiser,** *see* Wilhelm I; Wilhelm II. **Kandahar,** *29,* 59. **Kariba Dam,** 229. **Kashmir,** *221,* 222. **Kaunda, Kenneth,** 229. **Kellogg-Briand pact,** 171. **Kemal, Mustafa,** 138. **Kenya,** British settlement in, 81, *81;* and East African Federation, 228–9; and Germany, 89; independence of, 230; and Mau Mau, 207, 225–6; white settlers in, 228. **Kenyatta, Jomo,** 226, 230. **Keynes, J.M.,** 151, 169, 194, 248. **Khaki Election,** *see* general election (1900). **Khartoum,** 61–2, *61.* **Khedive** (of Egypt), 59–60. **Kikuyu people,** 225–6. **Kilmainham Treaty,** 39. **Kimberley,** *91,* 93–4, 95. **King David Hotel,** attack on, 224. **Kinnock, Neil,** 254. **Kipling, Rudyard,** 83–4. **Kitchener, Sir Herbert,** later Lord Kitchener, in First World War, 120, 126; in upper Nile valley, 89–90. **Korean War,** 199, 200, 235–6, *236.* **Kruger, Paul,** 93. **Kut-el-Amara,** siege of, 128, *128.*

labour exchanges, 98, 103, *103,* 158. **Labour party,** during 1918–24, 140, during 1930s, 164–5, during 1950s, 205; and Asquith Coalition, 123–4; and Baldwin, 139; and Beveridge Report, 188; and Central African Federation, 229; constitution (1918) of, 140; criticism of (during early 1950s), 198–200; and education, 213; and EEC membership, 244–5; and fall of first government, 142–3; and free trade, 139; and general election (1929), 152, (1945), 193–4, (1959), 207; and General Strike, 148; and government (1924), 140–4, *140,* (1929–31), 151–3, ‑‑‑s (1945–51), 193–4, (1964–70), 210–5, (1974–79), 247–8; and League of Nations, 170; and Liberal party, 101, 105; and Lloyd George Coalition (1916–18), 124–5, (1918–22), 134; and miners, 152, and ‑‑‑ strike (1984–85), 255; and Mosley, 163; and National government formation, 153–5; and Rhodesia, 232; and stronger foreign policy in 1930s, 173; and Suez crisis, 241–2; and technology, 210; and Thatcherism, 252. **Labour Representation Committee,** 53. **Ladysmith,** *91,* 93–4.

laissez-faire, 91. **Lancashire,** 14, 87. **Land League (Irish),** 37–8, 39, 41. **Land Purchase Acts (Irish),** 43. **land value tax,** 104. **landowners,** 19–20, 25, 36, 58, 66. **Lang, Cosmo,** 166. **Lansbury, George,** 154, 164, 171. **Lansdowne, Lord,** 113. **Laval, Pierre,** 172. **Lawrence, Colonel T.E.,** 128. **League of Nations,** and appeasement, 174; Britain and, 170; and Ethiopia, 172; and Labour party, 140; and Manchuria, 172, *172;* origins of, 167. **Leeward and Windward islands,** 228. **Legal Aid and Advice Act,** 198. **lend-lease,** 184, 194–5. *Let Us Face the Future,* 193. **Liberal party,** and Afghanistan, 29; and Asquith Coalition, 123–4; and Baldwin, 139; and British Empire and Commonwealth, 216; and death duty, 66; and decline (during inter-war years), 143, 164, (during 1950s), 205, 209; and economic protection, 123; and first Labour government, 140–3; and free trade, 139; and general election (1868), 16, (1874), 23–4, (1885), 40, (1929), 151, (February 1974), 247; and government (1868–74), 16–24, (1880–85), 57–62, (1886), 40–1, (1892–5), 43–4, 64–6, (1905–14), 79, 100–11; and Ireland, 36–46; and League of Nations, 170; and Lloyd George Coalition (1916–18), 124–5, (1918–22), 134; and 'methods of barbarism' (in Second Boer War), 94; and National government, 153–5; and Newcastle Programme, 65; and newspapers, 71; and Nonconformist Churches, 69; revival (in 1960s), 209; and Social Democratic party, 252; and suffragette campaigns, 108–9; and tariff reform, 98–101; and working classes, 52, 53. **Liberal Unionists,** 41–3, 45; and Conservatives, 63; and Whigs, 65. **Libya,** 81, 185, *185.* **licensing** (in First World War), 124–5. **Licensing Act** (1872), 24, (1904), 98. *Life and Labour of the London Poor,* 78. **literacy,** 71. **literature,** 149. **Liverpool,** 15, 90, 255. **Livingstone, David,** 80, 86. **Lloyd, Selwyn,** 208, 240, 242. **Lloyd George, David,** and Baldwin, 138, 139; collapse of his Coalition government (1922), 138; and Education Act (1902), 98; and general election (1929), 151; and Labour party, 140; and Mansion House speech, 116; as Minister of Munitions, 123–4, *124,* 127; and National government, 153; and National Insurance Act, 106–7, *107;* and old age pensions, 102; and Paris peace settlement, 167–9; and People's Budget, 104; as Prime Minister (1916–18), 124, 126, 127, 129, (1918–22), 134–8; and Second Boer War, 94. **local government,** 14, 63–4, 65–6; ___ Act (1888), 63–4, (1894), 65–6, (1929), 149; and education, 97–8; and Newcastle Programme, 65. **Locarno,** treaties of, 171. **London,** and Blitz, 182–3; ___ County Council, 64, 200; demonstrations in, 53, 107, 159; Festival of Britain, 200; and finance, 6; and immigration, 214; and newspapers, 71; and parliament, 8, 14; poverty in, 78–9; and riots, 255; and strikes, 50–2; ___ Transport, 152, 162, 196; Treaty of (1913), 117; and V1 and V2 attacks, 191. **Lords, House of,** and budgets, 66; functions of, 9–10, 104; and Irish home rule, 44, 110; membership a disadvantage to Curzon, 139, 210; opposition to government policy, 21–2, 44, 58, 65, 104, 152, 197; and Osborne judgement, 54; and Parliament Act, 105–6; and People's Budget, 104–5; and premiership, 139, 210; and Taff Vale case, 54. **low church** (members of the Church of England), 68. **Lowe, Robert,** 12, 18. **Lowlands,** Scottish, 14. **Ludendorff offensive,** 128–9. **Lugard, Lord,** 84–5, *85*. **Luxemburg,** *118, 122, 168,* 243. **Lyttleton, Oliver,** 228–9. **Lytton, Lord,** 172, *172*.

MacArthur, General Douglas, 236. **MacDonald, James Ramsay,** and India, 220; and international peace, 140, 171; and Labour party, on formation of National government, 153–4; and Labour Representation Committee, 53; as leader of the Labour party, 140–3; as Prime Minister (1924), 140–43, *141,* (1929–31), 151–3, (1931–35), 160–1; retirement of, 165. **McKenna, Reginald,** 123, 141. **Macleod, Iain,** 227, 229. **McMahon correspondence,** 223. **Macmillan, Harold,** becomes Prime Minister, 206; as Chancellor of the Exchequer, 206; and Cyprus, 226; and EEC, 244; as Minister of Housing, 202, 204, 205, 206; as Prime Minister, 206–10; *207;* retirement of, 210; and wind of change speech, 226–7. **Mafeking,** *91,* 93–4. **Mahdi, the,** 59, 60–2. **majority rule,** 227–8, 230. **Majuba Hill,** battle of, 59, 62, *91, 94*. **Makarios, Archbishop,** 226. **Malawi,** 230. **Malaya,** *82;* British settlement in, 81; and Second World War, 185; war in, 225, 226, 236. **Malaysia,** 225. **Manchester,** 49. **Manchuria,** 171–2, *172,* 173, 174. **mandates,** 168–9, 223, 230. **Mann, Tom,** 51. **Manning, Cardinal,** 51. **Mansion House speech** (of Lloyd George), 116. **Marne,** battle of the, 120, *122*. **married women,** 76; ___'s Property Act, 57, 76. **Marshall Aid,** 195, 234–5. **Mary, Queen,** Consort of George V, 165. **mass production,** 162. **mass-radiography,** 202. **Matabele and Mashona peoples,** 83. **Matrimonial Clauses Act,** 76. **Marx, Karl,** 52. **match-makers' strike,** 50–1, *50.* **Mau Mau,** 225–6. **Maudling,** 208, 210. **May committee,** 153, 154, 158. **means test,** 158–9, 248. **Merchant Shipping Act,** 27–8, 101. **Mesopotamia,** 128, *128,* 218. **Methodist Church,** 69. **Middle East,** and Paris peace settlement, 168–9; and Russia, 23, 31; and Suez crisis, 238–42, *239.* **Midlands,** 163. **Midlothian campaigns** (of Gladstone), 34, 57. **milk production,** 7. **Mill, J.S.,** 76. **Milner, Sir Alfred,** 92, 93, 94, 95. **mine owners,** 145, 146. **minerals** (in South Africa), 92. **miners,** conditions of, 144; ___ Federation of Great Britain, 144; and General Strike, 144–8; and Heath government, 247; and South Wales, 55; and strike (1921), 144–5, (1984–85), 254–5; and strikes before 1914, 54–5; and Triple Industrial Alliance, 55, 144; working day of, 103, 135, 146, 147, 152. *Miners' Next Step, The,* 55. **minority government,** 140, 151. **Minto, Lord,** 88. **missionaries,** 85–6. **mixed economy,** 209. **modernisation** (of industry), 157, 248, 252. **Mollet,** 240. **monarchy** (*see also* Edward VII; Edward VIII; Elizabeth II; George V; George VI; Victoria), 9. **Monckton, Walter,** 202. **Mond, Sir Alfred,** 148; ___ -Turner conversations, 148. **monetarist policies,** 207, 246, 250, 255. **money bill/budget,** 104, 105. **Mons,** battle of, 120, *122*. **Montagu-Chelmsford reforms,** 218, 219–20. **Monte Cassino,** battle of, *185,* 189. **Montenegro,** *33,* 117, *118*. **Montford reforms,** *see* Montagu-Chelmsford reforms. **Montgomery,** 185–6, 191. **Morant Education Act** (1902), 97. **Morley-Minto reforms,** 88, 218. **Morocco,** *81,* 113, 115–16, *118, 185,* 186. **Morrison, Herbert,** 152, 199, 200. **Morrison shelter,** 183. **Moslem League,** foundation of, 88, 221; and Pakistan, 221–3. **Mosley, Oswald,** and British Union of Fascists, 163–4, *163;* in Labour government, 152, 163. **motor cars,** early development of, 75; expenditure on, 203; and holidays, 163; production of (1930s), 162; tax on, 104; widespread use of (1950s and 1960s), 203–204. **motorways,** 203. **Mountbatten, Lord Louis,** 222–3, *222*. **Mozambique,** 81, 88, 231. **'mulberry' harbours,** 190. **multilateral disarmament,** 238. **Mundella Education Act** (1880), 57. **Munich,** summit meeting at, *175,* 176–7, *176,* 178–9. **munition workers** (in First World War), 123, 124, 125, 135. **Murder (Abolition of Death Penalty) Act,** 213–4. **music halls,** 33, 71–2, *72*. **Mussolini,** 164, 176, 178, 189.

Nagasaki (*see also* atomic bombs, use of), 237. **Nasser, Colonel,** 239–42. **Natal,** 31, 80, 91, *91,* 93, 95. **National Agricultural Labourers' Union,** 50; ___ Assistance Act, 197–8; ___ Economic Development Council, 208; ___ government, 153–5, *157,* 160–1, *161,* 220; ___ Health Act, 198; ___ Industrial Relations Court, 246; ___ Injuries Act, 197–8; ___ Insurance Act (1911), 106–7, *107,* 135, 149, 158, (1946), 197; ___ League (in Ireland), 39, 42; ___ Plan, 211; ___ Society, 17; ___ Unemployed Workers' Movement, 159, 164; ___ Union of Mineworkers, 255; ___ Union of Women's Suffrage Societies, 108. **nationalisation,** and Conservative consensus on, 197, 200; during First World War, 124; and Labour governments (1945–51), 193, 196–7, 199; and Labour party constitution (1918), 140, 209. **NATO,** *see* North Atlantic Treaty Organisation. **naval rivalry** (with Germany), 114–5, *115*. **Navy, Royal,** and Dardanelles campaign, 122–3; expenditure on, 66; and Falklands, 251–2; in First World War, 125–6; and Germany, 114, *115,* 169, 173; in Second World War, 181. **Nehru, Jawaharlal,** 222, *222*. **Netherlands, the,** *118;* and Africa, 80, 92; and EEC, 243; and Second World War, 181, 191. **Neuve Chapelle,** battle of, 122, *122*. **New Towns Act,** 201. **New Zealand,** as a dominion, 216; emigration to, 7, 50; and First World War, *119,* 122, 217;

relationship with Britain, 80. **Newcastle Programme,** 65. **newspapers,** before 1914, 71; campaigns by, 103, 205; censorship of, 124; circulation increases in, 16; and First World War, 123, 124; and Second Boer War, 94. **Nigeria,** British settlement in, 81, *81;* and France, 89; and independence, 230; and Lord Lugard, 84. **Nile,** upper valley of the, 61, 88, 89–90. **Nivelle offensive,** 127. **Nkomo, Joshua,** 229. **Nkrumah, Kwame,** 227. **no-man's land** (in First World War), 120–2. **Nonconformist Churches,** and Church of England, 69; and Education Act (1870), 17–9, 24, 69, (1902), 98; and Ireland, 42; and Liberal party, 16, 24, 69; and licensing, 69, 98; and trade unions, 50. **Non-Intervention committee** (in Spanish Civil War), 173. **Normandy,** 189, 190–1. **North** (of England), 10, 163, 254, 257. **North Africa,** 185–6, 189. **North Atlantic Treaty Organisation,** 235, 243. **North London Collegiate School,** 75. **North Sea,** 116, 126; ... oil, 255. **North-East** (of England), 161. **Northern Rhodesia** (*see also* Rhodesia), *81,* 228–30. **Northcliffe, Lord,** *see* Harmsworth, Alfred. **Northern Ireland,** 8, 161, 163, 254–5. **Norway,** *118,* 181, 244, 245. **Notting Hill disturbances,** 214. **Nottingham,** miners in, 255. **nurses,** 75, 125. **Nutting, Anthony,** 240. **Nyasaland,** *81,* 88, 207, 228–30. **Nyerere, Julius, 230.**

Oath Act, 70. **obstruction** (in parliament), 37, 39. **OEEC,** *see* Organisation for European Economic Co-operation. **Officers Training Corps,** 96. **offices,** women workers in, 75, 125. **oil,** 157; and Palestine, 169; price increases in, 247, 248; North Sea ..., 255. **old age pensions,** 102, 107, 149. **Omdurman,** battle of, *61,* 89. **OMS,** *see* Organisation for the Maintenance of Supplies. **Open University,** 213. **opinion polls,** 209. **Orange Free State,** 91, *91,* 93, 94. **Organisation for European Economic Co-operation,** 234, 243. **Organisation for the Maintenance of Supplies,** 145, 146. *Origin of Species, The,* 69–70. **orphans,** 149. **Orpington,** by-election at, 209. **Orwell, George,** 144. **Osborne judgement,** 54. **O'Shea, Kitty,** 42. **Ottawa conference,** 160, 218. **Ottoman Empire,** *118;* and Balkan Wars, 116–9; and Chanak, 138; and Dardanelles campaign, 122–3; and Eastern Question, 31–4, *33;* and First World War, 127–8, 223; and Paris peace settlement, 169; and Russia, 23. **overlords** (in Churchill's second government), 127. **Owen, Wilfred,** 127. **Oxford Movement,** 67–8; ... university, 20, 21, 24, 75, 152.

Pacific islands, 81. **pacifism,** 164, 171–2. **Pakistan,** 221–3, *221,* 238. **Palestine,** abandonment of, 195, 199, 224–5; as British mandate, *128,* 169, 223–4, *225, 230.* **Pankhurst, Emmeline,** and her daughters, 108, *108.* ***Panther,*** 115. **Paris,** 113, *118, 122;* and First World War, 120; and Second World War, 191; summit conference at, 242. **Parliament Act** (1911), 14, 105–6, 109, (1949), 197. **parliamentary committee of Trades Union Congress,** 48. **parliamentary government,** 10–1, 14. **parliamentary reform** (*see also* Representation of the People Act, 1918; Equal Franchise Act, 1928), First ___ Act (1832), 10, 14; and Newcastle Programme, 65; Second ___ Act (1867), *13,* 16, importance of, 14, passage of, 11–3, terms of, 13, and women, 76; Third ___ and Redistribution Act (1884–85), 14, 39, 53, 58, 61, 125. **Parnell, Charles,** 37–40, 42, 46. **partition,** of India, 222–3; of Palestine, 225. **partnership** (in Africa), 228. **Passchendaele,** battle of, *122,* 127. **patronage,** 21. **pay,** restraint of, 208, 247. **payment of MPs,** 54. **Peace Ballot,** 171. **peace conference,** Paris (1919–20), 167–9, *168.* **peasants,** Irish, 36, 43. **Peel, Sir Robert,** 15, 25. **Peel Commission,** 224. **Peelites,** 15, 16. **Peerage Act,** 210. **Pendjeh,** incident at, *29,* 62. **Pensions Act,** 1925 (*see also* old age pensions), 149. **People's Budget,** 104–5. **Persia,** 23, *29,* 114, *128.* **Phoenix Park murders,** 39. **Phoney War, the,** 180–1. **picketing** (*see also* secondary picketing), 48. **piece work,** 75, 103. **Plaid Cymru,** 254. **Plan of Campaign** (in Ireland), 42. **planning,** and Labour party, 211; local, 149; in Second World War, 187; after Second World War, 193, 199, 206, 208. **Plimsoll, Samuel,** 27–8; ___ Line, 28. **plural voting,** 152. **poetry,** of First World War, 127; of Swinburne, 70; of Tennyson, 70. **points, rationing,** 186. **Poland,** British support of, 178–9; and Czechoslovakia, 176–7; and frontiers (1945), 233; German invasion of, 179, 181; and Locarno treaties, 171; and Paris peace settlement, 168, *168,* 169. **police,** and crime, 214; Joynson-Hicks and, 149–50; and miners' strike, 255; and riots, 256; women as, 125. **political levy,** trade union (*see also* Trade Union Act, 1913; Trade Disputes Act, 1927), 54. **polls, opinion,** 11. **polytechnics,** 213. **Poor Law,** 149, 158. **population** (of Britain), 8. **Portugal,** 88, *118,* 244. **positive discrimination,** 256. **Potsdam conference,** 233. **poverty,** before 1914, 77–9, 102; and Beveridge Report, 187, 188; measurement of, 78–9, 180. *Poverty: A Study of Town Life,* 79. **Prayer Book** (of the Church of England), 68, 150, *150.* **prefabs,** 201. **prescription charges,** 200, 211. **Pretoria,** Convention of, 59. **prices and incomes,** 211–2. **Primrose League,** 77. **prison,** for conscientious objectors, 124. **privatisation,** 257. **probation service,** 198, 214. **'profiteering'** in First World War, 123. **Profumo scandal,** 209. **'property-owning democracy',** 205. **proportional representation,** 152, 252–3. **protection, economic** (*see also* safeguarding; tariffs), and Baldwin, 139; in First World War, 123; and National government, 160; and tariff reform, 99–100, *100.* **protectorates,** 81, 95. **Protestants** (in Ireland), 36, 41.

provided schools, 98. **Prussia,** 21, 22–3. **Public Assistance Committees,** 149, 158. **Public Health Act,** 26–7. **public schools,** 17; and Army, 96; for girls, 75; and imperialism, 85; and Labour party, 140. **public works,** 151. **Public Worship Regulation Act,** 68, *68.* **pubs,** 24, 71, *78,* 98, 124.

Quit India campaign, 221.

Race Relations Act, 215, 256. **Rachmanism,** 209–10. **racial discrimination,** 214–15; ___ tension, 214, 256. **radar,** 191. **Radicals,** 11–2, 16, 41, 57, 58, 70. **radio,** 139, 163, 213. **RAF,** *see* Royal Air Force. **railwaymen,** strikes of (before 1914), 54; and Triple Industrial Alliance, 55, 144. **railways,** accidents on, 73; amalgamation of companies, 73; contraction of, 203–4; development of (before 1914), 73–4, *73;* nationalisation of, 195; workers on, 50. **rates,** 10, 13, 19, 98, 149. **rationalisation** (of production), 162. **rationing,** and Butler, 204; and Cripps, 195, 199; in First World War, 125; in Second World War, 186, 193. **rearmament,** 165, 173, 174. **reconstruction** (in Second World War), 187. **Red Friday,** 145. **Red scare,** 142. **Redmond, John,** 46, 109, 111. **Reid committee,** 196. **religion,** 67–70. **religious teaching,** 17–9, 98. **Rent Act,** 209–10. **reparations,** 169, 171. **Representation of the People Act** (1918), 14, 125, 139. **republic,** demand for (in Britain), 9, 70. **revival, industrial,** in 1930s, 152, 154, 161–3, *162,* 165. **Rhineland,** 168, *168,* 169, 173, 174. **Rhodes, Cecil,** and Jameson Raid, 92; and Rhodesia, 83, 229; and South Africa, 92. **Rhodesia** (*see also* Northern Rhodesia; Southern Rhodesia; Zimbabwe), British settlement in, 81; ___ Front, 230; independence of, 232; Portuguese claims to, 88; and Smith government, 230–2. **riots** (in 1980s), 256, *256;* and Second Reform Act, 13. **Rippon, Geoffrey,** 245, *245.* **ritualism,** 67, 68, *68.* **River Pollution Act,** 27. **road haulage,** 196; ___ transport, 203–4. *Road to Wigan Pier, The,* 144. **Robbins Report,** 213. **Roberts, General,** in Afghanistan, 29, 59; in Second Boer War, 94. **Robertson, Sir William,** 126. **Rochdale,** 49. **Roebuck, John,** 47–8. **Roman Catholic Church,** 36, 41, 42, 51, 68, *68,* 150, 254. **Romania,** *33, 118, 168,* 169, 178, 233. **Rome,** Treaty of, 243. **Rommel,** 185. **Roosevelt, President,** 160, 184, 186. **Rosebery, Lord,** 44, 65, 101. **round-table conferences** (on India), 219–20. **Rowntree, Seebohm,** 79. **Royal Air Force,** *181,* 182. **Royal Commission,** on the Poor Laws, 49; on trade unions, 47–8. **Royal Family,** 183, *203,* 222. **Royal Navy,** *see* Navy, Royal. **Royal Niger Company,** 82. **Royal Titles Act,** 28. **Ruhr,** occupation of, 171. **Runciman Mission,** 175. **rural district councils,** 149. **Russell, Lord John,** 11, 13. **Russian Empire,** *118;* and Anglo-Russian convention, 113–4; autocratic rule of, 10, 114; and Balkans,

31–4, 116–8; British loans to, 142; and Civil War in, 170; and Eastern Question, 31–14, *32;* and First World War, 170; and Persia, *29,* 114; Revolutions in, 142; and Triple Entente, 113–4. **Russo-German Non-Aggression pact,** 178–9, 181. **Russo-Japanese War,** 112, 113.

safeguarding (*see also* protection, economic), 123, 141, *151,* 157. **Safety First election campaign** (1929), 150. **Sale of Food and Drugs Act,** 27. **Salisbury, Lord,** and Africa, 83, 88; background and attitudes, 62–3; and Ireland, 39–40; last Prime Minister in House of Lords, 139; as Prime Minister, 39–40, 42–3, 45, 62–4; retirement of, 97; and Splendid Isolation, 112; and Third Reform Act, 58. **Salvation Army,** 77. **Samuel, Sir Herbert,** ... commission, 145–6; and General Strike, 145, 147; and National government, 153; and Palestine, 224. **San Stefano,** Treaty of, 32–3. **sanctions,** and Falklands, 251; by League of Nations, 172; and Rhodesia, 231, *232.* **Sandon Education Act** (1876), 28. **Sankey report,** 144. **Sarajevo,** assassination at, 117–8, *118.* **Sassoon, Siegfried,** 127. **satyagraha,** 219. **Saunderson, Edward,** 44. **Scapa Flow,** 169. **Scarman, Lord,** report of, 256. **schools,** and discipline and standards in, 213, 257; and examinations, 213; and leaving-age, 152, 213; meals at, 101; and medical inspections, 101–2. **Scotland,** and Depression (1930s), 161, 163; and general election (1987), 254; population of, 8; relationship with Britain, 8–9; and Second Reform Act, 13. **Scottish Nationalist party,** 254. **scuttling** (of German ships), 169. **seamen,** strike by, 212. **seaside holiday towns,** 73, 163. **SEATO,** *see* South-East Asia Treaty Organisation. **Second Front** (in Second World War), 189–91, *190,* 192. **secondary** education, 98–9, 188, 213, 257; ... picketing, 254–5. **secret ballot,** for parliamentary elections, 19–20, *20,* 58; in trade unions, 254. **Secretary of State,** for India, 86; ... for War, 22. **self-determination,** 167, 168, 176, 178. **Selsdon policies,** 246, 248, 249. **Serbia,** 33, 117–9, *118.* **servants,** 75, *76,* 202. **Sèvres,** meeting at, 240; Treaty of, 138. **SHAPE,** *see* Supreme Headquarters of Allied Powers in Europe. **Sheffield outrages,** 47. **Shells scandal,** 123–4. **ship building,** 5, 157. **shipping,** 7. **shops,** 75, *78,* 162; ... Act, 103. **Sierra Leone,** 81, *81,* 230. **Silesia,** 168, *168.* **Silverman, Sidney,** 213. **Simon, Sir John,** commission of, 219–20; and General Strike, 147. **Simpson, Mrs Wallis,** 165–6. **Singapore,** 82, *82, 184,* 185, 225. **single-member constituencies,** 58. **Sinn Fein party,** and Lloyd George Coalition (1918–22), 134, 136–8; origins of, 46; and Third Home Rule Bill, 109–10. **Six Day War,** 212. **slump** (*see also* Depression), 156. **slums,** 27, 134, 152. **Smith, Herbert,** 146. **Smith, Ian,** 230–2, *231, 232.* **smoking,** 102. **Smuts, General,** 217. **Snowden, Philip,** as Chancellor of the Exchequer (1924), 140–1, (1929–31), 151–3; and crisis of 1931, 152–4. **Social contract,** 247. **Social Democratic Federation,** 52, 53. **Social Democratic party,** 252. **social security,** 140. **Socialism,** and Ballot Act, 20; and Death duty, 66; idea and early development of, 52–3; and Labour party constitution (1918), 140; and Labour party (in 1950s and 1960s), 200. **Solemn League and Covenant,** 110. **Somaliland,** 81, *81.* **Somme,** battle of the, *122,* 126–7. **South** (of England), 10, 257. **South Africa,** *81;* and annexation of Transvaal, 30; and apartheid, 231; blacks in, 30–1; Boer-British conflict in, 30, 31, 92–6; as a dominion, 216–7; early white settlement in, 80; emigration to, 7; and First World War, *119;* and Gandhi, 219; and Gladstone, 57; leaves Commonwealth, 231; minerals in, 30, 83; and Rhodes, 83; and Second Boer War, 91–6; and South-West Africa, 168; Union of, 95, 216–7. **South Atlantic,** 251–2. **South-East Asia,** 185, 236–7; ... Treaty Organisation, 238. **South-West Africa,** *81,* 89, 168. **Southern Rhodesia** (*see also* Rhodesia), *81,* 228; and Central African Federation, 228–30; and Smith government, 230–1. **Soviet Union,** 196; and approach of Second World War, 178–9; Britain's relations with, 170, 171; defectors to, 199; and Eastern Europe (after 1945), 233–5; first Labour government's relations with, 142, 171; influence in Britain, 150; and Second World War, 181, 184, 190; and Western Europe, 243. **Spanish Civil War,** 173, 174. **Speaker** (of House of Commons), 39, *44,* 70. **special areas,** 161. **special relationship** (with US), 242–3. **spheres of influence** (in Africa), 81. **Spitfires** (fighter aircraft), 182. **Splendid Isolation,** 112, *112.* **Sri Lanka,** *see* Ceylon. **St Germain,** Treaty of, 169. **Stalin,** 186. **Stalingrad,** battle of, 186, *189,* 190. ***Standard, The,*** 71. **Stanley, Henry,** 80. **staple industries,** 5, 7, 157, 161. **Stead, William,** 71. **steam power,** 7. **steel** (*see also* iron and steel), 197, 202. **sterling crisis,** 211. **stock market,** 203, 211, 257. **Stockton,** 206. **Stop-Go,** 206–8, 211, 212. **Stormont,** 254–5. **strategic bombing,** 191. **Stresa Front,** 173. **strikes,** and General Strike, 144–8; and industrial unrest (before 1914), 54–5, (after 1918), 135–6; by miners, 247, 254–5; and Thatcherism, 254–5; and trade unions (in nineteenth century), 47–8, 49–52; and 'winter of discontent', 249. **students,** 213. **submarines** (*see also* U-boats), 186, 191. **suburbs,** 73–4, 162. **Sudan, the,** British control of, 81, *81;* German threats to, 88; and Gladstone, 60–2. **Sudetenland,** 175–7, *175,* 178. **Suez Canal,** and Arabi Pasha rebellion, 59; construction of, 28, 238; crisis (1956) concerning, 205, 206, 207, 226, 228, *230,* 237, 238–42, *241;* ... group, 239; and India, 238; nationalisation of ... Company, 239–40; and Palestine, 169; purchase of shares in ... Company, 28, 238; and Second World War, 186; ... Users Association, 240; ... zone, 239. **suffrage,** *see* franchise. **suffragette activity,** 76, 108–9, *108,* 125. **suffragist societies,** 108.

summer time, 125. **summit conferences,** at Geneva (1955), 242; at Munich (1938), 176–8; at Paris (1960), 242. **super tax,** 104. **Supreme Headquarters of Allied Powers in Europe,** 235. **suspended sentences,** 214. **Swaziland,** *91,* 95. **sweated industries,** 103. **Sweden,** 118, 244. **Switzerland,** *118,* 224. **Swinburne,** 70. **Syndicalism,** 55.

Taff Vale case, 54, 98, 101. **Tanganyika,** *81,* 168, 199, 228–9, 230. **tanks** (in First World War), 127. **Tanzania,** 230. **tariff reform,** 98–100; ... League, 99. **tariffs,** 5–6, 99. **task force,** Falklands, 251, *251.* **taxation,** and Butler, 204, 206; and Cripps, 195; cuts in, 206, 207, 249–50; and death duty, 66; and Labour party (1964–70), 211, 212; and People's Budget, 104; and Second World War, 187, 193; and tariff reform, 98–100, *100;* and Thatcherism, 249, 250. **teachers,** 125, *180,* 257. **Technical Instruction Act,** 64. **Tel-el-Kebir,** battle of, 60, 61, *61.* **television,** 163, 213. **temperance societies,** 77, 98. **Temple, William,** 188. **Tennyson,** 70. **Territorial Army,** 96. **Test Ban Treaty,** 238. **textiles,** 5, 157. **Thatcher, Mrs Margaret,** becomes leader of the Conservative party, 249; as Prime Minister, 249–57, 249; and Thatcherism, 249, 257. **Thomas, J.H.,** 141, 151, 152. **Thorneycroft, Peter,** 207. **three-day week,** 247. **Three Fs Act,** 39, 42. **Tibet,** 23, 114. *Tiger* negotiations (on Rhodesia), 231–2. **Tillett, Ben,** 51. **time standardisation,** 73. *Times, The,* 71, 123. **tobacco,** 104, 203. **Tobruk,** fall of, 185, *185.* **Tory democracy,** 26–8, 63. **Tory party** (*see also* Conservative party), 15, 16, 25. **total war,** First World War as, 124–5; Second World War as, 174. **Town and Country Planning,** Acts, 201; Ministry of, 188. **Toxteth,** riots in, 255. **trade,** 5–7, *6,* 218, ... boards, 103; and First World War, 120. **Trade Disputes Act** (1906), 54, 101, 104, 148, (1927), 148, 152. **Trade Union,** Act (1871), 48, (1913), 54, 148, (1984), 254; ... Congress, 48–9, 53, 211; ... movement (to 1914), 47–55, *48,* 98, 101, 103, and Conservative government (1951–55), 202, 207, 208, (1970–74), 246–7, *247,* and Cripps, 195, and decline after General Strike, 148, and Gladstone, 16, 24, and miners' strike (1984–85), 254–5, and Social Contract, 247–8, and Thatcherism, 249, 254–5, and unemployed, 159. **Transjordan** (*see also* Jordan), *128,* 169. **transport,** and changes (before 1914), 73–5, (1950s and 1960s), 203–4; during First World War, 125; during inter-war years, 149, 163; in London, 152, 162; ... workers, 55, 144. **Transvaal,** annexation of, 30, *30,* 59; and Convention of Pretoria, 59; and First Boer War, 59; and gold, 92; and Second Boer War, 91, *91,* and Union of South Africa, 95; and Zulu War, 31. **trench warfare,** 120–2, *121,* 126–7, 128. **Trek, Great,** 91–2, 93. **Trianon, Treaty of,** 169. **Trinidad and Tobago,** 228. **Triple alliance,** 114. **Triple Entente,** 113–14,

115, 117. **Triple Industrial Alliance,** 54, 136, 144, 145. **Truman, President,** 234; doctrine of, 236. **tuberculosis,** 201–2. **Tunisia,** 81, *185,* 186. **Turkey** (*see also* Ottoman Empire), 195, 233, 238. **typhoid,** 202.

U-boats (*see also* submarines), 125–6, 128. **UDI,** see Unilateral Declaration of Independence. **Uganda, British settlement in,** 81, *81;* and East African Federation, 228–9, 230; and Germany, 89. **Uitlanders,** 83, 92. **Ulster** (*see also* Northern Ireland), *137;* after 1918, 136–7; ___ Defence Union, 44; and home rule, 41, 44, 108, 109, *110;* ___ Unionist party, 254; ___ Volunteers, 110–1. **Ulundi,** battle of, 31. **Unauthorised Programme** (of Joseph Chamberlain), 57. **unconditional surrender** (in Second World War), 186. **uncovenanted benefit** (*see also* dole, the), 135. **underground railway,** 74, 152, 162, 183. **undeveloped estates,** 90–1, 99. **unemployed,** the (*see also* unemployment), families of, 158; life of, 157–9; and means test, 158; protests by, 159; and Socialism, 53; ___ Workers' Dependants Act, 135; ___ Workmen Act, 98. **unemployment** (*see also* unemployed), before 1914, 7, 34, 98; during inter-war years, causes of, 156–7; extent of, 135, 151, 152, 156, 165, 254; and Labour governments, 141, 152, 163; and Liberal party, 151; protests about, 159, *160;* reality of, 157–9, *157;* after 1945, 207, 208, 212; in 1970s and 1980s, 248, 250, 252, 256, 257; ___ Act (1934), 159; ___ Assistance Board, 159; and Beveridge Report, 187, 188; and Conservative party, 193; ___ Insurance Act (1920), 135, 158; insurance against, 107, 135; and National government, 160–1. **Unilateral Declaration of Independence** (by Rhodesia), 231, *231.* **unilateral disarmament,** 237. **Union of Democratic Mineworkers,** 255. **Unionist party,** *see* Conservative party. **United Gold Coast convention,** 227. **United Nations,** and British colonialism, 227; and Falklands, 251; and Korean War, 235–6; origins of, 184; and Palestine, 225; and Suez crisis, 240, *241,* 242. **United States,** and *Alabama* settlement, 23; and atomic bomb, 237; and British colonialism, 227; and British economy, 194–5; declining economy of, 152–3; economy of, 157; and European unity, 244; and First World War, 126, 128–9; and Israel, 224–5; and League of Nations, 170; loan from, 194–5; and newspapers, 71; prejudices against people from, 166; relations with Britain (during inter-war years), 171, (after 1945), 205, and Second World War, 183–4, 186, 189–92; and Soviet expansion, 233–7; and Suez crisis, 242; system of government, 10, 12; as trade competitor, 6, 7. **universal suffrage,** 14. **universities,** new, 213; ___ Tests Act, 21, 69. **University, Open,** 213. **unskilled workers,** 49, 51–2. **urban district councils,** 149.

V1 and V2 attacks, 186, 191, 192. **Valera, Eamon de,** 136, 137–8. **Verdun,** battle of, *122,* 126. **Vereeniging,** Treaty of, 94. **Versailles,** Treaty of, 167–9, *168,* 173; and appeasement, 173–4. **Viceroy of India,** 86, 218. **Victoria, Queen,** and army reforms, 22; death of, 97; and Gladstone, 16, 34; and Gordon of Khartoum, 62; and India, 28, *28,* 86; and Jubilees, 9, *9,* 91; and ritualism, 68; and Rosebery, 65; as a widow, 9, *9.* **Vietnam,** 237, 243. **Vimy Ridge,** battle of, *122,* 127, 217. **vitamin supplements,** 186, 201. **voluntary schools,** 17.

wages, 7, 203. **Wales,** and Depression, 161, 163; and industrial unrest, 54; Lloyd George and, 104; population of, 8; relationship with Britain, 8–9. **Wall Street Crash,** 157. **War poets,** 127. **war-guilt** (German), 168. **water,** purity of, 26. **Warwickshire,** 50. *We Can Conquer Unemployment,* 151. **Welensky, Roy,** 229. **welfare state and services,** and Conservative consensus, 200, 202; and Labour governments (1945–51), 197–8, 199, *199;* and Liberal governments (1905–14), 101–3, 106–7, 197; and Thatcherism, 249. **West Africa,** 81, 84–5, *85,* 89, 90–1, 227–8. **West Germany,** 243. **West Ham,** 53. **West Indies** (*see also* Caribbean), 80, 214, 223, 228. **Western Front** (in First World War), 120–1, *121,* 122–3, *122,* 126–9, 218. **Westminster,** Statute of, 217. **'wets',** 249–50. **Wheatley,** 141; Housing Act of, 141. **Whigs,** 11, 15, 16, 41, 57, 58, 65. **'white man's burden',** 83–4. **widows,** 149. **Wilhelm I,** Kaiser, 22. **Wilhelm II, Kaiser,** 112, 113. **Wilkinson, Ellen,** 160. **Wilson, Harold,** and EEC membership, 244, *244;* as leader of Labour party, 209; as Minister of Trade, 200; and Ministry of Disarmament, 238; and Northern Ireland, 254; as Prime Minister (1964–70), 210–2, *212,* (1974–76), 247–8; and Rhodesia, 231–2. **Wilson, President Woodrow,** 129, 167–9, 170. **wind of change** (in Africa), 226–7, 229. **Windsor, Duke of,** *see* Edward VIII. **'winter of discontent',** 249, 254. **Wolseley, Sir Garnet,** 61–2. **women,** advance of (1970s and 1980s), 249; in the cabinet, 151; first woman Prime Minister, 249; during First World War, 125, *125;* and local government vote, 64, 66, 76–7; in match-makers' strike, 50, *50;* obtain parliamentary vote, 125, *134,* 149; and political parties, 77; position of (before 1914), 75–7; and Second World War, 187; and struggle for parliamentary vote, 11, 76–7, 106, 108–9, *108;* and varied employment, 75, *76.* **Women's** Auxiliary Army Corps, 125; ___ Liberal Federation, 77; Married ___ Property Act, 57; ___ Social and Political Union, 108. *Workers' Weekly, The,* 142. **workhouses,** 78, 102. **working classes,** activity among, 53; and Church of England, 77; conditions of, 65; and Conservative party, 26, 52, 53; distrust of, 12; and education, 17; exploitation of, 52; and General Strike, 146; and industrial unrest (before 1914), 54–5; and means test, 158; and National Insurance, 107; and Second Reform Act, 13, 52. **Workmen's Compensation Act** (1897), 64, 101, (1906), 101. **World War, First,** 22; Britain's involvement in, 120–9, *121;* causes of, 114, 117–9, 167–8; and dominions, 217; home life during, 124–5; pointless slaughter in, 171. **World War, Second,** 22; British involvement in, 180–92; causes of, 171, 173–4; and Commonwealth, 218, 221; home life during, 186–8. **Wyndham Land Purchase Act,** 45.

Yalta conference, 233. **York,** 79; ___shire, 14. **Ypres,** battles of, 122, *122.* **Yugoslavia,** *168,* 169.

Zambia, 230. **Zimbabwe,** 232. **Zimmerman telegram,** 128. **Zinoviev letter,** 142, 171. **Zionism,** 169, 223, 224. **Zulu War,** 31, 83.